THE I TATTI
RENAISSANCE LIBRARY

James Hankins, General Editor

BRUNI

HISTORY OF THE

FLORENTINE PEOPLE

VOLUME I

ITRL 3

LEONARDO BRUNI

✦ ✦ ✦

HISTORY OF THE
FLORENTINE PEOPLE

VOLUME I ✦ BOOKS I–IV

EDITED AND TRANSLATED BY

JAMES HANKINS

THE I TATTI RENAISSANCE LIBRARY
HARVARD UNIVERSITY PRESS
CAMBRIDGE, MASSACHUSETTS
LONDON, ENGLAND

Series design by Dean Bornstein

Library of Congress Cataloging-in-Publication Data

Bruni, Leonardo, 1369–1444
[Historiae Florentini populi. English & Latin]
History of the Florentine people / Leonardo Bruni;
edited and translated by James Hankins.
p. cm. — (The I Tatti Renaissance library; 3)
Includes bibliographical references and index.
ISBN 0-674-00506-6 (alk. paper)
I. Florence (Italy) — History — To 1421.   I. Hankins, James.
II. Title.   III. Series
DG737.A2 B813 2001
945'.51 — dc21

Second printing, 2001

Contents

ക്ട്ര

Introduction   ix

Maps   xxii

HISTORY OF THE FLORENTINE PEOPLE

Introduction

꽃쏀꽃

If boldness of conception, originality, style, and influence are any criteria of excellence, the *History of the Florentine People* by Leonardo Bruni of Arezzo (1370–1444) deserves to be considered the greatest historical work of the Italian Renaissance. That was the judgment of many contemporaries and it is the judgment of many modern students of Renaissance historiography as well.[1] But despite Bruni's brilliance as an historian, the modern reader is more likely to have heard of him as a figure in the history of political thought. He is today considered the most important representative of the "civic humanism" of the early Renaissance. Civic humanism in modern scholarship has come to stand for the view that, during the Italian Renaissance, there existed a powerful symbiosis between the republican traditions of city-states such as Florence and Venice, on the one hand, and that strain of Renaissance literary and intellectual life known as humanism, on the other. On this view there is something essentially republican, liberal, even egalitarian about Renaissance humanism and something essentially humanistic about Renaissance republicanism. The interpretation is debatable, but the terminology remains helpful.[2] In fifteenth-century terms civic humanism can be usefully identified with a literary and educational reform movement directed at the political classes of Italian city-states. Bruni's writings illustrate all the leading ideas of the movement. The great challenge of politics is not to improve laws or institutions, but the moral quality of the ruling class: it is not governments, but governors, who need reforming. The best way to reform civic leaders is to train them in virtue and eloquence, and virtue and eloquence are best learned from prolonged study of the classical authors. Classical scholar-

ship — indeed all scholarship — has therefore an important role to play in civic education. The Christian religion must guide us in preparing for the next life, but in this life (Bruni implies rather than states) our criterion of ethical value should be the good of the state. Hence acquiring wealth, maintaining a family, and involvement in public life — activities regarded with suspicion by ascetic forms of Christianity — take on value as positive duties which increase the security and power of the state. The needs of the state even confer value on the military life. If the medieval crusades had assigned new prestige to the soldier's life by giving it a spiritual justification, Bruni and his generation celebrated the secular glory that knights and condottieri could win by defending the liberty of the state and extending its power over other lands. So high was the value attached to military valor that praise of it could sometimes adopt the elevated language of civic religion.[3]

Such are the ideas for which Bruni has become famous in the last half-century. They help explain why he is today regarded primarily as a political thinker and only secondarily, if at all, as an historian. Yet in his own time, Bruni's *History of the Florentine People* was regarded as his greatest monument. At Bruni's state funeral in the church of Santa Croce, he was laid out on his bier holding a copy of the *History*, a pose that was preserved in stone in the elegant funeral monument later carved for him by Bernardo Rossellino. The *History* became a famous book in Quattrocento Italy and was widely imitated by humanists working for other republics and princes in Italy. It was required reading for every Florentine patrician as well as for men of state throughout the peninsula. Bruni had the idea to write it as early as 1404, when, in the course of composing his famous *Panegyric of the City of Florence*, he came to realize the richness of his theme.[4] Later, when Florence conquered Pisa in 1406, the similarities (as he saw it) between this victory and Rome's victory over Carthage in the second century B.C. once again whetted the young humanist's appetite to tell Flor-

ence's story. Finally in 1416, after circulating the first book of his history among some of Florence's leading citizens, Bruni was given a tax exemption to pursue his historical writing (an admirable custom), and thus, in effect, became the official historiographer of the Florentine state.

The composition of the work was a laborious process which occupied Bruni for the rest of his life.[5] Book II was finished by 1419, Book III by 1420, Book IV after 1422. We have reports of various occasions when Bruni presented portions of his great work to the Florentine town council (or Signoria): in 1424, probably on completion of the fourth book; in 1428, at a public ceremony marking the end of the Second Milanese War; and in 1439, when Bruni presented Books VII–IX to the city fathers during festivities associated with the Council of Florence. Copies of the first six books of the work were already circulating after 1428, and there is at least one professional copy of the work in nine books from the 1430s. The whole work was ready for copying in 1442, and the Signoria laid out sixty florins for a magnificent presentation copy to be prepared for its private use.[6] By then, in fact, the Signoria clearly regarded Bruni's work as an official history, as the property of the Florentine state, to be continued by other hands and disseminated as it saw fit. A copy of it was kept in the chapel of the Palazzo Vecchio along with other civic trophies such as the banners of defeated enemies and the original manuscript (as was thought) of Justinian's *Pandects*, taken at the conquest of Pisa. Around 1456 the Signoria encouraged Bruni's younger contemporary and friend, the humanist Poggio Bracciolini, to compose a continuation of Bruni's history to cover the first half of the fifteenth century. As early as 1442 the Signoria seems to have wanted Bruni's work translated into Italian, a desire that was at length fulfilled in 1473 when the patrician humanist Donato Acciaiuoli finished his official version. This was printed in Venice in 1476, together with Poggio's continuation.

Bruni was an appropriate choice to serve as Florence's official historian. He was born in 1370 in Arezzo, once the university town of Tuscany and still in Bruni's day a home to Latin letters. He was the son of an obscure grain dealer who had profited from the Florentine takeover of Arezzo in 1384. After the death of his parents, Bruni came to Florence in the early 1390s to study law, but fell in with the circle of young literary men who surrounded Coluccio Salutati. Salutati was the chancellor of Florence, a disciple of Francesco Petrarca, and the leading man of letters of his generation. He also had the best library in Tuscany (an invaluable asset in the age of the manuscript book), including an extraordinary collection of historical writings. Bruni, like Salutati's other disciples, had the free run of his library. It was Salutati who turned Bruni into a brilliant student of Roman history and literature. It was Salutati who encouraged him to learn Greek when the opportunity to do so appeared in 1398, when Manuel Chrysoloras, a Byzantine émigré, came to lecture at the University of Florence. And it was Salutati who in 1405 obtained for Bruni his first position, the post of apostolic secretary to Pope Innocent VII.

As papal secretary Bruni both witnessed and participated in the most dramatic and terrible events of his time. The decade he spent serving a succession of popes coincided with the end of the Great Schism of the Western church, that period when the loyalties of the Catholic Church were divided among two — later three — claimants to the See of Peter. It was not an edifying time to be in papal service and there is evidence that Bruni's later secularism was in part a response to the rampant corruption and lack of principle he observed firsthand in the papal curia, before leaving John XXIII's service late in 1414.[7] As a resident and later (after 1416) a citizen of Florence, Bruni witnessed some equally dramatic events: Florence's long, inconclusive contest with Duke Giangaleazzo Visconti of Milan, which ended in 1402; the conquest of Pisa in 1406; King Ladislas of Naples' threat to Florentine independence

in the second decade of the century; Florence's failed attack on its fellow-republic, Lucca, which ultimately brought down the old oligarchy in 1434; the rise of the Medici to power; and most of all, the long contest with Duke Filippo Maria Visconti of Milan which began in the early 1420s and continued, with various interruptions, until after Bruni's death. From December of 1427 to his death in 1444 Bruni served as chancellor (or as undersecretary for foreign affairs, as we might say) to the Florentine Signoria. From 1436 he began to occupy major offices in the Florentine regime, including two terms on the Ten of War, the most powerful of all civic magistracies. Bruni's youth, like Machiavelli's, was spent in the corridors of power, but unlike Machiavelli, the poor immigrant from Arezzo returned to public service in his late fifties and in his late sixties rose to the highest dignities of state. Bruni's lifetime was an age of wars, of political unrest, of imperial expansion in the Florentine state, and of revolution and ideological collapse in the Church. And he had a front-row seat.

Bruni's understanding of men and affairs is revealed again and again in the later books of his *History*. But in Book I of that work it is his scholarship and his powerful historical imagination that impresses above all. Bruni was among the greatest scholars of his day, and his extraordinary mastery of Latin and Greek historical sources enabled him to make short work of the luxuriant legends that had grown up concerning the founding of Florence. Bruni's crisp dismissal of civic myths enshrined in revered medieval chronicles such as that of Giovanni Villani is among the most impressive feats of humanist criticism in the fifteenth century, anticipating and rivalling Lorenzo Valla's more famous debunking of the Donation of Constantine in the 1440s. Florence was founded not by Trojans fleeing the fall of Troy, but by veterans of the Roman dictator Sulla as the result of a land distribution. Florence was destroyed not by Attila the Hun in the fifth century, but by the Gothic chieftain Totila in the sixth. The city was not so much

refounded as restored by Charlemagne. Bruni's history is full of clear-sighted historical revisionism of this sort, its conclusions often supported by documents from papal and Florentine official archives, to which Bruni was given privileged access.

But what is truly impressive in Book 1, what places Bruni in the class of Gibbon as an historical thinker, is his powerful recasting of the broad outlines of Etruscan, Roman, and medieval history. Ancient Christian and medieval historians, following their biblical sources, had seen world history as a succession of empires culminating in the Roman Empire and the Incarnation of Christ. It was the *pax romana* established by Augustus, under the guidance of Divine Providence, that made possible the spread of Christianity and its ultimate establishment as the state religion under the fourth-century emperors from Constantine to Theodosius. The Roman Republic was little more than a disorderly prelude to the grand period of imperial and Christian triumph. Bruni, wanting to establish the legitimacy and superior value of republican government, could not accept this story, deeply rooted though it was in ten centuries of Western historiography. He offered a much more complex and sophisticated picture, in part based upon classical historical sources and in part absolutely original. Bruni ignored the four empires of biblical history and began instead with an empire all but forgotten, the Etruscan empire. The Etruscans, who had controlled central Italy before the spread of Roman power, had been an alliance of free peoples centered in twelve city-states in Tuscany; they had enjoyed a superior culture and religious life later imitated by Rome herself. Rome, too, had once been a free city-state before her decline under the emperors. Her high virtue and superior unity in the days of the Roman republic had enabled her to defeat the Etruscan confederation. Bruni's story of Etruria's flourishing and decline, based on his reading of the patriotic Roman historian Livy, is an example of the Aretine's remarkable abil-

ity to reverse the ideological polarities of his sources, wringing new interpretations from hostile authorities.[8]

Eventually (Bruni tells us), Rome lost her political liberty and came under the rule of a series of corrupt emperors. Most of the emperors, indeed, were monsters of iniquity, and Rome rotted from within. A succession of barbarian invaders from Northern Europe at last shattered the empty shell of empire. Constantine transferred the capital to Byzantium, giving rise to the empire of the Greeks, but the true empire based in Italy was now dead. Charlemagne had tried to revive it, backed by the dubious authority of the popes, but failed. His successors were nothing but German barbarians; they gloried in the empty title of empire, but were rarely resident in Italy and exercised no real power there. The seat of universal empire remained empty. But the very weakness of the German empire made possible, little by little, the revival of the free cities of Tuscany. Some of them had died out since Etruscan times; some, like Bruni's native Arezzo, had survived in weakened form; some, like Florence, were Roman cities built on Etruscan foundations; some, like Siena, were essentially recent growths. The last scrabbling for power between the pope and the dying German empire had exacerbated the natural rivalries between these cities, and the struggle between Guelfs and Ghibellines had darkened the first centuries of the Tuscan revival. But by the later thirteenth century, the disease had largely run its course. The old German empire was little more than a memory. Tuscany was growing more and more unified under Florentine leadership. Florence was an ideal combination of Etruscan liberty and culture, and Roman virtue and unity. She was the New Rome, the center of a new Italian empire based in old Etruria. It does not take much imagination to guess that Bruni, like other Florentines of his generation, hoped that Florence had before her an imperial destiny to rival that of Rome herself.

Books II through XII tell the story of Florence's emergence as a free people and as the dominant power in Tuscany. Though the title of his work has often been shortened by copyists and editors to *The Florentine History*, Bruni himself insisted on the title *History of the Florentine People*. And with good reason, for the Florentine People is the chief actor in Bruni's story. The Florentines themselves used the word "people" (*popolo*) as a social description, indicating "the broad middle ranks of communal society . . . the regional merchants, notaries, moneychangers, manufacturers of cloth for the local market, retail clothdealers, and other professional groups of the major guilds who did not belong to lineages of great wealth or social prestige; and the shopkeepers, providers of services, builders, and artisans of various sorts in the minor guilds."⁹ But the term *popolo* also had a political meaning. In the thirteenth century, the middle ranks of society in city-states throughout northern and central Italy had organized themselves collectively to check the violence and political turmoil caused by rival factions of nobles, and to impose peace and civil order. Florence was no exception. Her *popolo* first organized itself around 1250, a movement referred to by modern historians as the *primo popolo*. The Ghibelline ascendancy of 1260–1267 destroyed this first popular movement, but it was revived again in 1282 with the regime of the Priors. The *popolo* took over the *comune*, that is to say the city government, and eventually, backed by the guilds, acquired institutional notes, including its own seal and coat of arms. From the 1280s down to the second half of the Quattrocento the governing body of Florence, officially at least, was the Priors of the Guilds of the Comune and People of Florence. That was the entity under whose authority the documents composed by Leonardo Bruni, in his role as chancellor of Florence, were transmitted to ambassadors and foreign powers; that was the entity which aspired to replace the Holy Roman Empire and the Papacy as the sovereign power in Tuscany. In Bruni's view, whatever was in practice the influence exercised on that gov-

ernment by the rich and powerful (including the Medici), it was nevertheless a free government, and therefore decisively different from the princely forms of government found elsewhere in Italy.

Political liberty is the key concept in Bruni's *History*, and refers both to independence from foreign rule and to internal self-rule. Self-rule does not mean political equality among citizens and representative government, as today, but rather broad consent of the middle and upper ranks of society to the policies of the political leadership. Political liberty also implies the freedom for qualified citizens to participate in city government (if not usually to exercise real political power) as well as protection from the arbitrary behavior of the powerful, as guaranteed by the rule of law. In Bruni's conception, however, political liberty is not merely a way of characterizing non-monarchical government; it is the key to explaining power and process in history. It was political liberty that made Etruria and the Roman Republic great; it was the loss of political liberty that, eventually, brought the Roman Empire down. The return of political liberty to the cities of Tuscany, after the withdrawal of the shadow of empire to Germany, had created the conditions leading to the present flourishing state of the Florentine empire. In a free state (as Bruni had learned from Sallust and Tacitus), great men competed for glory and made their city glorious and powerful as a result. Under tyrants, great men are cut down as a threat to the prestige of the ruler. Hence republican liberty was not only the best form of rule; it was the precondition of empire and the motor of historical change.

We can thus see in Bruni's *History*, for the first time in the Western tradition, the outlines of a conceptual framework that has dominated European historiography ever since: the tripartite division of history into an *ancient* period, for Bruni ending with deposition of the last Western Emperor, Augustulus, by Odoacer in A.D. 476; a *medieval* period, between the fall of the Roman Empire and the revival of city life sometime in the late eleventh and

twelfth centuries — a period marked by Germanic invasions and weak claims to imperial authority; and a *modern* period, beginning with the demise of the Holy Roman Empire as a force in Italian politics in the second half of the thirteenth century. This periodization (later adopted by Machiavelli) is not precisely the same as a modern historian would use, perhaps, but the underlying conception is the same. Insofar as the modern period is still today defined by the emergence of national states from the shadowy universal authorities of the High Middle Ages, the Empire and the Papacy, Leonardo Bruni may be said to be the inventor of the earliest political conception of the Modern. And though it was doubtless not Bruni's conscious intention to secularize history, his conception of the modern is, nevertheless, inescapably secular. Numerous commentators have noted that in Bruni's history, the rise and fall of political freedom takes the place that the fortunes of Christianity had held previously as an organizing principle in early Christian and medieval historiography. Divine providence is no longer, visibly at least, the prime mover in human affairs. Human beings themselves make their own history. It is for this reason, and not for any great formal or technical advances, that Bruni is rightly called the first modern historian.

If history is the result of human activity, both the historian and the citizen have a clear responsibility to learn from the past. In the Renaissance, as in antiquity, historical writing was looked upon as a way to extend greatly the natural memory of the human race and thus to acquire the virtue that grew from experience, careful thought and a well-stocked memory: namely, the virtue of prudence. Bruni's *History* is full of lessons for the citizens of a republic. For example: War is a hazardous enterprise that should be undertaken only with the advice of the wisest and most experienced citizens who understand motives and the underlying causes of events. In war, reason and a just estimate of one's strength and

one's true interests should always trump the lust for glory; the desire for honor is a poor excuse to undertake war. The aristocratic code of honor, however admirable in certain respects, is destructive when it issues in factionalism; unity is a precondition of success in both foreign and domestic affairs. Unity is promoted when the state alone is the font of honor, and citizens are allowed to compete freely for honor and offices. Only then is an ethic of public service created; only then is the republic on the road to greatness. A republic is better off when governed by the middling sort of citizen, frugal, hardworking, and peaceloving, for the citizen who is interested in business rather than conflict will be readier to put the good of the state ahead of private honor. At the same time, all the orders of society need to learn to live in harmony with each other. The popular rulers of the city should take the advice of their betters in wisdom and experience; aristocrats should learn to bridle their licentiousness and arrogance and accept popular rule; the lowest classes should be kept out of power at all costs. Such, for Bruni, were the main lessons history offered to the citizens of republics.

This volume is the first of three projected volumes. Volume 2 will contain Books v through viii of the *History*. Since Books ix through xii are considerably shorter than the previous books, volume 3 will be rounded out with a new edition and translation of Bruni's memoir, *An Account of the Events of His Own Time (Rerum suo tempore gestarum commentarius)*.

I could not have completed the work for this volume without generous help from a number of persons, whose assistance I gratefully acknowledge here. Abigail Fojas converted the relevant parts of Santini's Latin text to digital form for me, saving me the labor of retyping the text. Paola Tartakoff prepared collations of most of the witnesses I have used to establish the text, and I am most

grateful for her diligence and skill. My wife, Virginia Brown, read through the text and translation and made numerous suggestions for its improvement.

Neither this book nor the series in which it appears would have appeared without the enlightened support of Walter Kaiser, Director of the Villa I Tatti, of whom it may be truly said *nihil quod tetigit non ornavit*. The original impulse for the series and its ultimate form owe much to his shaping hand. I should like to dedicate the three volumes of this edition and translation to him as a token of gratitude for his help and wise counsel, his swift wit and unerring taste.

J.H.

Cambridge, Massachusetts

September 2000

NOTES

1. See especially Eric Cochrane, *Historians and Historiography in the Italian Renaissance* (Chicago, 1981), chapter 1.

2. For a summary and critique of the modern conception of civic humanism, see my essay "The Baron Thesis after Forty Years," in *Journal of the History of Ideas* 56 (1995), 309–338, and *Renaissance Civic Humanism: Reappraisals and Reflections*, ed. James Hankins (Cambridge, Eng., 2000).

3. In Bruni the most striking passage is the end of his *Oration for the Funeral of Nanni Strozzi*, in *Leonardo Brunis Rede auf Nanni Strozzi*, ed. S. Daub (Stuttgart and Leipzig, 1996), pp. 300–302; in the present text, note II.59, where the battle car of the Florentine state is treated as a kind of holy relic, kissed by soldiers on the point of death during the battle of Montaperti; or IV.11, where Bruni entertains the speculation that news of the victory of Campaldino was transmitted by divine messengers to the Florentine town council.

4. See my essay, "The Civic Panegyrics of Leonardo Bruni," in *Renaissance Civic Humanism*, p. 145.

5. The data regarding the composition of the *History* are summarized in my *Repertorium Brunianum: A Critical Guide to the Writings of Leonardo Bruni*, Istituto Storico Italiano per il Medio Evo, Fonti per la Storia dell'Italia medievale, Subsidia, vol. 2 (Rome, forthcoming).

6. R. Fubini, "Osservazioni sugli *Historiarum Florentini populi libri XII* di Leonardo Bruni," in *Studi di storia medievale e moderna per Ernesto Sestan* (Florence, 1978), p. 430, n. 82.

7. See for example Bruni's bitter remark about the modern popes in I.58, written just after he had left the papal service.

8. He did the same in his *New Cicero* (1413/14), where he used Plutarch to undermine Plutarch's own judgment about the relative merits of Demosthenes and Cicero, as well as in his *Commentary on the Punic Wars* (1420), where Bruni's pro-Roman account of the war reverses the slant Polybius had absorbed from his "Carthaginian" sources. The great student of Western historiography, Arnaldo Momigliano, writes of Bruni's historical writing: "This mixture of uncritical repetition of ancient sources and of very critical awareness that the ancient authorities themselves were conditioned by their own sources is the real beginning of historical criticism." See his essay, "Polybius' Reappearance in Western Europe," in *Polybe*, ed. E. Gabba, Entretiens sur l'antiquité classique, Fondation Hardt, XX (Geneva, 1974), p. 356.

9. The description is taken from John Najemy, "Civic Humanism and Florentine Politics," in *Renaissance Civic Humanism*, p. 82.

· Rome and the Etruscan Cities ·

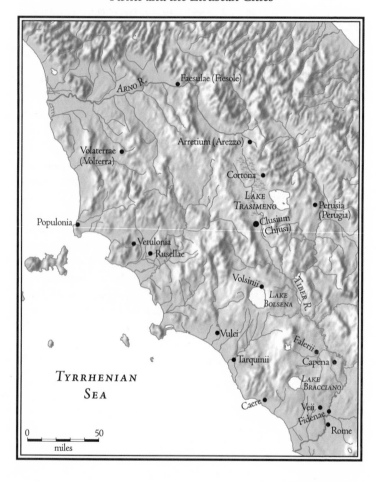

ARNO R.

Faesulae (Fiesole)

Volaterrae
(Volterra)

Arretium (Arezzo)

Cortona

LAKE
TRASIMENO

Perusia
(Perugia)

Populonia

Clusium
(Chiusi)

Vetulonia

Rusellae

Volsinii

LAKE
BOLSENA

TIBER R.

Vulci

Falerii

Tarquinii

Capena

LAKE
BRACCIANO

TYRRHENIAN
SEA

Caere

Veii

Fidenae

Rome

0   50
miles

· Italy in the Late Thirteenth Century ·

Trent

Milan

Pavia

Verona

ADIGE R.

Mantua

Venice

PO R.

Reggio Emilia

Ferrara

Modena

Bologna

Ravenna

Genoa

APPENNINE

Lucca

Florence

Pisa

ARNO R.

Siena

Città di Castello

Arezzo

LIGURIAN
SEA

Perugia

ADRIATIC
SEA

MOUNTAINS

Grosseto

Orvieto

Tiber R.

CORSICA

Viterbo

Tagliacozzo

Anagni

Montecassino
San Germano

Foggia

Capua

× Benevento

Naples

KINGDOM
OF
NAPLES

SARDINIA

TYRRHENIAN
SEA

IONIAN
SEA

MEDITERRANEAN

Palermo

Messina

Reggio Calabria

SICILY

SEA

- - - Boundary of the
Kingdom of Naples

× Battles

· Tuscany in the Late Thirteenth Century ·

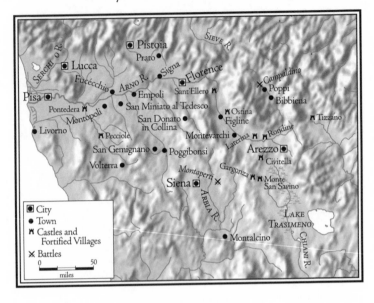

Pistoia

Prato

Lucca

SIEVE R.

SERCHIO R.

Fucecchio

Signa

Florence

Campaldino

Poppi

Pisa

ARNO R.

Empoli

Sant'Ellero

Bibbiena

Pontedera

San Miniato al Tedesco

Ostina

Figline

Tizzano

Montopoli

San Donato
in Collina

Livorno

Pecciole

Montevarchi

Laterina

Rondine

San Gemignano

Poggibonsi

Arezzo

Volterra

Gargonza

Civitella

Montaperti

Monte
San Savino

Siena

ARBIA R.

LAKE
TRASIMENO

Montalcino

CHIANA R.

City

Town

Castles and
Fortified Villages

Battles

0   50

miles

HISTORY OF THE
FLORENTINE PEOPLE

PROOEMIUM AUCTORIS

1 Diuturna mihi cogitatio fuit et saepe in alterutram partem sententia pronior faciundumne foret, ut res gestas florentini populi forisque et domi contentiones habitas et vel pace vel bello inclita
facta mandare literis aggrederer. Excitabat quippe me ipsarum magnitudo rerum, quibus hic populus primo inter se civili varioque
discidio, deinde adversus finitimos egregie gestis, tandem nostra
aetate potentia immodice adauctus et cum Mediolanensium po-
tentissimo duce et cum Ladislao bellicosissimo rege ita contendit,
ut ab Alpibus in Apuliam, quantum Italiae longitudo protenditur,
cuncta armorum strepitu quateret ac transalpinos insuper reges
magnosque exercitus ex Gallia et Germania commoveret.[1] Acce-
dunt ad haec Pisae captae, quam ego urbem vel diversitate animorum vel aemulatione potentiae vel exitu belli recte alteram Carthaginem, ut mihi videor, appellarim. Cuius extrema debellatio atque
obsidio pari obstinatione apud victos victoresque agitatae, ita multa[2] memoratu digna continent, ut antiquis illis maximis rebus,
quas legentes admirari solemus, nulla ex parte inferiores appareant.
Haec mihi perdigna literis et memoria videbantur ac earundem co-
gnitionem rerum utilissimam privatim et publice arbitrabar. Nam
cum provecti aetate homines eo sapientiores habeantur, quo plura
viderunt in vita, quanto magis historia nobis, si accurate legerimus,
hanc praestare poterit sapientiam, in qua multarum aetatum facta
consiliaque cernuntur, ut et quid sequare et quid vites faciliter su-
mas excellentiumque virorum gloria ad virtutem excitere?

Ex adverso labor ingens ac partim obscura, partim interrupta
2 quorumdam temporum notitia, nominum[3] denique asperitas vix
cuiuscumque elegantiae patiens, multae praeterea difficultates vehementer avertebant. Tandem vero his inter se multum diuque

PREFACE

It required long deliberation and many changes of mind before I 1
decided to write about the deeds of the Florentine People, their
struggles at home and abroad, their celebrated exploits in war and
in peace. What attracted me was the greatness of the actions this
People performed: first its various internal struggles, then its admirable exploits against its immediate neighbors, and finally, in
our own time, its struggle as a great power against the all-powerful
duke of Milan and the aggressive King Ladislas. Indeed, all Italy
from the Alps to Apulia rang with the sound of Florentine arms,
and even beyond Italy the People caused kings and vast armies to
cross the Alps from France and Germany. In addition there is the
conquest of Pisa, and if one considers the clash of characters, the
rivalry for power, and the ultimate outcome, I think it fair to call
that city another Carthage. In the final conquest and siege of Pisa,
victors and vanquished alike displayed an equal tenacity, and deeds
were performed that were every bit as memorable and important
as those great events we read about and admire so much in antiquity. These actions seemed to me very much worthy of record and
remembrance, and I thought that acquaintance with them would
serve both public and private ends. For if we think men of advanced years are wiser because they have seen more of life, how
much greater is the wisdom history can give us if we read it carefully! For there the deeds and decisions of many ages may be scrutinized; from its pages we may learn with ease what behavior we
should imitate and avoid, while the glory won by great men, as
therein recorded, inspires us to perform acts of virtue.

What held me back, however, was the labor involved in such an 2
enterprise, and the gaps and obscurities in our knowledge of certain times, the harsh sounding names that would hardly allow of
elegant treatment, and many other difficulties. Having weighed all

pensatis in hac potissimum sententia constiti, ut censerem quamcumque scribendi rationem torpenti silentio esse praeferendam. Itaque ea scribere aggressus sum, non ignarus quidem ipse mei nec quantum onus suscipiam nescius. Sed coeptis spero fautor deus aderit et, quando boni causa id ago, bene vertet. Quod si vires ausis non respondebunt meis, adnixum tamen conatumque iuvabit. Atque utinam superioris aetatis homines, utcumque eruditi atque diserti, scribere potius sui quisque temporis facta quam praeterire taciti maluissent. Erat enim doctorum, ni fallor, vel praecipuum munus, ut suam quisque aetatem celebrando, oblivioni et fato praeripere ac immortalitati consecrare niterentur. Sed puto alia aliis tacendi causa fuit; quosdam enim labore deterritos, quosdam facultate destitutos, ad alia potius scribendi genera quam ad historiam animum appulisse. Nam libellum quidem aut epistolam, si paulo coneris, faciliter transigas. Historiam vero, in qua tot simul rerum longa et continuata ratio sit habenda causaeque factorum omnium singulatim explicandae et de quacumque[4] re iudicium in medio proferendum, eam quidem velut infinita mole calamum obruente tam profiteri periculosum est quam praestare difficile. Ita, dum quisque vel quieti suae indulget vel existimationi consulit, publica utilitas neglecta est et praestantissimorum virorum rerumque maximarum memoria paene obliterata.

3   Ego autem non aetatis meae solum, verum etiam supra quantum haberi memoria potest, repetitam huius civitatis historiam scribere constitui. Pertinebit autem huius[5] cognitio et ad italicas res; nihil est enim iam diu per Italiam dignum memoria gestum in quo huius populi non intervenerint partes. Legationibus quoque vel missis vel acceptis explicandis magna ceterarum gentium notitia perstringetur. Sed antequam ad ea tempora veniam, quae propria sunt professionis nostrae, placuit exemplo quorundam rerum

these matters long and carefully, I came to feel that, on the whole, any plan for writing was better than silence and idleness. In starting to write, therefore, I have been aware of my own limitations and of the burdens of my task. But I hope that God will favor my enterprise and make it turn out well, since I am acting in a good cause. For if my abilities are not equal to the undertaking, He will nevertheless aid hard work and effort. Would that the men of earlier times, whatever the extent of their learning and eloquence, had recorded the events of their own day, instead of letting them pass by in silence! For if I am not mistaken, the special duty of scholars has ever been to celebrate the deeds of their own time and so to rescue them from oblivion and the power of fate — indeed, to render them hallowed and immortal. Yet I suppose that each man had his reasons for remaining silent. Some shrank from heavy labor; some lacked the ability; some applied themselves to other genres of writing. It is not hard, with some effort, to write a slim volume or a letter. History, however, requires at once a long and connected narrative, causal explanation of each particular event, and the public expression of one's judgment about every issue. With the unending burden of the task overwhelming the pen, a history is as dangerous a thing to promise as it is hard to perform. Thus, while everyone has pursued his personal comfort or considered his reputation, the public good has been neglected and the memory of remarkable men and heroic actions has been almost wholly lost.

I have decided, therefore, to investigate and write the history of 3 this city, not only in my own time but in earlier ages as far as memory has preserved it. The account will touch on the wider history of Italy as well, for nothing important has been done in Italy for a long time without the participation of at least some Florentines. To explain the various embassies sent out or received by this city, too, requires some notice of other nations. Before I come to the times that mainly concern me, however, I should like (following

scriptorum de primordio atque origine urbis vulgaribus fabulosisque opinionibus reiectis quam verissimam puto notitiam tradere, ut omnia in sequentibus clariora reddantur.

the example of certain annalists) to relate what I think is the most correct tradition concerning the city's founding and its origins. This will involve rejecting some commonly held but mythical beliefs, and will shed light on what is to follow.

LIBER PRIMUS

1   Florentiam urbem Romani condidere a Lucio Sylla Faesulas deducti. Fuerunt autem hi Syllani milites, quibus ob egregiam cum in ceteris tum in civili bello navatam operam, pars Faesulani agri est attributa et Faesulae una cum veteribus incolis sedes traditae. Has civium deductiones consignationesque agrorum Romani colonias appellabant, quod videlicet praedia quae colerent quibusque inhabitarent, sedes tradebantur. Quae autem occasio fuerit novos colonos in haec loca deducendi, pro rei notitia aperiendum est.

2   Haud multos ante Syllae dictaturam annos, cuncti ferme Italiae populi unum sub tempus a Romanis defecere, indignatione commoti quod ipsi una cum Romanis per singulas expeditiones militantes, laboresque et pericula pro augendo imperio subeuntes, praemiorum expertes angebantur. Quare saepius inter se conquesti, tandem legatis communi de re Romam missis, quasi civitatis membra, honores et[1] magistratus concedi sibi postularunt. Agitata ea res est per M. Drusi tribunatum, dubiaque spe aliquandiu protracta. Sed cum tandem eorum postulata reicerentur, aperte quasi ab ingratis rebellarunt bellumque gesserunt, quod quia a sociis gestum est, sociale bellum nuncupatur. In eo demum bello victor populus romanus, principes rebellandi provincias persecutus, multis illas cladibus afflixit. Sed praesertim in Picentes Tuscosque saevitum, nam et Asculum, florentissima Picentium urbs, hostilem in modum a Romanis vastata est et in Tuscis Clusium a solo eversum; Arretinis et Faesulanis, praeter belli damna et caedes,

BOOK I

The founders of Florence were Romans sent by Lucius Sulla to Faesulae.[1] They were his veterans who had given outstanding service in the civil war as well as in other wars, and he granted them part of the territory of Faesulae in addition to the town itself and its old inhabitants.[2] Such a relocation of citizens and assignment of lands was called a *colony* by the Romans, because the estates cultivated and inhabited by the citizens were granted to them as homes. Why new colonists were sent to this area, however, must be explained.

Not many years before Sulla's dictatorship, there was a general rebellion among the peoples of Italy against the Romans. They had been allied with the Romans on every campaign, had fought and labored by their side and shared the perils which attended their expansion, and yet, as they were distressed to find, they had not shared in the rewards. Hence their indignation. After much complaining among themselves, they finally sent a delegation to Rome to discuss their common problem, and to demand a share in honors and offices for themselves, as though they were themselves organic parts of the state. The question came up during the tribunate of Marcus Drusus, and for some time the petitioners were left in suspense. Their demands were ultimately rejected, however, and then the peoples involved rebelled openly and declared war on their ungrateful allies. Because the war was made by former allies of Rome, it is known as the Social War.[3] The Roman people emerged victorious and severely punished the leading provinces involved in the rebellion. They dealt most harshly with Picenum[4] and Tuscany. The flourishing city of Asculum in Picenum was razed like an enemy town, and in Tuscany, Clusium was likewise leveled to the ground. The people of Arretium and Faesulae also suffered heavy blows above and beyond the war dam-

magnae insuper calamitates inflictae per quas, publicatis multorum bonis multisque fugatis, civitates sunt paene habitatoribus inanitae.

3   Ea videlicet occasio fuit, et quasi invitamentum, ut Sylla postea dictator haec potissimum loca militibus suis tribueret. Per hunc igitur modum a L. Sylla militibus Faesulas deductis agrisque viritim divisis, eorum plerique urbem montanam et difficilem aditu, praesertim in illa securitate romani imperii, minime sibi necessariam arbitrati, relicto monte, in proxime[2] subiecta planitie, secus Arni Munionisque fluviorum ripas, conferre aedificia et habitare coeperunt. Novam urbem, quod inter fluenta duo posita erat, Fluentiam primo vocitarunt eiusque incolae Fluentini dicti. Et id quidem nomen per aliqua tempora urbi fuisse videtur, donec crescentibus rebus et civitate maiorem in modum adaucta, sive corrupto ut in plerisque vocabulo sive quod miro[3] floreret successu, pro Fluentia Florentiam dixere.

4   Meminerunt horum colonorum Tullius et Sallustius, duo praestantissimi latinae linguae auctores. Tullius optimos fuisse cives romanos et fortissimos viros affirmat, sed insperatis ac repentinis divitiis bello civili a Sylla locupletatos, modum in sumptibus servare nescisse; dum aedificant tanquam beati, dum magnis familiis magnisque conviviis et sumptuosis apparatibus violentius utuntur, in tantum aes alienum incidisse, ut si liberare se velint, rursus foret eis Sylla ab inferis excitandus. Equidem permagni facio quod latini parens eloquii de aedificiis scribit ac ex eo speciosa ab ipsis incunabulis fundamenta huius urbis fuisse coniecto. Et extant sane hodieque permanent vetustorum reliquiae operum vel in hac nostri temporis magnificentia civitatis admirandae: aquaeductus, per quem de septimo lapide accepti fontes in urbem ducebantur, et

age itself, for many people's property was confiscated and many were forced to flee, so that these towns were almost emptied of inhabitants.[5]

Such was the occasion—almost, in fact, the invitation—for Sulla's later action as dictator in granting his veterans these lands in particular. That is how Sulla's veterans came to Faesulae and divided the fields among themselves. Many of them decided, however, that amidst the security of the Roman empire it was unnecessary to inhabit an inaccessible hill town. So they left the mountain and began to form settlements along the banks of the Arno and the Mugnone in the plain below. The new city located between these two waterways was at first called Fluentia and its inhabitants Fluentini.[6] The name lasted for some time, it seems, until the city grew and developed. Then, perhaps just through the ordinary process by which words are corrupted, or perhaps because of the wonderfully successful flowering of the city, Fluentia became Florentia.

Both Cicero[7] and Sallust,[8] two great Latin writers, record the existence of these settlers. Cicero tells us, moreover, that the veterans, though excellent Roman citizens and the toughest of men, did not know how to control their spending when they found themselves suddenly and unexpectedly enriched by Sulla through civil war. They built grandly and created great households, gave large and luxurious banquets with abandon, and soon were buried in debt. To free them from this burden, Sulla himself would have had to return from the dead. What the father of Latin eloquence says of their buildings seems important to me, for it leads to the conclusion that the foundations of this city, from its very infancy, were magnificent. And there still exist today remains of ancient buildings that must command our admiration even amidst the present splendor of Florence. There is the aqueduct that brought water to the city from sources seven leagues away, and the great theaters, at that time placed outside the walls, for popular sports

3

4

theatri ingentis ad ludos populares tunc extra moenia positi, nunc intra urbem ipsam privatorum aedificiis occupati. Templum etiam, in quo nunc baptisterium est, vetustum sane ac egregium opus, Marti gentilitas consecravit.

5   Videntur autem hi coloni, sive levandi desiderii causa sive amore veteris patriae, pleraque Romanae urbis loca aedificiaque aemulari voluisse. Nam et capitolium sibi fecerunt et forum iuxta positum eo situ iisdemque regionibus inter se conversa, quis romanum forum capitoliumque videmus. Addiderunt thermas publicas ad populi lavacra; theatrum ad spectacula ludorum. Ex eadem aemulatione templum Martis est, in quem videlicet deum Romani genus, fabulosa licet credulitate, referebant. Usque adeo vero aemulandi studio provecti sunt, ut etiam minus necessaria opera maiori impensa non piguerit imitari. Productis ad septimum usque miliarium arcubus, fontes accepti in urbem ducebantur, qui ut Romae opportuni, ubi omnis aqua gypso corrupta solo profertur, sic Florentiae superflui, ubi purissimi latices tota urbe scaturiunt. Huic publicae magnificentiae privata quoque aedificia convenisse crediderim, quamvis in privatis minus appareat. Nam publicis quidem, ut supra diximus, non contemnendae reliquiae attestantur.

6   In his igitur aedificationibus ac cetero vitae splendore, quem Tullius memorat, occupatos, dum nec futurum prospiciunt nec parto parcunt, brevi, ut fit, tempore, pecuniae defecerunt, et simul unica largitionum spes, L. Sylla, non dictatura modo, verum etiam vita abierat. Itaque partim indigentia, partim consuetudine praemiorum adducti, novum aliquem motum exoriri optabant. Viri militares et civili bello assueti, quietes[4] esse nullo pacto sciebant; rursus novas dictaturas et nova belli praemia mente volutabant. Et

and spectacles. These theaters are now located within the city limits and built over with private residences. Also, the temple where the baptistery is now located is an outstanding ancient structure which the pagans dedicated to Mars.

Out of nostalgia or love for their old home, the colonizers seem 5 to have consciously imitated Rome in their planning of the city and in the construction of buildings. They built themselves a capitol and a forum, in the same configuration as was found in Rome, and they had baths for public cleanliness and an arena for watching games and spectacles. The temple of Mars was built in the same spirit of emulation, for it was to this god that the Romans, superstitiously, traced their ancestry. They were so eager to affirm their relationship to Rome, in fact, that they liked to copy less important structures as well, even at tremendous expense. They brought water in by aqueduct, which was reasonable in Rome where all the local water was chalky, but superfluous in Florence where perfectly pure water springs up in abundance. It seems likely, moreover, that their private houses matched their public buildings in magnificence, though the evidence that this was the case is less abundant. The above-mentioned ruins of the public buildings prove how ample those, at least, were.

Absorbed in their luxurious way of life and surrounded by 6 buildings such as these, the colonists lived, as Cicero tells us,[9] without thought of the future and without saving any part of their wealth, and, as usually happens in such cases, it was quickly spent. Meanwhile Sulla, their one source of largesse, not only left the dictatorship but passed out of this world. So, partly because of their poverty and partly because they were accustomed to getting rewards, they looked forward with eagerness to some new disturbance. Soldiers and men used to civil war, they had no idea how to live in peacetime. Their thoughts ran ever to new dictatorships and new booty. And debt was an added incentive to draw the

accedebat aes alienum, acer quidem stimulus et qui timidis etiam animos facere soleat ad otium perturbandum.

7   Forte per id tempus Romae L. Catilina res novare aggressus, magnam adversus rem publicam coniurationem inierat, in qua multi equestris, multi senatorii ordinis, quidam item patritii generis fuerunt. Tetigitque suspicio C. Caesarem, eum qui postea dictator fuit; tunc autem non privatus tantum sed et alieno aere onustus, res novas cupere putabatur. Multa igitur prius Romae efficere conatus, ubi tentata parum prospere succedebant, parte coniuratorum intra urbem ad patranda illa quae praescripserat relicta, ipse cum reliquis exire ac foris bellum concitare decrevit. Et primo quidem Praeneste nocturno impetu occupare, ibique sedem belli constituere⁵ cogitarat; mox vero, ut diligentius eam urbem custodiri sensit, mutato consilio pro Praeneste Faesulas delegit. Egressus itaque Roma et ad haec ipsa loca profectus, regionem totam bello armisque involvit.

8   Hoc primum periculum et ultimum paene discrimen tenerae adhuc urbi et modo conditae fuit, quod tamen ita evasit, ut commodius equidem posuerim accidisse. Nam Lentulus et Cethegus aliique coniurationis principes quos Romae Catilina reliquerat, dum plures secum in societatem facinoris adsciscere conantur, proditi a legatis Allobrogum et in senatu convicti, ultimo tandem supplicio affecti periere. Catilina vero, ut haec audivit, quando spes iam fractae et conatus in irritum casuri videbantur, in Galliam fugere conatus est, sed ab exercitibus romanis circumventus, et fortunam pugnae experiri coactus, una cum suis in pistoriensi agro occiditur. Haec ego, quamquam pervulgata harum rerum historia sit, tamen quia in hanc regionem et primordia huius urbis inciderunt, paucis commemoranda putavi.

9   Enim vero hic motus rerum ac belli vicinitas, ut non nihil detrimenti novae urbi incussisse, sic veluti quandam salutarem discipli-

sword, for debt is a sharp spur that drives even timid persons to make trouble.

At this very time, as it happened, Catiline in Rome was fo- 7
menting a revolt. He had embarked upon a vast conspiracy against 67 B.C.
the commonwealth, involving many knights, many senators, and
even some persons of patrician ancestry. Suspicion fell also on Ga-
ius Caesar, the one who later became dictator, although at this
time he not only held no public office but was burdened with debt
and was thought to be thirsting for revolution. Catiline had already made various attempts in Rome without much success. He
now left some conspirators in the city to carry out his instructions
and decided to go forth himself with the rest and start a war from
the outside. His first choice was to take Praeneste by a night attack and to establish a base there; but when he learned that that
city was well guarded, he changed his mind and opted for Fiesole.
He came to this region from Rome and involved the whole of it in
armed conflict.

The young city thus experienced its first danger and almost its 8
earliest crisis, but considering the happy outcome, I should say it
was a good experience. This was because Lentulus and Cethegus
and the other leaders of the conspiracy whom Catiline had left in
Rome, while trying to organise a larger revolt, were turned in by
the Gaulish ambassadors they had contacted. They were convicted
in the senate, were given the death penalty, and perished. When
Catiline heard this news, he saw that his hopes were dashed and
that his efforts would be to no avail. He gave up hope and tried to
escape to Gaul, but he was surrounded by Roman armies and was
forced to try his fortune in battle, with the result that he and his
followers were killed on the fields outside Pistorium.[10] The story is
familiar, of course, but I wanted briefly to retell it because it happened here and affected the beginnings of this city.

The disturbance and the proximity of war seem in fact to have 9
done some harm to the new city but also to have forced the people

nam hominibus attulisse videtur. Per aliena namque pericula, spe novarum dictaturarum praemiorumque quibus ante vehementius inhibant deposita, suis contentos esse rebus oportere tunc primum didicerunt, et spem in turbatione ponere vanum ac periculosum esse. Simul igitur cum animi proposito mutati mores. Terreri alieno aere, sua diligenter circumspicere ac perpendere, parsimoniae ac frugalitati operam dare, sobrietatem colere, disciplinam rei domesticae exercere, luxuriam et prodigalitatem viam ad perniciem existimare: haec ipsi facere, haec liberos edocere. Igitur civitas, emendatis moribus, robustius coalescere, et immigrabant frequentes, dulcedine loci amoenitateque pellecti. Surgebant aedificia; suboles augebatur.

10   Crescere tamen civitatis potentiam ac maiorem in modum attolli, romanae magnitudinis vicinitas prohibebat. Ut enim ingentes arbores novellis plantis iuxta surgentibus officere solent nec ut altius crescant permittere, sic romanae urbis moles sua magnitudine vicinitatem premens, nullam Italiae civitatem maiorem in modum crescere patiebatur. Quin immo et quae ante fuerant magnae, ob eius urbis gravem nimium propinquitatem, exhaustae porro diminutaeque sunt. Quemadmodum enim tunc cresceret civitatis potentia? Neque sane fines augere bello poterat sub imperio constituta nec omnino bella exercere nec magistratus satis magnifici, quippe eorum iurisdictio intra breves limites claudebatur, et haec ipsa romanis magistratibus erat obnoxia.

11   Mercaturae quoque, si quis forte eam partem ad incrementum civitatis attinere quidquam existimet, non alibi per id tempus quam Romae commodius exercebantur. Ibi frequentia hominum et venundandi facultas, eorum portus, eorum insulae, eorum portoria, ibi gratia, ibi publicanorum favor; alibi neque gratia neque potentia par. Itaque sicubi quisquam per propinqua loca nascebatur ingenio validus, is, quia domi has sibi difficultates obstare videbat, Romam continuo demigrabat. Ita quidquid egregium per Italiam nascebatur ad se trahens, alias civitates exhauriebat. Quod

to learn a good lesson. From the perils of others, they learned to give up their own overpowering desire for new dictatorships and new booty. For the first time they realized that they must build on what they already had, and that placing their hopes in political disturbances was both vain and dangerous. So all at once they changed, not only their ideas, but their way of life. They began to practice new mores themselves and trained their children in them. Now they feared debt, carefully watched and counted their possessions and cultivated thrift and frugal ways; they were sober, limited their spending, and saw luxury and prodigality as the road to ruin. Having mended its ways, the city became prosperous and immigrants crowded in, attracted by the beauty and charm of the region. New buildings arose and the fertility of the populace increased.

Only the nearness of Rome in her grandeur limited Florentia's 10 rise to power. As mighty trees overshadow young seedlings that grow nearby and keep them stunted, so did Rome overwhelm her neighbors with her sheer size, allowing no greater city to arise in Italy. Other cities that had once been great were oppressed by their neighbor Rome, ceased to grow, and even became smaller. How, then, might Florentia's power increase? Being under imperial rule she could not augment her borders by war, nor indeed wage war at all; nor could she boast splendid magistrates, since their jurisdiction was narrowly circumscribed and subject to Roman officials.

As to commerce—in case anyone thinks that this activity is 11 somewhat relevant to the growth of the city—in those days it could most profitably be carried on in Rome. That was the place where men gathered and where there were markets. Rome had ports, islands, tolls, privileges, official protection. Nowhere else was there so much privilege and power. If a man of solid worth was occasionally born elsewhere within the general region, he would see the difficulties that stood in his way at home and invariably move to Rome. Thus Rome drew to herself everything won-

antecedentia simul et secuta tempora manifestissime ostendunt. Etenim priusquam Romani rerum potirentur, multas per Italiam civitates gentesque magnifice floruisse, easdem omnes stante romano imperio exinanitas constat. Rursus vero posteris temporibus, ut dominatio romana cessavit, confestim reliquae civitates efferre capita et florere coeperunt, adeo quod incrementum abstulerat, diminutio reddidit.

12   Quoniam vero de civitatibus Etruriae multa dicturi sumus, utilissimum nobis videtur, ab ipsis vetustissimis incipientes, de tota etrusca re, qualis ante romanum imperium qualisque postea fuerit, quam brevissime fieri poterit, recensere. Et simul illud annectere, postquam romana potentia cessavit, quae civitates in ea floruerint, quae capita extulerint, quam potentiam habuerint, ut ex hac notitia et narratione rerum etruscarum peritiores instructioresque ad tempora usque nostra deducamur.

13   Ante romanum quidem imperium longe maximas totius Italiae opes maximamque potentiam ac prae ceteris vel bello vel pace inclitum nomen etruscorum fuisse, inter omnes antiquissimos rerum scriptores haud ambigue constat. Origo autem vetustissima eius gentis ex Maeonia est, unde Lydi multitudine ingenti ac praeclara bello manu Italiam navibus advecti, in ea parte quae nunc Etruria dicitur consederunt, pulsisque inde pelasgis ceterisque eius regionis veteribus incolis, a Tyrrheno eorum rege Tyrrheniam nuncuparunt. Aucta subinde subole et potentia simul cum multitudine in dies⁶ crescente, quantum inter Apenninum montem et inferum mare Tyberimque et Macram fluvios terrarum clauditur, id totum propagatis finibus tenuere, mox Etrusci a sacrifico, ut creditur, ritu, vel a sereni contemplatione coeli graeca lingua nuncupati, ipsaque regio Etruria dicta. Totam vero etruscam gentem in duodecim populos divisam fuisse veteres tradidere, sed eos omnes ab initio rex unus gubernabat. Tandem, ut regia potestas gravior illis visa, ex singulis populis singulos lucumones (sic enim magistratum

derful that was engendered in Italy and drained all other cities. The proof lies in any comparison of pre-Roman and Roman times. Before the Romans took over, many cities and peoples flourished magnificently in Italy, and under the Roman empire all of them declined. After the fall of Rome, on the other hand, the other cities immediately began to raise their heads and flourish. What her growth had taken away, her decline restored.

Since we shall be speaking at length about the cities of Tuscany, 12 it seems appropriate to summarize briefly the history of that whole region from its most ancient beginnings. We shall observe what Tuscany was like both before and after the period of Roman domination, and in the latter period, which of its cities flourished, which capitals became prominent, and what sort of power they exercised. We shall thus arrive at our own times with a knowledge and understanding of Tuscany derived from the facts of history.[11]

Before the Roman empire, the greatest wealth and power in It- 13 aly and the greatest fame in war and peace belonged to the Etruscans — such is the clear message of all the most ancient sources. The original home of this people was Maeonia, whence the Lydians, with a large populace and a famous band of warriors, sailed to Italy and settled in the region now called Tuscany. They expelled the Pelasgians and other previous inhabitants, and called the region Tyrrhenia after their king, Tyrrhenus. Their progeny increased and their power grew daily with their numbers, until they had extended their borders and controlled all the lands from the western shore to the Apennines, and from the Tiber to the Macra River. Later they received the Greek name, Etruscans, which referred either to their sacrificial rites or to their contemplation of clear skies.[12] The region itself acquired the name Etruria. According to ancient sources, the Etruscans consisted of twelve tribes. Originally, however, they all obeyed one king. Eventually, as royal power seemed burdensome to them, each tribe began to elect a separate *Lucumo*, as they called the magistrate who, with the help

vocitabant qui comuni consilio totam regeret gentem) creare coeperunt. Eorum unus certo tempore aliis praeerat, ita tamen ut
auctoritate et honore, non potentia princeps esset. Sub hoc igitur
magistratu per longa tempora pari voluntate auctoritateque duodecim populorum Etruria gubernata, qualis concordiae fructus esse
solet, in tantas opes potentiamque accrevit, ut non solum urbibus
passim opportunis locis per eam conditis virisque et divitiis intra
fines floreret, verum etiam extra longe lateque dominaretur.

14   Testes eius potentiae sunt duo maria, quibus Italia modo insulae cingitur; utraque sane non ab aliis populis quam ab Etruscis
nominata. Inferius Tuscum, idemque Tyrrhenum, vetusto gentis
nomine, quae appellatio, ut quibusdam Graecis placet, ab Sardinia
in Siciliam obtinet. Superius Adriaticum ab Atria, oppido quondam maritimis rebus maxime inclito, quod Etrusci per ea tempora,
iis quoque locis dominantes, iuxta litus superi maris non longe
a Padi ostiis⁷ condidere. Etenim Apenninum transgressi, omnia
primo cis Padum loca, mox et transpadanam regionem totam
usque ad Alpes praeter extremum Venetorum angulum, bello et
armis subacta, Etrusci possederunt. Inde per tractum adriatici maris descendentes, magnam eius litoris tenuerunt partem, pulsis
Umbris, gente per eam tempestatem maxima ac potentissima,
quorum supra trecenta oppida ab Etruscis debellata fuisse veteres
tradunt historiae. Cis Apenninum vero per inferiorem Italiae partem ad fretum usque siculum eorum potentia provecta est. Haec
autem per loca frequentibus missis coloniis, multae quidem urbes
ab eis conditae, multae etiam veteribus exactis possessoribus novo
colono repletae memorantur, quarum veluti indices eorum potentiae adhuc extant. Ab inferiori quidem Italiae parte Capua inter
inclitas quondam urbes perpaucas nominata; a superiori vero

of a communal council, ruled the whole tribe. One such *Lucumo* came to be supreme over the others, but in prestige only, not in actual power. Under this magistracy, Etruria was ruled for a long time by the equal will and authority of all its twelve peoples; and internal concord, as it usually does, gave them wealth and power. The various cities founded in suitable places within the borders of Etruria became large and prosperous, and eventually the Etruscans held sway over lands far beyond their own borders.

The two seas that nearly encircle Italy bear witness to the 14 power of the Etruscans, for both are named after them and no others. The lower sea was named the Tuscan or Tyrrhenian Sea after the old name of the people, and according to certain Greek sources, this name applied to it from Sardinia to Sicily. The upper sea was called the Adriatic, named after Atria, a famous port founded by the Etruscans on the coast not far from the mouth of the Po—for they ruled that area too.[13] Indeed, once the Etruscans had crossed the Apennines, they subdued in war and occupied, first of all, every place on their side of the Po, and later the whole region on the other side up to the Alps, except for the farthest promontory held by the Venetians. Moving down the sweep of the shore, they controlled the greater part of that coast and expelled the Umbrians, a people who were then numerous and powerful enough, as the ancient sources tell us, to lose over three hundred towns to the Etruscans. On our side of the Apennines they extended their power through the southern part of Italy down to the straits of Sicily. And wherever they went, they colonized. Historians preserve the memory of numerous towns which they founded, as well as numerous towns whose previous inhabitants they drove out and replaced with their own people. Some of those towns still exist, a continuing monument to their former power. Capua is mentioned among the very few once-famous cities of this kind in the south, while in the north there is Mantua, which started as an Etruscan colony. It is known that the Etruscans

Mantua et ipsa quoque Etruscorum colonia. Nam ex singulis Etruriae populis, quos duodecim fuisse supra docuimus, singulas colonias trans Apenninum missas constat, quarum praecipuae fuerunt urbes: Atria, ex qua Adriatico nomen est mari; item Mantua, quae ex transpadanis sola nunc extat.

15   Videtur autem huius gentis potentia vetustissimum quidem initium habuisse, utpote quae ante troiani belli tempora non aucta modo, verum etiam pollens florensque fuerit. Aeneam denique Troia[8] profugum cum a Latinis et Rutulis bello premeretur, ad florentes Etruscorum opes contulisse sese ac exinde auxilium petiisse Virgilius facit. Evandrus enim,[9] cum Aeneae roganti opem consilium[10] daret ac[11] sibi nequaquam tantas esse vires ut Latinis Rutulisque resistere quiret docuisset, ad Etruscos illum destinans, sic inquit:

> ast tibi ego[12] ingentis populos, opulentaque regnis
> iungere castra paro.

16   Et paulo post id ipsum explanans:

> haud procul hinc saxo colitur[13] fundata vetusto
> urbis Agillinae sedes, ubi Lydia quondam
> gens, bello praeclara, iugis consedit[14] Etruscis.
> hanc multos florentem annos rex deinde superbus[15]
> imperio et saevis tenuit Mezentius armis.

17   Quamquam ut alienior a poetarum figmentis, sic intemeratior ac purior historia tradit non Aeneam, sed Turnum bello superatum ad Mezentium et florentes Etruscorum opes confugisse atque inde adversus advenam ducem exercitumque auxilia supplicem implorasse. Sed utravis opinio praestiterit, troianum ante bellum floruisse etruscam rem fateamur necesse est. Duravit autem incolumis domique et foris usque ad transitum Gallorum in

(who, as we have said, consisted of twelve peoples) sent colonies from each separate people across the Apennines. Their principal cities were Atria, which gave her name to the Adriatic, and Mantua, which is the only one still extant of the Etruscan plantations beyond the Po.

It seems that the power of the Etruscans had an extremely ancient origin, that they were not merely an emerging force before the Trojan War, but already powerful and prosperous. Hence Aeneas, a refugee from Troy, turned to the Etruscan state for help in his war against the Latins and Rutulians, or so Virgil says. For Evander, when he was giving counsel in answer to Aeneas' plea for help, began by telling him that he himself did not have enough power to resist the Latins and the Rutuli, and then directed him to the Etruscans, saying: [15]

> And then I plan for a vast people and well furnished armies
> To join you.

A little later he explains: [16]

> Not far hence, founded upon an ancient rock,
> Rises the site of the Agyllan city, where once Lydia,
> A nation famous for war, settled on the Etruscan hills.
> This old and flourishing city, King Mezentius
> Has yoked by cruel arms under his proud rule.[14]

Another account, somewhat more removed from the inventions of the poets and therefore truer and less corrupt,[15] tells us that it was Turnus, not Aeneas, who turned to Mezentius after suffering defeat and who asked for help from the wealthy Etruscans against an invading chief and his army.[16] Whichever account we accept, however, we must admit that the Etruscan nation flourished before the Trojan War. And it lasted intact at home and abroad until the invasion of Italy by the Gauls, about six hundred years after the Tro- [17] *616 B.C.*

23

Italiam, annos post troianum bellum circiter sexcentos; post conditam vero urbem Romam centum fere et septuaginta.

18   Quo quidem tempore Galli maximis peditum equitumque copiis duce Belloveso Alpes transgressi, aliaque inde super aliam multitudine per priorum vestigia ex Gallis Germanisque confluente, eam omnem Italiae partem, quae nunc Gallia Cisalpina dicitur, Tuscis ademerunt. Novissimi vero omnium Gallorum Senones tractum maritimae orae, in quo Sena Gallia urbs est, occuparunt. Ab iis et aliis Gallis opes Etruscorum attritae et intra iugum Apennini post longa bella repressae. Romanorum insuper crescens potentia alia ex parte fines obtundebat. Ita in medio duarum validissimarum gentium constituti, Etrusci bifariam vexabantur. Mansit tamen etiam post per aliquot saecula robur et auctoritas gentis, ut foris imminutae, sic domi validae praepotentisque.

19   Enim vero longe alia ratione cum Romanis quam cum Gallis agebatur. Nam adversus barbaras illas et efferatas gentes implacabile bellum fuit Etruscis. Cum Romanis vero non odio neque acerbitate unquam pugnatum; plus etiam amicitiae quam belli interdum fuit.

20   Declarant imitationis studia, quae nemo ab invisis despectisque assumit. Constat autem Romanos praetextam et trabeas phalerasque et annulos, togas quoque pictas et palmatas tunicas, currus insuper aureos triumpho decoros, fasces denique et lictores et tubas et sellam curulem ac cetera omnia regum magistratuumque insignia ab Etruscis sumpsisse. Nam quod duodecim lictores apparebant regibus consulibusque romanis, id quoque inde sumptum traditur, quod cum ex duodecim populis Etrusci constarent, singulos singuli lictores regi dabant. Inde ab Romanis res accepta, nec numerus quidem imminutus est. Haec omnia, ne quis forte

jan War, and about one hundred and seventy years after the founding of Rome.

The Gauls, led by Bellovesus, had massive forces of infantry 18 and cavalry. They crossed the Alps and were followed by other populations migrating from Gaul and Germany. Together these peoples took from the Tuscans all that part of Italy which is still known as Cisalpine Gaul.[17] The last of the Gauls were the Senones, who occupied a tract of the coastline around the city of Senigallia. The wealth of the Tuscans was diminished by these and other Gauls, and after long wars Etruria was confined within the area bounded by the Apennine passes. Meanwhile the growing power of the Romans encroached on their borders from the other side. Thus the Etruscans were squeezed between two very vigorous peoples and were pressed hard on both borders. Still, for several centuries, the strength and authority of this people, though diminished outside Tuscany, remained vigorous and dominant at home.

The Etruscans behaved very differently toward the Romans 19 than they did toward the Gauls. Against those barbarian and savage peoples they waged implacable war. Against the Romans, they never fought with hatred and bitterness; in fact, from time to time they were more Rome's friends than her adversaries.

Rome's desire to imitate them proves this, for no people imi- 20 tates those whom they hate and despise. The Romans took from the Etruscans the toga praetexta and the phalera; the painted togas and embroidered tunics; the rings of office; the handsome golden chariots used in triumphs; the fasces, the lictors, the trumpets and curule chairs, and all the other insignia of kings and magistrates.[18] The twelve lictors who prepared the way for Roman kings and consuls are also said to be derived from the Etruscans. Since that nation consisted of twelve peoples, each people sent one attendant to the king. After the custom was adopted by the Romans, the latter kept the same number of lictors. Lest anyone think we are sim-

nosmet nobis blandiri existimet, graeci romanique vetustissimi scriptores tradidere. Nec imperii tantum insignia ceterumque augustiorem habitum sumpserunt ab Etruscis, verum etiam litteras disciplinamque. Auctores habere se Livius scribit, ut postea Romanos pueros graecis, ita prius etruscis litteris vulgo erudiri solitos. Nam caerimonias quidem ac religionem et cultum deorum, qua in arte Etrusci prae ceteris gentibus excelluisse traduntur, Romani sic ab illis susceperunt, ut tamen priores partes relictas penes auctores ipsos faterentur. Simul atque gravius quidquam rei publicae imminebat, in quo deum numina placandum censerent, vates et haruspices ex Etruria vocabantur. Denique omnis harum rerum cognitio etrusca disciplina apud Romanos vocitata est. Haec et huiusmodi[16] inde sumpta probare mihi videntur, Romanos etruscam gentem cum observantia quadam admiratos, a qua et ornamenta imperii et deorum cultum ac disciplinam litterarum, tria maxima ac praestantissima, sibi publice privatimque imitanda receperint. Nec pacis quidem artibus admirati sunt gentem, bello autem contempserunt. Probant obsidio urbis Romae et obsides Porsennae traditi, quod post transitum Gallorum in Italiam fuisse admirabilius est. Nec ob ullum magis quam ob[17] etruscum hostem Romae trepidatum reperies, neque dictatores saepius dictos. Primus Romanorum Etruscos bello attigit Romulus ipse, Romae[18] urbis conditor; mox et alii fere[19] omnes romani reges, praeter Numam Pompilium et Tarquinium Superbum, id bellum susceperunt.

21   Fuit autem inter Etruscos Romanosque prima belli origo ex huiusmodi causa. Fidenae Tuscorum colonia trans Tyberim fuit inter crustumerinum romanumque agrum. Qui eam incolebant

ply flattering ourselves, moreover, we may note that all this information comes from the oldest Greek and Roman sources. The Romans did not take from the Etruscans imperial insignia and other dignified forms of dress only, but also their letters and learning. Livy says that he has sources to show that Roman boys, before the period when they were given instruction in Greek literature, were commonly taught Etruscan literature.[19] The Romans also adopted their religious ceremonial and cultic practices from the Etruscans — and in these arts the Tuscans are reported to have excelled all other nations — doing this in such a way that they left the older rites in the charge of their Etruscan inventors. As soon as a serious crisis would threaten the commonwealth and the Romans decided that the spirits of the gods needed placating, priests and soothsayers would be summoned from Etruria. All such knowledge of religious matters was referred to by the Romans as 'Etruscan learning'. It seems to me that the Roman willingness to borrow these things shows that they had a certain respect for the Etruscans. Imperial insignia, religious ceremonies, and literary studies are excellent and important matters, things that relate to private as well as public life. Nor did the Romans admire Tuscany for the peaceful arts but despise her in war. The Etruscan attempts to besiege Rome and the hostages turned over to Porsenna in particular are recorded, which are all the more impressive because by that time the Gauls had arrived in Italy. Nor will you find that any enemies frightened the Romans more than the Etruscans, or forced them to adopt dictators more often. The first war of Rome against Tuscany was started by Romulus himself, the city's founder, and from then on almost all the kings of Rome took up this same war again, excepting only Numa Pompilius and Tarquinius the Proud.

The cause of the first war between the Etruscans and Romans was as follows. Fidenae was an Etruscan colony located across the Tiber, between the lands of Crustumerium and Rome. The Etrus- 21

c. 750 B.C.

Etrusci, urbem novam sibi finitimam immodice crescere suis inimicum commodis rati, priusquam ad summum plane robur, quod iam inde cernebatur, evaderet, praevenire festinantes, et suis ipsi[20] viribus et propinquis Etruriae opibus fisi, bellum Romanis, nulla prius accepta iniuria, intulerunt. Populato itaque romano agro ingentique abacta praeda, cum fuga agrestium urbem quoque metu ac tumultu complesset, Fidenas onusti rediere. At Romulus, ut has iniurias ultum iret, legionibus raptim eductis infesto agmine Fidenas contendit. Eo cum pervenisset, nec moram nec spatium Fidenatibus praebet auxilium ex Etruria arcessendi, sed ipsis adequitando portis, mox et fugam simulando, ira et indignatione ad pugnam excivit, tantusque fuit ardor militum et praestantia ducis ut cum Fidenates in insidias praecipitati effuso cursu urbem repeterent, victi victoresque uno impliciti agmine Fidenas intrarent. Captis igitur per hunc modum Fidenis et praesidio militum ab romano rege imposito, Veientes, qui propinquiores ex Etruriae populis Fidenatibus erant, cum indigno consanguineorum casu permoti, tum etiam quod propinquitatem Romanorum infestam sibi inquietamque putabant fore, armata iuventute emissa, discursionem[21] in agrum romanum praedabundi fecere. Adversus hos quoque Romulus resistendi ulciscendique gratia legiones eduxit. Haec prima Romanis Etruscisque origo fuit belli; quod tunc leviter coeptum,[22] leviter etiam terminatum est, mutuis dumtaxat populationibus, vastatis agris, parvaque admodum pugna tumultuario magis quam iusto proelio commissa. Indutiae in centum annos secutae.

22   Ceterum ex hoc ferme initio cetera post hoc bella inter Tuscum Romanumque oriuntur, quod vel exierat indutiarum tempus vel

cans who had colonized Fidenae thought that their new neighbor, the city of Rome, was growing immoderately and would become a threat to their own well-being. Gathering their own forces and those of their Etruscan neighbors in the region, they hastened to start a preemptive war against Rome before the latter gained what they already anticipated would be her full strength, and they attacked her without provocation. The men of Fidenae laid waste to Roman territory and took a lot of booty before returning home laden with spoils, while country people fleeing to Rome filled the city with fear and turmoil. Romulus quickly called out his legions to avenge these injuries and headed off to Fidenae with an attack force. He arrived so rapidly that he gave the men of Fidenae no time to summon help from Etruria. Romulus rode his men to the very gates of Fidenae, then feigned flight, which provoked the Etruscans to fight out of anger and indignation. Such was the Roman soldiers' ardor and their leader's excellence that when the army of Fidenae had been lured into the trap and had fled back to their city in a disordered rout, a confused throng containing both vanquished and victors entered Fidenae.[20] The town was thus taken and a garrison imposed by the king of the Romans. The people of Veii, the nearest Etruscan city to Fidenae, were troubled by the humiliation of their kinsmen, and now feared that they would have no more peace with the hostile Romans so near; so they sent out their young warriors to raid the Roman countryside and plunder the farms. Romulus led his legions to fight and take revenge on this people, too.[21] Such was the beginning of the first war between the Romans and the Etruscans. As it was rather lightly started, it was easily ended, with both sides merely suffering some plundering and destruction of farms, but with fights more like brawls than proper battles. A truce lasting one hundred years followed.

From this beginning, however, other wars arose later between 22 the Etruscans and the Romans, either because the truce ran out or

dictis conventisque non manebatur. Sub Romulo tamen et Numa
Pompilio indutiae valuerunt, nullo ab alterutris motu exorto. Tullio mox regnante Hostilio rursus exarsit bellum ob Fidenatum rebellionem. Defecerant enim Fidenates a Romanis. Veientes consilii
participes impigre tulerunt opem et asciverant in occultam belli
societatem Metium Fufetium Albanorum dictatorem. Hic enim
principatum romani populi, cui post Horatiorum pugnam se ex
foedere subdiderat, indigne ferens, clam cum Etruscis convenit ut
commisso proelio Romanos, quibus per speciem auxilii legiones
albanas coniunxerat, versis signis adoriretur. Infirmi tamen vir
animi, nec hostibus nec suis promissa servavit. Neque enim cum
Romanis quibuscum in arma venerat Etruscos invasit, nec rursus
ut promiserat Etruscis Romanos adortus est, sed inter spem et
metum fluctuante consilio, seorsum eduxit suos, quocumque victoriam inclinari vidisset et ipse eodem momento inclinaturus. In
ancipiti proelio vicit populi romani fortuna et bellacissimi Tullii
regis audacia. Fusis denique pugna ingenti hostibus, Fidenas recepit ac mox affecto poena Metio Albam Longam evertit.

23   Ancus inde Martius et Priscus Tarquinius romani reges bellum
deinceps etruscum ambo susceperunt. Sed de Martio quidem
haud ambigue constat; de Tarquinio autem varia apud scriptores
traditio est. Sunt qui non cum Veientibus modo, sed cum tota penitus etrusca gente bellum per novem annos gestum a Tarquinio
rege tradant. Sunt et qui rebus eius regis enarrandis, quasi nihil
fuerit cum Etruscis negotii, totam rem tacitam intactamque prae-
tereant. Sed ut de Tarquinio ambigitur, sic de Servio Tullio certis-

because the agreed-on conditions were not being observed. The peace held, however, under Romulus and Numa Pompilius, and neither side broke it. After that, in the reign of Tullius Hostilius, war broke out again because of an uprising of the men of Fidenae, who had rebelled against the Romans.[22] The men of Veii, who were privy to their counsels, helped them with alacrity and brought Metius Fufetius, the dictator of Alba, into a secret military alliance. He had been forced to submit by treaty to the hegemony of the Roman people after the battle of the Horatii. Resenting this, he made a secret agreement with the Etruscans that, once the battle had been joined, he would attach his Alban legions to those of the Romans on the pretext of bringing them aid, then change sides and attack them. Being a man of vacillating temperament, however, he kept his pledges neither to his enemies nor to his own side. He neither fell upon the Etruscans in company with the Romans, with whom he had joined forces, nor did he help the Etruscans attack the Romans. With a mind wavering between hope and fear, he kept his men out of the battle until he had seen who would win, so as to join the winning side at that moment. The opponents were evenly matched, but Roman fortune and the audacity of their fierce king, Tullius, triumphed. He routed the enemy in a terrible battle and retook Fidenae. He then executed Metius, and razed the city of Alba Longa.

The next two kings of Rome, Ancus Marcius and Priscus 23 Tarquinius, both continued the war with the Etruscans. This is perfectly clear in the case of Marcius, but we have different stories concerning the elder Tarquinius. Some say he fought for nine years, not only with Veii, but with almost all the Etruscan nation. Others, telling the story of this king, pass over the matter in total silence as though he had no business at all with the Etruscans. But if there is some doubt about Tarquinius, it is certain that Servius Tullius fought hard and long against the entire Etruscan people, and with a larger war-machine, than any king before him. Certain

simum est eum maiori quam quemquam superiorum regum apparatu, cum tota etrusca gente bello gravissimo et longissimo contendisse. Viginti annos continuatum a Servio id bellum quidam auctores ferunt.[23] Me quoque propensiorem ad credendum belli diuturnitatem facit, quod per annos quatuor et quadraginta (tot enim regnavit Servius) nullum aliud bellum quam etruscum ab eo rege susceptum memoratur. Quod tanta laude gessit, ut cum prius iniussu populi regnasset, vel eius belli a se gesti fiducia, de se referri ad populum et incerto multitudinis suffragio nomen regium committere non abnuerit. In eo tamen bello nec victi Etrusci nec aliquae eorum urbes captae traduntur; multis dumtaxat ultro citroque inflictis cladibus, illud modo effectum ut videretur superior Romanus fuisse. Haec regio dominatu Romae durante cum Etruscis gesta.

24 Exactis deinde regibus Tarquinius regno pulsus, ad Etruscos fiducia generis, quod ab iis oriundus erat, supplex confugiens, duos Etruriae populos, Veientes Tarquiniensesque, in arma concivit; qui romanum in agrum magnis copiis profecti, cum L. Iunio Bruto et M. Valerio, cui postea Publicolae nomen fuit (hi tum primi anni consules erant[24]), pugnaverunt. Proelium fuit atrox vehemensque ut nullum ante. Utriusque aciei dexterum vicit cornu; in maxima tamen hominum strage utrinque facta, creditum est uno plures ex Tuscis quam ex Romanis cecidisse. Maior autem Romanis inflicta clades, quod L. Brutus, qui auctor fuerat regis eiciendi, in eo proelio[25] interfectus est. Pugnae certe ea fortuna fuit ut utravis pars se victam putaret. Denique Romanis morte alterius consulis orbatis, plurimaque suorum caede territis, fugam ad primam lucem parantibus, Etrusci, priusquam illucesceret, abiere.

authors tell us that his war with Tuscany lasted continuously for twenty years.[23] I am disposed to believe that the war lasted so long because in the forty-four years of Servius' reign, he is not known to have waged any other war. He gained such a reputation for his conduct of this war that, although he had ruled at first without popular sanction, later, on the strength of his victories, he did not refuse to submit his rule to the people's approval and to expose the name of king to the unpredictable votes of the multitude. We are not told that the Etruscans were conquered in this war, however, or that they lost even one of their cities. It seems simply that over a long period each side inflicted great damage on the other, and that the ultimate result was a strengthening of Rome's position. These are the events relating to the Etruscans that occurred in Rome during the monarchical period.

When the monarchy ended and Tarquinius was driven out, he fled as a suppliant to the Etruscans.[24] He was counting on family loyalty, since he had sprung from them, and he managed to incite to arms two Etruscan peoples, the Veii and the Tarquinii. They sent a vast army to invade Roman territory and fought against Lucius Junius Brutus and Marcus Valerius, who was later known as Publicola (for these were the consuls in those first years of the republic). The battle was ferocious and cruel as no previous conflict had been. The right wing of both armies outflanked its opponents, but in the mutual slaughter, according to one source, the Etruscans lost many more men than the Romans. The greater loss, however, was inflicted on the Romans, for Lucius Brutus, the leader of the movement to expel the king, was killed in that battle. The outcome was certainly such that each side considered itself defeated. Finally the Romans, bereaved by the death of one of their consuls, were terrified by the enormous casualties among their men and prepared to retreat at dawn; the Etruscans left the field before daylight.

24

509 B.C.

25   Porsenna inde Clusinus rex, ob restituendum Tarquinium maiori apparatu renovavit bellum. Hoc duce Etrusci Romanos vicerunt, incluserunt, obsederunt, urbem etiam capturi, nisi Horatius Cocles pontem Sublicium, qui unus per id tempus Tyberi supererat, rescindi iussisset. Ostendunt periculi magnitudinem honores a populo romano Cocliti habiti, non ob victam subactamque hostium provinciam, sed ob id solum, quod rumpendi pontis moram facultatemque dedisset suis. At enim maiores, si vera loqui ius fasque sit, tyberino debebantur amni: nempe quam romana virtus tutari non poterat, tyberini gurgites urbem servarunt. Etrusci, Ianiculo et omnibus cis Tyberim locis occupatis, reliquam urbis partem longa obsidione pressam tenuere, donec deficiente obsessos cetera spe, in corpus regis grassandi consilium iniretur, ut cui aperto bello pares non essent, eum clam per insidias e medio tollere molirentur. Hinc illa scribae caedes et Mutii Scaevolae manus foculo iniecta.

26   Nec tamen his tot artibus prius etruscus rex ab obsidione destitit urbis quam obsides, non mares modo verum etiam feminas, dandi necessitatem expressit obsessis. Dati nobilissimi cuiusque nati, feminae etiam virgines; inter quas Valeria, Publicolae consulis filia, multaeque aliae patritiarum gentium. Haec praecipua de populo romano Etruscorum gloria fuit, nec cum aliquo quoquam communis; nunquam enim alii cuiquam imperatori vel genti populus romanus obsides dedit ob pacem impetrandam. Ipsi certe Romani iis quos vicerant nihil fere aliud quam obsides imperabant, in quo non solum cautio pacis, sed et confessio victoriae contineri putabatur. Foedus cum Porsenna initum mutua Etruscorum Ro-

Porsenna, king of Clusium, renewed the war to restore Tar-   25
quinius with greater forces at his disposal. Under this leader, the
Etruscans beat the Roman army, surrounded and besieged Rome,
and almost took the city. The only thing that saved Rome was the
order of Horatius Cocles to destroy the Pons Sublicius, which was
at that time the only bridge to span the Tiber.[25] How grave the
danger had been is apparent from the honors the Roman people
granted him, not for conquering and subduing an enemy province,
but merely for giving his own people the time and means to destroy a bridge. It would have been more appropriate (if it is not
irreverant to speak the truth) to honor the Tiber itself, for it was
the river's swirling waters that saved the city when Roman valor
could not. The Etruscans, who controlled the Janiculum and held
all the areas on the north side of the Tiber, long held the other
parts of the city in the grip of a siege. The besieged formed a plan
to attack the person of the king. This was their sole remaining
hope as they were unequal to open warfare. So they resorted to
cunning tricks to lure him furtively away from the main body of
his troops. Hence the murder of the secretary and story of how
Mucius Scaevola put his hand in the fire.[26]

But all these stratagems did not cause the Etruscan king to lift   26
the siege, and when he did go he insisted on taking both male and
female hostages from the besieged. Men of the noblest birth were
given, and high-born maidens. Among the latter was Valeria,
daughter of Publicola the consul, as well as many others from patrician families. This was a triumph for the Etruscans unequaled
by any other people. To no other ruler or people had the Romans
ever given hostages in order to sue for peace. They themselves, indeed, when they conquered others, demanded almost nothing but
hostages, for this to them meant not only a guarantee of future
peace but an admission of defeat. The treaty that was signed with
Porsenna was further stabilized by benefits which accrued to both
Etruscans and Romans. For the Etruscans were received with

manorumque beneficia secuta stabilius fecerunt. Nam et excepti
amice hospitaliterque Etrusci Romae, qui ad oppugnandam Ari-
tiam cum Arunte regis filio post romanum foedus profecti, mox
amisso duce redierunt, hisque vicus in celeberrima parte urbis datus, qui Tuscus propterea dictus est, ac Romanis post aliquot annos benigne a Porsenna obsides remissi. Tarquinius, qui ad eam
diem in Etruria fuerat, aliunde sibi quaerere auxilia iussus, ad Manilium Tusculanum[26] generum transiit.

27   Firma hinc pax quiesque romano populo et Etruriae fuit, quam
ad extremum Veientes turbarunt. Haec enim civitas agrum Romanis finitimum habens, ex communione, ut saepe fit, discordiis
haustis, post varias querelas aliquotiens ultro citroque iactatas,
tandem aperto certamine cum Romanis contendit. In eo bello,
prima quidem pugna, Romanos Vei superarunt. Secunda autem
pugna atrocissima fere omnium quae unquam memorantur fuit, in
qua Romani, primo proelio ab Etruscis victi, milites iurare coegerunt se nisi victores nunquam redituros. Itaque hac religione ob-
strictis animis, obstinatius quam ante pugnatum est, non sine
utriusque partis maxima clade. Interfecti sunt in eo proelio Cn.
Manilius[27] consul et Q. Fabius alterius consulis frater. Capta
etiam romana castra atque direpta ab Etruscis, sed mox fortuna
mutata pugnae, a romanis victoribus recuperata. Nec quicquam
magis ad victoriam obfuisse videtur Etruscis quam nimia festinatio
in castris oppugnandis, ad quae dum properant quasi victores, eorum acies plus iusto exhausta a Romanis superatur. Raro tamen
unquam incertior atque mobilior fortuna quam ea die fuit. Victi
procul dubio, Romani vicerunt. Tanto denique sanguine victoria
constitit ut, cum postea triumphus consuli offerretur, lugendum

friendship and hospitality at Rome when they, after the alliance with the Romans, went on an expedition against Aritia under Aruns, the son of Porsenna, and returned after his death in battle. They were given houses in a beautiful section of Rome, known thereafter as the Tuscan Quarter,[27] and Porsenna after some years kindly gave back the hostages to the Romans. Tarquinius, who was still living in Tuscany, was bidden to seek help elsewhere and went to Mamilius Tusculanus, his son-in-law.[28]

Afterwards peace and tranquillity reigned between Rome and Etruria until it was finally broken by Veii. Veii was a city bordering on Roman territory, and, as often happens, friction arose through contact. After various quarrels initiated at intervals by one side or the other, Veii finally started an open conflict with Rome. In the first battle of the war, the men of Veii overcame the Romans. The second battle, however, was perhaps the most horrible ever recorded. The Romans, after their first defeat, had made the soldiers swear that they would never return except as victors. The soldiers felt bound by this oath, and they fought with much greater tenacity than before, and there were extremely heavy losses on both sides. Killed in the battle were the consul Gnaius Manlius and Quintus Fabius, the brother of the other consul. The Roman camp was seized and plundered by the Etruscans, then the tide of battle turned and the Romans recovered it. Nothing seems to have contributed more to the Roman victory than the excessive haste of the Etruscans in sacking the Roman camp. For when the Etruscans, believing themselves victorious, made a rush for it, they relaxed their own battle-order more than they should have and so were beaten by the Romans. Hardly ever has fortune been so treacherous and so fickle as it was that day. It appeared certain that the Romans had been beaten, but they still won. The victory was so bloody that later, when the consul was offered a triumph, he would state that it was an occasion for weeping rather than for

27

482 B.C.

potius esse diceret[28] quam triumphandum. Non minori tamen dolore huius pugnae casus Veientes quam prioris Romanos affecerat.

28   Itaque accitis reliquae[29] Etruriae auxiliis (nam primo quidem
ipsi per se soli pugnarant), vindicabundi in hostem ruentes, trecentos et sex Fabios, ex una omnes familia, qui apud Cremeram
praesidium contra Veios munierant, cum magna clientium manu
ad quinque millia hominum fuisse ea traduntur, ad unum interfecerunt. Inde legiones romanas, quae cum L. Menenio consule non
procul a Cremera castra habebant, eodem impetu aggressi, non solum verterunt in fugam exercitum consulemque, verum etiam castris exuerunt. Mox fugientes palatosque non absque magna caede
Romam usque persecuti, Ianiculum montem, qui cis Tyberim contra capitolium maxime imminet, occuparunt tenueruntque aliquot
menses veluti obsessam urbem. Tyberi etiam traiecto et ad Portam
Collinam et ad alia diversissima a Tyberi loca sub ipsis romanis
moenibus pugnas conseruerunt. Tandemque ut ante Porsenna
eundem locum tenente, ad extrema digladiandi remedia ventum
est. Sic tunc iterum legionibus etruscis Ianiculum occupantibus,
premente urbem fame, necessitas Romanis expressa ut duo consules duoque consulares exercitus cum universa iuventute romana in
ipso Ianiculo monte ancipiti periculosoque certamine cum Etruscis confligerent. Nec ita prosper fuit eventus pugnae, quin alter ex
consulibus capitis reus ad populum fieret quod male pugnasset.

29   Denique, ne singula proelia consecter, haec una Etruriae civitas,
nunc ipsa per se, nunc et aliarum civitatum viribus adiuta, supra
trecentesimum et quinquagesimum romanae urbis annum bellum
extraxit. Victa interdum proeliis et ipsa saepe victrix. Extremum

triumphal celebration. And the outcome of the battle caused Veii as much sorrow as Rome.

Veii had fought alone before, but now they called for help from the rest of Etruria. They avenged themselves by attacking the enemy and killing, it is reported, all 306 members of the Fabii family (who had been fortifying a stronghold near the Cremera river against the men of Veii), together with a large band of their followers, in all some five thousand men. The Veian forces then directed a similar blow at the Roman legions posted near Cremera under the consul Lucius Menenius. Not only were army and consul forced to flee, but the whole camp was thoroughly plundered.[29] The retreating army and stragglers were pursued and cut down with great loss of life until they reached Rome. There the Etruscans again occupied the Janiculum Hill, which overlooks the north side of the Tiber across the river from the Capitoline Hill. For some months they occupied and held it as though they were besieging Rome. They would even cross the Tiber and engage in battles both by the Porta Collina and at various other places by the Tiber beneath the very walls of Rome. As when Porsenna threatened Rome from the same place, it came down in the end to sword-fighting at close quarters. As on that occasion, once again Etruscan legions held the Janiculum and threatened to starve the rest of the city. Rome was forced by extreme need to call out both consuls and two consular armies and the entire youth of Rome. They attacked the Janiculum in a dangerous struggle where the forces were evenly matched. Nor was the outcome favorable to the Romans. One of the two consuls was afterward arraigned before the people for military incompetence.

To summarize a great many battles, this one Etruscan city carried on the war against Rome down to 403 B.C. and beyond. Sometimes she had the help of other cities, sometimes she fought alone. Sometimes she was beaten in battle, sometimes she won. Her final overthrow, however, came when she decided on her own,

28

403 B.C.

29

autem in quo subacta est, nullo communi tuscae gentis decreto sed privato consilio, ipsa intulerat bellum. Itaque, mox prementibus Romanis, denegata sibi ceterorum populorum auxilia fuerunt, indignantibus aliis quod citra commune gentis decretum sua ipsi auctoritate bellum movissent, et metu insuper Gallorum ad sua quosque tuenda retinente. Responsum denique in communi tuscae gentis conventu Veiis auxilia flagitantibus datum: ipsi per se, quando ita placeret, adversus romanam vim resistere curarent, nec in eo bello socios periculi quaererent in quo speratae ab initio praedae socium habere nullum voluissent. Haec Romanis obsidendi Veios occasionem facultatemque dedere. Sustinuit tamen, quamvis deserta, suo proprio ac domestico robore aliquandiu bellum, nec nisi post decem aestates decemque hiemes continuas circumfessa, nec tunc[30] quidem vi, sed improvisa cuniculorum fraude, expugnata est.

30   Praedae tantum ex ea una urbe Romani cepere quantum ex omnibus superioribus bellis ad eam diem nunquam acceperant. Denique cum supra exercitum fortunae eius urbis putarentur, universus populus romanus publico edicto, quod nunquam alias factum est, ad praedam vocatus. Fuit enim urbs opulentissima atque maxima, ea situs laude eaque opportunitate ut saepe a victoribus cogitatum sit de relinquenda urbe Roma et Veios, tanquam in praestantiorem urbem, populariter commigrando.

31   Veiis captis, veluti claustra sibi Romanus patefecerat ad reliquos Etruriae populos subigendos. Itaque mox adversus Faliscos et Capenates, quos propinquitas Veientani belli haud intactos reliquerat, exercitus ducti, eorum urbes sine longo nimium certamine in potestatem romani populi dedere compulerunt. Quod tamen diversis rationibus factum est. Nam Capenatibus quidem per vastitatem agrorum vis expressa dedendi. Faliscos vero admirandae virtutis specimen in Furio Camillo praestantissimo Romanorum

not by agreement among the Etruscan peoples, to resume the war. Thus, when Rome pressed her hard, she was refused help by the other Etruscan peoples. They were angry because Veii had started a war on her own authority without seeking a general resolution of the Etruscan peoples, and they were also, in some cases, fearful of the Gauls and anxious not to leave their own territories unprotected. Their answer, when Veii sought their help, was given by a general council of the Tuscan peoples: "Resist the Romans yourselves, since that is your wish, but do not ask for allies to share the danger in a war where you originally had no desire to share booty with allies." This gave Rome the chance and the means to besiege Veii. Though abandoned by her allies, the city sustained the war a long time by her own strength alone. Only after ten successive summers and winters of siege was it taken, and then not by force but by a ruse: a surprise attack through underground tunnels.   *394 B.C.*

The Romans took as much plunder from this one city as they   30
had gained in all their previous wars put together. Since the wealth of the city seemed too much for the army alone, the whole Roman people was summoned, by a special edict, to come and take part in the plunder. This had never been done anywhere else. Indeed, Veii was a most opulent and impressive city, and its site was so fine and had such possibilities that the victors considered many times abandoning Rome and emigrating en masse to Veii, as to the more excellent city.[30]

Now the capture of Veii seemed to open the way for Rome to   31
subdue all of Etruria. The Romans attacked the Faliscans and the Capenates, peoples whom the war with nearby Veii had not left unscathed. They were both compelled to surrender their cities without a very long struggle. The collapse, however, occurred for different reasons in the two cases. The Capenates were forced to give up because of the devastation to their lands. The Falisci, on the other hand, were so impressed with the admirable virtue of the great Roman leader, Furius Camillus, that they surrendered to

duce conspectum, ut se sponte dederent, subegit. Et quos non ignis, non ferrum, non obsidio, non vastitas agrorum flectere potuerat, iustitiae et honestatis splendor inflexit. Gesta est autem res in hunc maxime modum.

32   Cum populato agro non longe a Faleriis castra Romanorum posita essent, magister quidam ludi, improbae fraudis mercedem sperans, principum filios sibi in disciplinam traditos, per diversam ab hoste portam quasi spatiandi gratia secum eduxit. Mox alio ex alio conserto[31] sermone, diversis ab urbe tramitibus stationi Romanorum quae inter castra et urbem posita erat, se cum discipulis obiecit. Captus itaque sponte sua et ad imperatorem perductus, "Falerios," inquit, "imperator, tibi hodie tradidi, quando hos pueros, quorum parentes principes sunt civitatis, in manus tuas adduxi. Tu huius tanti beneficii memor gratusque erga me esto." Quae ubi Camillus audivit, facinus improbi hominis despicatus, "Tu," inquit, "sceleste, ad tui similem te venisse putas, cui turpia non solum cordi sint, verum etiam praemio digna videantur? Mihi vero populoque romano longe diversa mens est. Colimus enim belli sicut et pacis iura, armaque adversus armatos hostes, non adversus imbelles pueros gerimus. Ita denique Faliscorum hostes sumus, ut humana tamen societate cum eisdem nos esse coniunctos meminerimus. Ego armis, patientia, virtute, quae romanae sunt artes, non improbando scelere Falerios vincam." Nudatum inde hominem et manibus post terga vinctum, discipulis verberandum reducendumque in urbem tradidit. Ex hoc tanta[32] mutatio Faliscorum ani-

him of their own free will.[31] Men who could not be subdued by fire or sword, or by siege, or by the devastation of their fields, were moved by the splendor of justice and honor. Here is the remarkable story.

The Romans had pitched their camp in a devastated area near 32 Falerii, and a certain Faliscan grammar teacher, hoping for gain from an act of wicked fraud, took some of the sons of the leading citizens who had been entrusted to him for their education and led them to the enemy camp. He started them off on a supposed walk through a gate facing away from the enemy, then, distracting them with his ceaseless chatter, brought them by various paths away from the city to a Roman outpost located between the Roman camp and the city. He was thus by his own intent captured and brought before the commander. "General," he said, "today I have given the Falisci into your hands by giving you these children, whose parents are the leaders of the city. No doubt you will remember to be grateful to me and reward my services." When Camillus heard these words, he showed contempt for the crime of this unscrupulous person. "Do you think, you rascal," he replied, "that you have come to criminals like yourself, who will not only embrace your act of wickedness but reward it? My attitude and that of the Roman people is quite different. We maintain the laws of war as we do those of peace, and fight our wars against armed enemies, not against harmless children. Though we are the enemies of the Falisci, we do remember that we are bound together with them by our common humanity. I shall conquer the Falisci with arms, with persistence, and with virtue. These are Roman qualities. I shall not conquer them by some rascally crime." Stripping the man naked and tying his hands behind his back, he then turned him over to his students to be beaten and brought back to the city. The result of this act was a great change of heart on the part of the Faliscans. While they had burned till then with incredible hatred for the enemy and had preferred ruin to a Roman

mis iniecta est ut qui modo incredibili odio accensi, exitium potius quam pacem romanam mallent, nihil aliud quam fidem et iustitiam imperatoris admirantes, sese atque urbem in potestatem populi romani tradiderint. Per hunc modum Falisci superati sunt.

33   Nec multo post Tarquiniensibus et Caeritibus arma illata. Ad Vulsinienses tandem transivit bellum, velut incendium quoddam alia subinde loca circumsumens; tandem ad intimas Etruriae gentes, Clusinos, Perusinos, Arretinos (hae tunc[33] potentissimae civitates erant), penetratum. Hic aliquandiu substitit vis belli, et cursus victoriae retardatus est, iam ipsis civitatibus commune periculum magis horrentibus damnantibusque errorem suum, quod non Veios et Falerios et Capenas, quae dudum oppida praeceperat hostis, quando in iis tutandis res quoque sua agebatur, ab ipso initio defendissent, sed negligendo et quiescendo in consanguineorum periculis, cum suae gentis minui vires, tum hostem[34] augeri passi essent.

34   Et profecto non ambigitur quin si omnes Etruriae populi uno consilio bellum gessissent, diuturnius ac magnificentius tota Etruria defendi potuisset. Sed sive Galli accolae perpetui hostes sive discordia quaedam civitatum sive fata cuncta iam ad Romanos trahentia sive haec simul omnia fecerunt, ut non una conspiratione ad bellum coirent. Haec certe causa Romanum superiorem dedit, quod ille et suis et sociorum viribus potens, non totam simul gentem, sed singulas civitates pervadebat. Reliquae vero, ceu ea res ad se non pertineret, nec primis quibusque absumptis ad proximos inde periculum foret venturum, otiosas expectactrices alienae calamitatis se praestabant. Neque enim Veios, ceteris Etruriae populis auxilia ferre paratis, tam longa[35] obsidione cepisset Romanus,

peace, now they gave themselves and their city into the hands of
the Roman people. Such was the strength of their admiration for
the good faith and justice of the Roman general. Thus were the
Faliscans conquered.

Soon after this, the Romans attacked Tarquinii and Caere. The 33
war spread to Volsinii, as fire will consume other places nearby,
and eventually it penetrated to the heartlands of the Etruscans,
Clusium, Perusia, and Arretium, which were most powerful cities
at that time. Here the violence of the conflict was briefly checked,
and the victorious advance of the Romans slowed, as the Etruscan
cities now began to tremble at their common danger. They cursed
their own mistake in not from the very beginning defending Veii,
Falerii, and Capena, the towns first seized by the enemy, for in
protecting those places they would have been acting in their own
interest as well. Through negligence and laziness in their kinsmen's hour of need, they had allowed their people's strength to decline and that of the enemy to grow.

Undoubtedly, if all the Etruscans had waged war with a unified 34
strategy, they might have defended themselves long and magnificently. Whether it was the presence of the Gauls as a permanent threat on their borders, or discord among themselves, or the
Fates now favoring the Roman side, or a combination of all these
things, they failed to go to war with a common plan. It was certainly this that gave the Romans the upper hand. Uniting their
own forces to those of their allies, they overcame, not the whole
nation at once, but each city in turn. The cities not directly involved acted as though the matter did not concern them and as
though they themselves would not be next after their neighbors
had been destroyed. Thanks to their idleness and hesitation, they
lent themselves to each other's destruction. For the Romans could
not have kept up the long siege of Veii if the other Etruscan cities
had stood ready to help her—indeed, they would not have dared
besiege Veii at all. In fact, as soon as even two of the other cities,

immo nec obsidere quidem ausus esset. Quippe duobus tantum populis, nec iis quidem maximis, Capenatibus et Faliscis opem ferentibus, obsidionem paene totam Romani dissolverunt. Sed dum integra fuit etrusca res, nunquam hic animus populis a diis datus; fracta vero atque imminuta, sero tandem saniora quidem, sed parum iam profutura consilia inierunt. Victa est ergo ad extremum multis atque ingentibus proeliis, quorum maxime insignia fuerunt, unum apud Sutrium, in quo sexaginta millia Etruscorum caesa traduntur, alterum ad Vadimonis lacum, in quo, fractis opibus et fortuna vetere amissa, in pace potius quam in armis reliquam spem habere coeperunt.

35   Venit autem tota in potestatem populi romani circiter CCCCLXX annum post Romam conditam, cum ab ipso conditore Romulo bella initium cepissent. His autem bellis romani duces plurimi claruerunt. Nam et primus rex et primus consul ac deinceps secuti reges consulesque, dictatores praeterea quidam et tribuni militum summa cum industria in illis versati, laudem amplissimam meruere. Sed e regibus quidem, praecipuam eius belli gloriam alii Prisco Tarquinio, alii Servio Tullio delegant. Ex consulibus autem M. Valerius Publicola de hac gente primus triumphavit; inde M. Fabius, P. Servilius, Mamercus Aemilius, A. Cornelius Cossus multique alii consules dictatoresque magnam sibi in iis bellis gloriam peperere. Excellentissima tamen omnium gloria fuit M. Furius Camillus, qui Veios et Falerios subegit, et Fabius Maximus, qui extremo fere tempore multis ac maximis proeliis, quantum nemo alter, Etruscorum opes[36] afflixit. Romani quamvis armis subactos Etruscos, tamen, postquam se suaque in potestatem populi romani dedidere, honesto vocabulo socios appellarunt.

and not the greatest ones but only Capena and Falerii, began to give some support, the Roman siege was almost broken. Yet the Etruscans, as long as the nation remained whole, were not blessed with this spirit of unity. Only when they had been divided and diminished did they finally — too late — take wiser counsel, but by then it was of little use. So the Etruscans were beaten at last in a series of great battles. The two most famous encounters took place at Sutrium, where 60,000 Etruscans, it is said, were left dead on the field, and at Lake Vadimonis,[32] where, their power broken and their old luck gone, they came to put their remaining hopes in peace rather than arms.[33]

311 B.C.

About four hundred and seventy years after the founding of Rome by Romulus, who also saw the beginning of these wars, all Etruria fell into Roman hands. These wars brought fame to many Roman leaders. The first king and the first consul, and all the kings and consuls after them, and the dictators, and the military tribunes, all gave their best efforts in campaigns against the Etruscans, and so earned notable glory. Among the kings of Rome, some authorities assign special glory in this contest to the elder Tarquin, some to Servius Tullius. Among consuls, Marcus Valerius Publicola had the first triumph, but later there were many others, such as Marcus Fabius, Publius Servilius, Mamercus Aemilius, Aulus Cornelius Cossus, and many other consuls and dictators who acquired great glory for themselves in these wars. The finest glory of all was won by Marcus Furius Camillus, the conqueror of Veii and Falerii. But that of Fabius Maximus matched it, for he, towards the end of this period, damaged the power of the Etruscans in more and greater battles than anyone else. And although they had subdued the Etruscans by arms, still, after the latter had surrendered themselves and their possessions into the hands of the Roman people, the victors gave them the honorable name of allies.[34]

35

283 B.C.

47

36   Remisso dehinc bellorum metu, secura quidem ab armis Etruria fuit, sed veluti marcescente otio oppugnata. Est enim hoc mor-
talibus natura insitum, ut via ad amplitudinem honoresque expo-
sita, facilius se attollant; praeclusa vero, inertes desideant. Tunc
igitur imperio ad Romanos traducto, cum neque honores capessere
neque maioribus in rebus versari liceret, etrusca virtus omnino
consenuit, longe plus inerti otio quam hostili ferro depressa. Bis
tamen, postquam in Romanorum potestatem concessit, rebellionem publice molita est. Primum sub Hannibalis tempore, ducibus
Arretinis; secundum sociali bello, quo Latini et Marsi et Umbria
Romanis defecere. Prima rebellio iam parturiens per Arretinorum
subitam oppressionem facile sopita est. Secunda vulneribus et
cruore extincta, Clusiumque et Faesulae gravissimis incommodis a
Romanis afflicta. Fuit autem post haec sub romano imperio firmi-
ter et indubitate usque ad Arcadii et Honorii tempora, annos
postquam subacta fuerat circiter septingentos.

37   Tunc enim primum Goti, Radagaso et Alarico ducibus, Italiam
pervasere, iam ante ab imperatoribus paene neglectam, fatiscenti-
bus certe opibus et potentia populi romani ad ruinam vergente.
Gothos Hunni secuti sunt; Hunnos Vandali; Vandalos Heruli;
post hos iterum Gothi; mox Langobardi multis sub regibus Italiam possidere.

38   Declinationem autem romani imperii ab eo fere tempore po-
nendam reor quo, amissa libertate, imperatoribus servire Roma incepit. Etsi enim non nihil profuisse Augustus et Traianus, etsi qui
fuerunt alii laude principes digni videantur, tamen, si quis excel-
lentes viros primum a C. Iulio Caesare bello, deinde ab ipso Au-

Thenceforward, fear of war receded and Etruria was safe from 36
armed attack, but now she was besieged, as it were, by debilitating
leisure. It is a fact of human nature that, when the way lies open
to greatness and honors, people are ready to better themselves;
when that way is blocked, they become lifeless and do nothing.
When their empire had been transferred to the Romans, and
the Etruscans could neither gain honors nor put their energies
into major enterprises, Etruscan virtue grew completely enfeebled.
They were brought low far more by inactivity than by the enemy's
sword. Twice after their surrender to the Romans, the Etruscans
tried to rebel. The first attempt came in the days of Hannibal's invasion, under Aretine leadership. The second revolt was during 209 B.C.
the Social War, when the Latins, the Marsi, and the Umbrians rebelled against the Romans. The first rebellion was easily strangled
at birth when the Aretines were rapidly crushed. The second rebellion was stamped out with much suffering and bloodshed, and
the Romans imposed heavy penalties on Clusium and Faesulae.
After this, however, Etruria remained firmly and unquestionably
under Roman power, down to the time of Arcadius and Honorius; at this point she had been subjugated for about seven hundred years.

It was then that the Goths, under their leaders Radagaisus and 37
Alaric, first ravaged Italy. Even before that the emperors had been A.D. 401
neglecting Italy, their resources were waning and the power of the
Roman people was in severe decline. The Goths were followed by
the Huns, the Huns by the Vandals, and the Vandals by the
Heruli, after which the Goths invaded again; then, shortly thereafter, the Lombards held Italy under the rule of their many kings.

Yet the decline of the Roman Empire ought, in my opinion, to 38
be dated almost from the moment that Rome gave up her liberty
to serve a series of emperors.[35] Even though Augustus and Trajan
may have been useful to Rome, and although other princes too
may have merited praise, yet we should consider the excellent men

cruelly cut down in the civil wars of Caesar and during the wicked triumvirate of Augustus. If one considers the savagery of Tiberius after that, the fury of Caligula, the insanity of Claudius, and the crimes of Nero with his mad delight in fire and sword; if one adds Vitellius, Caracalla, Heliogabalus, Maximinus and other monsters like them who horrified the whole world, one cannot deny that the Roman empire began to collapse once the disastrous name of Caesar had begun to brood over the city. For liberty gave way before the imperial name, and when liberty departed, so did virtue. Before the day of the Caesars, high character was the route to honor, and positions such as consul, dictator, or other high public offices were open to men who had excelled others with their magnanimous spirit, strength of character, and energy. But as soon as the commonwealth fell into the power of one man, high character and magnanimity became suspect in the eyes of rulers. Only those were acceptable to the emperors who lacked the mental vigor to care about liberty. The imperial court thus opened its gates to the lazy rather than to the strong, to flatterers rather than to the industrious, and as the administration of affairs fell to inferior men, little by little the empire was brought to ruin. Can one deplore a single instance where virtue is cast off and not deplore still more the destruction of the whole state? How many luminaries of the commonwealth were extinguished under Julius Caesar — of how many leaders was the city deprived? Under Augustus, whether from necessity or malice, what a host of proscriptions there were! How many citizens were eliminated and crushed! So that when he finally put an end to this bloodthirsty slaughter, it was thought to be attributable less to his clemency than to exhausted cruelty.[36] He chose as his son and his successor Tiberius, a man of disgusting character, who did not stop torturing and tormenting the citizens even while he took his meals. Caligula, the successor of Tiberius, killed just about everyone! Of whose blood did he not drink his fill? After Caligula there was the cruel folly of Claudius, who

mensas quidem unquam cessavit. Successor Tiberii Caligula, quem non occidit? Cuius sanguinem in civitate non hausit? Claudii post hunc crudelis amentia, non ad suum dumtaxat, sed ad uxorum et libertorum nutum, omnem romanam nobilitatem trucidavit. Hunc secutus Nero Caesar, cui pepercit, qui nec fratri nec uxori nec matri nec praeceptori nec urbi quidem ipsi pepercit? Quanta sub illo strages civium! Quanta caedes patrum facta est! Ut verissime a quodam sit dictum tunc Neronem periisse, cum cerdonibus timendum esse coeperat; absumpta videlicet romana nobilitate, plebecula et opifices in quos saeviret restabant. Longum foret singulos percurrere, sed tamen eadem omnibus mens fuit, ut et timerent cunctos in quibus excellens aliquid conspicarentur et quos timerent odissent et quos odissent[38] ferro trucidarent, donec superante odio metum, ipsi quoque trucidabantur.

39   Ut sic maius illis cum civibus bellum quam cum hostibus esset, quod paucis exemplis intelligi licet. Nam Iulius quidem Caesar interfectus est. Tiberio a Caligula manus iniectas putant. Ipse certe Caligula gladiis suorum peremptus. Claudius fungo boleto ab Agrippina uxore necatus. Neronem non febris sed gladius absumpsit. Galba Neronis successor ab Othone trucidatus est. Othonem Vitellius prostravit. Vitellium romani peremerunt gladii. Idem Domitianum exitus habuit, idem alios, quos enumerare prolixum magis quam necessarium esset.

40   Hae tantae[39] caedes revolutionesque rerum utcumque tandem essent, absque diminutione et quassatione imperii esse non poterant. Itaque paulatim evanescere vires et prolapsa maiestas interire coepit ac deficientibus civibus ad externos deferri. Sed primis quidem temporibus magnitudo potentiae incommoda tolerabat. Roma autem, etsi intestinis quae modo retulimus affligeretur in-

slaughtered the whole Roman nobility, not merely at his own wish, but even at the whim of his wives and freedmen. Nero was the next Caesar after him, and whom did he spare? He spared neither brother, nor wife, nor mother, nor teacher, nor the city itself. What a scourge of the citizenry did his reign become! He made such a slaughter of patricians (as someone said with perfect truth) that when he died the artisan class was beginning to fear for their lives. For as the Roman nobility had been eliminated, the rabble and the tradesmen were all that was left for him to rage at and ravage. It would take a long time to list their every crime, but the emperors were all of the same mind, fearing anyone in whom they could detect some excellence, hating whomever they feared, and killing with the sword whomever they hated. At last hatred would overcome fear, and they themselves would also be cut down.

Indeed, for them, the war they waged against their own citizens   39
was more important than wars waged against external enemies. A few examples may help make this clear. Julius Caesar was assassinated; Tiberius, it is thought, was acted against by Caligula; and Caligula is known to have been stabbed by his guards. Claudius was poisoned with a mushroom by his wife Agrippina, and Nero died, not of a fever, but by the sword. Galba, Nero's successor, was killed by Otho. Vitellius laid Otho low, and Vitellius in his turn was run through by Roman swords. Domitian too was murdered, and others as well. But it would be excessive and unnecessary to name them all.

So many murders and assassinations, and the revolutions that   40
in the end followed them, could not but lead to the weakening and decline of the Empire. Roman power began little by little to drain away and her grandeur to decline, eventually falling into foreign hands for lack of native citizens. Yet in earlier periods the vastness of Roman power withstood her misfortunes. Though badly afflicted with internal troubles, as we have shown, Rome still remained safe from external enemies. The Emperor Constantine,

commodis, ab externo tamen hoste tuta perstabat. Postquam vero Constantinus, amplificata Bizantio, ad orientem subsedit, Italia et ceterae occidentales imperii partes, quasi pro derelictis habitae, negligi coeperunt, ac tyrannorum barbarorumque invasionibus exponi; qui ceu in vacuam possessionem ruentes, variis temporibus, tamquam diluvia quaedam, has terras inundarunt. De quibus, quoniam illi multa per Etruriam gesserunt et hanc ipsam de qua scribimus everterunt urbem, brevi discursu, quantum necessitas flagitat, referemus.

41   Primi omnium barbarorum post imperii sedem Bizantium translatam Gothi, Radagaso et Alarico ducibus, Italiam pervasere. Gothos antiqui Getas dixerunt. Ea gens scythica est; incoluit autem primum eam Scythiae regionem, quae circa Maeotida paludem ad occasum spectat. Inde productis sedibus circa maris pontici litus magis consedit. Eam propterea oram scriptores quidam geticum litus appellant. Fama eorum potentiae antiquissima est,[40] quippe non vicinas dumtaxat Europae regiones, sed Asiam quoque populati, iam inde ab initio formidabiles erant. Lucullus Romanorum primus eos bello victos Moesia pepulit. Inde ab Agrippa aliisque romanis ducibus ultra Danubium amnem submoti. Sed propter ingentem multitudinem varia incolentem loca, nunquam penitus subacti. Quotiens romana cessabant praesidia, populabundi Moesiam Thraciamque et ceteras vicinas provincias consuerunt[41] irrumpere. Sub Gallo tandem et Volusiano principibus cum Gothis foedus est ictum. Quo mox post eorumdem principum mortem intermisso atque neglecto, usque ad Diocletiani et Maximiani tempora hostes magis quam foederati habebantur. Sub his rursus principibus renovato foedere, magna Romanis ad parthi-

however, enlarged the city of Byzantium and moved the capital to the east. The emperors thereafter began to view Italy and the western part of the empire almost as the abandoned part, to be neglected and left exposed to the invasions of tyrants and barbarians. The latter rushed into the deserted property, as it were, at various times like the waters of a flood and inundated these lands altogether. I shall briefly describe the barbarians here, as necessity requires, since they were active in Tuscany and even devastated the city of which we are writing.

A.D. 324

Of all barbarians who overran Italy after the capital was moved to Byzantium the first were the Goths, led by Radagaisus and Alaric.[37] These people were the same whom the ancient writers call the Getae. They were Scythian by descent, and they once inhabited the part of Scythia which borders the western shores of the Sea of Azov. Then they migrated east, coming to a halt around the shores of the Black Sea instead. Hence some writers refer to this coast as the Getic Coast. From remotest times they had been famous for their power; indeed, they were a formidable race from the very beginning, having brought devastation to Asia as well as Europe. Lucullus was the first Roman to defeat them in war and expel them from Moesia. Later Agrippa and other Roman leaders pushed them back across the Danube. As their numbers were enormous and they dwelt in a variety of regions, however, they could never be altogether subdued. Whenever the Romans would relax their guard, they would burst into Moesia and Thrace and other nearby provinces and plunder them. Under the emperors Gallus and Volusianus a pact was finally made with the Goths, but it was suspended and fell into desuetude soon after the death of these emperors, and down to the time of Diocletian and Maximian, the Goths were more often thought of as enemies of the Romans than as their allies. Under the latter emperors, however, the alliance was renewed, and the Goths sent large forces of auxiliaries to the Romans during the Parthian campaigns of

41

cum bellum, quod Maximianus susceperat, miserunt auxilia. Constantino etiam adversus Licinium gerenti bellum aliisque interdum principibus opitulati sunt.

42 Hac igitur cum Romanis amicitia constituta per multosque servata annos, domesticis cladibus laborare coeperunt. Hunnorum namque gens et ipsa Scythica praevalens armis et hominum feritate Gothos superiora Scythiae loca incolentes, quos Ostrogothas vocant, aggressa, multis proeliis superatos parere sibi coegit. Hoc itaque metu perculsi inferiores Gothi, cum Hunnis resistere posse nequaquam confiderent, ad Romanorum gratiam conversi Valentem imperatorem per legatos rogant, ut eos dudum amicos ac saepe opitulatos Danubium transire ac in romani solo imperii, quo Hunnorum furorem servitutemque evadant, recipere dignaretur. Suam cladem, non sine periculo Romanorum futuram, docent; se, si eos recipiant, in potestate principis mansuros legibusque quas eis dederit parituros.

43 Valens igitur etsi periculosam rem in tanta barbarorum multitudine suspicabatur, tamen, ut adversus Hunnorum potentiam ex ea parte imperium communiret, Gothos cum coniugibus et liberis transire amnem benigne permissos intra Moesiam recepit. His autem locis Maximum quendam cum aliquot cohortibus praefecit, eique mandavit ut, quae ad usum victumque necessaria forent, importanda curaret. Per doctos etiam homines religione christiana, qua ipse princeps imbutus erat, Gothos curavit imbuendos. Sed multitudinem ingentem et advenam confestim rerum inopia[42] subsecuta intolerabiliter premere coepit, quam avaritia Maximi, quaestum in commerciis procurantis, durius acerbabat. Hanc itaque passi aliquandiu Gothi, tandem vulgo conqueri fortunas

Maximian. They also aided Constantine when he was warring against Licinius, and supported other emperors from time to time.[38]

The long-standing friendship between the Goths and the Romans was eventually strained by great internal troubles that came upon the Goths. For the Huns, another Scythian people outstanding in arms and in ferocity, attacked those Goths, called Ostrogoths, who dwelt in the highlands of Scythia, and after a number of battles forced them into slavery. The lowland Goths were stricken with fear, and since they were by no means sure they could resist the Huns, they had recourse to their friendship with the Romans. They sent legates to the emperor Valens asking that, as old friends and frequent allies, they might be permitted to cross the Danube onto the soil of Roman Empire and so to escape the fury and the slavery that threatened them from the Huns. They spoke of their own disasters, which would soon threaten the Romans as well, and they promised to accept the emperor's rule and to obey the laws he gave them if the Romans would let them in.

42

Valens saw some danger in such a host of barbarians, but he hoped they would protect that region of the empire from the power of the Huns. So he generously permitted the Goths with their wives and children to cross the Danube into Moesia. He put a certain Maximus with some regiments of guards in charge of the region, and commanded him to import whatever provisions would be needed by the newcomers. He also sent the Goths learned men to teach them the Christian religion, which he himself professed. But the great influx of foreigners soon produced an intolerable shortage of goods, and the avarice of Maximus, who was making a profit on commercial transactions, aggravated the shortage. So after suffering these conditions for some little time, the Goths finally began to complain en masse and to bewail their fate, blaming Maximus, now for corruption, because he had been prohibit-

43

A.D. 376

suas misereri coeperunt, et modo improbitatem Maximi, quod importari non permitteret, modo avaritiam, quod carius venderet accusare: iam sibi, mancipiis suppellectilique exhaustis, liberos dumtaxat coniugesque superesse; eos iam ipsos a venditoribus exposci; statim videlicet atque illi defuerint, sese tamquam pecora abductum iri; praestitisse autem vel Hunnis servire vel pugnando cecidisse quam vel fame tabescere vel hanc tantam avarissimorum hominum contumeliam perferre.

44   His et huiusmodi vocibus vulgo miserebantur. Reguli erant Gothorum Phritigernus et Alatheus, viri bellaces otioque infensi. Hos cum suopte ingenio feroces, tum popularium querelis incensos, novarum rerum stimulabat cupiditas. Eorum opera tandem Gothi Romanos invadunt; milites cum praefecto quot assequi possunt trucidant. Superatis inde in congressione cohortibus, per Moesiam Thraciamque et ripensem Daciam fusi, omnia populantur. Fit provincialium magna caedes; multi in servitutem trahuntur. Denique Gothi, beneficiorum principis obliti, non iam precario, sed veluti propriis regionibus dominantur.

45   Per id tempus Valens apud Antiochiam erat. Qui ubi haec audivit, confestim, ut tantis resisteret cladibus, in Thraciam cum exercitu properavit. Commisso proelio, mala malis aggerantur. Equites enim Valentis a Gothis superati, cum peditem destituissent, circumventae legiones a barbaris usque ad internecionem caeduntur. Valens autem ipse cum sagitta[43] saucius fugeret et ob dolorem nimium saepe equo laberetur, ad cuiusdam villulae casam deportatus est, quae mox a barbaris persequentibus incensa una cum imperatore crematur.

46   Gothi victores totam vastantes Thraciam a Constantinopoleos expugnatione aegerrime repelluntur. Quae ubi Gratiano Valentis

ing imports, and now for greed, because he was selling provisions too dearly. They had already been compelled to sell their slaves and furniture, and had only their wives and children left; the provisioners were now demanding they sell their families as well; and once the latter had been sold, they would themselves be led away like sheep. They said they would rather serve the Huns, or die fighting them, than starve to death or be thus brought low by the greediest of men.

Such were the pleas for mercy that were spreading openly   44
among the Goths. Their princes, Phritigern and Alatheus, were warriors who hated idleness; they were fierce by nature and had in addition become incensed over the grievances of their people. So a lust for revolt spurred them on. Thanks to them the Goths finally attacked the Romans and massacred as many Roman soldiers as they could catch, including the governor. The Goths then encountered and defeated the Roman garrisons and began spreading devastation throughout Moesia, Thrace, and the regions of Dacia near the Danube. There was great slaughter among the provincial people and many were taken as slaves. Forgetting the favor the emperor had bestowed on them, the Goths no longer held these provinces at the emperor's pleasure but ruled them as their own.

The emperor Valens was in Antioch at this time. When he   45
heard what had happened, he hurried to Thrace with an army to deal with the catastrophe. The battle that ensued, however, made a bad situation worse. Valens' cavalry were beaten by the Goths, leaving the foot soldiers to fend for themselves; and so the legions were surrounded by the barbarians and slaughtered.[39] Valens himself fled with an arrow wound, but owing to the great pain he was in, he kept slipping from his horse. He was carried into a certain village house, which the pursuing barbarians burned down with   A.D. 378
the emperor himself inside it.

The victorious Goths, having devastated all Thrace, were   46
driven off from the siege of Constantinople with bitter fighting.

nepoti, qui in occidente regebat imperium, nunciata sunt, luctu simul ac periculo anxius, cum de reparando rei publicae statu consultaret, placuit tandem ut quemadmodum Nerva quondam Traianum, sic ipse tunc Theodosium virum praestantissimum ex Hispania in consortium regni assumeret. Igitur Theodosius unica rei publicae spes, adversus gothicum tumultum imperator creatus, purpuraque apud Sirmium a Gratiano indutus, ubi in Thraciam cum exercitu pervenit, summa industria atque felicitate Gothos superavit, multisque ac ingentibus proeliis victos Thracia pepulit. Sed cum ulterius barbaros insequeretur, morbo correptus aegrotare coepit. Eaque causa fuit Gratiano, ut desperata Theodosii salute, cum Gothis pacem firmaret. Quam mox et Theodosius ipse morbo liberatus, ob collegae honorem sine controversia secutus est, Gothosque, ut primo inimicos armis pepulerat, sic postea amicos gratia et benevolentia in fide retinuit, eorumque opera in rei publicae necessitatibus saepe utiliter usus est.

47 Gratiano deinde apud Lugdunium, Galliae urbem, ac post aliquot annos Valentiniano eius fratre apud Viennam interfectis, Theodosioque subinde apud Mediolanum vita functo, ad Arcadium et Honorium Theodosii filios devenit imperium. Sub his tandem principibus, Gothorum magna pars novarum sedium avida, Alarico viro impigro sibi duce constituto, per Pannonias ac Sirmium intravit Italiam. Alia item eiusdem gentis multitudo sub Radagaso duce eadem loca penetravit. Hi duo Gothorum duces duoque exercitus, uno atque eodem anno, qui fuit Stilicone et Aureliano consulibus, Italiam ingressi memoriae produntur. Sed exercituum et ducum fortuna diversa admodum fuit.

48 Radagasum enim ingenti multitudine Apennini iuga transgressum, cum per Etruriam barbarico furore debaccharetur et iam Roma propinquo trepidaret metu, Stilico Honorii dux, vir per

When Valens' nephew Gratian, the emperor of the West, heard this news, he was filled with sorrow and anxiety. Having considered what he should do to save the state, he finally decided to do what Nerva had once done in appointing Trajan, namely, to elevate an outstanding man, the Spaniard Theodosius, to rule the empire as his associate. Thus Theodosius was made emperor as the only hope of the empire, the man who would quell the Gothic uprising. He took the purple from Gratian at Sirmium and from there marched into Thrace with an army, where he fought the Goths with great energy and success. He won numerous great battles and expelled the Goths from Thrace. But as he was pursuing the barbarians still further, he fell ill. That was why Gratian made peace with the Goths: he had despaired of Theodosius' life. And when Theodosius did recover from his illness shortly thereafter, he accepted the peace without protest in order to maintain his colleague's honor. As he had defeated the Goths in war when they were his enemies, so now he kept their friendship by his good faith and generosity, and he frequently found their services useful to the commonwealth in its hour of need.[40]

Gratian was killed at Lyons in Gaul; his brother Valentinian, several years later at Vienna. When Theodosius himself died thereafter at Milan, the empire devolved upon his sons, Arcadius and Honorius. During their reign, a large part of the Gothic host grew hungry for new land, and under Alaric, a man of great energy who had made himself their leader, they invaded Italy via Hungary and Sirmium. Another horde of Goths entered the same region under Radagaisus. So the record shows that two Gothic leaders and their armies invaded Italy in one year during the consulate of Stilico and Aurelian. Their fortune, however, was very different. 47

A.D. 395

Radagaisus crossed the Alpine passes with an enormous following and rampaged through Etruria with barbaric fury. Rome was already trembling at his fearful approach when he was defeated in 48

eam tempestatem egregius, bellando superavit, tandemque in Faesulanis montibus qui Florentiae imminent redactos hostes et omnium rerum inopia maceratos ita delevit, ut ex ducentis Gothorum
millibus (non enim pauciora in Radagasi exercitu fuisse traduntur), nemo incolumis evaderet. Magna pars caesa, reliqui capti
atque venundati. Ipse quoque Radagasus cum suos, fractis iam rebus, turpi fuga desereret, captus a nostris et in vincula coniectus,
postquam victorum spectacula satiavit, occiditur. Hanc Gothorum
stragem tantamque de hostibus victoriam partam fuisse octavo
Idus octobris quidam putant, atque ex eo festum diem Florentiae
institutum, temploque inde nomen inditum, quod videlicet ea die
victoria egregie parta, maximo barbarorum metu civitas liberata
esset. Nos vero diligentius perquirentes, hanc victoriam de Gothis
habitam sub Arcadii et Honorii tempore,[44] Stilicone iterum et
Antemio consulibus, decimo post Theodosii mortem, octavo supra quadringentesimum christianae salutis anno comperimus; de
die autem nihil certi potuimus reperire. Quare illa quae de institu-
tione festi et templi vocabulo dicta sunt, in medio relinquantur.

49   Radagasus ergo et Gothi qui sub illo erant hunc in Etruria
finem habuere. Alaricus vero aliam Gothorum manum per Italiam
rapiens, ab ipso fere ingressu castris non procul Ravenna positis,
per legatos ad Honorium missos sedes ad inhabitandum sibi
suisque poposcit, impetravitque volente Honorio ut ad eas Galliae
partes, quibus Vandali Alanique imminebant, per favorem et amicitiam eorum qui romano parebant imperio proficisceretur. Hoc
itaque foedere cum barbaris icto, cum illi in Galliam contenderent
et iam apud Pollentiam urbem sub ipsis Alpibus exercitum de-
duxissent, nihilque hostile metuerent, quidam ex Honorii ducibus

battle by Stilico, a general of the Emperor Honorius and the outstanding man of his day. At last, having driven the enemy into the
mountains of Fiesole overlooking Florence, he starved them of
supplies and wiped them out so completely that of two hundred
thousand Goths (no fewer, they say, were in Radagaisus' army) not
one escaped unscathed. The majority were killed, the rest captured
and sold. Radagaisus himself, his venture now in ruins, deserted
his own troops in shameful flight, but was captured by our forces
and thrown into irons. The victors gloatingly displayed him in triumph, then slew him. This great defeat and slaughter of the Gauls
some think to have occurred on October 8th,[41] and that is why
(they say) the day became a holiday in Florence[42] and why this legend was inscribed on the Florentine temple, namely, that 'this date
saw a glorious victory wherein the city was freed from great dread
of the barbarians'. Our own more diligent researches have established that this victory over the Goths took place in the reign
of Arcadius and Honorius, in the consulship of Stilico and Anthemius, ten years after the death of Theodosius, in the four hun-   A.D. 408
dred and eighth year of Christian salvation. We have not found
any reliable evidence regarding the precise day. For this reason we
shall leave unresolved the claims that have been made about the
institution of the holiday and the inscription on the temple.

Such was the end that Radagaisus, and the Goths who fol-   49
lowed him, met in Etruria.[43] Alaric swept into Italy with another
band of Goths and set up camp near Ravenna. Almost as soon as   A.D. 403
he had entered he sent ambassadors to Honorius to ask for places
where his people could settle. With Honorius's approval he obtained permission to set out, with the favor and friendship of all
Roman subjects, for the regions of Gaul threatened by the Vandals and the Alans. Such was the agreement made with the barbarians. Then, as they were marching on Gaul and had brought
their army to the city of Pollentia at the foot of the Alps, expecting no hostilities, the Goths were suddenly attacked by certain

Gothos improviso impetu contra fidem aggressi, magnam eorum stragem primo ediderunt.

50   Erat profecto militum firmissima spes omnes barbarorum copias ea die tolli posse, quando illi, sive contemptu disciplinae militaris sive nimia pacis fiducia, non delecto castrorum loco neque aggere et fossa munito, passim inter iumenta impedimentaque per agrum iacebant. Itaque magna prius ab aggressoribus edita caedes, et quacumque pervaserunt, plurimus barbarorum manabat cruor. Sed maior erat multitudo quam ut uno impetu trucidari posset. Et iam circa regem trepida quidem sed magna convenerat manus. Quo in loco cum inter sese quid agendum foret quasi attoniti sciscitarentur, tenuisse dicitur aliquandiu suspensos Gothos diei religio. Nam ne quid sceleri deesset, sacrum paschae diem, quo minus caveret hostis, ad tantam caedem Honoriani delegerant. Quare Gothi, nefas ea die pugnare credentes, se primo continuerunt a pugna et sponte sua cesserunt hosti. Tandem vero, ut aggressores nihilo segnius instare et suos ferociter insequi conspiciunt, ira simul et indignatione furentes, veluti caeca rabie in hostes feruntur. Illi autem, qui in improvisa dumtaxat caede spem victoriae posuerant, ut iusta supervenit acies, facile superantur. Gothi modo victi, mutata pugnae fortuna, repente victores fiunt; varie dissipatos Honorianos incredibili caede prosternunt; cadaveribus et cruore omnia complent.[45] Hinc tumentes ira victoriaque elati, iustam paene rabiem contra nostros exercent. Omisso namque in Galliam itinere ac pactas sedes valere sinentes, infesto agmine per Italiam ruunt, omnia quacumque incedunt late ferro igneque vastantes.

of Honorius' generals, despite the previous assurances of safe conduct.

At first the attackers slaughtered a multitude of Goths. The 50 soldiers were sure that on that day they could wipe out the whole host of the barbarians since the latter, whether from contempt for military discipline or from over-confidence in the treaty, had not chosen a fortified encampment nor protected themselves with defense works, but lay scattered around a field with their baggage train. Thus the aggressors caused great slaughter at first, and barbarian blood flowed copiously wherever the attackers penetrated. But the host was too great to cut down in a single assault. Frightened but numerous they huddled around their king. In their astonishment they were divided as to what to do, and religion, it is said, held them back for a time. For, to complete the tale of crime, Honorius' troops had chosen Easter Sunday for the massacre, to be sure to catch the enemy off guard. The Goths, considering it an inauspicious day for fighting, at first held back from battle and willingly gave way before the enemy. After a while, however, when they saw the attackers come on unrelentingly and ferociously attack their families, they grew mad with anger and indignation and struck back at their enemies in blind rage. Honorius' men, who had pinned their hopes of victory solely on unexpected slaughter, were easily defeated once the righteous army turned on them. The fortune of battle changed, and the Goths turned suddenly from vanquished into victors. They defeated utterly Honorius' scattered forces with incredible carnage, strewing the field with corpses and gore. And from this place, swollen with wrath and elated with victory, they turned their righteous fury on our nation. They abandoned the march on Gaul and renounced the agreement concerning areas of settlement. Sweeping through Italy with frightful force, they wrought devastation wherever they marched with fire and sword.[44]

51   Adversus hunc barbarorum furorem Stilico novo exercitu opponitur. Is eorum furentes impetus primus repressit; quin etiam bellandi peritia fretus, saepe barbaros inclusit, saepe circumvenit, saepe contrivit, plenam habiturus victoriam, si mens sana fuisset. Sed iam pridem imperio inhians, has per Italiam clades nutrire cupiebat. Quare Gothos nec vinci nec vincere patiebatur, sed occulte quidem illos fovens, aperte autem belli et pacis copiam denegans, cum abire cuperent, in Italia sustentabat. Quae ubi Honorio patefacta sunt, Stiliconem cum Eucherio filio, cui sceleste parabatur imperium, interfici iussit.

52   Iustam certe principis iram et dignam tanti sceleris vindictam acerbiora mox incommoda subsecuta sunt. Gothi enim, sublato Stilicone maximo duce romanisque ob eius mortem turbatis animis,[46] liberius iam per Italiam ruentes, urbem denique illam victricem orbis (quod et scripsisse pudet) hostiliter ingressi, praeter sacra loca, quae barbari licet venerabantur, caedibus omnia et cruore foedarunt. Direpta inde[47] et quibusdam locis incensa urbe, non multos postquam intraverant[48] dies, cum inaestimabili praeda et magna captivorum multitudine egrediuntur. Fuit inter captivos Placidia Galla, Theodosii filia, Arcadii et Honorii soror, quam ex augustalis palatii deliciis per horrida Gothorum castra abductam (adeo sors cuncta etiam incredibiliter interdum miscet), barbarum sequi dominum omnipotens fortuna compulit. Egressi Roma Gothi, per Campaniam, Lucaniam, Brutios simili clade bacchantur. Emensos Italiae longitudinem, in Siciliam traiicere conantes, aestus et naufragium salutare Siculis reiecit.

Against this barbarian fury the emperor pitted Stilico with a 51
new army. At first he stopped their wild attacks. Relying on his
expert knowledge of warfare, he would often surround them, often
cut them off, often wear them down, and he would have overcome
them completely if his intentions had been sound. But he had long
aspired to become emperor himself, and he actually wanted to fos-
ter calamity in Italy. For this reason he would let the Goths neither win nor lose; he would covertly support them while openly
refusing them the resources to make either war or peace, and when
they wanted to leave Italy he kept them there. When all this was
revealed to Honorius, he ordered the death of Stilico and his son
Eucherius, for whom Stilicho was wickedly trying to obtain the
throne.

The just wrath of the prince and the righteous vengeance he 52
took for such treason led very soon to worse troubles. For, when
Stilico, the greatest Roman general, was removed and the Romans'
courage was dulled by his death, the Goths swept freely over Italy
and at last (it shames me to write) furiously invaded that city
which had conquered the world, defiling everything with slaughter A.D. 410
and bloodshed — except the sacred places, for which they did show
some respect, barbarians though they were. The city was seized
and some parts of it were burned. Then a few days later the barbarians departed with priceless booty and a great crowd of captives. Among their prisoners was Galla Placidia, the daughter of
Theodosius and sister of Arcadius and Honorius. She was
dragged from the luxury of the imperial palace to the rough camp
of the Goths (so strangely does Chance sometimes mix all things
together), and almighty Fortune constrained her to follow the barbarian lord.[45] When they had left Rome, the Goths wrought similar disasters elsewhere, storming through the provinces of Campania, Lucania, and Calabria. Having measured the length of Italy,
they tried to cross over into Sicily but stormy seas and a fortunate
shipwreck kept them out of that island.

53   Consultantibus inde rursus, ne refectis navibus traiicerent an
retro iter verterent, inter huiusmodi moras consultationesque Alaricus apud Consentiam moritur. Gothi regis corpus, ne quis vel in
mortuum vindictam exercere posset, maximo captivorum et militum opere, derivato Basento amne, in medio alveo cum ditissimis
hostium spoliis et omni regia gaza reponunt, flumenque mox in
solitum restituunt cursum. Captivos post haec italici generis, vel
pro magnificentia regii funeris vel ne quis efferre docereve locum
possit, ad unum omnes trucidant. Inde Athaulfo Alarici propinquo sibi rege subrogato, Romam iterum petunt, et quod reliquum
fuerat praedae abradunt. Populata dehinc Etruria ac ceteris propinquis regionibus afflictis, in Galliam tandem, veluti procella
quaedam malam secum tempestatem ferens, abiere.

54   Capta est autem Roma a Gothis anno, postquam condita fuerat, millesimo centesimo sexagesimo quarto; postquam vero a Gallis capta fuerat, octingentesimo. Placidia autem Galla, quam supra
a Gothis captam abductamque ostendimus, ab Athaulfo rege in
matrimonium accepta est. Haec etiam post mortem Athaulfi regis,
qui Barchinoniae suorum dolo interfectus est, Constantio viro
praestantissimo coniugata, Valentinianum peperit, qui post Honorii mortem imperavit.

55   Attila post haec, Hunnorum rex, quanto nullus ante terrore Italiam ingreditur. Hunnorum gentem scythicam fuisse supra ostendimus. Incoluit[49] autem primo supra Maeotida[50] paludem; inde
mutatis sedibus intra Pannoniam consedit. Post amplificatam potentiam imperiumque super multas gentes longe lateque exten-
sum, ad Attilam et Bledam fratres regnum devenit. Sed Attila, per
dolum Bleda necato, solus regnavit; potentissimus quidem omnium regum qui ante ipsum fuerant. Parebant enim sibi immanis-

They were discussing whether to rebuild their ships and try 53
again or to journey back whence they had come, when amidst the
discussions and delays Alaric died at Cosenza. The Goths buried A.D. 412
their king where no vengeance could be taken on his body, divert-
ing the river Busento with the labor of many soldiers and prisoners, putting his body in the center of the river bed with the richest
spoils of their enemies and all the royal treasure, then redirecting
the river back into its original course. They then took all their Italian captives and, whether for the glory of the king's burial or to
prevent them from revealing the whereabouts of the grave, killed
them down to the last man. Ataulf, a relative of Alaric, was now
elected king in Alaric's place, and they went again to Rome and
scraped up whatever booty was left to take. Thereafter, having
plundered Etruria and afflicted other regions near it, they finally
went into Gaul like some storm bringing evil weather.

Rome, then, was sacked by the Goths one thousand one hun- 54
dred and sixty-four years after its founding and eight hundred
years after it had been taken by the Gauls. Galla Placidia, moreover, whose seizure and abduction by the Goths we have described, was taken in marriage by Athaulf. After his death (he was
murdered at Barcelona as a result of a plot by his own people) she
was married to Constantius, a remarkable man, to whom she bore
Valentinianus, the next emperor after Honorius.[46]

After this came the invasion of Attila, king of the Huns, who 55
spread unprecedented terror through Italy. We have said that the A.D. 452
Huns were a Scythian people. At first they settled on the northern
shores of the Sea of Azov, then they migrated into Hungary.
When they had grown more powerful and extended their rule far
and wide over many peoples, the throne came to two brothers, Attila and Bleda.[47] Attila, however, killed Bleda by trickery and ruled
alone. He was the most powerful king ever seen. Great and powerful nations obeyed him. Cruel and fearsome by nature, he seemed
born to be the terror of the world. Having devastated Macedonia,

simae fortissimaeque nationes; ipse quoque truci pavendus ingenio, ad terrorem orbis terrarum natus videbatur. Hic igitur
Macedonia, Moesia, Thracia Illyrioque[51] vastatis, tandem perva-
gata Germania, in Galliam transiit. Addidit viribus dolum. Quod
enim Romanos Gothosque persequebatur, ne in unum eorum potentiae convenirent, Romanis per litteras ostendit se Gothos, gentis suae antiquos hostes et veluti fugitivos servos, toto orbe perquirere atque ulcisci velle; Romanos rogare vel arma secum iungant
ad inimicorum vindictam vel otiosos spectatores se praestent. Gothis vero se adversus Romanos dumtaxat hostilia ferre arma confirmavit; proinde quiescerent aut se ipsi coniungerent.

56   Haec a Romanis Gothisque deprehensa, amicitiae iungendae
causa fuere. Quare in unum convenientes Theodoricus Gothorum
rex ac Aetius patritius, a Valentiniano iuniore in Galliam missus,[52]
Romanorum[53] Gothorumque exercitus adversus Attilam coniunxerunt. Quae ubi Attilae nunciata sunt, truculentior iam inde factus, omnia vastat; urbes quot expugnare per Galliam potest, ad
solum usque subvertit, templa incendit, igne et ferro cuncta ab-
sumit. Committitur tandem proelium maximum atque atrocissi-
mum, in quo supra CLX millia cecidisse traduntur. In eo proelio
Theodoricus Gothorum rex ab Hunnis occiditur; Attila ipse
usque ad castra cum ingenti suorum caede fugatur. Ab oppugna-
tione castrorum mors sui regis Gothos avertit. Itaque quasi aequo
Marte discessum est, cum alteri regem amisissent, alteri castris inclusi se inferiores proelio faterentur.

57   Attila igitur haud multo post tempore in Pannoniam reversus,
cum exercitum reparasset, non iam Galliam, sed Italiam ipsam invadere decrevit. Quare profectus cum Hunnorum et aliarum gen-

Moesia, Thrace and Illyria, he marched through Germany into Gaul. He combined cunning with violence. Since he was attacking both Romans and Goths, he did not want them to combine their forces. So he wrote to the Romans to explain that he wished to pursue the Goths across the globe and avenge himself upon them, as they were ancient enemies and, as it were, escaped slaves of his people. He asked the Romans to join him in the fight and gain vengeance on their enemies, or else to observe but take no active part. To the Goths, meanwhile, he gave assurances that he was merely moving his troops against the Romans. They should either remain passive or join him.

When this duplicity was detected, it led the Romans and 56 Goths to form an alliance. Theoderic, king of the Goths, and the patrician Aetius, who had been sent to Gaul by the younger Valentinian, joined together and united their armies against Attila. The news made Attila still more aggressive, and he proceeded to devastate everything. He razed to the ground every city he could take in Gaul, burning the churches, and consuming everything with fire and sword. Then the greatest and most terrible battle occurred, in which over one hundred and sixty thousand men are said to have fallen. In that battle Theoderic, king of the Goths, was killed by the Huns. Attila for his part suffered great losses and was forced to flee to his encampment. The Goths were prevented by the death of their king from besieging the camp. Thus the outcome of the battle was indecisive, for one side lost its king, while the other admitted its inferiority in battle by taking refuge in its camp.

Attila, therefore, not long after this, went back to Hungary and 57 then, when he had restored the strength of his army, decided to invade Italy herself rather than Gaul. To this end he set out with a great host of Huns and other peoples and besieged Aquileia, a city on the Italian border. Attila wasted much time on this siege, for all of three years were consumed before the city fell. They say that

tium maximis copiis, Aquileiam urbem in ipso Italiae limine obsedit. Diutius obsidio eius urbis Attilam remorata est; triennio toto
circa illam consumpto expugnatur. Ferunt cum iam barbaros tae-
dium desperatioque capiendae urbis cepisset et infecta re abeundum putarent, Attilam, speculandi gratia circa urbem obequitan-
tem, animadvertisse ciconias ex altis turribus pullos efferre. Quod
simul atque vidit, constitit laetus suisque ostendens, "Aspicite," inquit, "commilitones: praesciae futurorum, aves filios deportant et
quam perituram sciunt, deserunt urbem. Agite iam nunc mecum:
destinata nostrae victoriae moenia invadite. Haec dies finem labo-
rum et praedam abunde vobis tradet." His adhortationibus incensi
barbari arma corripiunt et acrius solito moenia circumstant. Nec
defuit augurio fides. Urbs diu obsessa, brevi expugnatur. Attila
captam Aquileiam, trucidatis civibus, solum adusque subvertit.
Mox inde movens exercitum, Vicentiam, Veronam, Mediolanum,
Ticinum pari terrore pervadit ac post multam oppidanorum diripit
caedem.

58   Exanimata itaque metu reliqua Italia victoremque terribilem
horrendo pavore expectante, Leo pontifex maximus (nondum
enim haec intolerabilis, quam nunc videmus, superbia pontificatum irrepserat, sed in humilitate et sanctimonia praesidebant) pro
salute cunctorum legatione ad Attilam suscepta, cum apud Mincium amnem castra habentem Attilam reperisset, facundus praesul
feritatem victoris orando mollivit ac ut, omissa Italia, ad propria
regna reverteretur obtinuit.[54] Cogitantem post haec rursus imperium Romanum concutere variasque iactantem minas, mors opportuna e medio sustulit. Nam post convivium laxius hilariusque
celebratum, resupinus cum dormitaret, sanguis e naribus fluens vi-
talibus oppletis meatibus repente necavit.

59   Post Hunnorum feritatem Vandalorum furor exarsit. Haec
gens ab extremis Oceani Arctoi finibus excita, per multas vagata
terras, tandem, permissu romanorum principum in Pannoniis

the barbarians had begun to be seized with boredom and to despair of ever taking the city, and they were thinking that the enterprise should he abandoned, when Attila, riding around to the city to make a reconnaissance, noticed some storks taking their young off its high towers. As soon as he saw it he stopped in delight and said to his companions: "Look, fellow soldiers, this is a portent; the birds remove their children and abandon the city they know will he destroyed. Now strike with me; attack the walls; they have been marked out for our victory. This day shall bring the end of your labors and rich plunder." Excited by his urging, the barbarians seized their weapons and swarmed over the walls with renewed vigor. Nor was their faith in the omen vain. The city which they had besieged for so long was taken in a moment. Attila killed the citizens and razed the captured city to the ground. Then he moved the army on, and marched through Vicenza, Verona, Milan, and Pavia with equal terror, slaughtering the townsmen and plundering their houses.

The rest of Italy was stricken with fear and expected the terrible conqueror with fear and trembling, but Pope Leo[48] (in those days popes presided with humility and holiness, not with the intolerable arrogance that has crept into the pontificate today) took it upon himself, for the security of all, to go on an embassy to Attila. When Leo had come upon him in his camp on the Mincio River, the eloquent leader softened the victor's savage ferocity by his prayers and persuaded him to leave Italy and return to his own dominions. After this, Attila threw out various threats to return and strike the Roman Empire again but his death fortunately intervened. After a feast that he had celebrated with too much self-indulgence and merriment, he fell asleep on his back, choked on the blood flowing from his nostrils, and died instantly.[49]

After the savagery of the Huns, the fury of the Vandals burst into flame. This people, having been dislodged from the northernmost shores of Ocean, had wandered through many lands, settling

consedit. E Pannoniis rursus Stilicone solicitante Rhenum transisse dicitur, biennio fere ante quam Roma a Gothis caperetur. Inde
aliquot annis in Gallia commorata, in Hispaniam primo, mox in
Africam transgressa, circa Hipponem consedit. Nec multo post,
Carthaginem et plerasque Africae urbes occupatas, multos annos
detinuit. Cum hac autem gente Valentinianus imperator, qui Honorio successerat, foedus iecerat, sed eo mox Romae a suis inter-
fecto, cum Maximus quidam imperio occupato Eudoxiam Valenti-
niani uxorem per violentas sibi nuptias coniunxisset, Vandali ab
Eudoxia solicitati, Genserico rege eos ducente, Italiam navibus advecti, Romam intrarunt tertio et quadragesimo anno postquam a
Gothis capta fuerat. Nihil eorum ingressus ab hostili defuit: capti
cives, urbs spoliata, templa quoque, quae prius Gothi intacta reli-
querant, a Vandalis direpta. Satiatos denique praeda Vandalos,
cum Eudoxia, sive capta sive recepta, Gensericus in Africam reduxit.

60   Ad has Gothorum, Hunnorumque et Vandalorum calamitates
Odoacer quartus accessit. Hic Toralingorum et Herulorum magnis copiis in Italiam ductis, cum Orestem patritium sibi cum
exercitu occurrentem apud Ticinum superasset et Augustulum
mox Romae ab imperio, quod post Maioranum et Antemium oc-
cupaverat, deiecisset, non solum Italiam, sed Romam quoque ipsam possedit. Adversus hunc tertio decimo iam anno Italiam occupantem, Zeno imperator, qui apud Constantinopolim orientem
regebat, Theodoricum Gothorum regem, iam ante apud se magno
in honore habitum, ad liberandam Italiam misit. Erat autem
Theodoricus ex his Gothis qui olim in suis sedibus remanentes
Hunnis Attilaeque servierant. Qui cum valido exercitu Italiam ingressus, Odoacrem primo non longe ab Aquileia iuxta Sontium

finally, with the permission of the Roman emperors, in Hungary. At the request of Stilico they are said to have gone from Hungary back across the Rhine almost two years before Rome was sacked by the Goths. They remained some years in Gaul, then crossed into Spain, and afterwards into Africa, to settle around Hippo. Not much later, they occupied Carthage and many other African cities and remained there for many years. Honorius' successor, Valentinian, made an alliance with this people, but he was soon killed for that reason at Rome by members of his household, and when his successor, a certain Maximus, forced Valentinian's widow, Eudoxia, to marry him, Eudoxia called on the Vandals for help. Genseric, their king, led them in a naval expedition to Italy, and they entered Rome forty-three years after the Goths had sacked it. Their entry in no way differed from that of an enemy: citizens were taken captive, the city was looted, and even the churches, which the Goths had left intact, were torn apart by the Vandals. Then Genseric led them back to Africa, sated with plunder, having liberated or perhaps taken captive Eudoxia.[50]

The fourth invader, after the calamities wrought by the Goths, Huns, and Vandals, was Odoacer.[51] He came into Italy at the head of a vast army of Toralingi and Heruli, met and defeated the patrician Orestes and his army at Pavia, and then overthrew Augustulus, the Roman emperor who had succeeded Majorian and Anthemius. Thus he took control not only of Italy but of Rome itself. After Odoacer had occupied Italy for thirteen years, Zeno, the eastern emperor at Constantinople, sent against him Theoderic, king of the Goths, a man already of very high standing in the imperial court, who was to liberate Italy. Theoderic came of that nation of Goths which had formerly remained in its own dwelling-places and had been enslaved by Attila and the Huns.[52] He entered Italy with a powerful army and first defeated Odoacer not far from Aquileia, on the Sontius River.[53] He beat him again in a critical battle near Verona, and finally besieged him at Ravenna,

60

amnem, deinde apud Veronam gravi proelio superatum, tandemque Ravennae obsessum et ad deditionem coactum occidit, Romamque et Italiam recepit cum summa alacritate omnium populorum. Verum laeta huius principia tristissimos exitus habuere. Nam post victoriam multitudine Gothorum undique diffusa, quas receperat urbes veluti captivas possedit, ut non liberati ab eo Italiae populi, sed saeviorem etiam dominum accepisse viderentur. Huic tandem post multas Italiae clades apud Ravennam defuncto, Attalaricus nepos ex filia puer adhuc cum Amalthea[55] matre in regno successit. Attalarico inde mortuo Theodasus, post hunc Witiges, post Witigem Hildebadus, mox Erarius, post Totila, omnium crudelissimus, regnum obtinuit. Hi omnes Gothorum reges Italiam tenuere. Sed adversus Theodasum, quem in ordine tertium regem fuisse diximus, Iustinianus imperator (ad hunc enim post Zenonis et Anastasii et Iustini mortem imperium devenerat) Belisarium cum exercitu in Italiam misit, ex huiusmodi causa permotus.

61   Amalthea Theodorici regis filia, quam una cum Attalarico eius nato in regno successisse ostendimus, mortuo filio, Theodasum consobrinum suum in consortium regni adscitum, regem creavit. Qui, beneficii immemor, haud multo post, ut solus regnaret, in Vulsinii lacus insula, ubi domus et thesauri regii fuerunt, reginam occidit. Id quidem factum animos Gothorum sic alienarat ab rege ut parum a seditione abessent. His igitur cognitis imperator, tempus liberandae Italiae venisse ratus, Belisarium cum exercitu misit. Qui postquam in Italiam copias traiecit, Neapolim urbem, partes Gothorum pertinacissime retinentem, obsedit expugnavitque, non absque ingenti caede Neapolitanorum Gothorumque, qui ab initio obsidionis se urbe incluserant.

62   Inter haec Gothorum copiae adversus Belisarium a Theodaso missae, cum in Campania essent, ob eas quas supra memoravimus

forced him to surrender, and killed him. He recovered Rome and Italy, receiving a most enthusiastic welcome from all its peoples. His auspicious beginnings led, however, to an unfortunate outcome, for after his victory, a multitude of Goths spread out everywhere and took control of the cities that he had recovered, treating them like conquered towns. So it seemed to the peoples of Italy that they had not been liberated, but rather had acquired a still more savage master. When he finally died at Ravenna after doing much harm to Italy, he was succeeded by his grandson, Attalaricus, son of his daughter, Amalasuntha, who ruled with her son as he was still a child. When Attalaricus died, Theodasus followed, then Witiges, Huldebatus, Erarichus; finally Totila, the cruelest of all, became king. All these Gothic kings ruled Italy. But Justinian, emperor of the east (to whom the empire fell after the deaths of Zeno, Anastasius and Justinus) sent Belisarius with an army to Italy to fight Theodasus (the third king of the Goths, as we said). He did so for the following reason. | A.D. 535

As we have remarked, Amalasuntha, the daughter of Theoderic, had succeeded together with her son Attalaricus to the kingship. When her son died she took Theodasus, her cousin, as co-ruler and made him king. He was ungrateful and wanted to rule alone, so after a short time, he killed the queen on an island of Lake Bolsena where the royal palace and treasure were. But this action so alienated the Goths from the king that they came near to revolt. Thus Justinian, informed of the situation, decided it was time to liberate Italy and sent Belisarius with an army. When he had ferried his troops to Italy he first laid siege to Naples, a city with a strong partisan attachment to the Goths. He besieged and captured the place, causing a great massacre of Neapolitans and Goths who had shut themselves inside the town from the beginning of the siege.[54] | 61

In the army Theodasus sent against Belisarius there was a military mutiny. It happened in Campania and was provoked by the | 62

causas infensae regi, seditione militari Witigem, egregiae nobilitatis hominem et regia stirpe antiqua natum, sibi regem creaverunt. Witiges ergo rex per hunc modum ab exercitu factus, ut regnum sibi stabiliret, propere in Etruriam et Flaminiam copiis reductis, Theodasum occidit. Moxque Ravennam ingressus, Amaltheae filiam, Theodorici neptem, sociam regni uxoremque adsumpsit. Dum haec apud Gothos geruntur, Belisarius felicitate discordiarum fretus, Romae exercitu admoto, volente populo romano, intra urbem recipitur. Varia post hoc fortuna belli fuit. Witiges enim compositis rebus nonnumquam ita praevaluit, ut Belisarium intra urbem Romam diu obsideret, tanta fame populum romanum exercitumque intra moenia premente, ut aegre sit urbis sustentata defensio. Sed tolerantia Belisarii cunctas difficultates superavit, adauctisque tandem copiis obviam Gothis egressus, mira felicitate per Etruriam et Flaminiam cum hoste conflixit. Ad extremum vero omnibus Gothorum copiis profligatis, Witigem apud Ravennam captum simul cum regina uxore Constantinopolim abduxit.

63 Liberata penitus videbatur Italia, et profecto erat, modo vel parum temporis ad solidandam victoriam Belisarius impendisset. Sed dum eadem magnitudine animi qua hostium copias vicerat, reliquias contemnit, semina maioris incendii et duriorum calamitatum ab eo relicta vastitatem et ruinam Italiae brevi tempore pepererunt. Gothi enim qui per Italiam, praecipue autem per transpadanas partes quae longius abfuerant a bello, remanserant, ut Belisarium abesse cognoverunt, in unum convenientes ac se ipsos cohortantes, Hildebadum primo quendam, moxque Erarium, ac

causes we have alluded to above. The army made Witiges their king. The latter was a man of extraordinary nobility and was descended of of old royal stock. Witiges, then, made king in this fashion by the army, brought his troops quickly back to Etruria and Flaminia and, to stabilize his rule, killed Theodasus. Soon he entered Ravenna and made Amalasuntha's daughter, another grandchild of Theoderic, his wife and co-ruler. While the Goths were thus engaged, Belisarius took happy advantage of their discord to move his army to Rome and was welcomed within the city by the Roman people. The fortunes of war after this varied. Witiges, having put his affairs in order, was able sometimes to prevail over Belisarius, to the extent that he besieged him for a long time in Rome, starving the people and the army within so that the A.D. 538 defense of the city was sustained only with great suffering. But the fortitude of Belisarius overcame all difficulties. Finally he received reinforcements and, marching out to meet the Goths, battled the enemy throughout Etruria and Flaminia with great success. In the end all the forces of the Goths were crushed, and Witiges, with his wife and queen, was captured at Ravenna and taken off to Constantinople.[55] A.D. 547

All Italy seemed to be liberated, and so it was, but Belisarius 63 spent far too little time consolidating his victory. The same greatness of soul that made him a conqueror led him to scorn what was left of his enemy; and the seeds he had left behind of still greater conflagrations and still harsher calamities in a short time gave rise to destruction and ruin for Italy. For the Goths who remained in Italy, especially north of the Po, far from the war, when they learned that Belisarius was gone, banded together and urged each other on. They elected as king, first a certain Huldebatus, then Erarichus, and then — when both of these kings were killed within two years in revolts of their own men — Totila was chosen. He restored Gothic strength and appeared with vast forces at the gates of the Etruscan cities which had revolted against the Goths after

illis subinde infra biennium seditione suorum interfectis, Totilam regem creaverunt. Hic reparatis Gothorum viribus magnoque conflato exercitu adversus Etruriae civitates quae post Belisarii victoriam a Gothis defecerant, plus quam barbarica feritate[56] desaevit. Urbes multas evertit, multas incendit, quasdam omnino cum omni subole delevit.[57] Denique potentia simul atque ingenio ferox, Italiam totam, quae paulo ante a Belisario liberata gaudio exultabat, duriore servitute rursus oppressit; urbem quoque romanam diu obsessam hostiliter ingressus, totam diripuit, eversaque murorum parte, civibus aut interfectis in captivitatem abductis, ita vastavit ut quadraginta amplius dies sine ullo penitus habitatore fuisse quidam auctores sint. Supra decem haec pestis annos Italiam tenuit, donec per Narsem eunuchum a Iustiniano cum exercitu missum, bello victus et interfectus est, ac omnes Gothi ad internecionem deleti. Hic fuit Totila, quem ob saevitiam inflictarum cladium dei flagellum quidam appellant, genere quidem Gothus, sed in Italia natus educatusque (de quo monuisse ista voluimus, quod plerique vulgo secuti famam longe aliter opinantur).

64   Liberatam Gothorum dominatu Italiam paucis post annis Longobardorum furor oppressit. Ea gens ab extremis Germaniae finibus Oceanique protinus litore originem traxit. Egressi autem patrio solo novarum sedium quaerendarum gratia, Ibore et Aione ducibus, Vandalos, Herulos et Gepidas aliasque vicinas gentes saepe bello superarunt, mutatisque frequenter sedibus, tandem intra Pannonias constiterunt. Inde rursus excitos Italiam venisse constat, a Narse sollicitatos arcessitosque. Nam mortuo Iustiniano, cum Iustinus eius successor Narsem ab administratione Italiae parum grate revocaret, commotus iniuria Narses, creditur barbarorum concitatione vel sui desiderium vel certe vindictam ingratitudinis procurasse. Sophiae denique Augustae Iustini uxori Narsem, quod erat eunuchus, ad pensa per contumeliam revocanti, talem se illi telam ordiri respondit quam donec vivat non sit expeditura.

Belisarius' victory. Totila ravaged them with more than the usual barbarian fury. Numerous cities were sacked, many were burned, and some were completely wiped out with an entire generation of their people. Using both force and fierce cunning, he subjugated anew all of Italy—which had but a short while before been celebrating its liberation by Belisarius—and imposed a still harsher servitude. After a long siege he, too, entered Rome and tore the whole city apart, knocking down part of the walls. Its citizens were either killed or captured, and he devastated the city so completely that, according to some authors, it lay for more than forty days without a single inhabitant. This plague controlled Italy for more than ten years, until the eunuch Narses, whom Justinian sent with an army, defeated and killed Totila and massacred the entire Gothic army. Such was Totila, whom some called the Scourge of God because of the savagery with which he inflicted carnage. He was of the Gothic race, though born and educated in Italy—we should like to note this because many persons, misled by vulgar traditions, have held quite different views about him.[56]

A.D. 546

A.D. 552

Now freed from the rule of the Goths, Italy was overwhelmed a few years later by the fury of the Lombards. This people originated in the northernmost reaches of Germany, right by the shores of Ocean. They left their native soil, led by two chiefs, Ibor and Aion, seeking new lands for settlement. They often defeated the Vandals, the Heruli, and the Gepidae in war, as well as other neighboring peoples. After many migrations, they finally settled in Hungary. From there they were evidently encouraged to come into Italy at the invitation and request of Narses. For after Justinian died, his successor Justin ungratefully recalled Narses from the administration of Italy, and Narses, offended, is believed to have aroused the barbarians to activity, either because he simply wanted to, or at any rate because he wanted to revenge himself on the imperial ingratitude. Justin's wife, Sophia Augusta, recalled Narses (who was a eunuch) to his weaving in order to insult him; he re-

64

A.D. 568

65   Hinc odio simul ac metu anxius Albuinum Longobardorum regem sollicitare non destitit, identidem monens ut inopibus Pannoniae ruribus omissis, ad Italiae opulentiam se suosque conferret. Albuinus igitur his adhortationibus inductus, Longobardos cum coniugibus et liberis ad iter parat; quoque certius Italiam retinere in potestate possit, viginti Saxonum millia, item alias barbaras gentes eadem spe opimarum sedium pellectas, sibi coniungit. Profectus inde magno agmine virorum, mulierum, puerorum, iumentorum, secus Adriatici sinum maris, qua planissimus in Italiam aditus est, cum omni suorum multitudine ingreditur. Inde late diffusus omnia populatur. Venetiae atque Galliae urbes, praeterquam quod Gothorum cladibus admodum afflictae erant, pestis insuper recens exinanierat. Itaque nullo fere negotio sibi metu aut vi cunctas parere Albuinus compellit. Veronam, Vicentiam, Mediolanum et alias subinde vicinas urbes capit. Papia vero[58] tres annos obsidionem perpessa, tandem Longobardis deditur. Denique ante Albuini regis mortem, quem sexto supra triennium mense postquam Italiam ingressus erat periisse constat, omnis fere Italia usque Ravennam et Etruriam, praeter admodum paucas munitissimas arces, in Longobardorum potestatem devenit. Nec ambigitur quin idem rex totam penitus subegisset, si vel paucis fuisset annis vita superstes. Periit autem in medio victoriarum cursu apud Veronam, dolo uxoris interfectus. Causa eius mortis in hunc modum traditur.

66   Ante adventum Longobardorum in Italiam, inter Albuinum et Cunemundum Gepidarum regem grave exarsit bellum. Productis mox in aciem utrinque copiis, rex Gepidarum ab Albuino cominus

plied that he was preparing a loom for her that she would not be able to finish weaving in a lifetime.[57]

Thus filled with hate and fear, he kept calling for help from   65 Alboin, the king of the Lombards, advising him over and over to leave the poor back-country of Hungary and come with his people to the wealth of Italy. Alboin was persuaded by these pleas, and he got the Lombards and their wives and children ready. To be quite sure he could hold on to Italy, he had twenty thousand Saxons join him as well as other barbarian peoples, moved by the same hope of finding rich dwelling-places. Thus he set out with a vast train of men, women, children, and draft animals along the Adriatic shore, which is the easiest path into Italy, and the whole multitude invaded. They spread out from there in all directions and devastated everything. Venice and the cities of northern Italy had been afflicted by the Gothic scourge and further weakened by the recent plague. Thus Alboin was able to make them all submit by threats and by force, almost without negotiations. He took Verona, Vicenza, Milan and other cities of the region.[58] Pavia, it is true, required three years of siege but it finally surrendered to the Lombards. Thus by the time of Alboin's death, which evidently   A.D. 572 occurred three and a half years after he had entered Italy, almost all Italy down to Ravenna and Tuscany, except for a few well-fortified castles, had come under the power of the Lombards. And there is no doubt that the king, had he lived even a few more years, would have subjugated the whole country. But he died in the midst of his victories, at Verona, killed by a trick of his wife's. The cause of his death is reported as follows.

Before the arrival of the Lombards in Italy a great war erupted   66 between Alboin and Cunemundus, the king of the Gepidae. Both sides brought their troops into battle, and the king of the Gepidae was killed by Alboin in hand-to-hand combat. The Gepidae were crushed and their property lay in ruins, while their king's daughter, Rosamunda, a virgin of great beauty, was taken away by

pugnante occiditur. Profligatis inde Gepidis eorumque rebus eversis, Rosemundam regis filiam, praecipuae pulcritudinis virginem,
inter captivos Albuinus abduxit, captusque splendore formae,
paulo post eam suscepit uxorem. Erat Albuino, ut Germanorum
mos fuit pro ostentanda virtute, ex regis a se caesi calvaria poculum argento auroque addito fabrefactum; eo solemnibus fere
conviviis, quotiens regina abesset, utebatur. Hilariori igitur caena
apud Veronam urbem per id tempus instituta, poculum poscit,
dumque reginam praesentem graviter ferre animadvertit, vino simul et cursu victoriarum superbus, reginae propinari illamque una
cum patre bibere iubet. Regina dolorem alto premens corde, beni-
gno affatu quando ita iubeat, regi paret. Moxque, velut paternis
exagitata furiis, duobus militibus quorum alterum regi infensum,
alterum amore sui devinctum pereuntemque sciebat, in consilium facinoris assumptis, per illos in cubiculum clam receptos dor-
mientem interficit regem. Ipsa vero navim ingressa, per Athesim
fluvium Ravennam aufugit. Longobardi, Albuini corpore regio funere sepulto, Dephonem[59] praecipuae nobilitatis hominem sibi regem praefecerunt. Hic fuit et virtute longe inferior Albuino et natura crudelior. Itaque mox eo intra biennium defuncto, per decem
fere annos absque rege Longobardi fuere, ducibus gentis, qui iam
varie per urbes Italiae sparsi erant, ita impigre bellum gerentibus
ut nunquam sit regia desiderata potestas. Per hos duces Longobardorum gens alia post alia appetendo loca Brundusium usque Ta-
rentumque subegit, praeter urbem Romam, quam constat in huius
gentis potestatem nullo unquam tempore devenisse.

67   Post decennium rursus placuit regem creari, quod mox per
omne tempus usque ad Desiderium, qui ultimus eorum rex in Italia fuit, observatum est. Cumque Gothi primo apud Ravennam sedem regni statuissent, Longobardi apud Ticinum regia constituta,

Alboin among the captives. But he was himself captured by her loveliness and shortly thereafter took her to wife. Alboin, following the German custom of parading his warrior prowess, had a bowl made from the skull of the king he had slain, plated with silver and gold, and he made use of this bowl at solemn feasts when his queen was not present. So it was that he asked for his bowl at an uproarious feast in Verona, but on this occasion the queen was present, and he saw that she was deeply troubled. Being full of drink and his recent successes, he ordered a toast to the queen and bade her 'drink with her father'. The queen's manner was affable as she obeyed the king's order but her proud heart was anguished. Soon, as if driven by paternal furies, she took two soldiers into her confidence; one she knew was hostile to the king and the other entirely enslaved by love for her. She secretly let them into the bedroom while the king slept, and they killed him for her. Then she got into a boat and fled down the Adige River to Ravenna. The Lombards buried Alboin with royal splendor and elected Clepho, a man of high nobility, their king. He was far inferior to Alboin in virtue and far crueler. So when he died within two years, the Lombards went for almost ten years without a king. Their leaders, scattered across the various cities of Italy, waged war so strenuously that there was never any desire for royal authority. Under these leaders the Lombards satisfied their continual hunger for more land, and they subjugated Italy as far as Brindisi and Taranto, except for the city of Rome, which, it appears, never at any time came under their rule.[59]

After ten years they decided to elect a king once more, and this 67 would be the rule in Italy thereafter, down to Desiderius, the last king of the Lombards. As the Goths had first made Ravenna the capital of their kingdom, the Lombards established their royal residence at Pavia and through their chiefs governed Etruria, Flaminia, Umbria, Samnium, and other regions of Italy. It is clear

Etruriam, Flaminiam, Umbriam, Samnium reliquasque Italiae regiones per suarum gentium duces gubernabant. Quatuor supra ducentos annos in Italia dominatam Longobardorum gentem constat, ac multorum regum successionem per hoc tempus habuisse.

68 Tandem cum gravioris iniurias populo romano pontificibusque inferret, Carolus Francorum rex, cui postea ex rebus gestis Magno fuit cognomen, in Italiam precibus Adriani pontificis maximi evocatus, Desiderium Longobardorum regem post aliquot prospera proelia apud Papiam obsessum, ad deditionem coegit; ipsoque cum uxore ac[60] liberis in Galliam deportato atque reliquis Longobardorum ducibus varie profligatis, gravem eius gentis dominatum a cervicibus Italorum dimovit. Ob quae et alia subinde merita ab Adriano evocatore multis ac maximis privilegiis ornatus, mox a Leone eius successore Augustus appellatus, imperatorium nomen dignitatemque suscepit. Hinc nata est, quae hodie quoque perdurat, imperii romani divisio, aliis in Graecia, aliis in Gallia Germaniaque romani principis nomen usurpantibus. De quo non ab re fuerit pro cognitione rei pauca repetere.

69 Romanum imperium a populo romano institutum atque perfectum est. Nam reges quidem non ita late possederunt ut imperium meruerit appellari. Sub consulibus ac dictatoribus tribunisque militaribus, qui fuerunt libero populo magistratus, et res et nomen emersit imperii, Africa paene tota magnaque Asiae parte ultra Armeniam et Caucasum montem armis subacta. Europae vero, Hispaniis, Galliis, Graecia, Macedonia, Thracia aliisque subinde partibus bello domitis, Rheno et Danubio imperium terminarunt. Maria insuper insulaeque et litora a Bosphoro in Britanniam cuncta paruerunt.

70 Haec omnia per quadringentos sexaginta quinque annos ab unius urbis libero populo perfecta. Externis invictum bellis, intes-

that the Lombard race dominated Italy for more than two hundred and four years and had a long line of kings during that time.

Eventually, because the Lombards were inflicting grave harm on the Roman people and the popes, Charles, the king of the Franks, who was later for his deeds known as the Great, was called into Italy by the entreaties of Pope Hadrian.[60] He fought several successful battles with Desiderius, the Lombard king, and finally forced him to surrender at Pavia after a siege. He deported him with his wife and children to France, whilst variously crushing the other Lombard leaders, and so finally lifted the heavy yoke of this race from the necks of the Italians. For this and other subsequent achievements, he was adorned with many privileges by Hadrian, who had summoned him, and afterwards he was named Augustus by Leo,[61] Hadrian's successor, who crowned him with the imperial name and office. Hence was born the division of the Roman empire which still exists today, with some arrogating to themselves the title of Roman emperor in Greece, others in Gaul and Germany. For a clearer picture of this subject, it will not be amiss to say a few words.[62]

The Roman Empire was founded and perfected by the Roman People. The early kings never attained such wide domains as to merit the name of empire. The reality and the name of empire emerged under the consuls and dictators and military tribunes, the magistrates of a free people. It was created by the armed conquest of almost all Africa and a great part of Asia to beyond the mountains of Armenia and the Caucasus. The parts of Europe subdued in war included Spain, Gaul, Greece, Macedonia, Thrace, and later other regions, and the Rhine and the Danube became the borders of the empire. The seas with their islands and their shores all obeyed Rome, from the Bosporus to Britain.

All this was accomplished in four hundred and sixty-five years by the free people of a single city. Unconquered by external foes, this people was overwhelmed at last by internal discord and civil

68

A.D. 774

A.D. 800

69

70

tinae civilesque discordiae oppressere. Imperatores hinc creari coepti, quod ante armorum castrorumque nomen fuit, id tamquam intestino vigente bello intra moenia inductum; verbo quidem legitima potestas, re autem vera dominatio erat. Stipati armorum caterva, metu servire compellebant cives. Ab his imperatoribus Germania et quibusdam provinciis ad imperium adiunctis, foris quidem potentia non nihil extensa est; domi autem vires imperii assiduis paene caedibus imminutae. Sed ab initio quidem singuli imperabant; Nerva autem, qui duodecimus ab Augusto successit, primus sibi consortem delegit imperii. Quo postea exemplo duo interdum principes eodem tempore extiterunt. In partitione tamen rerum usque ad Constantini tempora, praecipua Romae servabatur auctoritas; post Constantinum vero sedemque imperii Bizantium translatam, maxime factitatum est ut duobus imperatoribus institutis, alter Romam atque Italiam, alter Orientem susciperet gubernandum. Sed fere apud Constantinopolim summa rerum habebatur: qui illic imperabant, saepe alio sibi[61] adiuncto Romam Italiamque solebant committere. Iamque ex consuetudine sequestratum, illud orientale, hoc occidentale vocabatur imperium. Occupantibus deinde Italiam barbaris occidentale cessavit imperium, nec post Augustulum illum, quem ab Odoacre deiectum ostendimus, quisquam, ne tyrannice quidem, per Italiam et Occidentem id nomen suscepit usque ad Carolum Magnum, quem a Leone pontifice imperatorem diximus appellatum.

71   Inter Augustulum vero et Carolum per trecentos fere annos imperium cessavit, quod hinc intelligi licet. Odoacer Torcilingorum rex, deiecto Augustulo, tredecim annos Romam Italiamque possedit. Gothi, qui cum Theodorico rege Odoacrem oppressere, sexa-

war. From that time forth, emperors began to be chosen, and the word *imperator*, which before had meant arms and forts, was brought, as it were, within the city walls as though to signal continuous civil war. The word still referred to a legitimate function, but in reality it signified lordship and domination. Surrounded by armed troops, the citizens were cowed into subservience. Germany and certain provinces were added to the empire by the emperors, so the empire's external power was somewhat extended, but the strength of the empire at home was diminished by almost continual assassinations and slaughter. When they began the emperors reigned alone, but Nerva, the twelfth emperor after Augustus, was the first to choose a co-ruler. Thereafter two emperors from time to time ruled simultaneously as colleagues on this model. Until the time of Constantine, however, the division of business did not alter the primary authority of the city of Rome. After Constantine moved the capital to Byzantium, it became the habitual practice to have two emperors, one to rule Italy and Rome, the other to rule the east. The highest power was soon felt to belong to Constantinople, as those who ruled there often entrusted Rome and Italy to their co-ruler. Once the empires were divided in practice, moreover, they came to be called the eastern and western empires. When the barbarians then took over Italy, the western empire ceased to exist. After Augustulus was overthrown by Odoacer, as A.D. 476 we have shown, no one, not even as an act of tyrannous usurpation, took up the name of emperor in Italy and the West until Charlemagne, to whom, as we have said, Pope Leo gave the title.

Between Augustulus and Charlemagne, then, the empire ceased 71 to exist for almost three hundred years, and this may be calculated as follows. Odoacer, the king of the Toralingi, ruled Rome and Italy for thirteen years after dethroning Augustulus. The Goths, who defeated Odoacer under King Theoderic, ruled this region for almost sixty years. Narses took it away for a short time. Then the Lombards held Italy for two hundred and four years. After de-

ginta fere annos in his locis dominati sunt. Nonnihil temporis
Narses intercepit. Mox Longobardi ducentos et quatuor annos tenuerunt Italiam. Post Longobardos a se oppressos fugatosque vige-
simo quinto fere anno, Carolus imperator Romae creatus obliteratum nomen imperii dignitatemque resumpsit. Enim vero prius,
etsi bini imperatores rem publicam gubernabant, tamen alter ab altero dependebat, consortesque ambo erant imperii. Post Carolum
vero neque consortium ullum, nec ulla penitus remansit commu-
nio: divisi animi, divisa item signa. Nam ante Carolum, imperatores vexillo rubro, quod populi romani antiquum fuit insigne, aquilam auream addiderant; qui postea successerunt Carolo, fuscam
aquilam fulvo gestarunt vexillo, quo quidem insigni nullo unquam
tempore usus fuerat populus romanus.

72   Fuit praeterea disceptatio varia, cum alii veterem imperatorum
seriem et antiquum succedendi morem servandum censerent; alii,
etsi alienum a iure, tamen quia expediret, novum electionis exem-
plum a pontifice introductum probarent. Nobis autem plurimum
videtur referre, populus romanus hortatu pontificis an pontifex
ipse iniussu populi imperatorem crearit. Constat enim nullius magis quam populi romani id munus esse. Nam pontificatus per illa
tempora magis ab imperatoris auctoritate pendebat, nec quisquam
praesidebat, nisi quem post senatus, cleri et populi romani[62] electionem imperatoria comprobasset auctoritas. Verum haec censurae illorum, qui iuris pontificii peritiores habentur, subiicimus.

73   Carolo certe ipsi, utcumque tandem electo, divina porro huma-
naque faverunt, et fuit profecto vir dignus imperatorio culmine et
qui non solum rerum gestarum magnitudine, verum etiam pluri-
marum virtutum excellentia, Magnus meruerit[63] appellari. Idem
fortissimus atque mitissimus, summa iustitia nec minori sobrie-

feating and pursuing the Lombards for almost twenty-five years, Charlemagne was crowned emperor in Rome and restored the forgotten name and office of the empire. While it is true that at an earlier time there had been two emperors who governed the commonwealth, one depended on the other and they were associated in the rule of a single empire. After Charlemagne there was no association at all, and nothing remained in common between the eastern and western empires; they were divided in spirit, divided even in their emblems. Before Charlemagne, the emperors had added a golden eagle to the old red banner of the Roman People. The successors of Charlemagne, however, displayed a black eagle on a tawny yellow banner, a symbol never used by the Roman people.

There was also a complicated dispute about imperial elections. 72 Some thought that the old series of emperors and the old customs of succession should be maintained while others approved, as an expedient procedure, a new form of election introduced by the pope, even though it lacked a legal basis. To us it seems highly debatable whether the Roman People creates the emperor on the urging of the pope, or the pope himself, without instruction from the Roman People, creates the emperor, since it is evident that this office most properly belongs to the Roman People. In those times, it was more the case that the papacy depended on the emperor, and no one presided over the Church unless, after election by the senate, the clergy, and the people of Rome, he had been approved by imperial authority. But we submit these questions to the judgment of those who are considered more learned in canon law.

Charlemagne himself, whatever the means of his election, certainly enjoyed both divine and human favor. He was truly worthy of the high position of emperor. He deserved to be called "The Great" not only for the greatness of his deeds but for excellence of his many virtues. He was most strong and most merciful, just in the highest degree and equally temperate in his habits. To the

tate, ad gloriam rei bellicae, quae in illo[64] maxima fuit, liberalium artium studia et doctrinam litterarum adiunxerat. Ter in Italiam cum exercitu venit. Primo adventu Desiderium Longobardorum regem apud Ticinum subegit. Secundo adversus Araisum bene-ventanum ducem Capuam usque profectus est. Tertio Leonem pontificem a Romanis per iniuriam eiectum, in urbem restituit, quo tandem tempore[65] imperatorium nomen dignitatemque pro-meruit. Bella praeterea multa ac maxima contra Hunnos, Saxones, Aquitanos et alias quasdam nationes per se et filios ac praefectos felicissime gessit.

74   Huius successores quidam eam Italiae partem in qua Longobar-dorum regia fuit possidentes, se reges Italiae nuncuparunt, quo-rum e numero fuerunt Pipinus Caroli filius, item Bernardus et Lo-tharius nepotes ac Ludovicus Lotharii filius. Quorum Lotharius et Ludovicus non solum Italiae reges, sed etiam imperatores Roma-norum fuere. Sed et alii Caroli successores in Gallia primo, mox et in Germania romanum velut per manus traditum gubernarunt im-perium usque ad Arnulfum Germaniae regem, qui septimus a Ca-rolo successor et ultimus eius sanguinis imperator fuit. Postquam igitur in Germaniam imperium abiit ac pauci ex iis in Italia sta-tione continua, plurimi vero adventiciis, cum erat opus, exercitibus ad tempus morabantur, civitates Italiae paulatim ad libertatem re-spicere ac imperium verbo magis quam facto confiteri coeperunt, Romamque ipsam et romanum nomen, veneratione potius an-tiquae potentiae, quam presenti metu recognoscere.

75   Denique quotcumque ex variis barbarorum diluviis superfue-rant[66] urbes per Italiam, crescere atque florere et in pristinam au-ctoritatem sese in dies[67] attollere. Sed in Etruria quidem, a primis illis Romanorum bellis usque ad haec tempora, civitates multae oppidaque magna, quorum prius fuerat auctoritas, interierant. Nam et Caere et Tarquiniae[68] et Populonia et Luna, quae urbes quondam magnae iuxta litus inferi maris positae fuerunt, et per

great glory he had won in war, he added zeal for the liberal arts
and literary learning. Thrice he came to Italy with his army. The
first time he subdued Desiderius, king of the Lombards, near
Pavia. The second time he marched down as far as Capua against   A.D. 773–74
Araisus, the duke of Benevento. The third time he restored to
Rome Pope Leo, who had been unjustly expelled by the Romans.
That was the occasion on which he earned the imperial title and
office. In addition to all this, Charlemagne and his sons and gener-   A.D. 800
als waged many great wars with the utmost success against the
Huns, the Saxons, the Aquitainians, and certain other nations.[63]

Some of his successors, who possessed that part of Italy where   74
the royal court of the Lombards had been located, called themselves kings of Italy. Among them were Pepin, the son of Charlemagne, and Bernard and Lothair, his grandsons, and Louis, the
son of Lothair. Lothair and Louis were not only kings of Italy, but
also Roman emperors. But these and other successors of Charlemagne governed the Roman empire first from Gaul and later from
Germany, until the time of Arnulf, the king of Germany, who was
the seventh successor and heir of Charles and the last emperor of
his line.[64] After that, the empire was far away in Germany, and
few of the emperors maintained a lasting presence in Italy, though
many dwelt in it temporarily with foreign armies when the need
arose. Little by little, the Italian cities began to pay heed to liberty
and to acknowledge the empire's authority nominally rather than
in practice. The city of Rome and the name of Rome were vener-
ated for their ancient power but were no longer regarded as formidable.

At last those Italian cities that had survived the various floods   75
of barbarians began to grow and flourish and gradually regained
their ancient prestige. In Tuscany, however, many cities and large
and important towns had perished between the time of the first
Roman wars and this new era. For Caere, Tarquinii, Populonia,
and Luna, which had once been great cities along the Tyrrhenian

mediterraneam regionem Veii, quam urbem decennio supra obsessam a Romanis ostendimus, item Rusellae, Capenae,[69] Faleriae,[70] omnino defecerant. Clusium et Faesulae parum ab interitu distabant.

76 Florentiam vero quidam ab Attila Hunnorum rege, alii a Totila eversam, inde longum post tempus a Carolo Magno restitutam, prodidere. Nobis autem satis superque exploratum est Attilam Hunnorum regem nunquam Etruriam intrasse, sed nec citra Mincium amnem, qui ex Benaco in Padum influit, unquam progressum. Totilam vero Gothorum regem contra Etruriae civitates, quae post victoriam Belisarii a Gothis defecerant, desaevisse ostendimus. Eo adducor ut confuso nomine pro Totila Attilam a quibusdam acceptum per errorem credam. Incendisse autem Totilae animum ad delendam hanc urbem, praeter novam defectionem, vetus quoque dolor existimatur, quod videlicet dudum apud eam tot Gothorum millia cum Radagaso duce occubuissent; itaque refricante memoriam animo Florentiam tolli voluisse, qua stante velut trophaeum de sua gente in Etruria positum extabat. Haec si ita sunt, supra ducentos annos, qui Totilam inter Carolumque[71] fuere, eversam iacuisse hanc urbem necessarium est. Qua in re illud non immerito quem movebit, si per tam longum tempus vacua populo relicta sit urbs, quibus interea locis cives fuerint adservati? Nam novos quidem ex Romanis habitatores a Carolo ductos credere vanissimum est, praesertim tot calamitatibus involuta atque ita iam pridem multis cladibus urbe Roma afflicta, ut supplemento habitatorum ipsa potius indigeret quam aliis dare posset. Denique ad Ostiam urbem adeo Romanis necessariam per haec ipsa fere tempora cum deficerent incolae, propter vacuitatem romanae urbis colonos e Sardinia positos memoriae proditum est.

coast; and in the central region Veii (which, as we have said, was besieged for ten years by Rome), Rusellae, Capena and Falerii — all these cities had become totally extinct. Clusium and Faesulae were barely alive.

Florentia was razed (according to some) by Attila the Hun or (according to others) by Totila and later restored by Charlemagne after a long period. To us, however, it seems abundantly clear that Attila the Hun was never in Tuscany at all, and that he never crossed to this side of the river Mincio, which flows from Lake Garda to the river Po. Totila, king of the Goths, did, as we have shown, ravage the Tuscan cities which had rebelled against the Goths after Belisarius' victory. I am convinced, therefore, that a confusion of names has led some authors erroneously to mistake Totila for Attila. It may plausibly be supposed that, quite apart from Florentia's recent defection, an old rancor burned in Totila's heart and made him want to destroy this city, for it was here that, still earlier, so many thousands of Goths under Radagaisus had been killed. The memory of it would have rubbed raw in his mind, and he would have wished to destroy Florentia, a city that stood like a monument to the defeat of his people in Etruria. If so, Florentia must have lain in ruins for two hundred years, from Totila to Charlemagne. Anyone will justly be struck by the question of where the citizens lived in the meantime if the city lay empty of its people for so long. For it is completely useless to imagine that Charlemagne brought new inhabitants in from Rome, especially as that city had been recently involved in great calamities and had already been so much afflicted by earlier devastation that it needed to gain new inhabitants itself and could not possibly supply them. About that time, in fact, it is recorded that Ostia, a city critical to the Roman state, needed inhabitants, and that colonists were brought there from Sardinia because the city of Rome itself was empty.

76

77   Ego igitur magnas quidem inflictas a Totila clades, plurimam caedem factam civium et eversa moenia existimo, sed neque urbem funditus deletam neque per medium illud tempus sine habitatoribus omnino fuisse. Video namque dives illud ac praecipuum Martis templum et alia quaedam aedificia supra aetatem Totilae vetusta extare, quae cum incolumia relicta conspiciam, totam urbem deletam credere non libet, neque haec ipsa absque habitatoribus tamdiu stetisse. Quare moenia potius a Carolo restituta et nobilitatem, quae diffisa munitionibus urbis frequentia in praediis suis castella munierat, intra urbem revocatam; urbem denique ipsam varie disiectam in formam urbis redactam, sed reparatam magis quam rursus conditam existimo.

78   Urbes igitur quae per Etruriam perierant, supra ostendimus. Ex his vero, quae per tot adversas tempestates emersae, ad extremum evaserant, Pisae, Florentia, Perusia, Senae plurimum eminebant. Sed Pisani classe potentes late mari dominabantur eo facilius, quod maritima ex tuscis urbibus haec sola remanserat, Tarquiniis, Luna et Populonia iam pridem absumptis. Florentini autem industria terra praevalebant. Perusini ubertate soli et opportunitate loci crescentes, magnam potentiam habuere. Senas splendor[72] urbanarum rerum et familiarum excellentia longe nobilitarunt, et attulerunt potentiae materiam Rusellae et Populonia finitimae quondam urbes eversae. Proximi erant Arretini, bonitate agrorum et amplitudine territorii omnibus fere praestantes, sed inter Florentinos et Perusinos constitutis, duarum validissimarum civitatum officiebant potentiae. Nam Cortona quidem in Arretinorum potestate diu permansit, nomine etiam civitatis amisso, donec haud multo supra nostram aetatem pristinum locum recuperare promeruit. Hos proxime sequebantur Lucenses, Volaterrani, Pistorienses,

I think, therefore, that Totila had indeed done great harm to 77
Florence, slaughtering many of her citizens and tearing down her
walls, but I don't believe that he destroyed the city altogether nor
that it was entirely without inhabitants in the intervening period. I
see standing yet the rich and extraordinary temple of Mars and
other buildings from before the age of Totila, and when I consider
these unharmed remains I cannot believe that the whole city was
destroyed nor that it stood uninhabited for so long. More likely, I
think, the walls were restored by Charlemagne and he recalled
the nobility, which, lacking confidence in the city's fortifications,
would have defended the numerous castles on their estates. I
think, therefore, that the city was put back together as a city after
having been variously dismembered. Rather than refounded, in
my opinion, it was essentially restored.[65]

I have mentioned the Tuscan cities that perished. The main 78
ones which finally re-emerged after being so long swamped by calamity were Pisa, Florence, Perugia, and Siena. The Pisans had a
powerful fleet and enjoyed dominance at sea the more easily as
theirs was the only Tuscan maritime city that remained after
Tarquinii, Luna, and Populonia disappeared. The Florentines
were the dominant land power thanks to their diligent activity.
The Perugians prospered and acquired great power because of
their fertile land and their strategic location. Siena became prominent for the splendor of her urban wealth and her excellent families, and the resources freed by the destruction of her near neighbors, Rusellae and Populonia, added to her power. Arezzo was
next door, and nearly surpassed all other cities by the quality of
her land and the size of her territory, but she lay between Florence
and Perugia and the power of these two sturdy neighbors stood in
her way. Cortona, for instance, had a long time before lost her status as an independent city-state and had become a dependency of
Arezzo; she only recently reacquired her ancient autonomy. Next
after these cities came Lucca, Volterra, Pistoia, Orvieto, and

Urbevetani, Viterbienses; nam Sutrinos et Nepesinos atque omnem illam Etruriae partem quae romanae urbi adiacet, ut secunda
primo Romanorum fortuna, sic postremo adversa magis afflixerat.
Hae igitur civitates memoratu dignae post longas tempestates et
multiplicia pericula superstites erant. Sed ex omnibus quos supra
memoravimus, Perusinorum antiquissima potentia est. Haec enim
civitas et[73] ante romanum imperium inter capita Etruriae una e tribus nominata, et ad extremum secundum vel tertium potentiae
semper obtinuit locum, quod neque Clusio neque Arretio, quae
olim capita quoque et ipsa fuerunt, ad extremum contigit. Nam
Pisanorum quidem non antiqua sane fuit potentia nec ullam fere
apud veteres haec civitas habuit auctoritatem. Omne eius robur citra Caroli tempora floruit, mari tamen[74] quam terra longe nobi-
lius. Nec eius pristina origo a nostris est, sed a Graecis. Eo factum
reor ut florente quondam mari terraque Etruria, nullam ipsa partem auctoritatis teneret; eversis autem nostris maritimis urbibus,
dominandi susceperit facultatem. Senensium autem novam esse
civitatem Florentini et Arretini veteres agri ipsis paene Senarum
moenibus contermini ostendunt. Crevit tamen[75] postea et plurimum floruit, splendore ac magnificentia nulli maximarum non ae-
mula. Arretii vero et Clusii et Volaterrarum vetustissima origo est.
Tyrrhenorum ea oppida constat fuisse, quos troianum ante bellum
in Italia floruisse supra ostendimus. Cortonam ante etiam Tyrrhenorum adventum a Pelasgis conditam quidam auctores sunt, sed
eam Pelasgis pulsis mox Tyrrheni habuere. Viterbienses ab Arretinis ortos vetusta apud utrumque populum fama obtinuit.

79   Fuerunt praeterea inter civitates per superiora illa tempora con-
iunctiones quaedam: Florentini, Perusini et Lucenses sese mutuo
dilexerunt. Credo quod hinc pistoriensis, illinc aretinus interiectus
ager fines communionesque promiscuas, ex quibus discordiarum
materia plerumque oriri solet, utrinque sequestrabant. Inter Senenses item et Pisanos volaterrano divisos agro concordia viguit.

Viterbo; for Sutrium and Nepete and all of Tuscany in the vicinity of Rome had been badly hit, first by the good fortune of Rome and afterwards by her sufferings. These are the cities worth noting of those which survived the long period of storm and danger. But Perugia was the oldest power among the cities I have named. Even before the Roman empire it was referred to as one of the three capital cities of Etruria and to the end it always held the second or third place in terms of power. Neither Chiusi nor Arezzo, which too were once ancient capitals, continued as such to the end. Pisa was not a great power in ancient times and seems not to have had much standing in the eyes of the ancients. All her strength has developed since the time of Charlemagne, but far more prominently at sea than on land. And her oldest origins are not native but Greek. That is why, I believe, as long as the Etruscans flourished by sea and land, Pisa enjoyed no prestige. When our maritime cities were ruined, however, she was able to dominate. It is clear that Siena's status as a city-state is new, for the ancient territory of the Florentines and Aretines ran right up to her walls.[66] Later she grew and flourished, with splendor and magnificence to rival any. Arezzo and Chiusi and Volterra are the oldest. They were evidently towns of Tyrrhenia, which flourished in Italy even before the Trojan War, as we have remarked already. Cortona, according to certain writers, was founded by the Pelasgians even before the arrival of the Tyrrhenians, but it was soon captured by them, and they expelled the Pelasgians. Viterbo was an offshoot of Arezzo's according to the ancient traditions of both towns.[67]

In earlier times there were alliances among these towns, and 79 Florence, Perugia, and Lucca were mutually very friendly. This was so, I think, because the territories of Pistoia and Arezzo separated these three cities, and there could be none of the border disputes which commonly bring trouble. Siena and Pisa, divided by the territory of Volterra, also enjoyed harmonious relations. But partisanship and factionalism often altered their mutual relation-

Sed haec vel studia partium vel factionum respectus saepenumero variabant. Etenim quod cuiusque rationibus aptissimum est, id promptissime populi amplectuntur. Atque ego puto per prima illa tempora post barbarorum cessationem inter civitates nostras concordiam viguisse; mox vero, ut crescere coeperunt, vacuas ab externo metu, invidia et contentiones transversas egere.

80   Attulerunt autem his bellorum et discordiarum abundantissimum fomitem[76] crebrae inimicitiae inter pontifices romanos imperatoresque coortae. Nam imperium illud, quod in Carolo Magno maxime propter tutelam romanae ecclesiae fundatum ab initio fuit, in Germaniam ut supra ostendimus delatum, tales plerumque habuit successores ut ad nullam rem magis quam ad persequendos evertendosque pontifices creati viderentur; adeo unde salus petita erat, scelus emersit. Causa fere inimicitiarum illa suberat, quod ecclesiastica quaedam iura hi ut sua retinere, illi antiquata licentia usurpare nitebantur. In eos itaque pontifices sententiis et censuris, quae sola eorum tunc erant arma, ut severe poterant, animadvertebant, civitates et principes adversus illorum vesaniam concitabant, et ne quis eorum pareret edictis, sub gravissimarum denuntiatione poenarum deterrebant. Illi contra armis terribiles aderant. In re ambigua variae inclinationes animorum his vel illis faventium reperiebantur.

81   Haec itaque magnis saepe studiis per Italiam agitata, eo demum contentionis processere ut non solum civitates singulae, verum etiam populi intra una moenia constituti, vario favore dividerentur. Ita per Etruriam natae sunt factiones duae: una fautrix pontificum, imperatoribus adversa; altera imperatorio nomini omnino addicta. Sed ea, quam imperatoribus adversam supra ostendimus, ex iis fere hominibus[77] conflata erat qui libertatem populorum

ships. For peoples are quick to embrace whatever course of action suits their interests. During the first period after the barbarian invasions had ceased, our cities shared a strong sense of harmony, I believe, but as soon as they had begun to grow larger, with no fear of external enemies, they started to behave in an envious and competitive way.

The many disputes between the Roman pontiffs and emperors 80 brought plentiful tinder to our local wars and quarrels. For the empire which began with Charlemagne and was founded mainly for the protection of the Roman church, once it was, as we have explained, transferred to Germany, fell into the hands of successors whose main purpose in life seemed to be the persecution and overthrow of the popes. What had once been a source of security became a vortex of evil. The cause of the hostility was essentially that the popes tried to hold on to certain ecclesiastical rights while the emperors tried to usurp them on the basis of outmoded prerogatives. Against the emperors the popes therefore directed the strongest possible condemnations and censures, which at that time were their only arms, and urged cities and princes to oppose the imperial excesses, threatening them with heavy punishments if any of them should obey the emperors' edicts. The emperors, terrible in arms, marched against them. As the facts of the dispute remained ambiguous, attitudes varied; some favored the popes, some the emperors.

These issues were the subject of such frequent and heated quar- 81 rels throughout Italy that not only individual cities but even peoples living within the same walls were divided into parties. Two factions appeared in Tuscany: one favored the pope and was opposed to the emperors, the other was entirely devoted to the imperial name. But the side which, as we said, opposed the emperors was essentially composed of those who were more inclined to embrace the liberty of peoples: they considered it degrading for Germans and barbarians to rule over Italians under the pretext of the

magis complectebantur; Germanos autem barbaros homines sub praetextu romani nominis dominari Italis perindignum censebant. Alia vero factio ex iis erat qui imperatorio nomini addicti, libertatis et gloriae maiorum immemores, obsequi externis quam suos dominari malebant. Hinc studia partium coorta, magnarum calamitatum initia fuere. Nam et publicae res contentione et cupiditate magis quam bono et honesto tractabantur, et privatim odia inimicitiaeque in dies crescebant. Ita privatim et publice simul invaserat morbus, qui primo enutritus contentionibus, tandem exacerbatus odio ac letifer factus, ad arma et caedes ac vastitatem urbium ad extremum prorupit.

82   Maxime vero eius[78] morbi vis per Federici secundi tempora in Etruria exarsit. Licet enim eius avus, qui item Federicus appellatus est, pulsis Urbe pontificibus contra eorum fautores pluribus locis intulerit arma ac Mediolanum diu obsessum ad solum everterit Parmamque et Placentiam longo afflixerit bello et quatuor falsos pontifices contra veros perfoverit, ac postea Herricus pater non minori acerbitate animi desaevierit, tamen quantum ad res etruscas attinet, secundus Federicus principium et causam attulit civilium externarumque calamitatum. Hic paterna quidem origine a Svevis ortus, materna autem a siculis regibus, antequam ad imperium vocaretur, Siciliae regnum cum matre Constantia possidebat, maxime pontificum romanorum tutela in eo defensus. Sed postquam Ottone amoto ad imperium assumptus est, confestim avi ac patris vestigia ingressus, per tres et triginta (tot enim regnavit) annos maximis calamitatibus sedem romanam affecit, tres per id tempus pontifices persecutus, Honorium, Gregorium, Innocentium. Privatus autem ad extremum lugdunensi concilio ac imperiali et regia potestate depositus, non quemadmodum avus eius, tandem post multa errata se ipsum humilians ad gremium rediit,

Roman name. The other faction consisted of men who had bound themselves to the imperial cause and had forgotten the liberty and glory of their ancestors—men who preferred to serve foreigners rather than be ruled by their own people. Hence partisanship arose and this was the beginning of great calamities. For public affairs began to be conducted more in accordance with greed and rivalry than with goodness and honor, and in private life hatred and enmity increased daily. Thus the disease took hold of private and public life at the same time. First it was nurtured by quarrels, then it worsened and became deadly hatred, finally it burst out in arms and slaughter and the devastation of cities.[68]

This fever reached its height in Tuscany during the time of Frederick II.[69] His grandfather, whose name was also Frederick, had expelled the popes from Rome and had attacked their supporters in numerous places; after a long siege he had razed Milan to the ground and had done much harm to Parma and Piacenza in the course of a long war, while setting up four anti-popes. Frederick II's father, Henry, had been no less bitter a foe of the church. But as far as Tuscany was concerned, it was Frederick II who was chiefly responsible for the outbreak of civil and foreign calamities. On his father's side, he was of Swabian origin, but on his mother's he was Sicilian. Before being called to the empire, he had enjoyed joint possession of the kingdom of Sicily with his mother Constance, being protected in this position by the popes. But after Otto was removed from the scene and Frederick became emperor, he immediately followed in his father's and grandfather's footsteps and inflicted great calamities on the Holy See throughout the thirty-three years of his reign. In this time he persecuted three popes: Honorius, Gregory, and Innocent.[70] When at last he was deposed by the Council of Lyons and deprived of both his imperial and royal powers, he did not, like his ancestor, humiliate himself after his many errors and return to the fold. Instead he showed contempt for the council and its decrees. He tried not

82

A.D. 1212–50

A.D. 1245

sed et concilia et decreta contemnens, non solum ea quae tenebat restituere, sed insuper alia occupare perrexit. Siciliam igitur et Apuliam ac proximas Italiae partes ex materna ut diximus haereditate possidens, ac ex propinquo magis adhaerens, civitates Etruriae curiosius observavit, illas denique nudare adversariis ac suarum partium facere instituit. Hoc ille non solum in praesentia, verum etiam in futurum existimavit conducere. Nam quod[79] filiis abundabat, ut est hominum mens sibi ipsi nimis assentatrix et credula, longam illis in Italia successionem parare constituerat. Id ita demum contingere existimavit posse, si diversae factionis hominibus per Etruriam depulsis, amici et fautores eius haud ambigue civitatibus praesiderent. Hac itaque mente Etruriam cum exercitu ingressus, per singulas urbes auxilia subministrando ac ipsas per se et filios adeundo, monendo denique et irritando ut hi qui imperatorias fovebant[80] partes adversarios pellerent effecit. Nec id quidem persuadere difficile fuit, tumentibus iam pridem animis et multifariam inimicitiis inter cives vigentibus.

83 Quo quidem tempore multa intestina proelia, multae caedes civium et domorum incendia atque alia quae civilis ira ferre solet, per singulas fere urbes perpetrata traduntur. Nec tamen hi qui pulsi erant quieverunt, sed castella quaedam suarum civitatum invadentes ex illisque cientes bella, caedibus et rapinis omnia infestabant. Adversus hos Federicus ipse tantorum malorum auctor et rogatu civitatum et sua ipsa[81] sponte, quasi contra imperii turbatores et laesae maiestatis reos insurgens, pleraque rebellantia obsedit loca. Et si quibus ex oppidis adversa factio pelli non potuit, ea tota oppida pro hostibus habuit, ferroque et igne populatus est. Ita partium studia, quae prius civili modo[82] et urbanis contentionibus ad id tempus per Etruriam agitata fuerant, per huius Federici rabiem ad caedem et sanguinem ac expulsionem civium et vastitatem urbium compulsa fuere. Ipse certe tanta immanitate in his rebus versatus est ut quosdam diversae factionis homines captos a se et in Apuliam sub custodia missos, sive ut propriam satiaret iram

only to reassert the prerogatives he was holding but even to usurp others. Since he ruled in Sicily and Apulia and neighboring regions of Italy, as we have said, through his mother's hereditary rights, and spent time nearby, he watched the cities of Tuscany carefully, deciding finally to strip them of his adversaries and add them to his own party. He believed this would be of use to him not only in his present circumstances but also in the future. For he had plenty of sons, and since the human mind is all too self-flattering and credulous, he set on foot plans for them to acquire hereditary powers in Italy. He thought all he needed was to get rid of opposition in Tuscany and to make sure his friends and followers totally controlled those cities. For this purpose he entered Tuscany with an army, supplying aid to his party in each city, visiting the cities himself along with his sons, warning them and inciting his imperial supporters to expel the opposing faction. Nor was A.D. 1238 it difficult to persuade them, for their heads were hot enough, and lively enmities were ripening among the citizens already.

At this time, it is recorded, there were in almost every city great 83 numbers of street battles, citizens assassinated, houses burned and other marks of urban passion. The exiles, moreover, did not go quietly away; rather they occupied certain castles belonging to their cities and from these spread war, slaughter, and plunder through the countryside. Frederick himself, the real author of the evils, would then, on the request of the cities or of his own will, mount sieges against the rebellious places as harboring insurgents against the empire and persons guilty of treason. And if there were any towns from which the opposing faction could not be expelled, he would declare the whole town his enemy and devastate it with fire and sword. Thus the factiousness which earlier had merely aroused civil and urban quarrels in Tuscany, now, through Frederick's fury, issued in slaughter and bloodshed, expulsion of citizens, and utter devastation. He himself, certainly, practiced great cruelty in these matters. For instance, when certain

sive ut partium suarum hominibus gratificaretur, effossis prius oculis membrisque mutilatis per varia tormentorum genera occiderit. Cuius rei vindicta nequaquam diu dilata est, cum et ipse et filii male perierint et illa ipsa quam persecutus fuerat adversa Etruriae factio, armata ad eversionem sui generis potenter affuerit, scelerati sanguinis poena gloriose exacta.

men of the other faction were captured and sent to him in Apulia under guard, whether to satisfy his own anger or to please his followers, he first put out their eyes and mutilated their limbs, then killed them with various tortures. The vengeance for such actions was not long in coming, for both he and his sons came to a bad end. And the very faction he had persecuted in Tuscany acquired powerful arms with the aim of overthrowing his family and, to its glory, exacted a penalty in blood for that family's crimes.[71]

LIBER SECUNDUS

1 Pervagatiorem nobis historiam superioris libri necessitas fecit. Nam neque tantum opus aggressos, originem urbis indictam illibatamque praeterire fas putavimus, neque post illam enarratam, statim sine aliquo nexu rerum ad propria fuit tempora siccis, ut ita dixerim, pedibus transeundum. Itaque brevi discursu longa pervagati tempora, quaecumque ad notitiam dicendorum necessaria fuerunt, quasi argumentum praetexentes uno in libro collegimus, ut neque civitatum Etruscarum initia atque progressus, neque imperii romani declinatio atque divisio, neque haec ipsa, quae mox omnia quassarunt, studia partium factionesque, unde ortum augmentumque habuerint, ignota essent. Iam vero non cursu, sed incessu erit utendum.

2 Post Federici obitum, cuius de nefando scelere supra diximus, florentinus populus, iam pridem illorum qui rem publicam occuparant superbiam saevitiamque exosus, capessere gubernacula rerum ac tueri libertatem perrexit civitatemque totam omnemque eius statum populari arbitrio continere. Ea de causa robuste insurgens domique et foris multa duxerat providendum. Domi quidem, reducta nobilitatis ea parte quae dudum sub Federico exularat, et beneficio sibi illam coniunxit et partem huic adversam per huius reductionem reddidit imbecillam. Rei publicae vero gubernandae duodecim viros suffragio populi creatos praefecit, quos ab honoris antecellentia[1] vulgari quidem nomine antianos dixere. Urbe autem tota in sex regiones divisa, earum ex singulis magistratus sumebantur ac cetera omnia rei publicae munera. Multitudinem vero urba-

BOOK II

In the previous book necessity imposed upon us a wide-ranging 1
style of history. Having undertaken so vast a work, we thought it
wrong to omit any account of the city's origins, and equally wrong,
having recounted them, to pass immediately to the story of our
own times without wetting our feet, as it were, in the intervening
period. So we ran quickly through long periods of time, as in a
summary, collecting in one book whatever was necessary to understand what would be said later. For this reason we treated the beginnings and progress of the Etruscan cities, the decline and division of Roman power, and the origins and growth of that
partisanship and those factions which were afterwards to convulse
the world. But now we must walk, not run.

After the death of Frederick, whose shocking crimes we have al- 2
ready described, the Florentine People, having long been con- *1250*
sumed with hatred for the arrogance and ferocity of those who
had seized the commonwealth, roused itself to take the reins of
government, defend liberty, and to direct the affairs of the city-
state in accordance with the popular will. Rising up vigorously, it
took the lead in dealing with numerous foreign and domestic affairs. With regard to domestic affairs, it restored that party of the
nobility which not long since had been exiled under Frederick. By
this act of favor it attached that party to itself and weakened the
party that was opposed to popular rule.[1] It put Twelve Men,
elected by popular franchise, in charge of governing the commonwealth, who were distinguished by the honorable title of *Anziani* (a
word from the common tongue). The city was divided into six regions, and the magistrates and all other public offices were chosen
from each region. The urban multitude was enlisted under the
military standards of the several regions so that they might act simultaneously as a garrison against any plots by the nobles and also

nam per easdem regiones sub vexillis descripsit, ut esset simul domi praesidium, si quid contra nobilitas moliretur, simulque militiae, cum bellum posceret, designatus exercitus. Ab his initiis profectum, mirabile dictu est quantum adoleverit populi robur. Homines enim, qui dudum aut principibus aut eorum fautoribus, ut vere dixerim, inservierant, gustata libertatis dulcedine, cum populus iam ipse dominus auctorque honoris esset, totis se viribus attollebant, quo dignitatem inter suos mererentur. Igitur domi consilium et industria; foris autem arma fortitudoque valebant.

3   Prima huius populi post libertatem receptam expeditio suscepta est adversus Pistorienses; nec ea quidem ambitione vel dominandi cupiditate, sed provida cura libertatis retinendae. Pistoriensium enim per superiora iam inde tempora eadem quae Florentinorum conditio fuerat. Imperatorii nempe fautores nominis adversarios pepulerant; ipsi dominabantur, neque per mortem Federici statum mutaverant. Vulgabat vero tunc fama Corradum Federici filium suscepto imperatoris nomine magnas in Germania copias paravisse, Italiam regnumque paternum haud dubie petiturum. Ad huius igitur rei famam excitus florentinus populus, civitatem tam propinquam durare in partibus sibi periculosum arbitratus, reducere Pistoriensium exules per factionem dudum pulsos populumque ac libertatem in ea quoque urbe asserere constituit. Hac de causa in Pistorienses exercitus ductus est, multum admodum reclamante ea civium parte, quae fautrix imperii habebatur. Quin etiam cum perstaret in proposito populus armaque expediret, signa publica efferret, plerique principes eius factionis sequi recusarunt, sed nihilo magis ob eam rem profectio retardata est. Ingressi Pistoriensium fines, cum obviam fuisset hostis, pugnam conseruerunt. In qua usque adeo superior virtute et audacia Flo-

as a regular army in wartime. It is wonderful to relate how great the strength of the People grew from these beginnings. The People was now itself a lord and a font of honor, and men who only a short while before had been (frankly) servile towards princes and their supporters, now, having tasted the sweetness of liberty, bent all their strength on raising themselves up and acquiring an honorable standing in their own community. Thus the People grew strong in prudence and industry at home, in courage and arms abroad.[2]

The first enterprise of this People once it had received its liberty was undertaken against the Pistoiese. Its motive was neither ambition nor a desire for domination but a prudent concern for preserving its own liberty. The condition of the Pistoiese in the previous period was similar to what the Florentine condition had been until recently. Supporters of the Empire had expelled the enemies of that name, they themselves ruled, and the regime had not changed as a result of Frederick's death. But the report was then spreading that Conrad, Frederick's son, had assumed the imperial title and was readying vast forces in Germany with the aim, undoubtedly, of recovering Italy and his paternal kingdom. Roused by this report, the Florentine People, believing it would be dangerous to itself for a neighboring city to remain factionalized, decided to restore the Pistoiese exiles, who shortly before had been expelled in party strife, and to defend popular government and liberty in that city as well. So the army was led out against the Pistoiese, to the loud protests of that part of the citizenry which favored the empire. But the People persisted in its purpose, stockpiling arms and mustering its troops. Many leaders of the imperial faction refused to follow, but this did nothing to slow down the expedition. Having crossed into Pistoiese territory, they met and engaged the enemy in battle. In this battle, the Florentine People was so superior in strength and daring that it put the beaten Pistoiese to flight, driving them with great slaughter back to the

rentinus fuit, ut profligatos Pistorienses magna cum strage urbem adusque praecipites ageret; moenia finem insequendi fecere. Ab hac victoria elatus populus, cum in urbem rediisset, cives qui sequi publica signa recusarant, verbis minisque exagitatos abire in exilium compulit. Hi ad Senenses Pisanosque ob partium studia confugientes, illorum sublevati opibus, bellum Florentiae intulerunt. Ex hoc iam florentinus populus adversam imperio factionem palam adsciscere visus est et ad favorem eius plane respicere.

4   Per idem fere tempus Arretinis, qui dudum sub Federico pulsi exulabant, praebita auxilia sunt, quo in urbem regrederentur.[2] Convenerant enim illi magna multitudine apud Rondinem castellum arretini agri bellumque Arretio tumultuosius inferebant. Itaque eadem ratione fovendos civitas duxit, qua exules Pistorienses. Quatuor praeterea populi eodem anno in societatem assumpti: Lucenses et Miniatenses, odio Pisanorum; Urbevetani et Alcinates, qui Senensibus adversabantur. Cum enim Pisani et Senenses exulibus faverent auxiliaque submitterent, pari versura illorum inimicos fovere visum est.

5   Post haec eodem anno bis exercitus eductus: primum in mugellanum agrum, cum exulum fautores Accianicum magnis copiis obsessuri adventassent; secundo ad Montaream, quo ex castello nuper occupato exules bellum tumultuosius ciebant. Utroque in loco prospere gesta res, dispari tamen facilitate. Nam in mugellano quidem confestim fusae fugataeque sunt hostium copiae, Montarea vero per mediam hiemem dura atque aspera obsidione domita, frustra conantibus reliquis exulum obsessis auxilium ferre. Captum denique[3] id castellum, ad solum diruitur.

6   Eodem anno societas inita est cum Ianuensibus adversum Pisanos ac magno elatoque animo bellum undequaque susceptum. Haec fere priori anno digna memoratione gesta.

walls of their city. The People were elated by their victory, and when they returned to their own city they harassed with threatening words those citizens who had refused to muster, compelling them to go into exile. The political sympathies of the latter led them to the Sienese and the Pisans, whose resources enabled the exiles to make war on Florence. From this time forward the Florentine People were perceived as open adherents of the anti-imperial faction, openly courting its favor.[3]

Around the same time, in order to help them return to their 4 city, aid was offered to some Aretine exiles who had been expelled under Frederick. They had assembled in great numbers at the castle of Rondine in the Aretine territory, and from there they were conducting an irregular war against the Aretines. The City felt they should be supported on the same grounds it had supported the Pistoiese exiles. Alliances were formed as well with four other peoples that same year: the peoples of San Miniato and Lucca out of hatred for the Pisans, and the peoples of Orvieto and Montalcino who were resisting the Sienese. The Pisans and the Sienese had been aiding and abetting the exiles of these four towns and so by the same token were regarded as fostering the four towns' enemies.

Later this same year the army was marched out twice: first to 5 the Mugello, where supporters of the exiles had arrived in force to besiege Accianico; secondly to Montaia where from a recently-occupied castle the exiles were mustering for a guerilla war. The affairs of the People prospered in both places, but not with the same ease. In the Mugello the forces of the enemy were instantly broken and put to flight, while Montoio was conquered only after a hard and bitter siege in the middle of winter, and despite the vain efforts of the rest of the exiles to bring aid to the besieged. But at length the castle was captured and razed to the ground.[4]

In the same year an alliance with the Genoese against the 6 Pisans was formed and a war on multiple fronts was begun with

7   Proxima dehinc aestate in Pistorienses exercitus reductus, cum hostes superiori proelio fracti sese moenibus continerent, vastato circa urbem agro ad Titianum consedit. Id castellum, quia munitissimum erat, aliquot dies obsidionem pertulit, nec prius quam vi machinarum domitum, in potestatem pervenit. Florentino ad Titianum sedente Pisani cum exercitu adversum Lucenses congressi proelium non procul Toporio commiserunt. In eo proelio fracti Lucenses fugatique sunt, magnaque eorum multitudo a victoribus capta trahebatur. Quod postquam in florentino exercitu auditum est, sociorum dolentes casum, movere illico signa ac succurrere perditis rebus statuerunt. Profecti igitur rapto agmine victrices Pisanorum copias ad Heram fluvium consequuntur. Ibi sistere hostem ac pugnare invitum compellunt. Raro unquam atrocius quam ea die pugnatum tradunt, cum et Pisanus recenti victoria superbus fortiter dimicaret et Florentinus odio doloreque incensus obstinatissime niteretur. Post longum certamen superati ad extremum Pisani terga verterunt, quos profligatos palantesque secuti victores, magnam caedem edidere. Captivorum ad tria millia cum plerisque signis militaribus relata sunt, fuitque ingentis solatii loco, quod Lucenses captivi, qui modo trahebantur, exempti vinculis multos Pisanorum ipsi ceperunt ac versa fortuna vinctos traxerunt.

8   Per haec ipsa ferme tempora exules florentini duce Guidone comite, cui Novello cognomentum fuit, Fighinum ingressi bellum

bravery and high spirits. Such were the deeds most worthy of record from the foregoing year.

The following summer the army was marched out against the 7
Pistoiese. Having been beaten in the previous battle, the enemy 1252
were staying behind their walls. The Florentines laid waste to the
land around the city and encamped by Tizzano. This castle, being
very well fortified, held out against the siege for several days, and
came under the control of the Florentines only after it had been
conquered by siege-machines. With the Florentine army
encamped at Tizzano, the Pisans with their army engaged the
Lucchesi and began a battle not far from Montópoli. In this battle
the Lucchesi were broken and put to flight and a great number of
them were taken captive by the victors. When this became known
in the Florentine army, there was great grief at the plight of their
allies, and it was decided on the spot to march out and assist them
in their desperate situation. The Florentines set out in a flying column and pursued the victorious forces of the Pisans to the river
Era, where they compelled the unwilling enemy to stop and fight.
Rarely has there been more bitter fighting, it is said, than on that
day. The Pisans in the pride of their recent victory strove bravely,
while the Florentines fought with obstinate resolution, burning
with hatred and grief. After a long contest the Pisans were finally
overcome and turned tail. The victors followed the scattered and
fleeing enemy, slaughtering large numbers of them. Up to three
thousand prisoners were brought back as well as numerous battle-
standards. It was a source of great comfort that the Lucchesi,
who but a little while before were being dragged off as prisoners,
were now freed of their chains, and reversed their ill fortune by
themselves taking prisoner many Pisans, whom they bound and
dragged away.[5]

Around this same time the Florentine exiles under the leader- 8
ship of Count Guido Novello entered Figline and from there conducted irregular warfare. For this reason yet another expedition

inde tumultuosius inferebant. Quare paulo post reductas ex agro pisano copias, alia rursus expeditio[4] indicitur, profectique equites peditesque urbani ad Fighinum castra posuere. In eo obsidendo, cum apparatus maiores fierent (erat enim id oppidum per ea tempora in primis nobile), orta pacis mentio est demumque recepta his ferme conditionibus: ut exulibus reditus in urbem esset, utque Novello abducere militem sine fraude liceret. Ea fide servata sunt, receptum tamen oppidum a Florentinis, illico eversum oppidanique ipsi magna ex parte Florentiam traducti hisque locus in urbe ad inhabitandum[5] datus, nec multo post in partem rei publicae aequa cum aliis civibus conditione recepti.

9   Confecto fighinensi bello, antequam reducerentur copiae, Alcinatibus opem ferre placuit. Hi enim socii iam pridem a Senensibus obsidione pressi, extremo in discrimine versabantur. Itaque Fighino profecti, per arretinum agrum ad hostes[6] duxere. Pugna ingens commissa est non longe ab oppido, superatique in ea pugna Senenses, magna suorum clade terga dare ac obsidionem solvere coacti sunt. Ita liberatis periculo sociis, exercitus praeclaris rebus una aestate locis pluribus gestis in urbem rediit.

10   Hoc igitur victoriarum successu elatus populus, ut primum ver advenit, magnis rursum copiis egressus Pistorium circumsedit. Pistorienses vero, cum neque in se quicquam spei nec in amicis superesset, ne ad extremam dimicationem perducerentur, cedere tandem Florentinorum voluntati statuerunt. Eius rei causa legatus cum potestate publica missus est: Ildebrandinus Ottoboni filius, vir per ea tempora magnae in re publica auctoritatis, cumque eo

was announced shortly after the troops had returned from Pisan territory. Urban horse and foot companies set out and pitched camp near Figline. In the course of the siege, while larger war-engines were being readied (for at that time Figline was among the noblest towns), talk of peace arose. It was at length agreed to on approximately these conditions: that the exiles should return to the city, and that Novello should withdraw his army without fraud. This engagement was observed, but the Florentines, having taken the town, immediately demolished it and removed the greater part of the townsmen to Florence. There they were given a place to dwell and soon were accepted as part of the commonwealth on an equal footing with the other citizens.

Once the Figline war had been brought to a conclusion, it was 9 decided to bring aid to Montalcino before marching the troops back. These allies had for some time been hard pressed by a Sienese siege and their affairs were now at a critical juncture. So the Florentines set out from Figline and marched towards the enemy through the Aretine territory. A great battle began not far from the town in which the Sienese were overcome and put to flight with great destruction to their forces. And so they were compelled to lift the siege. Having thus freed its allies from peril, the army returned to the City. It had performed famous deeds in many places in the space of a single summer.[6]   1253

The People were elated at this series of triumphs and as soon as 10 spring came they went out in force once more and encamped around Pistoia. The Pistoiese had no hope left either in themselves or in their friends and decided at length to give way to the will of the Florentine people rather than fight it out to the end. So the Florentines sent out to draw up an agreement an ambassador named Ildebrando di Ottobono, who at that time was a man of great authority in the commonwealth, together with two judges. They allowed peace to the Pistoiese on the following conditions: that the league and friendship between the Florentine and

iurisperiti duo ad formulam concipiendam. Hi pacem Pistoriensibus his conditionibus permisere: ut foedus et amicitia posthac Florentino Pistoriensique perpetua foret; exules omnes Pistorienses in urbem reciperent; bona restituerent; bellum inferrent omnibus qui florentini nominis hostes essent, praeterquam adversum Pisanos et Senenses; captivi omnes utrinque dimitterentur.

11   Post haec rursus Alcinum copiae reductae et commeatus eo delatus, quo socii bello pressi assiduo sustentarentur. Hae commeatu exposito cum expedite redirent, aliquot hostium castellis in via expugnatis ditatae praeda in urbem rediere. Et iam fervebant animi maiora in dies capessere. Itaque secuta mox aestate, quanto numquam prius apparatu in Senenses proficiscuntur. Cum omnia late vastarent castellaque urbi finitima expugnare adorirentur, conterriti Senenses pacem quaesiverunt, quae haud cunctanter illis data est. In ea ita convenit, ut Senenses posthac Alcinatibus bellum ne inferrent neve hostibus florentini populi[7] sociorumve faverent. Inde Bonitium copiae traductae. Id oppidum sine ulla mora Florentinis deditur.

12   Post haec in Volaterranos transitum est, quae civitas non satis pacata florentino nomini credebatur et favisse quondam Pisanis ceterisque hostibus, ac diversarum partium homines in ea tunc urbe praevalere constabat. Eo igitur cum perventum esset, quamquam montis altitudo oppidique conspecta omnem expugnationis adimebat spem, ascendere tamen placuit et quam proxime urbi si-

Pistoiese people should henceforth be perpetual; that the Pistoiese should take all exiles back into their city; that they should restore the possessions of the latter; that they should make war on all enemies of the Florentine name, with the exception of the Pisans and the Sienese; and that all captives on both sides should be released.[7]

After this the troops marched back once more to Montalcino, bringing provisions to support the allies, who were hard pressed by continuous warfare. Having delivered the provisions they immediately marched back, capturing several enemy castles along the way, and returned to the City enriched with plunder. Now their spirits yearned every day for still greater enterprises. So when summer came they marched out against the Sienese with the greatest apparatus of war they had yet assembled. Laying waste all about them, they started to besiege the castles bordering on the city. The terrified Sienese sued for peace, which was granted them without delay. In the peace it was agreed that the Sienese should henceforth not make war on Montalcino, nor should they give aid to enemies of the Florentine People or its allies. Next the troops marched on Poggibonsi, which immediately surrendered to the Florentines.

After this they moved against Volterra, a city which was thought to be ill disposed to the Florentine name, having in times past brought aid to the Pisans and other enemies; and it was evident that men of the Ghibelline party had the upper hand at that time in the city. So when they arrived and saw the situation of the town, set high on a mountain, they lost all hope of storming it, but decided to march up anyway and show the standards as close to the city as possible. When this had been done, and the soldiery was spreading out to lay waste to the countryside, the Volterrans burst out of the town in a great mob and fell upon the Florentines with a sudden assault. The nature of the place itself added to the terror. The way down from the town was by a sheer cliff and it

11

1254

12

gna ostendere. Id cum factum esset ac diffusus miles popularetur, Volaterrani magna multitudine ab oppido irruentes repentino impetu Florentinos invasere. Adiuvabat terrorem natura ipsa loci. Declivis enim praecepsque ab oppido descensus est facilisque telorum de superiori parte coniectus, ut primo statim impetu coacti sint Florentini pedem referre. Sed conscia virtutis mens insignisque victoriarum memoria adversissimis etiam locis superare hostem in animum induxit. Itaque sese invicem cohortati, facto globo sursum versus signa intulerunt. Volaterrani, utpote qui neque duce certo neque ordine ullo, sed ut quemque tulerat casus in hostem descenderant, ubi contra quam rati fuerant, dirigi in se aciem ac signa inferri viderunt, parumper tolerantes proelium, referre primo pedem, mox effuso protinus cursu ad oppidum refugere, quos insecuti victores usque ad portas ceciderunt terga. In ipsis vero portarum angustiis maxime tumultuatum est, conantibus aliis super alios irrumpere. Tantaque fuit trepidatio, ut desertam omni praesidio portam mixti simul victi victoresque intrarent. Antesignani ad portam subsistentes grave agmen expectarunt, quod postquam advenit, signa illata sunt et intra urbem penetratum.

13   Nulla post haec fuit dimicatio. Volaterrani enim, ubi captam viderunt urbem, abiectis supplices armis ad placandam victoris iram convertuntur. Matresfamilias passis crinibus, sacerdotes veneranda manibus sacra praeferentes misericordiam implorabant. Haberent, quando superi ita voluissent, urbis dominatum; civibus et innocenti parcerent turbae; culpa factum esse paucorum, quod alienas ab utilitate sua partes Volaterrani suscepissent; in auctores modo culpae recidere poenam oportere. Ea dicentibus haud difficile fuit veniam impetrare. Neque sceleris enim neque acerbitatis quicquam Volaterrani admiserant; partium modo studia agebantur eaque mens civitatis ab initio fuerat, ut reductos mallet quam

was easy to throw spears from the higher positions, so the Florentines were compelled to give way immediately under the brunt of the first attack. But the consciousness of their own bravery and the memory of their famous victories strengthened their resolve to overcome the enemy even amid the most adverse circumstances. So, exhorting each other, they formed themselves into a body and carried the standards back up the mountain. The Volterrans had come down against their enemy as chance directed each of them, with no established leader and no order of battle. Now, contrary to their expectation, they saw formed troops and standards being led in their direction. They bore up under the assault for a little while, then gave ground. Soon they were fleeing in a disorderly run straight for the town, pursued by the victors, till they reached the gates where they were cut down from behind. The greatest uproar took place at the narrow gates where the Volterrans trampled each other in the struggle to get back inside. So great was their fear that the gate was left unguarded and victors and vanquished entered it simultaneously. The skirmishers posted themselves by the gate and awaited the main body of troops; when it arrived the standards were brought forward and the army made its way inside the city.

After this there was no further fighting. Indeed, when they saw 13 their city captured, the Volterrans threw down their arms and, becoming suppliants, turned to the task of placating the victors' anger. Mothers with flowing locks, priests bearing holy objects in their hands, pleaded for mercy. The Florentines (they said) had conquered the city by the will of the gods; they should spare the citizens and the innocent mob; it was the fault of a few persons that the Volterrans had received factions alien to their own interests; punishment should fall only on those responsible for the fault. It was not difficult for the Volterran spokesmen to find forgiveness. The Volterrans had not given way to criminal acts or bitterness; they had acted solely from party zeal. From the beginning it had been the intention of the City to subdue rather than destroy

perditos Volaterranos. Itaque nemo post ingressum violatus est, nemini bona ablata, pauci modo principes diversae factionis in exilium acti formaque rei publicae constituta. Ad ea conficienda aliquot dies absumpti.

14 Post haec in Pisanos copiae traductae sunt. Pisani in tanto Florentinorum successu pugnae fortunam minime experiundam rati, sese moenibus continebant, missisque in castra oratoribus pacem et ipsi poposcerunt. Dictae conditiones durae quidem multaque Pisanis per eam pacem adempta obsidesque ob ea implenda suscepti.

15 Haec permulta quidem et egregia mirabili felicitate una aestate a florentino populo gesta sunt, adeoque prosper fuit omnium coeptorum cursus, ut is fuerit annus victoriarum nuncupatus. Ex pisano demum agro laeta plaudentiaque agmina triumphantium more domum redierunt.

16 Eodem anno, crescente populi auctoritate aedes publicas, ubi nunc praetorium est, aedificare placuit. Cuius rei causa, cum a locorum dominis facta redemptione solum publicum effecissent, aedes praestanti magnificentia fundaverunt ac rostra et iudicia in his constituerunt, cum ante id tempus praesides domibus fere privatis uti consuevissent, consilia vero populi per templa agitarentur. Ita et foris et domi eo anno populi maiestas exaltata est.

17 Altero dehinc anno, cum deesset belli materia domi, Urbevetanis postulantibus missi equites quingenti. Hi cum forte Arretium pervenissent, Arretini guelfarum partium (iam enim per favorem florentini populi in urbem redierant) equitatus praesentia sublevati

the Volterrans. Hence no one was injured after Volterra was entered; no one's goods were taken; only a few leaders of the Ghibelline faction were sent into exile and a republican constitution was set up. Several days were spent making these arrangements.[8]

Then the troops marched to Pisa. The Pisans, after so many 14 Florentine successes, thought it best not to try the fortunes of battle. They shut themselves behind their walls and sent ambassadors to the Florentine camp to sue in their turn for peace. The conditions fixed were very hard indeed. The Pisans lost a great deal by that peace, and hostages were taken to ensure that the conditions were fulfilled.

These numerous great deeds were accomplished by the Floren- 15 tine People with marvelous good fortune in the space of a single summer: so prosperous was the course of all their undertakings that the year became known as the Year of Victories. And at last 1254 the army, happy and rejoicing, returned home in triumph from Pisan territory.[9]

In the same year it was decided, in view of the growth of popu- 16 lar authority, to construct public buildings where the Palace of the Podestà[10] now stands. For this purpose public land was created by purchase from its owners and a building of extraordinary magnificence was begun in which assembly-rooms and courts were laid out. Before this time judges were for the most part accustomed to use private dwellings and the councils of the People were held in churches. Thus was the majesty of the People raised high that year both at home and abroad.

The next year, in the absence of any grounds for war at home, 17 five hundred knights were sent to the Orvietans at their request. 1255 By chance they passed through Arezzo. The Aretines of the Guelf Party (who by now had returned to the city through the influence of the Florentine People) were encouraged by the presence of the Florentine knights and, seizing their arms, they expelled forthwith from the city the men of the opposite faction who had ruled the

raptis confestim armis diversae factionis homines, qui per Federici tempora rem publicam gubernarant,[8] urbe pepulerunt. Creditum est Guidonem cognomento Guerra (is enim praefectus equites ductabat) auctorem adhortatoremque pellendi fuisse, et submissa ab eo invadentibus auxilia et formidinem illatam adversariis palam constabat. Ea re Florentiae cognita, etsi non ingratum erat illarum partium homines pulsos esse, tamen verebantur ne id civitatis consilio contra fidem machinatum crederetur. Erat vero periculum, quoniam et Pistorii et Volaterris eadem quoque factio Florentinorum praesidiis sustentabatur, ne in suspicionem versa cuncta turbaret. Quocirca rem corrigendam rati, indicto exercitu in Arretinos egrediuntur. Cum ad urbem pervenissent, partim terrendo, partim cohortando, effecerunt ut pulsi Arretio cives ab illis ipsis, qui pepulerant, reciperentur. Ita pacatis rebus foedus cum Arretinis renovatum est et societas in quinquennium inita, idque in foedere ascriptum, ut Arretini magistratum qui peregrinus eligi consueverat de Florentinis in triennium susciperent. Quod ea de causa tunc provisum est, quo concordia civium servaretur et quae redierat factio, sub tutela magistratus secura[9] perstaret. Susceptus est autem primus Florentinorum ab Arretinis Teglarius Aldobrandi[10] filius Adimar, eques florentinus.

18   Eodem anno foedus cum Senensibus renovatum est, legati vero ad hoc missi, Oddo Altovita et Iacobus Ceretanus. In eo foedere multa ultro citroque conventa fuere, et illud in primis, ne Florentinus[11] Senensium, neve Senensis[12] Florentinorum exules reciperent neve faverent, et si postulatum foret, ab alterutra civitate expellerentur; subsidia invicem exhiberent ad ea quae quoquo modo possessa forent retinenda. Ictum est hoc foedus apud Donatianum oppidum, legatique Senensium iecerunt Provincianus Ildobrandi

commonwealth during the time of Frederick. It was believed that Guido Guerra, the leader of the Florentine knights, had been responsible for encouraging the expulsion, and it was obvious that he had given aid to the uprising and had intimidated its adversaries. When this became known in Florence, although there was no displeasure at the expulsion of men belonging to the Ghibelline party, it was nevertheless feared that the event would be seen as a treacherous plot planned by the City.[11] And there was the danger, since the Guelf faction was also being supported by Florentine aid in Pistoia and Volterra, that the suspicions aroused would lead to general disturbances. On this account the Florentines thought the matter should be put right, and so they summoned the army and marched out to Arezzo. Arriving there, they saw to it, through a mixture of threats and persuasion, that the citizens expelled from Arezzo were received back by the very citizens who had expelled them. The matter being thus settled, the treaty with the Aretines was renewed and an alliance for five years formed. It was stipulated in the treaty that the Aretines should receive a Florentine as their foreign official[12] for the space of three years. This was done, in that instance, in order to preserve civic concord and to guarantee under the protection of the magistrate the security of the restored faction. The first Florentine so received by the Aretines was Tegghiaio Aldobrandi de'Adimari, a Florentine knight.[13]

In the same year the treaty with the Sienese was renewed; the legates sent for this purpose were Oddo Altoviti and Jacopo Cerretani. In this treaty there were a number of reciprocal agreements, and chiefly this: that neither the Florentines nor the Sienese should take in or aid each other's exiles, and that if either city should request it, the other city should expel them; and that they should help each other in every possible way to keep what they possessed. This agreement was struck in the town of San Donato; the Sienese representatives were Provinciano di Ildobrando Sal-

18

filius Salvanus et Berengarius senensis. Ita quietis pacatisque rebus, optima inde spe discessum est.

19   Per haec ipsa tempora, cum viderentur omnia pacata maximaque florentino populo ex rebus gestis auctoritas accessisset, nova rursus turbationum fomenta in Apulia oriuntur. Federico enim superstites filii duo fuerant, Corradus legitimis[13] ex nuptiis et Manfredus ex concubina matre, ceterum admodum nobili. Huic, quia ingenio acri et forma conspicuus erat ac liberalibus studiis ingenue eruditus, favor hominum plurimus sequebatur, vivensque Federicus in honore habuit et moriens Tarentinorum principem illum reliquit. Ad Corradum vero regni ac potentiae omnis pertinebat successio. Is igitur non multo post obitum Federici ex Germania movens, cum superatis Alpibus in Venetos descendisset, per Adriaticum mare in Apuliam transiit. Ibi cum regnum aliquod tempus administrasset, in aegritudinem incidit adversam, qua dum curatur, veneno extinctus creditur[14] medico eius a Manfredo fratre corrupto. Successorem sibi Corradus Corradinum filium, tunc admodum puerum sub tutela matris in Germania degentem, testamento reliquit. Et quia suspectum habebat Manfredi animum, curam tuendi administrandique regni propinquis uxoris, quos secum e Germania duxerat, quoad filius adolesceret, demandavit. Horum in manibus arces armaque ac potestatem summam in regno reliquit.

20   Quae cum intueretur Manfredus, quoniam haec omnia contra se provisa intelligebat, confestim ad ingenium versus, Innocentio pontifici romano, qui quondam Federici, postea Corradi persecutione exagitatus fuerat, reconciliatus est, partesque romanae sedis prae se ferens, adeo gratam operam pontifici exhibuit, ut non solum in principatu a patre suscepto confirmaretur, verum etiam

vani and Berengario of Siena.[14] Their affairs thus settled and put to rest, the two sides departed with good hope for the future.

About this same time, when all seemed to be at peace and when 19 the deeds of the Florentine People had brought it to the height of its authority, new fuel for trouble once more appeared in Apulia. Frederick[15] had two surviving sons: Conrad, the issue of a legitimate marriage, and Manfred, whose mother was a concubine, though one of noble blood. The latter was much the more popular figure, as he was obviously brilliant and handsome as well as nobly educated in the liberal arts. While Frederick was alive he held Manfred in esteem and at his death made the young man Prince of Taranto. It was to Conrad, however, that the full succession to the kingdom and to power belonged. Not long after the death of Frederick, Conrad left Germany, crossed the Alps and went down into the Veneto, passing via the Adriatic into Apulia. There, after ruling his kingdom for some time, he fell sick. While being treated for this illness, he was poisoned, it was thought, by his doctor who had been bribed by his half-brother Manfred. In his will Conrad had made his son Conradin his successor; the latter at that time was a boy living in Germany under the tutelage of his mother. And because he had been suspicious all along of Manfred's intentions, until such time as the boy should grow up, he had entrusted the protection and administration of his kingdom to relatives of his wife whom he had brought with him from Germany. In their hands he left his citadels and arms and the supreme power in the kingdom.

When Manfred saw this, he understood that it was all directed 20 against him. Unhesitatingly he relied on his wits and was reconciled with Pope Innocent[16] who had been persecuted by Frederick and later by Conrad. Manfred showed himself a partisan of the Holy See and performed works so pleasing to the pontiff that he was not only confirmed in the principality he had received from his father, but was also endowed with further titles of honor.

aliis titulis dignitatibusque augeretur. Pontifex denique ipse Manfredi favore sublevatus fines regni intrare ausus est; brevique deiectis Corradini tutoribus cuncta in suum nutum potestatemque recepit.

21 Ceterum haud multo post Manfredus obortis adversum pontificem discordiis ac manifeste dissentiens Luceriae copias parare ac bellum movere constituit. Nec pontifex ipse segnis militem contrahere et conatum omnem adhibere pergebat. Inter hunc apparatum belli Innocentius Neapoli moritur. Quam veluti oblatam sibi fortunae beneficio facultatem arripiens Manfredus ita per vacationem romanae sedis vires extendit, ut creatus mox Alexander pontifex, diffisus regni negotiis excederet finibus ac se[15] Ananiam cum omni curialium turba reciperet. Missus autem adversus Manfredum legatus Octavianus romanae ecclesiae cardinalis, quamquam praevalidis copiis insignique omnium rerum apparatu, usque adeo tamen inferior bello fuit, ut magnam de se apud multos suspicionem relinqueret, ne studio partium, quo ex genere inficiebatur (erat enim Ubaldinae gentis), Manfredo faveret. Denique sub hoc legato, sive sponte sua cedente sive per vim pulso, plerasque regni partes Manfredus occupavit potensque inde factus suo iam nomine regnare incepit.

22 Huius igitur successum deiectionemque pontificis Pisani Senensesque ac ceteri eius per Etruriam factionis adeo laetis percipiebant animis,[16] ut prae gaudio exultare triumphareque viderentur impetumque susciperent rerum novandarum. Quare sequentis anni initio Pisani, spreto foedere cum Florentinis sociisque nuper

At length the pontiff himself, encouraged by Manfred's support, dared to cross the border of the Kingdom[17] and in a short time Conradin's tutors were driven out and the pope took everything under his power and command.[18]

However, a little while later there arose resistance to the pontiff, 21 and Manfred, now openly at variance with him, decided to mobilize his forces in Lucera[19] and start a war. The pope collected his forces and applied himself to the enterprise with equal alacrity. In the midst of these war-preparations, Innocent died at Naples. Manfred seized the opportunity offered him, as it seemed by Fortune's favor, and so extended his power during the vacancy of the Holy See that shortly afterwards, when Alexander[20] was created pope, the latter lost confidence in his affairs in the Kingdom, left its territory, and betook himself to Anagni with his whole court. He sent out against Manfred his legate Ottaviano, a cardinal of the Roman church. Ottaviano, despite powerful and well-equipped forces, performed so badly in the war that the strong suspicion arose in many minds that he was taking Manfred's side thanks to partisanship arising from a family relationship (Ottaviano being a member of the Ubaldini family). In the end Manfred wrested the greater part of the Kingdom from the control of this legate, either by force or by the latter's willing consent. Having achieved power, Manfred now began to rule in his own name.[21]

When they learned of Manfred's success and the expulsion of 22 the pontiff, the Sienese and the Pisans and the rest of the Tuscan Ghibellines were so delighted that they seemed to leap for joy and triumph, and the news encouraged them to attempt a revolution. Hence at the beginning of the following year, the Pisans, spurning 1256 the treaty recently made with the Florentines and their allies, marched into Lucchese territory and laid waste to everything along the river Serchio; they also tried to capture certain castles. At this news the Florentines and Lucchesi sprang to arms and, joining

icto, in agrum lucensem intulerunt arma lateque circa Auserim fluvium omnia popularunt; castella etiam quaedam expugnare adorti sunt. Ad huius rei nuncium Florentini Lucensesque in armis fuerunt, coniunctisque una copiis ad hostem profecti signis collatis dimicarunt. Proelium atrox fuit, sed tandem impares viribus Pisani in fugam vertuntur. Capti ex his ad tria millia, caesi autem permulti, multi etiam dum fugerent vorticibus amnis absorti periere. Victores traiecto Auseri Pisis copias admoverunt, omniaque circa urbem ferro igneque vastantes ad iniquissimam Pisanos compulerunt[17] pacem. Supra illa quae in priore foedere convenerant, Mutronae oppidum cum libero maris litore aliaque complura castella multumque agri dimittere coacti sunt et immunitatem Florentinis permittere; illud praeterea victis expressum, ut ponderibus et mensuris florentino more Pisani uterentur.

23   Per hunc modum immaturus Pisanorum impetus tunc repressus est. Fama tamen Manfredi in dies crescebat multaque Senenses moliri machinarique ferebantur. Qui rumor cum increbresceret, timentes Florentini ne Bonitium ab se deficeret, praesertim cum incolae eius oppidi partes omnino diversas prae se ferrent, subitaneo profecti milite, nullo tale aliquid suspicante Bonitium occuparunt et parte murorum deiecta in potestatem continuerunt.

24   Per haec ipsa fere tempora Arretini ob easdem suspiciones commoti arma corripuerunt, egressique omnibus copiis Cortonam urbem finitimam, quae per successum Manfredi minime quietura credebatur, expugnare adoriuntur. Urbs erat arduo situ et defensorum plena, sed tantus fuit impetus tamque audax Arretinorum coeptum, ut pluribus simul locis intra moenia penetraretur. Inde pugna per urbem commissa facile Cortonenses superati sunt, abiectisque tandem armis sese victoribus permisere. Arretini ar-

forces, set out to fight the enemy in a pitched battle. The battle was a terrible one, but at last the outnumbered Pisans turned and fled. Up to three thousand of them were captured; many were slaughtered; many also perished in flight, drowned by the river's swirling waters. The victors bridged the Serchio and marched their troops to Pisa, laying waste the lands around the city with fire and sword. The Pisans were compelled to accept a very one-sided peace. In addition to what had been agreed upon in the earlier treaty, they were forced to give up the town of Mutrone with free access to the coastline, many other castles and much territory; and they were to grant immunity to Florentines. This further condition, too, was extracted from the vanquished: that the Pisans should observe Florentine customs with respect to weights and measures.

Thus was the premature attack of the Pisans put down. Yet 23 Manfred's fame grew daily, and the Sienese were said to be plotting and setting afoot numerous schemes. When this rumor began to circulate, the Florentines grew fearful lest the Poggibonizi should defect, especially as the inhabitants of that town were showing themselves sympathetic to the opposite party. So the Florentines set out with a hastily-gathered force and occupied Poggibonsi by surprise. They threw down part of the defensive wall and continued their control of the town.[22]

1257

Around the same time the Aretines were aroused by similar 24 suspicions. They fell to arms and marched out with all their forces to capture the neighboring town of Cortona. It was believed that the latter town was about to make trouble owing to Manfred's success. The city was strongly situated and full of defenders. But so furious and daring was the Aretine attack that they breached the walls in many places simultaneously. Then they began to fight their way through the city and easily overcame the Cortonans, who eventually threw down their arms and surrendered. The Aretines strengthened the guard of the citadel at the top of the

cem in summa urbis parte munitam praesidiis confirmarunt, moenia vero ab inferiori parte urbis quibusdam locis diruerunt, quo rebellandi Cortonensibus adimerent potestatem.

25   Dum haec a Florentinis sociisque adversus suspiciones Manfredi providentur,[18] intestina intra urbem oritur seditio. Ea siquidem pars nobilitatis quae dudum sub Federico plurimum potuerat, successu Manfredi elata sese in spem attollere coepit, iam pridem infensa populo, cum ob partium studia, tum quod reductis adversariis se ab re publica exclusam dolebat. Igitur indignatione saucia et in spem elata compellare invicem, cohortari et liberius commonere, ne ea contumelia diutius perferatur, adsciscere homines eius factionis, captare rumores ac se in dies magis erigere. Haec cum suspicionem populi augerent,[19] magistratus ex eo numero principes quosdam ad se vocat, qui praecepta contemnentes se suis aedibus continebant, nec magistratui parebant vocanti. Praecipui inter hos erant Uberti, genus per ea tempora longe potentissimum. Id cum maxime contumax appareret, populares quorum in manibus res publica erat, adiuncta sibi nobilitatis ea parte quae suo dudum beneficio in urbem redierat, corripiunt arma ac facto agmine ad expugnandas Ubertorum aedes ire pergunt. Illi iam pridem haec praevidentes sese ad proelium comparaverant, non solum armatorum globo, verum etiam saxis e superioribus aedium locis impetum populi arcentes. Sed adversus tantam multitudinem frustra conati demum franguntur: caesi alii, alii pulsi, nonnulli etiam capti, de quibus est postea supplicium sumptum. Ex hoc ceterarum quoque familiarum homines illius factionis, populares etiam permulti, studio diversarum partium infecti, omnes denique hi qui aut ipsi aut sui multum sub Federico potuerant,

city, but knocked down the walls defending the lower part of the city in certain places so that the Cortonans should be unable to rebel.[23]

While the Florentines and their allies were taking precautions against suspicious activity connected with Manfred, a domestic insurrection arose within the City. That part of the nobility which a short while before had had the upper hand under Frederick became emboldened, encouraged by Manfred's success. It had long been hostile to the People both from partisanship and because it was unhappy at being excluded from the state after the return of its adversaries. So, between hope and indignation, they roused themselves, openly encouraging and inciting each other not to suffer insult any longer. They scouted the men of their faction, snatched at rumors, and grew bolder day by day. This activity aroused the suspicion of the People, and the magistrates summoned certain leaders of this noble party, who, defying their command, remained within their dwellings in disobedience to the magistracy. Chief among them were the Uberti, who were by far the most powerful family of the time. At the moment when this family seemed at the height of its insolence, the populist elements who controlled the commonwealth made adherants of that part of the nobility which had been restored through their favor, and proceeded, armed and in battle array, to storm the Uberti dwellings. The Uberti had long foreseen this eventuality and had prepared themselves for battle; they protected themselves against the People's attack not only with a mob of armed men but also with rocks thrown down from the top of their dwellings. But their efforts were useless against so numerous a force, and they were finally subdued: some slaughtered, some expelled, others captured and punished. Immediately thereafter, men from other families of that faction, and many popolani,[24] too, infected by partisan spirit — all those, in short, who themselves had been influential under Frederick or whose relatives had been — all these were driven out of the

urbe tunc eiecti, Senas, quod per id tempus ea civitas partium illarum fautrix habebatur, populariter confugerunt.

26   Non erat dubium quin Senensibus ex foedere quod triennio
ante cum Florentinis ictum fuerat, recipere exules non liceret.
Itaque civitas illa, expectatione aliquandiu suspensa, ubi Senas
convenisse audivit, oratores mittere statuit qui iniuriam quereren-
tur. Missi sunt autem florentini populi nomine oratores duo, Albicius Trinciavelliae, Iacobus Gherardi, et quidem ambo peritiam iuris habentes, ut si de foedere disceptandum foret, ius civitatis
tutarentur. Hi Senas profecti, cum magistratum populumque
adiissent, et foedus recitarunt et postularunt ut exules secundum
conventa pellerentur. Senenses vero, cum gratia exulum, qui am-
biendo rogandoque multos flectebant, tum Manfredi fiducia, reperire exceptiones ac demorari exules, trahere denique rem in longum pergebant. Quod postquam a Florentinis satis animadversum
est, bellum illis aperte indicitur.

27   At exules, quando tantam[20] belli molem sua causa imminere
cernebant, ad Manfredum conversi, respicere regem atque opem illius exposcere. Quod etsi ante[21] per litteras crebro fecerant, tamen
quia parum momenti in litteris suspicabantur fore, legatos mittere
placuit. Princeps eius legationis fuisse traditur eques florentinus
apprime nobilis ex familia Ubertorum. Farinatae[22] illi nomen erat.
Item alii ex singulis familiis, prout quisque vel auctoritate vel rerum gerendarum experientia praestabat, ad id munus delecti,
hisque communi omnium exulum consensu permissum, ut quae in
rem putarent fore, ea dicenda apud regem agendaque curarent.
Profecti ergo magnis itineribus ad ea loca in quibus rex erat pervenerunt. Ibi, postquam dicendi tempus illis datum, in hunc modum
locutos accepi:

28   "Si nulla tecum, praestantissime rex, neque voluntatis neque
obsequii nobis anteiret coniunctio, sed nunc primum novi et inau-

city and fled in a body to Siena, a city which at that time was believed to be a supporter of such parties.[25]

There was no doubt that, according to the treaty they had   26
made three years earlier with the Florentines, the Sienese were
wrong to receive the exiles. So, after a period of doubt, when Florence learned that the exiles had indeed gone to Siena, they decided
to send ambassadors to protest the injury. Two ambassadors were
sent in the name of the Florentine people, Albizzi Trinciavalle and
Jacopo di Gherardo, both lawyers, so that they might protect the
City's rights if the treaty should be disputed. They went to Siena,
came before its magistrates and people, read the treaty, and demanded that the exiles should be expelled in accordance with its
covenants.[26] But the Sienese had faith in Manfred and had been
influenced by the lobbying activities of the exiles. They continued
to raise legal objections and to harbor the exiles, dragging the matter out. As soon as the Florentines grasped the situation, they
openly declared war on the Sienese.   1259

When they perceived that the full weight of war was hanging   27
over their cause, however, the exiles turned to Manfred, paid their
respects, and sought his aid. They had done this repeatedly before
by letter, but now, suspecting that letters would have little weight,
they decided to send representatives. It is reported that the leader
of their delegation was an exceedingly noble Florentine knight of
the Uberti family whose name was Farinata. Other representatives
of each family were chosen for this task, men who held to be
the most outstanding for their influence or experience of affairs.
By common consent of all the exiles, these men were allowed to
take charge of doing or saying in the king's presence whatever they
thought would be to the purpose. They set out on their journey
and rapidly arrived at the place where the king was staying. There
they were granted time to speak and spoke, I am told, as follows:

"If, most excellent king, there were no prior connection of good   28
will and service between us, if we were seeking help now for the

diti homines auxilium peteremus, dicendum, ut videtur, nobis foret, quid utilitatis esset ad te, postulata si annueres, perventurum. Nos et paterna coniunctione tecum astricti ac toto animo domui tuae dediti regium limen advenimus, iam pridem noti fidique, nunc etiam, quando fortuna ita vult, eiecti et supplices. Ratio tamen amicitiae minus valeat, nisi utilitatem manifestissimam ostendamus. Duas esse per Italiam factiones, alteram paterno nomini totique generi tuo infensam inimicamque, alteram amicam et tota mente addictam, quis ignorat? Nec illud sane obscurum qualis per hoc tempus sit earum partium conditio. Profecto si dissimulare non oportet nec nosmetipsos blandiendo decipere, post divi Federici (quam numquam sine lacrimis recordabimur) mortem et pontificis in Italiam reditum, inimicorum animi supra modum crevere. Non esse iam contentos rediisse in urbes, sed ad vindictam erigi et nova moliri, eiectio nostra documento esse potest. Pontificem romanum habent fautorem; huius illi praesidio superbiunt; ad hunc tamquam ad aliquod columen omnia eorum consilia factaqua referuntur. Tu, quali in te animo pontifex sit, paulo ante expertus cognoscis. Tuum regnum, suum esse contendit. Ubi autem de regno contentio est, ibi fida pax esse numquam potest. Ipsi certe adversarii (quod exploratum certumque habemus) te ac domum tuam capitali odio persequuntur; quid a proavo, quid ab avo, quid a patre denique tuo perpessi sint, meminerunt. Ardet nunc in filium[23] ulciscendi libido, nec se consistere posse arbitrantur, donec progenies vestra[24] in propinquo consistet. Hos tu si crescere ac dominari, et simul te in Italia tuto consistere posse, praesertim adversa pontificis voluntate, credis, vehementer erras. In te illi atque in regnum tuum nunc crescunt, ubicumque crescunt, et ubicumque illis resistitur, illic res agitur tua.

first time as outsiders and unknown persons, we should surely be obliged to state why it might be useful to you to grant our requests. In fact we come to your royal doorstep as persons bound to you by ancestral ties, devoted whole-heartedly to your house, long known and long trusted—and now, since Fortune has so willed it, as castaways and suppliants. Yet arguments based on friendship are of little force unless accompanied by the clearest proofs of utility. Who does not know that there are two factions throughout Italy, one which hates and opposes your paternal name and your whole house, and another which is wholeheartedly pledged and attached to it? Nor is it hidden from view what the condition of both parties is at this time. Let us not pretend or deceive ourselves with flattery. Since the death of the divine Frederick (which we can never recall without tears) and the return of the pope to Italy, the arrogance of our enemies has grown immoderately. Now, not content with having been restored to their cities, they have risen to revenge and revolution, as our exile proves. The Roman pontiff is their supporter; under his protection they grow arrogant; to him, as though to some pillar, they refer all their counsels and deeds. You know from recent experience what the pope's intentions are towards you. Your kingdom is his, he contends. And where there is contention about kingdoms, there can be no reliable peace. There is no doubt—this is an established fact—that your adversaries persecute you and your house with mortal hatred. They remember what they endured from your great-grandfather, your grandfather and your father. Now they are aflame with lust to avenge themselves on the son, and they believe they cannot stop until your line, in the near future, shall cease. You are thoroughly mistaken if you believe that you can remain safe in Italy while they grow ever greater and more dominant, especially given the ill-will of the pontiff. They are growing strong against you, against your kingdom, everywhere; and wherever they are resisted is where your affairs are being prosecuted.

29   "Nostris autem (nam id quoque considerare dignum) per singulas urbes vires non desunt, sed perculsi dudum tepent animi et quodammodo delitescunt, nullius, ut ita loquamur, capitis favore calentes. Etenim caput praeter te nullum est ad quod respicere debeant. Tu dudum in purgando tutandoque regno tuo occupatus, hoc illis, quod eorum fides et genus tuum polliceri videbatur, praestare supersedisti. Nunc vero summa tua virtute ac felicitate superatis adversariis stabilitisque regni negotiis, quoniam domesticum intestinumque incendium extinxisti, iam impigre ad vicinum extinguendum concurre, ne forsan neglectum a te vires assumat ac rursus in tecta tua deferatur.[25] Levis est prudentia, rex, quae praesentibus tantum medetur; futura prospicere atque inde[26] contemplari sapientem decet. Nullus enim morbus, postquam advenit, sine corporis detrimento repellitur; at ne adveniat, tutior et salubrior provisio est. Quod si ullo in loco opportuna sit haec tua providentia, eam profecto Etruria Florentiaque expostulant: regio et civitas nullo modo abs te negligendae. Non sine optima ratione pater tuus, vir sapientissimus, cum de longa possessione huius regni ad posteros suos transmittenda cogitaret, ut in potestate haberet Etruriam maximo semper studio diligentiaque curavit. Videbat enim in hac pontificum romanorum cupiditate totam fere huius regni defensionem ex Etruriae statu pendere. Haec siquidem Italiae pars urbem romanam attingens velut a tergo illi imminet, ut, si tecum sentiat, nullus inde contra te movere se possit. Florentia autem quasi domina quaedam regionis est et, quacumque inclinat, magnam eius partem suo velut pondere secum rapit. Nec regionem unquam tecum habere videberis nec illa ipsa quae adhuc in partibus durant consistent, nisi Florentiam habeas; habebis vero, si nos tuo beneficio patriae restituti in tuo obsequio civitatem

"We ourselves in individual cities are not without strength (a   29
thing also worth considering), but spirits once daunted soon lose
their heat and die down into embers; and no leader can strike fire
into them again. In truth, you are the only leader they must respect. Occupied as you have been with liberating and protecting
your kingdom, you have refrained from offering them what their
loyalty and your ancestry seemed to promise. But now through
your great power and good fortune you have overcome your adversaries and stabilized your kingdom's affairs. You have put out the
fire at home; now hurry and put out the one next door. Don't let it
gain force and bear down on your own house again. It is a frivo-
lous prudence, O King, that takes thought only for present ills; it
behooves the wise man to look ahead and consider the future. No
illness, once contracted, can be expelled without damage to the
body; the safer and healthier plan is to avoid it in the first place.
And if there is any place that needs and demands the exercise of
your prudence, that place is surely Florence and Tuscany. On no
account must you neglect that region and city. When your father,
the wisest of men, laid plans for the long-term control of this
Kingdom in order to pass it down to his descendents, it was for
excellent reasons that he devoted the greatest zeal and industry to
keeping Tuscany in his power. For he saw, in view of the cupidity
of the Roman pontiff, that almost the whole defense of the Kingdom depended on the condition of Tuscany. Indeed this part of Italy, bordering as it does on the city of Rome, threatens the Kingdom from behind, as it were; but by the same token no one can
attack you from that direction if Tuscany is your ally. Florence is
mistress of the region. Whichever way she inclines, her weight
takes a great part of the region with her. Unless you hold Florence,
you will never be seen to have the region with you and the places
still wracked with party strife will never stabilize. But you *shall*
have Florence if your favor restores us to our fatherland and we
hold the City in obedience to you. In short, we are asking for

tenebimus. Denique nos vetusti fidique amici, qui nuper in patria florentes patri atque domui tuae per omnia bella obsecuti sumus, nunc a communibus inimicis eiecti opem rogamus, ea petentes quae tu ratione utilitatis etiam non petentibus nobis ultro afferre deberes."

30   Haec cum dixissent, ad pedes regios supplices advolvuntur. Rex assurgere iussos paucis illos verbis consolatur, et sese propediem ex consilio suorum ad ea quae postulent responsurum pollicetur. Expectantibus inde legatis incertum qua de causa non satis ampla spe rem[27] in longum protrahebat. Sunt qui putent Manfredum se ac sua reputantem nimiam erga Federicum ac domum eius affectionem quam in illis cernebat suspectam habuisse, nam ipse ex concubina genitus contra suorum voluntatem regium nomen invaserat; nec erat ambiguum, quin inter ipsum et nepotem, cum ille adolevisset, bellum ea de causa esset futurum; itaque de vindicanda sibi adversa factione saepius cogitasse. Alii longo intra regnum bello fatigatum, cum iam quietem amaret, haud libenti animo res novas capessere voluisse, quae plerumque ab incepto longius protrahunt. Quacumque tandem ratione id ageret, certe neganti propiorem[28] fuisse constat, nec quicquam ad apertam detrectationem magis quam verecundia obstare videbatur. Tandem instantibus legatis per praefectum respondet: se, etsi multis simul rebus impediatur, tamen ob veterem amicitiam alam germanorum equitum illis sub vexillo daturum.

31   Quod postquam legati accepere, seorsum, ut fit, consultandi gratia in unum coactis eorum plerique auxilii parvitatem ceu ridiculum existimantes abeundum e vestigio, nec quicquam ab ingrato rege suscipiendum censebant. At Farinata, quem inter legatos

help — we, your old and loyal friends, who served your father and your house through all the wars when we flourished in our fatherland, we who are now exiled by our common enemy. We seek what you yourself ought to be offering in your own interest, even if we were not the ones seeking it."[27]

When they had spoken, they prostrated themselves in suppliant 30 fashion at the royal feet. Bidding them rise, the king spoke a few words of cheer and promised them they would soon have a response to their request from his council. To the waiting ambassadors it was unclear why they were dragging out at such great length a matter of no tremendous consequence. Some thought Manfred was suspicious of the great affection he saw in them and their families towards Frederick and his house. He was, after all, the offspring of a concubine who had usurped the royal name against the will of his relations, and there was no doubt that for this reason there would be a war between him and his nephew when the latter grew older. So he must often have thought of punishing a faction hostile to himself. Others thought he was tired after a long war within the Kingdom; now he wanted peace, and was therefore reluctant to take up fresh enterprises, which, once begun, generally dragged out far too long.[28] For whatever reason, it was evident he was close to saying no, and that it was shame, more than anything, which stood in the way of an open refusal. At last, at the insistence of the legates, he responded through an official that, though entangled simultaneously in many affairs, for the sake of old friendship he would nevertheless grant them a squadron of German knights under his royal banner.

After the legates had received the offer, they gathered off to one 31 side in the usual way to consult. Most of them thought the offer of aid was laughably small and advised leaving forthwith without taking anything from the ungrateful king. But Farinata (who was, as we said, among the legates), a prudent and high-minded man, declared this to be bad advice: one should never give way to anger

fuisse diximus, vir prudens et alti animi, nullum id consilium esse ait; nusquam enim indignationi concedendum, ubi utilitas perquiratur. "Det modo," inquit, "suorum aliquos et vexillum mittat. Nos profecto in eum locum deducemus, ut regi, si modo ulla regiae dignitatis tuendae cura sit, maiora mittere auxilia necessitas exprimatur." Traductis celeriter omnibus in hanc sententiam laeto vultu sibi quae rex offerret placere gratoque illa animo accipere respondent; regique[29] mox amplissimis verbis gratias agunt. Profectique inde cum germanis equitibus Senas rediere.

32   Dum haec ab exulibus geruntur, Florentini iam parato exercitu fines Senensium ingressi cuncta populantur; castella etiam quaedam parum munita expugnant; tandem peragrata regione, cum obviam nusquam prodiret hostis, ad ipsa prope Senarum moenia copiis admotis castra non longe ab urbe posuerunt. Senenses, quod neque conducto milite per id tempus abundabant neque sane in ipso populo universam pugnae fortunam experiri satis videbatur tutum, sese moenibus continebant. Levia dumtaxat proelia promptissimis utrinque peditum equitumque prodeuntibus inter castra et portam crebro committebantur.

33   In hunc modum cum aliquot dies perstitissent, tempus venisse rati exules quo regis auxilia periculis obiectarent, invitatos benigne Germanos hilariori convivio largaque vini copia, cuius gens appetentissima est, longe perfundunt. Hinc dedita opera repente ad arma discurritur.[30] Exules ipsi in primis armantur ac magnum ali-

when interest is at stake. "Let him, for now, give us a few troops and send a banner," he said, "for we shall surely be brought to a place where necessity will force the king to send more substantial aid if he has any concern at all for saving his royal dignity." Everyone was quickly converted to this view, and so they responded smilingly to the official, saying they were pleased with the king's offer and accepted it with thanks. Soon after, they thanked the king fulsomely. Then they set out with the German knights and returned to Siena.[29]

Meanwhile, the Florentines had already mobilized their army, entered Sienese territory, and were laying waste to everything. They had also captured several poorly-defended castles. Finally, having passed through the region without the enemy coming out to meet them, they moved their troops right up to the walls of Siena and pitched camp not far from the city. The Sienese at that moment were not exactly awash in mercenary soldiers, and it did not seem to them advisable to hazard the outcome of the war on the military skills of the populace. So they had taken refuge behind their city walls. The keenest cavalry and infantry skirmishers on both sides engaged in frequent minor clashes in the area between the camp and the city gate. 32 1260

After having held out in this way for several days, the exiles decided the time had come when the royal auxiliaries should be exposed to danger. The Germans were cordially invited to an uproarious banquet and vast quantities of wine, for which Germans are particularly greedy, were poured out. Then there was a sudden—but carefully planned—rush to arms. The exiles were the first to arm themselves, each one boasting of some great and famous deed he would perform that day against the enemy. They all gathered at the gate opposite the Florentine camp. The gate was suddenly thrown open and the Germans, who by now had warmed to their work, charged with great spirit in their battle array, taking everyone by surprise. Coming down ferociously on the 33

quod praeclarumque facinus ea die in hostem edi posse pro se
quisque iactat. Convenerunt omnes ad portam castris oppositam,
qua mox repente patefacta Germani iam olim calentes suo ipsi agmine, ne expectatis quidem ullis, acerrime ruunt; delatique ferociter in hostem, non solum primam stationem turbarunt, verum
etiam munimenta castrorum transgressi maiorem quam pro numero procellam fugamque primo impetu edidere. Nam et improvisa fuit eruptio et tantam audaciam non sine maiori consilio suspicabantur esse. Itaque totis castris trepidatum est et foeda
quibusdam locis fuga fieri coepta. Tandem vero, ubi paucitas in
medio multorum conspicua fuit nec alii eadem alacritate sequebantur, conversi in Germanos alii undique circumveniunt, alii Senensibus exulibusque oppositi, quot[31] subsequebantur facile ad
portas repellunt. Sed ex Germanis nemo evasit; omnes, cum aliquandiu restitissent, ad unum oppressi sunt. Vexillum regis, quod
illi secum attulerant, a Florentinis captum pro antiquo gentis odio
et praesentis exultatione victoriae omni dedecore afficitur, tractum
per contumeliam totis castris et perverse suspensum. Morati post
haec eodem loco aliquot dies, cum iam nemo amplius obviam prodiret, Florentiam copias reduxere.

34   Eodem anno (nam aestatis magna pars adhuc supererat) exules
et Senenses ad Manfredum, legatione iterum missa, casum Germanorum et contumeliam hostium enarrando animumque regis
quam maxime incendendo, maiori iam fiducia postularunt auxilia.
Rex, quod non nihil dedecoris sibi inflictum existimabat et quod
spes vindictae celerrima[32] ostendebatur, Iordanum quendam ex
suis ducibus cum magnis equitum copiis in Etruriam misit. Horum adventu sublati Senensium et exulum animi quam maximas
item possunt copias parant, Pisanos et alias suarum partium civi-

enemy, they not only threw the pickets into confusion, but broke right through the camp's defenses, causing at their first onset far greater uproar and flight than their numbers should have warranted. For the charge was unexpected and its great boldness raised apprehensions that there existed some larger plan behind it. So the whole camp was thrown into a state of fear, and in some places, shamefully, desertions began. In the end, however, it became evident that the Germans were badly outnumbered, and that no forces of equal ardor were behind them. At this point some turned on the Germans and began to surround them, while others blocked the exile and Sienese forces behind them, driving them easily back to the gate. Of the Germans, none escaped; they resisted for some time, but were crushed down to the last man. The royal banner they had brought was captured by the Florentines who treated it with dishonor, moved by their past hatred for the German race and their present joy in victory. The flag was insulted by being dragged through the camp and hung upside down. Afterwards the Florentines spent a few more days in the same place; then, since no one else came forth to challenge them, they marched their troops back to Florence.[30]

In the same year (since much of the summer[31] was still left), the exiles and the Sienese sent another legation to Manfred to tell him what had happened to his Germans and how his enemies had insulted him. Having angered the king as much as possible, they now demanded help from him with greater confidence. The king, reckoning he had suffered significant dishonor and having had the hope of speedy revenge held out to him, sent into Tuscany one of his commanders, a certain Giordano, with a large force of knights. Their arrival raised the spirits of the Sienese and the exiles, who proceeded in turn to raise the greatest forces they could. They called upon the Pisans and the other cities of their party for aid, and many noble and powerful persons were summoned. All these forces came together at Siena: German knights, as many as 1500

34

tates auxilia rogant; multi etiam nobiles potentesque evocantur. Conveniunt omnes copiae Senis: equites germani, bellaces viri ad mille quingentos, peditum ingentes copiae, praeterea Senensium et exulum florentinorum evocatorumque magnus equitum numerus. Hoc apparatu quam celeriter in discrimen pugnae rem adducere cupiebant, veriti ne, si longius protraheretur bellum, auxilia regis, quibus tres dumtaxat menses nec ultra commorari in Etruria praescriptum erat, re infecta discederent. Itaque, quo maturius agant, haec machinantur.

35   Oppidum est Alcinum trans urbem Senas diversissima regione a florentino agro. Id, quod amicum foederatumque florentini populi erat, obsidere atque oppugnare Senenses parant, publiceque ad id oppidum expeditio indicitur. Haec eo consilio fiebant, ut Florentini procul domo exire ac in sociorum periculis auxilium ferre cogerentur. Florentini vero iam inde ab initio hunc apparatum hostium intuentes et ipsi se compararant et sociis amicisque ut praesto forent edixerant. Quid tamen[33] agendum esset, varia inter cives disceptatio erat. Alii exeundum totis copiis et opes[34] sociis impigre ferendum; alii, quoniam paulo ante ad ipsa prope Senarum moenia exercitum admovissent ac satis eo anno rei publicae dignitati factum esset, subsistendum in praesentia censebant; ferre autem tam procul domo auxilium et ad nutum hostis circumagi periculosissimum arbitrabantur. Ea rursus sententia quemadmodum tutior, ita minus speciosa videbatur; peritis tamen rei militaris magis placebat.

36   At contra magistratus ad exeundum pronior erat. Inclinabat autem ad id consilium cum gloriae cupido, tum falsa proditionis spes. Nam viri quidam ficte compositi in ipsa disceptatione rerum ab exulibus submissi, quam occultissime Florentiam profecti, cum

mercenaries, masses of infantry, and in addition a large number of knights from among the Florentine exiles, the Sienese, and the others who had been summoned. With such an array of forces they were eager to settle matters in a decisive battle as swiftly as possible. They were afraid that the war would drag out too long and that the royal auxiliaries, who had been instructed to spend no more than three months in Tuscany, would withdraw without the matter being settled. So they hatched the following plot to bring matters to a head.

The town of Montalcino sits opposite the city of Siena in a region quite remote from Florentine territory.[32] The Sienese prepared to besiege and assault this town, which was a friend and ally of the Florentine People, and an expedition was publicly declared against the place. This was done with the aim of forcing the Florentines to go far from home to bring aid to their allies in peril. The Florentines, however, who had from the very beginning observed the preparations of their enemies, had made their own preparations, and had alerted their friends and allies to be ready for action. But there was some difference of opinion among the citizens about what should be done. Some were for marching out all the troops and aiding their allies without delay. Others thought they should sit tight for the moment, seeing that they had just recently brought their army to the very walls of Siena and had done enough to satisfy the honor of the commonwealth for one year; it would be extremely dangerous, they believed, to bring aid so far from home and to be driven hither and yon at the pleasure of their enemy. The latter view, being safer, was less attractive, though it was preferred by the military experts.

The magistrates, on the other hand, were more inclined to venture forth. They were predisposed to this course of action both by desire for glory and by false hopes of treachery. In the midst of the Florentines' debate the exiles had quietly sent out certain men under false pretenses who arrived in Florence with the greatest se-

se recentes a Senis grandia quaedam afferre dixissent, ceterum ta-
citurnitate opus esse, tandem, iureiurando ne in plures efferant in-
terposito, magistratibus pandunt esse compluris[35] senenses cives
eosque apprime nobiles quibus displiceat bellum ac discordia civitatum; ceterum omnem eius rei culpam penes unum Provincianum Salvani[36] existere; eum iam non pro cive sed pro domino sese
gerere ac proprio privatoque nutu cuncta moderari; favere exulibus
ac bellum nutrire, ut per eam occasionem externis saeptus auxiliis
dominari civibus possit; eius intolerabilem arrogantiam cives amplius pati nolle; itaque coniurasse contra illum egregios quosdam,
quorum sigilla ac litteras pro fide attulissent; eaque de causa missos se, ut edicerent, si appropinquent Florentini et opem ferre velint, se arma confestim rapturos ac Provincianum ipsum exulesque opprimere haud cunctaturos; fore autem peropportunum
patrandae rei tempus, quod per speciem opis ferendae sociis quibus obsidio paretur, citra ullam suspicionem adventare cum exercitu possint.

37   Ad haec cum pleraque de secretiori mente hostium, falsa veris
miscentes, protulissent ac sigilla quaedam ostentassent, homines
plebeios ac bellicarum artium[37] ignaros, quales plerumque in magistratu esse solent, tanta spe extollunt, ut nec saniora quidem
consilia audire vellent, sed advocata protinus concione exeundum
totis copiis et opitulandum sociis pronunciarent.

38   Haec populus multitudoque gratis excipiebat animis, at illustres
viri et rei militaris periti, quorum magna tum copia in civitate erat,
ut periculosam et inutilem profectionem improbabant. Itaque varie

crecy. They said they were fresh from Siena bearing news of great import, but that they required strict confidentiality. Finally, after an oath had been sworn to keep the matter *in camera*, they revealed to the magistrates that there were numerous Sienese citizens, and those exceedingly noble, who disliked the war and the strife between their cities. Furthermore, the affair was entirely the fault of one Provinciano di Salvano. He was now acting like a lord rather than a citizen and had taken control of everything in accordance with his private pleasure. It was he who was helping the exiles and nurturing the war; he aimed to take advantage of the situation, surrounded as he was by foreign troops, to lord it over his fellow citizens. The citizens were no longer willing to bear his intolerable arrogance, so certain distinguished persons, whose sealed letters they had brought as proof, had conspired against him. They themselves had been sent to assure the Florentines that, should they come thither bringing aid to Montalcino, the Sienese conspirators would immediately take up arms and crush Provinciano and the exiles without delay. And this would be an excellent opportunity to compass their purpose, since under the cloak of bringing aid to besieged allies they could arrive in Siena with their army before suspicion had been aroused.

The emissaries offered further information about the secret intentions of their enemies, mixing truth with falsehood, and displayed certain seals. They raised such hope in these plebeian men, ignorant of the art of war — the sort who tend to predominate in magistracies — that the latter would not even listen to sounder counsels, but immediately summoned the assembly and proclaimed that they should march out with all their forces and help their allies.[33]   37

The People and the multitude received this announcement   38
gladly, but the men of distinction and the military experts, of whom there was a great number in the city at that time, condemned the expedition as dangerous and useless. Having first de-

primum inter se de consilii temeritate[38] conquesti, tandem una cunctorum sententia placuit magistratum adire et quando periculum grandius vertebatur, aperte quid ipsi de tota re sentirent expromere.[39] Pro cunctis omnium consensu verba fecit Teglarius Aldobrandi filius Adimar, vir disertus et magnae per id tempus auctoritatis, qui cum coetu nobilium ubi ad magistratum pervenit, in hunc modum locutus est:

39   "Ne excusare quidem libet nec aut verecundia aut ignavia deterreri, si patriae caritate adducti et invocati consilium exhibemus. Cum enim vel mortem pro illa subeundam leges imperent, quis levitatem pudoris, si prodesse viderit, extimescat? Vobis quoque, fortissimi praesides, non ingratum esse debet quicquid sincera voluntate affertur, quippe communis utilitas in medio iacet. Nemo autem usque adeo gnarus rerum unquam fuit, quin eidem longe plura ignota quam cognita essent. Itaque si aedificandum quid est, fabros et architectos; si navigandum, gubernatores in consilium adhibemus. In bello autem tanto diligentius id agendum, quanto periculum in illo vertitur maius. Nempe aliarum rerum omnium levissima, ut ita dixerim, iactura est, quoniam malefacta tolli emendarique possunt; belli vero errata, praeter aeternum dedecus, mortes et vulnera ac eversiones rerum subsequuntur. Ea malorum extrema nec tolli nec emendari unquam possunt, quo maturius a vobis[40] consulendum est ac eos qui huiusce rei experimentum quoddam habent diligentius audiendum.

40   "Quid ergo? dicet quispiam. Tu rei militaris peritiam et bellorum artem profiteris? Nihil loquor ipse de me,[41] quamquam dura temporum[42] conditio et eiectio quondam familiae nostrae me quoque diutius quam vellem arma tractare ac multa variis in locis experiri coegerunt. Sed sunt in hoc coetu quem videtis praestantis-

plored the rashness of the scheme severally among themselves, they finally agreed, since the danger was becoming very serious indeed, to go before the magistrates and give their frank opinion about the whole matter. By common consent Tegghiaio d'Aldobrando Adimari, an eloquent man of great authority at that time, spoke for them all. He went before the magistrates with a group of nobles and spoke as follows.

"When summoned and prompted by love of country to give 39 counsel, one is unwilling to make excuses or be deterred by shame or sloth. Since the laws command us to endure even death for our country, who will fear a little thing like shame, if her interest is at stake? You, too, most powerful Signori, should welcome any counsel that in a spirit of sincerity and good will is offered you, inasmuch as the common interest is everyone's concern. There has never been an expert whose ignorance does not far outweigh his knowledge. If we have to build something, we take advice from builders and architects; if we travel by ship, we employ pilots. In war one should be all the more careful to take advice as the stakes are much greater. In all other affairs the cost of failure can be easily borne (if I may put it this way), since what has been done badly can be taken away and fixed; mistakes in warfare are followed by deaths, wounds and universal destruction, quite apart from lasting shame. Extreme evils of this sort can never be taken away and fixed. So it behooves you to take seasonable counsel and listen carefully to men who have had some experience of such affairs.

"'What are you saying?' somebody will ask. 'Are you claiming 40 expertise in military affairs and the art of war?' I am saying nothing about myself, although hard times and the late exile of my family compelled me to handle arms longer than I should have liked and to have had many experiences in different places. But there are in the group you see before you outstanding men practised in arms from their youth. Love of country has impelled these

simi viri ab ipsa adolescentia in armis versati. Hos et usu doctos et longa experientia callentes patriae caritas impellit, ne in gravi periculo conticescant, et quoniam singulos prolixum nimis esset, me unum pro universis verba facere iusserunt.

41   "Convenere Senis hostium copiae et Alcinum oppidum obsidere parant. Vos exire totis viribus et auxilium ferre cogitatis. Altus nempe animus et coeptum audax! Nam quid aliud dici potest, tam praevalido hoste circumstrepente? Sed videndum est. Dicam equidem audacter quod patriae caritas dicendum suadet, ne plus audaciae quam prudentiae id consilium habeat. Nam si absque profectione illuc vestra sociorum salus tuta esse non potest, nihil novi afferimus. Cedant enim dignitati et fidei pericula nostra et pro sociorum salute devoti in proelium ruamus. Sin autem et oppidum illud citra profectionem nostram servari posse constat et has urbanas copias absque magno discrimine illuc duci non posse, tutam securitatem periculosae ferociae censemus praeferendam. Docebimus autem utrumque.

42   "Obsidere parant socios nostros. Quid? vos, simul atque circumsteterint, captos etiam putatis? Num moenia, num aggeres, num fossas habent? Num in monte constituti, situ etiam adiuvantur? Et tempus muniendi providendique legitimum habuere. Improvisa haec fortibus viris periculum afferre solent, provisa vero numquam. At longa obsidione macerabuntur! Id profecto, ut nunc sunt res, fieri non potest. Primo enim Germani a Manfredo missi quibus maxime hostis fidit, tres dumtaxat menses commorari in Etruria iussi sunt. Hoc enim tempus, ut vulgatum, satis et anxie quidem exules pepigere; eius iam media ferme pars transacta est

men, schooled in practical activity and astute from long experience, not to remain silent amid such grave peril. Since it would be too long a business for each of them to speak, they have bidden me speak for us all.

"The forces of the enemy have come together at Siena and are   41
preparing to besiege the town of Montalcino. You plan to march out with all our forces and bring them aid. Your spirit is lofty and your enterprise bold. Can it be called anything else, with so powerful an enemy making an uproar all around us? But look, let me make bold to say what love of country persuades me must be said: this course of action is more audacious than prudent. We should have nothing to say if the safety of our allies could not be maintained without this venture. Our own risks would take second place to honor and loyalty, and we would charge faithfully into battle to save our allies. But if it is evident both that that town *can* be saved without our going there, and that this City's troops *cannot* be brought there without extreme risk, we believe it is better to be safe and secure than fierce but at risk. We shall demonstrate both propositions.

"The enemy are preparing to besiege our allies. Well, what of   42
it? Do you think they are going to be captured as soon as they are surrounded? Do they not have walls, ramparts, moats? Are they not helped by their situation on top of a mountain? They have had the normal amount of time to fortify themselves and lay in provisions. Unforeseen attacks commonly present danger to brave men, but foreseen ones, never. 'But' (it will be objected) 'they will be reduced by a long siege!' Surely, as things now stand, this is impossible. In the first place, the Germans Manfred sent, on whom the enemy chiefly relies, have been ordered to stay in Tuscany for three months only. As is common knowledge, the exiles agreed to this length of time with considerable anxiety; almost half the time is now up and the siege has not yet begun. The rest of the troops will never remain once the Germans have left. It wouldn't be safe

obsidione nondum coepta. Reliquae vero copiae discedentibus
Germanis numquam manebunt, neque enim tutum illis esset et simul hiems aderit, quae paratas etiam structasque obsidiones frangit. Quid, si vos copias in finibus vestris, per ea castella, quae
proxima sunt agro hostium, ostenderitis? An illos in obsidione
permansuros putatis; ac non potius de tutandis suis quam de oppugnandis alienis cogitaturos? Profecto, aut non obsessum ibunt,
imminentibus copiis nostris, aut mox irrumpentibus in eorum
agrum, revocabuntur.

43   "Nec ulla certior quam haec defensio sociorum esse potest.
Nam si illuc exercitum ducetis, vobis pariter atque illis incerta pericula imminebunt. Nos quidem non ambigimus, quantum conie-
ctura haberi potest, quin hostes rem in discrimen pugnae adducere
quam maxime cupiant. Stimulat enim pudor superioris offensae et
ulciscendi libido solicitat animos, simulque cernunt, nisi priusquam Germani a Manfredo missi discedant, fortunam pugnae ex-
periuntur, sibi posthac vincendi spem nullam reliquam fore. Ut
igitur illis conducit accelerare pugnam, sic nobis differre. Nam
mora illis socios, nobis hostes detractura probatur. Nec illud sane
dici potest, ut ire quidem liceat, a pugna vero abstinere. Si enim in
hostili fuerimus, nutu illorum pugnandum erit.

44   "'Quid ergo? Tu virtuti nostrorum diffidis et Germanos paves-
cis?' Equidem virtutem nostrorum egregiam esse scio et simul hostis[43] non contemnendos duco, nam vires adversariorum in consilio
deprimere, id se ipsum decipere est. Verum communis mars et
omnis fortuna pugnae anceps; copiae hostium tales, quas nemo so-
brius aspernetur. Hi et moenia habebunt et commeatu abunda-
bunt, et pugnabunt et quiescent arbitrio suo. Nostros et commeatus cura et impedimentorum labor distrahet, non muris cinctos,
non parietibus tutos, sed die noctuque ad hostilem impetum expo-

for them: at the same moment winter will be upon them, which breaks down even careful and orderly sieges. Why don't you make a display of your forces within your own territory, putting them in the castles nearest enemy territory? Do you think they will stick to the siege then? Won't they, [in that case], think of safeguarding their own possessions rather than attacking others? Surely they will either not go to the siege at all, under threat from our troops, or they will be recalled as soon as we make incursions into their territory.

"And this is the surest way to defend our allies. Indeed, if you 43 lead the army there, you will only put yourselves as well as them at risk. It is clear to us, as far as we may conjecture, that the enemy is extremely eager to decide the issue in battle. They are goaded by the shame of their previous affront, and vexed by the desire for revenge. At the same time they realize they must try the fortunes of battle now, for they will have no hope left of winning once the Germans sent by Manfred depart. It is to their advantage to hasten the battle, it is to ours to delay it. Delay can only take allies from them and enemies from us. Nor can it be maintained that we might go out there without fighting. Once we are in hostile territory, we shall have to fight them whenever they choose.

"'Well, what of it?' someone will say. 'Do you doubt our cour- 44 age, are you afraid of the Germans?' For my part, I know our troops are outstandingly brave, yet I think the enemy is not to be despised, either. To underestimate the strength of one's adversaries when taking counsel is to deceive oneself. War plays no favorites[34] and the fortunes of battle are double-edged. The forces of the enemy are such that no sober man should despise them. They will have both fortifications and abundant provisions; they will fight and stop fighting at their pleasure. Our troops will be distracted by worry about provisions and the effort of hauling equipment; they will not be protected by walls or lie safe indoors, but will be exposed day and night to hostile attack. Thus even if the courage

sitos, ut etiam si maiori virtute sint nostri, tamen rerum ipsarum iniquitate premantur.

45   "An igitur ego[44] usque adeo stulte audax sim, ut, cum moram parvi temporis profligaturam hostis[45] cernam, malim properando incerta pericula quam cunctando certam victoriam complecti? Quid, si dum[46] apud Alcinum fuerimus, hostis ipse averso itinere Florentiam petat? Volumus et regionem et urbem illorum impetu exponere ac tunc demum ad vim arcendam redire cum populatio agrorum et villarum incendia revocabunt? Enim vero magis[47] e dignitate florentini populi fuerit in agrum hostium transisse! Satis est,[48] arbitror, quod hac ipsa aestate illum vastavimus, quod castella in eo cepimus, quod castra paene moenibus Senarum coniuncta habuimus, quod paratis ad dimicandum nobis per multos dies nemo obviam prodierit. Denique ego dignitatem in victoria maximam pono; victoriam autem non tam properatio quam cunctatio, nec tam ager hostium quam fines nostri nobis certissimam pollicentur. Malle autem periclitari quam vincere dementissimum est.

46   "Illud praeterea me valde terret quod equidem non silebo: vos autem vereor, quemadmodum accepturi estis. Scitis studia partium et civium vestrorum animos. Principes tantum diversae factionis urbe pepulimus; ceteros eiusdem animi intra moenia sustinemus. Si proficisci libeat, hos ducetis, quaeso, an domi relinquetis? Atqui, utra in parte maius periculum sit, diiudicare nequeo. Relicti enim, urbem prodere hosti poterunt; ductis autem, non tam pectus quam terga nobis erunt protegenda.

47   "His rationibus adducti, nec exercitum nunc procul domo ducendum nec fortunam pugnae experiundam[49] censemus, sed armandam iuventutem et per ea loca quae proxima sunt agro

of our troops is greater, they may still be overwhelmed by the sheer inequality of circumstances.

"When I see that a short delay will utterly ruin my enemies, 45 should I be so foolishly bold as to rush into uncertain dangers? Should I not prefer to grasp certain victory through delay? What if the enemy takes the opposite road and attacks Florence while we are at Montalcino? Do we want to expose our hinterland and the City to attack? Shall we return to ward off their attack only when summoned by the devastation of our fields and the burning of our country estates? 'But,' you will say, 'it will be more in keeping with the dignity of the Florentine People to enter enemy territory!' In my view it is enough that we have laid waste to their territory this very summer, that we have seized castles in it, that we pitched camp practically under the walls of Siena, that for many days we were ready to fight there and no one came out to challenge us. My view, in short, is that victory is the highest honor of all, and it is not haste but delay, not enemy territory but our own borders that promises the most certain victory. To prefer danger to victory is sheer madness.

"I shall not hide, moreover, what truly fills me with dread: it is 46 *you* I am afraid of, as you shall hear. You know the partisan fervor and the animosities of your citizens. It is only the leaders of the opposing faction that we have expelled; we harbor others of the same mind within our walls. Let me ask you: if it is your will to venture forth, will you take them with you or leave them at home? Either way, I couldn't say on which side the danger is greater. If they are left behind, they could betray the City to the enemy; if we take them with us, we shall need to shield our backs as much as our breasts.

"For these reasons we are proposing that the army should not 47 now be marched far from home, and that we should not try the fortunes of war. Let the young men be armed and show themselves in places near enemy territory. In this way, either the enemy

hostium ostendendam, ut sic vel proficisci impediantur ad obsidendum socios vel profecti per vastationem agrorum et pericula
suarum rerum revocentur."

48   Teglarius igitur nobilesque viri qui cum illo erant ita monue-
runt. Magistratus autem non aequis auribus hanc orationem exce-
pit, utpote quae imprudentiam eius arguere videbatur. Ac forte per
id tempus magistratum una cum aliis gerebat Expeditus quidam,
vir ferox ac[50] protervus, qualis nonnumquam immodica libertas
ferre solet. Is iam pridem recta monentem vix sustinebat ac mox,
ut finis dicendi ab eo factus, vultu et gestu maiorem in modum
commotus, "Quin[51] tu," inquit, "Teglari, quaeras? Num te metus
iam nunc foedarit? Enim vero magistratus non pavorem tuum, sed
dignitatem florentini populi intuebitur. Tibi, si prae metu torpet
animus, vacationem militiae damus."

49   Ad haec Teglarius nec se vacationem postulare inquit nec, si ultro concedatur, ea uti velle; se, quae meliora putaverit, sincera fide
quemadmodum debuerit pro patria monuisse; quacumque tamen
populus iverit, impigre secuturum; quin se pro certo habere eum
qui tam insolenter verba iactet numquam eo processurum in proelio quo ipse procedet.[52]

50   Frementibus dehinc aliis ac sententiam defendere parantibus
magistratus multam statuit, si quis amplius super ea re disceptaret.
Et iuvabat sane magistratus temeritatem populus ferox ac multis
victoriis superbus qui, non tam periculis sociorum anxius nec spe
aliqua oblata ductus quam ne hostem formidare videretur, exire in-
trepidus ac ultro se certamini cupiebat offerre.

51   Explosa itaque meliori sententia, profectio obstinate paratur.
Amici certiores facti auxilia rogantur. Illud interim agitatum, du-

will be hindered from setting out to besiege our allies, or, if they have already set out, they will be summoned back by the devastation of their fields and the danger to their property."

Such was the counsel of Tegghiaio and the noblemen who accompanied him. But the magistrates did not give the speech a fair hearing, as it seemed to expose their own imprudence. And it was perhaps at this time that a fierce and shameless fellow named Expeditus, the sort of person unrestrained liberty can sometimes produce, was serving as a magistrate with the rest.[35] For some time he had barely been able to contain himself as he listened to this good advice. As soon as Tegghiaio had finished speaking, he shouted—his limbs and voice shaking with passion—"What are you after, Tegghiaio? Have you turned into a filthy coward? This magistracy isn't going to pay any attention to your fears and quakings. It's going to consider the dignity of the Florentine people. If you're paralyzed with fear, we'll let you off military service."

Tegghiaio responded that he was not asking for an exemption, nor, were one offered him, would he wish to make use of it. He had given what he thought to be the best advice for his country with frankness and loyalty, as he ought, but wherever the People should lead he would unhesitatingly follow. Indeed he was sure that the man who had insulted him would never venture in battle where he himself would venture.

Then, when the rest of those present fell to grumbling and began to defend their decision, the magistrates fixed a fine for anyone who debated the matter further. The rashness of the magistrates was assisted by a fierce people, proud of its many victories. They wished to march out fearlessly and expose themselves voluntarily to battle, not so much out of concern for their allies' perils, nor led by any particular goal, but simply to avoid the appearance of being afraid of their enemies.

The best course having thus been shouted down, the expedition was prepared with resolve. Friendly powers were notified and

cerenturne in arma cives diversae factionis qui in urbe remanserant, an domi relinquerentur. Tutius visum est magnam eorum partem educere, ne relicti occasionem rerum novarum vacua in urbe nanciscerentur.

52   Postquam convenerunt socii et cuncta ad iter parata fuerunt, profecti ab urbe agrum senensem ingrediuntur. Ibi Arretinorum copiae magno equitum peditumque numero sese illis coniunxerunt. Sed antequam domo proficiscerentur Arretini, cunctos diversae factionis homines urbe pepulerunt, ne quid per absentiam exercitus moliri possent. Illud etiam ab iisdem provisum est, ne quamdiu exercitus abesset, una amplius porta in urbe aperiretur. Ex quo constat eos populariter abfuisse.

53   Florentini igitur cum Arretinis et Lucensibus ceterisque sociis iuxta flumen Arbiam, quatuor fere passuum millibus a Senis ex ea parte qua Arretium iter est, consederunt, intentis maxime ducibus, an quisquam civilis motus secundum traditam spem intra urbem oriretur. Senenses primo adventu copias intra moenia continebant. Mox vero, ut quidam e castris studio partium ad exules transfugit atque illorum hortatu (quo magis acceleretur pugna) in concionem ductus discordiam civium trepidationemque, ut ab exulibus edoctus erat, cuncta exaugens nunciavit, confestim magno ardore ab armatis simul inermibusque pugna deposcitur.

54   Cum ergo statuissent fortunam proelii experiri, Iordanus quem a rege Senas missum ostendimus (is enim summae rei bellicae praefectus a Senensibus erat) clausis portis ne quid efferri posset, aciem intra moenia silentio struxit ac cetera quae agenda erant pro tempore sine ullo tumultu praeparavit. Ubi vero cuncta satis com-

asked for aid. Meanwhile there was some discussion whether the citizens of the opposing faction who had remained in the city should be armed and marched out or left at home. It was thought safer to bring along a sizeable portion of them, since if they were left behind they might seize the opportunity in the empty city to carry out a coup.

The allies were mustered and everything was made ready for 52 the journey. Setting out from the city, they entered Sienese territory, where they were joined by a large contingent of Aretine horse and foot. Before the Aretines had left home, they had expelled from the city all the members of the Ghibelline faction in order to prevent a coup in the absence of the army. They had also arranged that, so long as the army was away, no more than a single gate should be left open. From this circumstance it is evident that their expedition had popular support.

So the Florentines, with the Aretines, Lucchesi and other allies, 53 pitched camp by the river Arbia, about four miles from Siena on the road from Arezzo. The leaders were eager most of all to learn whether an uprising was going to occur within Siena, as report had given them to hope. From the moment of their arrival, the Sienese had been keeping their troops within the city walls. Soon, however, there were eager calls for battle from the armed and the unarmed alike. A certain Ghibelline partisan had deserted to the exiles from the Florentine encampment, and at the exiles' urging (in order to hasten the battle) this man was brought before the Sienese assembly. He told of fear and discord among the Florentines, as the exiles had instructed him to, exaggerating everything.

Thus it was decided to try the fortunes of battle. Giordano, 54 who (as we said) was sent by the king to Siena, had been put in charge of military affairs by the Sienese. He had the gates shut to maintain secrecy, quietly set up his order of battle within the walls, and made the rest of the preparations necessary under the circumstances with no noise whatever. Now all seemed ready and

posita videbantur nec quicquam praeter signum proficiscendi ex-
spectaretur, volens urbanam multitudinem quae pugnatura erat
cohortari convocatam in unum, sic allocutus est:

55 "Ardor flagitatae pugnae, o Senenses, nulla cohortatione vobis
in proelium ituris opus esse ostendit. Attamen unumquemque
vestrum reputare secum oportet, quibus de rebus certamen sit
hodie futurum; sic enim et quanta vincendi necessitas incumbat
vobis intelligetis. Non solum enim de fama et gloria (quamquam
ista fortibus viris vel ipsa quidem per se ingentissima sunt), sed de
patria, de libertate, de coniugibus et liberis vestris, de bonis denique omnibus utrum vestra vel in hostium potestate futura sint,
paulo post dimicaturi estis. Ea quippe omnia, cum pugnare coepe-
ritis, in medio iacere campo putandum est; eorum futura, qui for-
tius vibraverint gladios. Ceterum, spem optimam atque firmissi-
mam debetis concipere. Habetis hostes in vestibulo paene urbis,
vestro potius quam suo consilio perductos, de quorum trepidatione atque discordia modo a transfugis audivistis. Eos improvidos
imparatosque, vobis affatim structis paratisque, insigni, ni fallor,
strage occidendos tradam. Ite igitur mecum fausto pede atque uti
dignum est maioribus vestris utque patriae huius dulcissimae caritas exigit, pugnatote."

56 His dictis aperiri portam iubet. Prima acies germanorum equitum fuit. His effusissimo cursu in hostem deferri et quam tumul-
tuarie possent turbare praeceptum erat. Post hos, senenses equites

the troops were waiting only for the signal to advance. Giordano, wishing to harangue the urban multitude that was about to fight, called them together and addressed them as follows:

"Your ardor in demanding battle, O men of Siena, shows you 55 have no need of exhortation as you go into battle. Yet each of you should reflect on what you are fighting for today, for in this way it will be borne in upon you how necessary it is for you to be victorious. You shall shortly be fighting, not only for fame and glory — though these things in themselves are of enormous importance to brave men — but also to decide whether your country, your liberty, your wives and children, and all your possessions shall be under your own control or under that of your enemy. You must know that when you begin to fight, all these things shall be wagered on the field of battle and shall belong to those who swing their swords the more stoutly. At the same time, you should be utterly firm and confident. You have your enemies practically on the doorstep of your city; they have come on your terms, not theirs; and you have just heard from deserters how wracked they are with fear and discord. I shall hand them over to you: they are unsuspecting and unprepared; you are abundantly prepared and in battle array; and if I mistake not they shall be cut down in a famous slaughter. So come with me and good luck! Fight and be worthy of your ancestors! Fight as your love for this sweetest of countries requires of you!"

Having thus spoken, he ordered the gate opened. The German 56 knights were in the van. They had been instructed to charge the enemy in a broad and loose formation so as to cause the maximum confusion. They were followed by the Sienese and exile knights. Close on the heels of the second line of knights a large number of infantry under their banners was hastening along the hilltops and higher elevations. When the German knights were spotted from the camp, they caused first hesitation, then uproar. But the Florentines were slow to react since no one suspected that the decisive

cum exulibus sequebantur. Peditum multitudo sub vexillis per eminentiora loca collesque mixta fere equitibus secundae aciei contendebat. Conspecti e castris germani equites dubitationem primo, mox et tumultum excitarunt, segnius tamen quod nemo fere de tota re certamen eo die, sed levia magis proelia, ut inter propinquos hostes oriri solent, suspicabatur fore. At postquam peditem sequi et aliam super aliam aciem properare cernunt, cognito hostium consilio ubique trepidatur. Praecipuus tamen apud duces pavor, qui secretorum conscii fraudem intelligebant. Et iam hostis aderat infestus, neque struere aciem neque affari militem duces poterant; caeco et incerto tumultu cuncta miscebantur.

57 Germani ferociter in primam stationem advecti magnam primo impetu procellam edidere et fuga quaedam inde fieri coepta, turbassentque latius, ni florentini equites obviam progressi impetum Germanorum egregie sustinuissent. Eorum concursu aequata pugna et adiuvabant fortissimi peditum, ut in tumultuaria re equitibus permixti. Stetitque id certamen, quoad Senensium exulumque ac mox peditum supervenit acies. Tunc pluribus simul locis pugnari coeptum; meliori tamen spe Senensis pugnabat. Nam in Florentinorum exercitu propter subitam vim nec struere acies nec affari militem duces potuerant; forte potius quam consulto, ut quemque casus tulerat, ipse sibi quisque dux adhortatorque erat. Resistebatur tamen nec pauciora inferebantur vulnera quam accipiebantur, donec transfugia fieri coepta sunt. Ea primum Florentinos turbarunt. Nam plerique diversae factionis, quos ductos in castra supra docuimus, sive iam ante corrupti sive tunc primum nocendi tempus nacti, foedo exemplo a suorum acie ad hostes transfugerunt. Tantumque valuit rabies et certamen partium, ut

encounter would be fought that day; they were expecting only the sort of light skirmishing that usually occurs when enemies are close to each other. But when they saw the infantry follow and rank upon rank of troops rapidly advancing, they grasped the enemy plan and were stricken everywhere with fright. Their commanders, however, were even more alarmed as they had been privy to the secret intelligence and realized that they had been tricked. Now the enemy was upon them, ready for battle, while they themselves had been unable to put their forces in battle-order or address their troops; everything had fallen into a blind and bewildering uproar.

Fiercely the Germans galloped up to the first guardpost and attacked it with a mighty charge, causing a flight of sorts to begin. The confusion would have been more widespread had not the Florentine knights come up and checked admirably the German attack. Once the Florentine cavalry had engaged, the battle became more equal. They were supported by the bravest members of the infantry, who mingled with the cavalry in the uproar. So the fight continued until the arrival of the Sienese and exile [cavalry], with the infantry on their heels. Then it began to break up into a number of different, simultaneous fights. But the Sienese had the advantage. Owing to the surprise attack the Florentine army did not have the chance to set its ranks in order and its leaders had been unable to address their troops; every man had to be his own general and his own orator, acting by chance, not design, as the situation directed him. Still, the army fought back, giving as good as it got, until the desertions began. This was what first caused the Florentine lines to break. As we have already described, many Ghibellines had been brought along in the Florentine camp, and — whether they had been bribed beforehand, or had just then for the first time found an opportunity to cause harm — they set a disgraceful example and began to desert from their own lines to the enemy. So maddened were they by party strife that they would

57

patriae decus dignitatemque prodere hostibus mallent quam sibi cives invisos praeesse.

58   Praecipuum tamen in ea pugna scelus unius Buccae Abbatis emicuit. Is natus e familia nobili, ceterum diversarum in re publica partium, prope signiferum astabat. Signifer erat eques illustris ex urbana familia quibus Pactii cognomentum est. Bucca igitur non transfugio solum, sed et insigni aliquo facinore exulibus gratificari cupiens, signiferum pone aggressus, manum qua tenebat vexillum improviso ictu abscidit vexillumque ipsum quod modo sequebatur, hostis e cive factus, prostravit. Eo casu turbata acie, cum iam nec quibus fidere nec a quibus cavere oporteret dignosceretur, fugam equites arripiunt, cedentes magis quam superati. Pedites equitum praesidio destituti, crebra etiam inter acies suorum transfugia cernentes, proditione conspecta et ipsi dilabuntur.

59   Nec fere posthac alicubi praeterquam ad signa pugnatum est. Currus fuit ingenti robore insignique ornatu, in quo vexilla florentini populi praealto hastili sublata ferebantur. Hunc in ceterorum fuga et trepidatione magna civium manus, quos patriae caritas tangebat, devota circumstetit, decus et gloriam hosti numquam sine sanguine relictura, castigabantque se ultro et invicem hortabantur, ne currum illum ac signa, per tot iam bella victricia, turpi fuga desererent ac tanto dedecore florentinum nomen dehonestarent; praestare denique pro patria mori quam tantae infamiae superesse. His vocibus generosissimus quisque flectebatur et fuga omissa circa signa subsistebat. Plerique robora ipsa currus complexi quasi supremis rebus osculabantur. Itaque iam pridem aliis locis profligato exercitu ad currum tamen acriter resistebant, quoad conver-

rather betray to the enemy the honor and glory of their own country than help fellow-citizens they hated.

In that fight the wickedness of a man named Bocca degli Abati[36] was particularly striking. Though a Ghibelline, he was posted near the standard-bearer owing to his noble lineage. The standard-bearer was an eminent knight of the Pazzi family of Florence.[37] Bocca wanted to win the favor of the exiles not only by his desertion, but by some notably outrageous deed. So he attacked the standard-bearer from behind, and with a sudden blow cut off the hand with which the latter was holding the standard. Transformed from a citizen into an enemy, Bocca knocked down the standard he had been following but a little while before. This misfortune threw the ranks into confusion, as they now could not tell friend from foe. The cavalry took flight, though it was more a retreat than a rout. The infantry, left without mounted support, seeing the numerous desertions from their ranks, and having observed Bocca's act of treachery, now themselves began to slip away.

By then practically the only fighting was taking place around the standards. There was an enormously strong and bravely decorated battle-wagon[38] upon which there used to be borne the standard of the Florentine People, attached to a very tall pole. A handful of citizens, moved by patriotism, stood faithfully around it in the midst of the general alarm and flight; they were not about to leave honor and glory to the enemy without bloodshed. They held themselves back by their own free will, exhorting each other not to desert in foul flight that wagon and that standard, victorious in so many battles; not to bring such disgrace upon the Florentine name; urging, in short, that it was better to die for one's country than to survive in ignominy. The noblest among them were moved by these words, abandoned flight, and stood firm around the standard. Many held fast to the very oaken beams of the wagon as though to kiss it in their final act. Thus when the rest of the army had long since fled elsewhere, there was still bitter resistance

58

59

sis in eos omnibus copiis corona ab hoste circumdati, cum undique telis impeterentur, magno prius edito certamine ad unum
omnes interfecti sunt.

60 Supra tria millia hominum[53] caesa in ea pugna referuntur, captivi ad quatuor millia ex fuga retracti. Castris et omni apparatu
Senenses potiti, cum finem persequendi fecissent, praelatis hostium spoliis et longo captivorum agmine in urbem copias reduxere.

61 Haec ubi Florentiae audita sunt, horror ac metus civitatem pervasit. Publice maestitia, privatim per singulas domos luctus utque
est proclivior ad malum suspicio, vivi simul mortuique complora-
bantur. Mulieres in publicum diffusae,[54] filios aliae, aliae parentes
fratresque velut praesenti funere clamitabant. Redeuntium vero
foedi vultus ac tristis oculorum deiectio, nec eos qui in acie ceci-
dissent, sed vivos se redeuntesque lugendos monebant; illos enim
functos fato, praestanti mortis genere pro patria interiisse; se ludibrio adversariorum servatos.

62 His querelis cum finem demum fecissent, circumspicere sese ac
intueri reliquam fortunam suam coepere. Venturos exules cum victore exercitu ac victoria crudeliter usuros nemo ambigebat. Eadem in urbe quae in castris extiterat proditio timebatur; nam et
plebs facile cum fortuna mutat animos et diversae factionis homines, quorum pars quaedam remanserat domi, minime quieturos
apparebat. His rationibus relinquere urbem ac demigrare tutius visum. Inde luctus renovari coeptus patriam, penates ac cetera quae

around the wagon. At last the enemy turned all its forces on it and surrounded it. Attacked with spears on every side, its defenders put up a tremendous fight and were killed to the last man.

It is said that more than three thousand men were slaughtered in this battle and that about four thousand fugitives were taken prisoner. The camp and all its equipment fell into Sienese hands. When they had put an end to their pursuit, the Sienese marched their troops back to the city, displaying the spoils of their enemies and a long line of captives.[39]

When the news was heard in Florence, fear and horror stalked the city. Public gloom and private grief swept through every house, and, as people are readier to suspect bad fortune than good, the living were mourned along with the dead. Women poured into the streets, some bewailing their sons, others fathers and brothers, as though they were attending a funeral. The shame-filled faces of those who had returned and their sorrowful, downcast eyes were a reminder that it was not those who had fallen in battle who were to be mourned, but those who had come home alive. The former fulfilled their destiny and died admirably for their country; the latter had saved themselves only to be objects of mockery to their adversaries.

When at last they had finished their laments, they began to look about them to see what fortune had left them. No one doubted that the exiles would be coming along with the victorious army and that they would make cruel use of their triumph. The same treachery which had showed itself in the camps was feared also in the city. For the passions of the common people are easily swayed by success, and it was evident that the Ghibellines, some of whom had remained at home, were going to cause trouble. For these reasons it seemed the safer course to leave the city and emigrate. Thereupon grief began anew for those who were leaving behind in one moment their country, their homes,[40] and everything they held dear. The men who emigrated were those so famous for

60

61

62

hominibus carissima sunt uno in tempore cuncta relinquentibus. Migraverunt omnes qui studio partium ita insignes erant, ut se adventante victore tutos fore desperarent. Plerique coniuges liberosque secum traxere. Maxima eorum pars Lucae, multi etiam Bononiae, utraque in urbe hospitaliter amiceque recepti constitere.

63 Non sum nescius a quibusdam magnis viris hoc eorum factum imprudens timidumque censeri, quod munitam urbem ac validis cinctam moenibus, antequam adventaret hostis, nullo certamine deseruissent; potuisse enim aliquod tempus defendi; in dies autem multa, interdum etiam minime sperata, ad salutem emergere. Ego illustres viros, quorum postea res fortiter gestae per totam fere Italiam claruere, numquam ignaviae imprudentiaeque damnarim; potius illorum conditionem temporum non satis notam reprehensoribus puto. Novo enim partium studio fervescente eminentiores quidem[55] cives in diversum abierant; plebs autem incerta, necdum[56] longa possessione alterutri addicta parti, ad victores semper nutabat, nec minus cives suos putabat qui exules erant quam qui infra moenia tenebantur. Quod si cum externo penitus et alieno hoste ac non cum civibus fuisset certamen, commune optimatium plebisque periculum et obstinata pro patria voluntas ad defensionem animos coniunxisset. Cives autem nuper pulsos regredi in urbem, ut maximum adversariis, sic nullum plebi periculum afferebat; nec urbs in potestatem hostium venire, sed in manus civium redire videbatur. Ea de causa plebs multitudoque nec obsidionem pati nec famem aut cetera incommoda subire volebat. Quamobrem expectare hostem ac se intra moenia abdere nihil erat aliud egregiis viris quam se certissimae neci offerre; cedere autem ac sese ad me-

their partisan zeal that they despaired for their safety when the victor should arrive. Many took with them their wives and children. The largest group settled in Lucca, and many, too, went to Bologna; in both places they were received in a friendly and hospitable spirit.

I am well aware that certain great men have judged this action 63 of theirs imprudent and timid: abandoning without a fight a fortified city, girt with powerful walls, before the enemy had even arrived. They could have defended it for some time (it is alleged); and the passage of time can extricate you from many desperate situations. For my part I should never condemn for cowardice and imprudence illustrious men whose brave deeds were later famous throughout Italy; I prefer to think that the condition of those times is imperfectly understood by those who do condemn them. With partisan passions boiling up anew, certain of the more eminent citizens had gone over to the other side. The common people could not be counted on; they had been pledged to neither party for any great length of time, and always tended to favor the victorious party. They considered the exiles their fellow-citizens no less than those who were staying inside the walls. If there had been a fight with some entirely foreign, external enemy and not with fellow-citizens, the common danger both to the ordinary folk and to the optimates and a resolute devotion to country would have united them in the common defense. The return of exiled citizens to the city, while it presented great danger to their adversaries, presented none to the commons; to them it appeared that the city was returning to the control of citizens, not coming into the power of enemies. Hence the commoners and the masses were unwilling either to undergo a siege or subject themselves to hunger and other discomforts. So for the men of distinction to hide within the walls awaiting the enemy was simply to offer themselves up to certain death; to withdraw and preserve oneself for a better fate

liorem servare spem, cum prudens, tum animosum videbatur consilium.

64   Exules, paucis diebus ad sectionem praedae intermissis, magnis equitum peditumque copiis Florentiam profecti nullo penitus obsistente apertis portis urbem intrarunt. xv Kalendas octobris ingressos Florentiam constat, cum apud Arbiam pridie Nonas septembris pugnatum fuisset, anno christianae salutis ducentesimo sexagesimo supra mille. Ex hoc civitas statum mutavit finemque habuit potentia eius populi qui post Federici mortem decem per annos ingenti pollens gloria ac multis victoriis superbus rem publicam gubernarat, nulla alia re quam nimia ferocia culpatus.

65   Posthac non iam populi, sed Manfredi nomine cuncta gerebantur. Potestas intra urbem Guidoni comiti, cui Novello cognomentum fuit, demandata est; Iordanus rei bellicae praeerat; stipendia ex aerario florentini populi Germanis promebantur. Per idem tempus omnes cives qui in urbe remanserant, fidem promittere coacti, in Manfredi nomen iuravere; bona quoque[57] civium qui demigrarant publicata et turres domusque eorum in urbe agroque eversae. Legatis etiam ad Manfredum missis gratiae regi actae, quod eius opera in patriam restituti essent; laudes amplissimae Iordani ducis ac Germanorum qui cum illo pugnarant additae; postulatumque est, uti ducem ipsum cum equitibus ultra praescriptum morari in Etruria pateretur.

66   Per haec ipsa tempora gravissimum apud Arretinos bellum gerebatur. Cives enim qui a pugna superfuerant in urbem regressi, quamquam perditis rebus permagnam impendere sibi tempestatem cernebant, consistere tamen in loco ac tutari sua statuerunt, erecti maxime in eam spem situ urbis, qui facile defendi posse videbatur, et rei frumentariae copia, qua plurimum ea civitas abundabat. Igitur his qui remanserant e diversa factione urbe de-

seemed to be a course of action that was at once prudent and bold.

The Ghibelline exiles spent a few days dividing the spoils, then set out for Florence with large forces of foot and horse. They entered the city without opposition; its gates were wide open. As is well known, they entered Florence on the seventeenth day of September in the year 1260 of Christian salvation; the battle of the Arbia had been fought on the fourth day of that month.[41] After this date there was a change of constitution, and the power of the People came to an end. For ten years after the death of Frederick it had governed the commonwealth, powerful, glorious, and proud of its many victories; its one fault was a fierce excess of warlike spirit. 64

1260

Henceforward public affairs were conducted in the name of Manfred, not in that of the People. Power in the city was turned over to Count Guido Novello, Giordano was in charge of military affairs, and the Germans were paid from the treasury of the Florentine People. About the same time all the citizens who were left in the city were compelled to swear a loyalty oath to Manfred. In addition, the property of the citizens who had emigrated was confiscated, and their towers and dwellings in the city and countryside were destroyed. Legates were sent to Manfred to thank him for his aid in restoring the exiles to their country; praise was heaped upon Duke Giordano and the Germans who had fought with him; and it was requested that the Duke himself and his knights be permitted to remain in Tuscany beyond the appointed period.[42] 65

During this same time a grievous war was being waged in Arezzo. The citizens who had survived the fight returned to the city, although they realized that with the defeat a great tempest hung over them. But they decided to stand fast and guard their property, encouraged most of all by the city's situation which made it easy to defend, and by the abundance of its grain supply. So they expelled the remaining Ghibellines, repaired the walls 66

pulsis, moenia, si qua in parte minus firma videbantur, repararunt, fossasque purgarunt; vallum etiam quibusdam locis addiderunt. Ad haec facienda duodecim viri creati, qui una cum magistratu singulis diebus circumirent urbem et quibus factu opus foret providerent. Contra vero cives diversae factionis ab iis pulsi, Senensium Florentinorumque adiuti viribus, urbi terribiles imminebant, proximisque occupatis castellis atrox erat certamen ac proelia prope quotidiana inter eos committebantur. Haec eo anno, quo pugnatum est apud Arbiam, fere gesta sunt.

67   Principio insequentis anni legati a Manfredo reversi cetera grata regi fuisse retulerunt, sed de Iordano non ultra impetrari quivisse quam uti paucos insuper menses commorandi facultas ei permitteretur. Itaque voluntate regis haud ambigue cognita, placuit ante illius decessum principibus in unum coactis communi sententia de statu Etruriae deque partium studio consultare. Conventus ad eam rem Emporii indictus est, qui locus inter civitates fere medius habetur. Eo cum legationes singularum civitatum ac principes eius factionis magna frequentia convenissent, proposita est regis voluntas, et quando abeundi necessitas Iordano incumbat, ipsi quid agendum providendumque sit pro salute partium statuerent. Tractari inde coepta res est, dictaeque variae sententiae pro cuiusque animo ac voluntate. Una tamen vox omnium erat, nulla ex re tantum suis partibus quantum a Florentia periculum imminere: eam urbem caput diversae factionis in Etruria esse; cives qui pulsi sunt[58] numquam quieturos; plebem etiam ac multitudinem cum diversa factione magis sentire; et rebellasse quondam post Federici

where they seemed weak, cleaned out the moat, and added a rampart in certain places. A board of twelve men was created for this task; they went around the city each day with the magistrates and oversaw the defense works. On the other side, the Ghibellines whom they had expelled, aided by Sienese and Florentine forces, became a terrible threat to the city. Occupying the nearby castles, they fought bitterly and engaged the Aretine Guelfs in battles nearly every day. Such, more or less, were the deeds done in the year when the battle of the Arbia was fought.

At the beginning of the following year, the legates returning from Manfred reported that the king was in general pleased, but with respect to Giordano he could be persuaded only to allow the latter the option of remaining a few months longer. Once the will of the king had been made abundantly clear, it was decided that before Giordano left there should be a meeting among the leaders to reach a common decision about the state of Tuscany and its partisan divisions. A meeting at Empoli was announced for this purpose, a place located almost in the middle of the Tuscan cities. When legations from the individual cities and the leaders of the Ghibelline faction had assembled there in great numbers, the king's will was set forth, and, as the necessity of Giordano's departure was pressing, they had to decide (it was thought) what should be done and planned for the welfare of their party. A debate on the subject began, and various opinions were stated that reflected the attitudes and desires of the speakers. There was nevertheless one point of agreement: that the greatest danger threatening their party came from Florence. That city was the capital of the Guelf party in Tuscany; the citizens who had been driven from thence were bound to make trouble; the commons and the urban masses were more sympathetic to the Guelfs; they had rebelled once before, after the death of Frederick, and, it would be remembered, they had eagerly recalled those same Guelf leaders (who at that time had also been in exile); if the situation should change — and

67

1261

mortem, et hos ipsos[59] homines tunc quoque eiectos praecupide revocasse memorabant; si quid contingat, qualia multa possunt, redeantque iterum, omnia turbaturos; quare si salvos esse vellent, si partes suas omni tempore superiores fore, si non modo se, verum etiam filios liberare periculis cuperent, Florentiam tollerent atque delerent. Eius enim casu et ruina penitus obrui diversam in Etruria factionem; stante vero praevalituram aliquando ac exitio partium futuram.

68 Haec Pisanorum Senensiumque legati, haec ceteri quot aderant in conventu fremebant et adhaerebant plerique nobiles qui per agrum florentinum arces munitaque habebant loca, per illius occasum potentiam suam augeri sperantes. Vicissetque tandem ea sententia, ni unus Farinata contra omnium impetum restitisset. Hoc uno tum cive patria stetit. Nam, cum eam sententiam placituram tandem nec ullum omnino repugnaturum appareret, assurgens gravi et indignante vultu, cum de his rebus dicere se velle significasset, expectatione pro viri dignitate facta in hunc modum locutus est:

69 "Numquam putavi fore post arbiensem pugnam ac praeclaram illam de hoste victoriam me ut vitae poeniteret meae. At iam poenitet et quod non in ipsa pugna oppetierim doleo. Nihil adeo rerum humanarum stabile est, et quae plerumque laeta credideris, maerorem subinferunt. Nec vicisse plane, ut videtur, satis est, sed refert plurimum quibuscum viceris. Iniuriam ab hoste quam a socio aequiori perferimus animo. Nec equidem nunc patriae casum deploro. Illa enim, utcumque tandem res sint, me superstite numquam tolletur, sed eorum sententias, qui ante me dixerunt, indignor. Scilicet, ad hoc[60] convocati estis, ut tollenda an relinquenda sit Florentia consultare deberetis, ac non potius quemadmodum illa cum ceteris stet ac duret in partibus cogitare? Non didici rhe-

many things *could* change—the émigrés might return and throw everything into confusion. So if they wanted to be safe, if they wanted their party to remain on top forever, if they wanted to free not only themselves but their children from peril, they should abolish Florence and wipe her out. With her fall and destruction the Guelf party in Tuscany would be entirely destroyed, but so long as Florence stood, the Guelfs could grow strong again and destroy the Ghibelline party.

Such were the howls of rage uttered by the legates of the 68 Sienese and Pisans and by everyone else present; and many of the nobles who held castles and fortified places in Florentine territory agreed with them, as the latter hoped to increase their own power through Florence's fall. This view would have triumphed in the end had not Farinata, alone, resisted the universal attack; our country survived because of this one citizen. For when it began to appear that this view would in the end win approval and that no one was going to put up any opposition to it, he rose up with a grave and outraged countenance, making a sign that he wished to speak about the matter. Out of respect for the man they waited, and he spoke as follows.

"After the battle of the Arbia, that famous victory over our ene- 69 mies, I never thought I should be sorry to be alive. But now I *am* sorry to be alive, sorry that I didn't die in that battle. Nothing at all is stable in human affairs; even the things you thought would make you happiest conceal within them sources of grief. It is not enough to have won, it seems; it matters more with whom you win. We bear injury more calmly from an enemy than from an ally. I am not now going to lament the fate of my country; however matters turn out, she shall not be destroyed while I am alive; but I am outraged at the views expressed by the preceding speakers. So *this* was the reason you had this meeting, to decide whether to destroy Florence or leave it alone? It wasn't to consider how it might coexist with other cities and remain Ghibelline? I am no

torum artes; nec verborum ornamenta, ut hi qui ante me dixerunt, meditatus sum, sed ut habet vulgare proverbium, quemadmodum sapio, ita loquor. Dicam igitur aperte quod sentio.

70   "Ego non urbem meam solum, verum etiam me ipsum ac meos cives miseros nimium abiectosque putarem, si de illa tollenda vel relinquenda statuere vobis liceret. Sed certe non licet, nec quicquam tale vestri arbitrii est. Nam et nos aequo iure in foedus venimus, et foedus ipsum non pro eversione civitatum, sed pro conservatione est ictum. Itaque sententiae quidem vestrae nescio magis vanissimae an acerbissimae sint. Utrumque certe, cum et ea censeant quae in vestra non sunt potestate, et nihil ultra proficiant quam ut acerbitatem animi erga socios ostendant. Atqui probabilius erat, praesertim communi pro salute in consilium vocatos, vetusta odia simultatesque omittere, nec sub alio praetextu alienam cladem eversionemque perquirere. Numquam enim non male consulit qui odio consulit, nec qui nocere socio cupit, utilitatem communem prosequitur.

71   "Sed, quaeso, quid iam oderitis? Urbemne? At quid mali unquam moenia tectaque fecerunt? An homines? Nos qui intus sumus an eiectos? Si nos, iam noster hic error est qui cum hostibus ita coivimus quasi cum sociis; vestrum autem scelus qui amicitiam simulantes, cum animus esset hostilis, foedus nobiscum inistis. Si eiectos, quid urbem persequimini?[61] Non enim moenia pro illis stant, sed contra illos; nec eos circumdant, sed arcent. Itaque, cum de illa evertenda cogitatis, non adversum hostes, sed adversum socios cogitatis. 'Caput est,' inquit,[62] 'diversae factionis.' Erat, puto, cum illi urbem tenebant; at nunc tenentibus nobis, quid magis di-

trained orator, I have not prepared any verbal tricks like the previous speakers; 'I talk what I know', as the common expression has it. So I shall say frankly what I think.

"I should think not only my city but myself and my fellow citizens miserable and cowardly if it should become yours to decide whether our city shall be destroyed or left alone. But it is certainly none of your business to decide this or any such matter. We Florentines, too, entered this league on an equal basis, and the league was formed not to destroy cities but to save them. I can hardly say whether your decision shows more falseness or more bitterness. Surely it shows both, since you pass judgement on matters that do not lie within your competence and that serve no purpose but to reveal your bitterness towards your allies. It would have been more acceptable, especially when summoned to give counsel for the common welfare, to have laid aside your ancient hatreds and feuds and not sought another's defeat and destruction under a different pretext. The man who gives advice out of hatred always gives bad advice, and the man who wants to harm his ally is not seeking the common good.

"But let me ask you what it is that you hate. The city itself? But what wicked acts have walls and houses ever done? Its population? Do you mean us who are inside the city or those who have been driven from it? If it is we whom you hate, the mistake is now ours for having joined ourselves to enemies in the belief that they were allies — though you too are guilty of a wicked act for entering with simulated friendship into a league with us when your intentions were in fact hostile. If it is the Guelf exiles whom you hate, why are you persecuting the city? Its walls are not surrounding and protecting them, they are resisting them and keeping them out. So when you plot to tear down those walls, you are plotting against your allies, not your enemies. Someone will say that the city is the capital of the Guelf faction. Yes it was, I believe, when they held the city, but now, when we hold it, why is it not rather

70

71

versae factionis est quam nostrarum partium caput? Nam muri quidem et turres perinde sunt ut hi a quibus tenentur. Ipsi per se nihil sentiunt. 'At populus multitudoque urbana cum diversa factione magis sentit'. Quid igitur? Proximo apud Arbiam proelio, cum magna pars civium ad nos transfugiens, in illos arma convertit, satisne ostendit magis nobiscum quam cum adversariis sentire? Quid? Quod ipsi adversarii sponte sua deseruerunt urbem, nonne satis indicio est eos[63] multitudini urbanae diffisos, quod nostrarum partium fautricem sciebant, migrandi consilium assumpsisse? Denique sit suspecta multitudo, quamquam est nostra. Sed sit suspecta: num etiam nos qui vicimus suspecti aut abiecti sumus? Et hoc vestrum remedium est, ut urbs, ne gravius dicam, nulli etruscarum postrema, ob hanc suspicionem tollatur? Quis unquam isto modo consuluit? Quis tantam acerbitatem, et si animo concepisset, verbis patefacere ausus est? Vestrae scilicet stabunt urbes; nostra autem ruet? Et vos in vestris florebitis; nobis autem qui una vicimus hoc praemium erit, ut pro exilio tunc perpesso, nunc eversionem patriae omni acerbiorem exilio patiamur?[64] Per deos immortales! Quisquamne vestrum sic me abiectum putavit, ut haec, non dicam assensurus vobis, sed aequo animo fuerim auditurus? Nempe quod nuper[65] arma adversus tuli. At ego inimicos meos persecutus sum; patriam vero semper dilexi. An igitur quam adversarii servabant, ego nunc perdam et futura saecula illos patriae conservatores, me eversorem nominabunt? Quid hoc infamius dici aut excogitari potest? Quid magis pusillanimum quam metu hostium tua delere? Denique, quid ego verbis moror? Erumpat tandem[66] digna vox. Ego, quamdiu unus e florentino nomine superfuero, numquam patiar neque permittam patriam meam tolli, et si millies mori liceret, millies morti me offeram."

the capital of our own party? Walls and towers belong to those who hold them; in themselves they have no sympathies. 'But the People and the urban masses are more sympathetic to the Guelfs' (you say). How so? What about the late battle of the Arbia, when a great part of the citizenry deserted to us and turned their arms against the Guelfs—doesn't this show that they are more sympathetic to us than to our adversaries? What about when our adversaries of their own free will deserted the city—isn't this sufficient proof that they decided to emigrate because they mistrusted the urban masses, knowing they favored our party? But let's grant that the loyalty of the masses is suspect—in fact it is on our side, but let's grant it anyway. Are we, too, the victors, to be held suspect and cast aside? And this is your remedy, that the city, which is second to none in Tuscany (to make no stronger claim), is to be destroyed on account of this suspicion? What sort of advice is this? Who ever dared express such bitter counsel, even if he secretly thought it? Your cities shall stand while ours is to be ruined? You shall be left to flourish in your city, while we who triumphed alongside of you shall have as our reward, in return for the exile we then endured, the destruction of our country, a suffering more bitter than any exile? By the immortal gods! Who among you thought me so base that I could listen calmly to these plans, let alone agree with them? Yes, I bore arms against Florence a short while ago. But I was persecuting my enemies; my country I have always loved. Shall I now squander what my enemies preserved? Shall future ages call them saviors of their country; me, her destroyer? Can anything more infamous be said or imagined? Is there anything lower than to destroy what is yours out of fear of an enemy? There is no point in further talk, but this sally is worth making nevertheless: if I were the last Florentine on earth, I should never endure or allow my country to be destroyed, even if I had to die a thousand times over."

72   Ea cum dixisset, e consilio se proripuit. Perculit omnium animos Farinatae oratio, et auctoritas eius commovit plurimos. Constabat enim studio illarum partium neminem unum praestantiorem esse virum verebanturque omnes, ne indignatio eius aliquid communi causae detrimenti afferret. Itaque suppressa statim eius rei mentio est dataque opera quibusdam gravioribus, ut lenienda re mitibus verbis in consessum reducerent. Fuit enim vir celsi animi et altiora semper intuentis; in adversarios tamen acerbior quam civilis modestia postulabat. In hoc autem periculo patriae vel summe laudandus, nisi ipse idem causa, ut in id periculum deduceretur, fuisset.

73   Contentione ergo, quoniam exitio partium futura videbatur, omissa, praeter domesticum equitatum ad mille insuper equites mercede conductos communi civitatum impensa alere statuerunt. Hisque et aliis copiis Novellus praeficitur summaque imperii illi demandatur. Dissoluto inde concilio Iordanus, uti a rege praeceptum erat, discessit.

74   Novellus autem quem praefectum bello diximus, haud multo post equitum peditumque copiis, quas e singulis populis acciverat, in unum coactis Lucensium fines, quod hi diversae factionis erant ac exules Florentinorum receperant, ingressus circumferendo bello, cum aliquot castella cepisset, maiori tandem apparatu Fucetium aggreditur. Id erat oppidum per eam tempestatem in primis nobile. Cum ab exulibus florentinis, quorum magna vis in eo tunc erat, itemque ab eius loci oppidanis egregie defenderetur ac Novellus admotis machinis pertinacius instaret, magnis coortis imbribus

With these words he flung himself out of the council chamber. 72
Everyone was daunted by Farinata's speech, and many were swayed
by his authority. It was well known that there was no more outstanding partisan than he, and everyone was afraid that his anger
would damage the common cause. So discussion of the matter was
immediately suppressed, and certain important persons were given
the task of smoothing over the matter with soft words and bringing Farinata back to the meeting. He was truly a man of lofty
spirit who always kept his eye fixed on nobler things, yet he behaved more unforgivingly towards his adversaries than is consistent with the moderation of civilized conduct. In this moment of
danger to his country he would have been deserving of the highest
praise had he not himself been at the same time a cause of his
country's having been endangered.

The debate was therefore abandoned as likely to destroy the 73
party. It was decided to hire up to a thousand mercenary knights,
in addition to the local cavalry, to be paid for in common by all the
cities. Guido Novello was put in charge of these and other forces,
and the high command was entrusted to him. The council then
dissolved itself and Giordano departed, as the king had instructed
him.[43]

Soon afterwards, Guido Novello (who as we said was in charge 74
of the war) collected the troops of horse and foot that he had
mustered from the individual cities and entered Lucchese territory.
He did this because the Lucchese were Guelfs and were harboring
the Florentine exiles. Spreading war on all sides, he captured several castles, then assaulted Fucecchio with more elaborate siege engines. Fucecchio at that time was a comparatively fine town. The
place was admirably defended by the Florentine exiles, a large
number of whom were there at the time, and also by the inhabitants of the place itself. Novello harassed them steadily with his
siege engines, but abandoned the siege after great rainstorms came

et solum (est enim palustre) multis locis praepedientibus, mense fere circa illud frustra consumpto obsidionem dissolvit.

75 Per idem tempus Lucenses exulesque florentini legatione in Germaniam missa, cuius principes fuerunt ex utraque civitate amplissimi viri, Corradinum Corradi filium, ad quem regni Siciliae pertinere ferebatur successio, contra Manfredum concitare tentarunt. Neque sane id negotium temere vel contra partium studia susceptum est ab exulibus. Nam post regni invasionem a Manfredo factam, cum iam plane illius fraudes vaframentaque detecta essent, oratores Corradini nomine ad pontificem venerant et erat iam coniunctio quaedam inita adversus Manfredum. Qua fiducia legatio est tunc in Germaniam missa. Principes eius legationis fuerunt Simon Donatus et Bonacursius Adimar Belincionis filius, equites florentini. Hi cum transmissis Alpibus ad ea tandem loca in quibus puer erat pervenissent, opportuna compererunt omnia praeter aetatem: nam et in Manfredum ardens odium apud matrem propinquosque pueri et praecupidos ad ulciscendum animos et potentiae satis. Aetas modo differendum suadebat, quae tenera adhuc et tantis impar negotiis videbatur. Tempus itaque expectare iussi, pleni quidem ingenti spe, sed vacui rebus legati rediere.

76 Proximo subinde anno Florentini qui Lucae erant, clam coactis copiis, nocturno et improviso impetu Signiam occuparunt. Perlatus inde in urbem rumor cives conterruit, veritos ne opportunitatem loci exules nacti maiorem in modum regionem turbarent. Constat autem nullum fere circa urbem locum inferendo bello opportuniorem esse. Itaque auxiliis propere accitis obsidere atque oppugnare Signiam pergunt. Ad eam rem cum machinae, tormenta, vineae ac cetera huiuscemodi enixiori studio pararentur, magnitu-

up and made the marshy soil impassible in many places. He wasted nearly a month on this operation.

Around this same time the Lucchesi and the Florentine exiles 75 sent a diplomatic mission to Germany whose leaders were distinguished citizens from both cities. Their aim was to stir up against Manfred Conradin, the Emperor Conrad's son, to whom the succession to the kingdom of Sicily appeared to belong. The exiles did not take up this business rashly or in violation of their partisan loyalties. In fact, after Manfred's invasion of the Kingdom, when his acts of deceit and cunning had been clearly exposed, ambassadors had been sent in Conradin's name to the pope, and there existed already a kind of entente against Manfred. It was on this understanding that the Lucchese and Florentine mission was sent to Germany. The leaders of the mission were the Florentine knights Simone Donati and Buonaccorso di Belincione de'Adimari. When these men had crossed the Alps and had at length arrived where the boy was, they found all the conditions to be favorable apart from the boy's age. The boy's mother and relatives showed a burning hatred of Manfred and they were longing for power and revenge. Only the boy's age argued for delay. He seemed tender still in years and unequal to great affairs. The legates were told to bide their time and returned home full of hope, but empty of concrete assistance.[44]

The next year the Florentines at Lucca secretly collected their 76 forces and occupied Signa after a surprise attack at night. When 1262 the tale was told in Florence, it terrified the citizens, who were afraid lest the exiles, having acquired a base, would create a great disturbance in the region. As is evident, hardly any place near the city could make a better base of operations for a war. So auxiliary forces were quickly called up and went out to besiege and storm the town. For this purpose they prepared with particular zeal siege engines, catapults, mantlets and similar apparatus of war. Those

dine apparatus conterriti illi ipsi qui occupaverant sponte sua reliquerunt.

77 Post fugam hostium Signiamque receptam Novellus cum iis quas obsidendi causa contraxerat copiis fines Lucensium (iam enim maturescebant segetes) ingressus est. Cum agros infestius vastaret, Lucenses cum exulibus sese obviam obtulerunt, neque multitudine neque viribus pares. Nam Pisani quidem finitimi populariter fere in castra ad Novellum confluxerant, et ipse praeter Germanos mercede[67] conductos optimum quemque e civitatibus delectum adduxerat. Commisso itaque proelio Lucenses exulesque facile superati in fugam vertuntur. Caesi complures, capti etiam frequentes in adversariorum manus pervenerunt et commissa in nonnullos foeda crudelitatis exempla.

78 Post hanc pugnam omnia ferme Lucensium castella in deditionem hostis accepit. Amisso agro, civibus etiam multis, qui et arbiensi et proximo adverso proelio capti fuerant, in potestate hostium constitutis, cum extrema cuncta proponerentur, Lucenses de pace cum victoribus agere coeperunt. Protracta res est in sequentem annum tandemque foedus ictum: ut pulsis exulibus ipsi in societatem foederis reciperentur aequo iure cum aliis civitatibus; utque cives omnes lucenses, qui ubicumque apud hostes captivi forent, gratis remitterentur; agerque et castella vel ea vel superiori aestate adempta redderentur. Has fere conditiones pax habuit. Ceterum transacta res arcane ac celeriter est, nullo penitus exulum gnaro. Itaque mox insperato abire iussi, nec satis temporis ad componendas fortunas concesso, fracta ferme omni spe cum coniugibus et liberis per proximum Apennini iugum Bononiam migravere.

who had occupied the town were terrified by the scale of these preparations and abandoned it of their own accord.

After his enemies' flight and the recovery of Signa, Novello entered Lucchese territory (it was now near harvest time) with the forces he had put together for the siege. While he was furiously laying waste to the fields, the Lucchesi and the Florentine exiles came out to challenge him. The latter were inferior both in numbers and in strength, for the neighboring Pisans poured out practically en masse to join Novello's camp, and he had brought with him, in addition to his German mercenaries, picked forces from the rest of the cities. The battle was joined, and the Lucchesi and the exiles were easily overcome and turned to flight. Great numbers were slaughtered while many others were captured and came into the hands of their adversaries. Against some of them horrible acts of cruelty were committed.

Following the battle, the enemy accepted the surrender of nearly all the Lucchese castles. The Lucchesi had lost their territory; many of their citizens were now in the hands of their adversaries, having been captured either at the Arbia or in the recent battle; and their affairs were all in a desperate state. So they began to negotiate a peace with the victors. The matter was dragged out into the following year, but finally a treaty was made. It provided that the Lucchesi would be received into the treaty alliance on the same footing with the other cities once they had expelled the exiles; that all Lucchese citizens who were anywhere in enemy hands would be released without ransom; and that the Lucchese territory and castles, even those taken the previous summer, would be returned. Such, broadly, were the peace conditions. The matter was settled swiftly and secretly, without the knowledge of the exiles. So presently, without warning, they were ordered to leave, without being allowed enough time to settle their affairs. In a nearly hopeless state they departed with their wives and children for Bologna by the nearest Appennine pass.[45]

77

78

79   Per idem fere tempus Arretinis qui urbem tenebant longo assi-
duoque bello fatigatis, cum adversarii magnis Florentinorum Senensiumque contractis copiis urgere violentius pararent, nec plebs
multitudoque urbana obsidionem latura videretur,[68] praestantes
studio partium cives migrandi consilium assumpserunt. Quo quidem facto diversae factionis homines in eam quoque urbem recepti, ut alias Etruriae civitates, sic illam sub Manfredi nutu postea tenuere.

80   Mutato igitur per Etruriam statu Florentinorum ac ceterarum
civitatum exules recens pulsi magno Bononiae numero (nam cis
Apenninum consistere vix[69] erat) convenerunt. Ibi cum aliquod
tempus non rei solum, verum etiam consilii inopes constitissent,
fortuna divitiarum simul et gloriae materiam obtulit.

81   Mutinensium proxima civitas intestinis seditionibus iactabatur.
Duae erant partes. Utraque armata pellere alteram urbe aut intra
moenia opprimere nitebatur. Neque causae discidii studiaque partium dissimilia nostris; quippe eadem fere tabes cunctam pervase-
rat conflictabatque Italiam. Exules igitur ab ea factione quae idem
sentiebat Mutinam arcessiti, cum impigre auxilium tulissent, magno partibus addito momento adversam factionem urbe pepulerunt. Pulsorum praeda omnis a Mutinensibus illis concessa, ditari
sunt coepti armis et equis splendidioribus comparatis, et numero
undique ad famam excitis pluribus adaucto.

82   Permovit eadem seditio et Regium Lepidum, finitimam urbem.
Pars enim victoribus congruens armis raptis Mutinensium exem-

Around this same time the Aretine Guelfs who were holding 79
on to their city grew tired of the long and unremitting warfare.
When their adversaries, collecting forces from Florence and Siena,
were preparing to set upon them with still greater fury, and when
it became evident that the commoners and the urban masses were
not going to put up with a siege, the leading Guelf partisans
adopted a plan to emigrate. This done, the Ghibellines returned to
this city as well, as they had already to the other cities of Tuscany,
and held it thereafter in the name of Manfred.

With conditions thus changed throughout Tuscany, the exiles 80
recently expelled from Florence and other cities came together in
great numbers in Bologna, as they could hardly maintain a foot-
hold on this side of the Apennines. After they had remained
there for some time, lacking not only resources but even a plan,
fortune offered them the means to acquire riches and glory simultaneously.[46]

The neighboring city of Modena was being rocked by internal 81
strife. There were two parties. Both were armed, and each was trying to expel the other from the city or destroy it within the walls.
The causes of the dissension and partisanship were not dissimilar
to ours; indeed, the same fever had spread everywhere and was
tormenting all of Italy. So the Florentine exiles were summoned to
Modena by the faction that was sympathetic to them.[47] The Florentines' tireless assistance added great force to the party, and the
Ghibellines were expelled from the city. The Modenese gave them
everything plundered from the banished men and the Florentines
now acquired riches in the form of arms and richly caparisoned
horses, and their number was greatly increased by men who joined
them on all sides, eager to share their fame.

The same strife was causing disturbances in the nearby city of 82
Reggio Emilia. The Guelfs there had seized arms and were trying
to expel their adversaries, following Modena's example. But the
Ghibellines were resisting stoutly. Among them was a man as bold

plo pellere adversarios perrexit. Sed resistebant illi audacius. Et erat in his[70] vir procero corpore, nec minus audacia manuque praecellens. Cascam vulgo appellabant. Hic saepe in adversarios delatus, admiranda fortitudinis facinora edebat; multis ab eo occisis contritisque ceteros formido exagitabat. Vocati igitur ab Reginis Etrusci, ut nuper Mutinensibus, ita tunc Reginis suarum partium hominibus auxilium attulere. Pugna in foro atroci commissa, unus Casca plurimum resistebat, et quacumque impetum faceret, suarum virium conscios palantes agebat. Eo denique uno stabat adversa factio, nec foro cedebat. Hunc igitur conspicantes Etrusci delectos e suis robustissimos iuvenes in eum mittunt. Illi agentem per forum cuneos Reginorum, uti praeceptum erat, Cascam invadunt, cumque alios submovisset ac ipse viribus ferox longius a suis pugnaret, conglobati in eum iuvenes latera mucronibus exaugent ac tandem confectum multis vulneribus in medio foro magna occupantem spatia prosternunt. Casca viro immanissimo necato statim adversa factio Regio pellitur. Florentinos et aliarum civitatum exules, ut Mutinensium nuper, ita tunc[71] Reginorum praeda ditavit. Multae nobilium ignobiliumque fortunae illis concessae arma et equos et pecunias abunde suppeditarunt. Dux Etruscorum ad Regium fuisse traditur Foresius Adimar, eques florentinus, iuvenis quidem, sed admodum bello praestans. Ad Mutinam vero quis eorum dux fuerit, memoriae proditum non est. Sunt etiam qui tradunt[72] manu Foresii Cascam procubuisse, cum in medio foro congressi spectantibus suis egregie dimicassent.

83   Et in Gallia quidem huiusmodi fortuna rebus erat. In Etruria vero omnia ferme loca Manfredo parebant; adversa pontifici fa-

and powerful as he was gigantic; his name in the common speech
was Casca. This fellow was frequently deployed against adversaries
and would perform prodigious deeds of courage: after he had
killed or worn down numerous opponents, fear would drive off
the rest. So the Tuscans were summoned by the Reggians and
they brought aid to the Reggian Guelfs as they had to the
Modenese. A bitter battle broke out in the forum, where Casca, all
by himself, put up a stiff resistance. Wherever he struck, he scattered his opponents, who were aware of his strength. Thanks to
this one man, the Ghibellines were kept going, and did not yield
the forum. So the Tuscans looked him over and picked out their
most powerful young men to send against him. Following instructions, they attacked Casca as he was leading a wedge of Reggians
through the forum, and separated him from the rest of his men.
He fought with the strength of a wild animal, but too far from his
men. The Tuscan youths surrounded him and wounded him in
his flanks with their swords, till at last, stricken with many blows,
he fell to the ground, his body measuring a vast area in the middle
of the forum. Once this enormous man was slain, the Ghibellines
were immediately driven from Reggio. The Florentine and other
Tuscan exiles were enriched by plunder taken from the Reggian
Ghibellines, as they had recently been by the Modenese plunder.
The numerous fortunes of nobles and non-nobles alike that were
allotted to them supplied them abundantly with arms, horses and
money. It is reported that the leader of the Tuscan forces at Reggio
was Foresi de' Adimari, a Florentine knight who, though still a
youth, was an outstanding warrior. Who their leader was at
Modena is not recorded. Some reports have it that Casca was cut
down by the hand of Foresi in a brilliant single combat in the middle of the forum, with their troops looking on.[48]

While Guelf affairs were prospering in Gaul,[49] almost all of 83
Tuscany was under Manfred's rule; the anti-papal faction was
dominant everywhere. The pontiff himself, terrified by Manfred's

ctio ubique dominabatur. Ipse autem pontifex Manfredi potentia conterritus tenui admodum spe apud Urbevetanos se receperat. Erat autem pontifex[73] Urbanus quartus, natione Gallicus.[74] Alexandro enim nuper defuncto hic in pontificatu romano successerat. Qui cum occupari pontificalia iura cunctaque in deterius labi cerneret et suo ipse motu et assiduis exulum querelis adhortationibusque impulsus, cum ad comprimendam Manfredi potentiam validiori aliqua vi opus fore arbitraretur, unicum tantis futurum malis remedium, Carolum Ludovici Francorum regis fratrem, virum bello egregium, in Italiam advocare, eique regnum Siciliae, quod a Manfredo occupabatur, iustis ac legitimis titulis concedere statuit. Nulla igitur solemnitate circa id praetermissa, legati ad Carolum profecti electionem regni et advocationem pontificis detulere. Nec defuit oblatis Carolus, sed suscepto deiciendi Manfredi onere magnas equitum copias summa vi parare contendit.

84 Per haec ipsa tempora elatis in expectationem animis et coepta Caroli quorsum evaderent, intuentibus fulgor, quem graeco nomine cometen vocant, praegrandibus ac lucentibus radiis per nonaginta fere dies in caelo emicuit. Multa, ut est hominum mos, et pleraque vana super eo dicta agitataque.[75] Et cecinere vates et varie, pro cuiusque ingenio, spe vel metu animos affecerunt. Enim vero multa subinde secuta veterem eius famam experimento certissimo comprobarunt regna mutare asseverantem. Mutatae enim post illum continuo res et Italiae status omnis renovatus:[76] pontificis mors, Caroli adventus, proelium adversus Manfredum, ipsius[77] Manfredi nex et conversio civitatum brevi subsecuta.

85 Ceterum ipse pontifex, vixdum[78] extinctis cometae ignibus, e vita migravit. Quae res primo formidinem incussit, ne coepta Ca-

power, had retreated to Orvieto, but with slender hope. The pope was Urban IV, a Frenchman.[50] He had succeeded to the Roman pontificate after the recent death of Alexander. He saw his pontifical authority being usurped and conditions deteriorating everywhere, and realized that some stronger force would be needed to curb Manfred's power. So, impelled both by his own free impulse and by the unceasing complaints and exhortations of the exiles, he decided that the only remedy for so many evils would be to summon to Italy Charles,[51] brother of King Louis of France and a famous soldier, and to confer on him by just and and legitimate titles the Kingdom of Sicily that had been usurped by Manfred. No formalities were omitted to this end, and legates were sent out to Charles informing him of his election to the Kingdom and of the papal summons. Charles was equal to the prize being offered him and took on the burden of deposing Manfred, striving with all his might to raise a great force of mounted men.[52]

At this very time, when spirits had been raised in expectation   84
to see how Charles' undertaking would turn out, a shining star,   1264
which the Greeks call a comet, shone in the heavens with enormous, brilliant rays for nearly three months. As is the way of mankind, there was much talk and analysis of the apparition, most of it vain. Seers prophesied, affecting minds variously with hope or fear, in accordance with each man's natural temper. Though indeed, many events that followed hard upon it proved by a most certain test the ancient reputation of comets as changers of kingdoms.[53] For after the comet things changed immediately, and the condition of Italy was entirely renewed. The death of the pope, the advent of Charles, the battle against Manfred and his murder, revolutions in the cities—all these followed the comet within a short period of time.

However that may be, scarcely had the comet's fires gone out   85
when the pope himself died, which raised fears that Charles' plans would be hampered. Yet not only was Urban's death not a hin-

roli impedirentur. At enim non modo non obfuit coeptis Urbani mors, verum etiam illa iuvit. Creatus est enim successor vir, ut ita dixerim, e Caroli sinu. Clementem quartum hunc pontificem vocavere, sed ante pontificatum Guido Fulcodii nuncupatus, e provincia quidem oriundus narbonensi et secularis dudum advocationibus clarus, in regia Francorum fere nutritus, demumque uxore defuncta narbonensis praesul, mox sabinensis episcopus cardinalisque effectus, per omnes dignitatis gradus ad pontificatum ascendit: vir procul dubio egregius ac multarum rerum experientiam callens. Hic ergo simul ac pontificale fastigium suscepit, incredibili favore in Carolum versus accelerare eius adventum ac illi copias amicosque per Italiam parare contendit. Cognita huius voluntate (neque enim minori odio quam Urbanus in Manfredum flagrabat) exequi coepta Carolus properavit. Validis igitur praemissis copiis quae per Alpes ac citeriorem Galliam penetrarent, ipse triginta navibus longis Massilia solvens per varias hostium insidias, qui tyrrhenum mare grandi observabant classe, ad tiberina incolumis ostia pervenit. Susceptus magno honore a populo romano et senatoria dignitate ornatus, adventum copiarum, quas per terram iter facere iusserat, expectabat.

86   Haec ab initio cernentes Florentini per adversam factionem domo eiecti magnam in spem venerant in sua redeundi. Itaque studio et diligentia praeveniendum rati, per legatos ad Clementem missos et operam suam contra Manfredum polliciti sunt et ut eos novo regi commendatos faceret postularunt. Percontanti Clementi de illorum statu haec ferme[79] referuntur: viros esse militares, grandi numero, armis equisque affatim structos; hos clientium magnam item sequi manum; seniorum praeterea ac eorum qui bello gerendo minus apti viderentur magnum numerum superesse; hanc totam multitudinem urbibus Etruriae a Manfredo suisque quod

drance to his undertaking, but it even helped. For the successor who was elected was a man after Charles' own heart. They called this pontiff Clement IV, but before his pontificate he had been known as Guy Foulques.[54] He was originally from the province of Narbonne and had enjoyed a long and distinguished career as a lay lawyer, having practically been raised in the royal court. After his wife's death he became bishop of Narbonne, then cardinal bishop of Sabina, rising through every rank of honor to the pontificate. He was beyond doubt an exceptional man who displayed skill and experience in a wide range of subjects. He had no sooner reached the heights of the papacy than he turned to Charles and with unbelievable partiality strove to hasten his arrival in Italy and to prepare troops and friends for him here. When he had understood Clement's intentions (and Clement's hatred of Manfred was no less burning than Urban's), Charles hastened to carry out his plans. He sent on ahead powerful forces by way of the Alps and Cisalpine Gaul, while he himself left Marseilles with thirty galleys. Despite various stratagems of the enemy, who were patrolling the Tyrrhenian Sea with a large fleet, he arrived safe at Ostia. Having been received with great honor by the Roman people and decorated with the rank of senator, he awaited the arrival of the troops he had ordered to make the journey by land.[55]

The Florentine Guelfs in exile watched these developments 86 from the beginning and began to nourish great hopes of returning to their own land. Believing their zeal and earnestness might precipitate matters, they sent legates to Clement promising their help against Manfred and asking to be recommended to the new king. In response to Clement's inquiries about them, they told him (more or less) that they were a large company of military men, well equipped and mounted; that they also had a large force of retainers in train as well as a large number of older people and other unwarlike folk; that this whole multitude, because it was Guelf, had been expelled from the Tuscan cities by Manfred and his

diversa sectaretur expulsam, in exilio ipso nomen et gloriam sibi per virtutem armaque peperisse; iam vero in Gallia horum opera non stetisse solum romanae sedis fautores, verum etiam depulsis adversariis superiores esse. Pontifex excellentiam virorum admiratus magnumque eius belli momentum in eorum fiducia reponens, oblationem grato se recipere animo et sibi commendationem curae fore respondit. Cohortatus deinde ad prosecutionem virtutis, quo eos sibi partibusque suis magis coniungeret, insigne suae gentis proprium illis perpetuo ferendum donavit. Ea est imago rubentis aquilae caeruleum draconem unguibus prementis. Id tunc insigne de pontifice susceptum exules habuerunt in eo bello hodieque habent duces partium optimarum, collegio postquam redierunt publice apud urbem instituto. Tunc igitur et sua ipsi sponte et pontificis hortatu se egregie praeparantes Guidonem cui Guerra cognomentum fuit, virum consilio simul manuque praestantem, sibi ducem praefecerunt ac ubi primum regis copias appropinquare cognitum, obviam illis in agro mantuano profecti Gallos in admirationem decoris sui converterunt. Ornati siquidem armis equisque[80] et ceteris quibus militares insigniuntur viri, etiam inter Gallos longe conspicui erant.

87　　Suscepti igitur benigne a praefectis regiis et una iter facere rogati, quod Etruria validis adversariorum praesidiis tenebatur et simul quod in ea implicari bello haudquaquam Galli volebant, per Flaminiam atque Umbriam Romam petiere. Gratissimus fuit Carolo Etruscorum adventus, utpote qui primi ex Italicis sese illi con-

Ghibelline followers; that even in exile they had won reputation and glory through courageous feats of arms; that, thanks to their help, the supporters of the Roman See in northern Italy were now not only holding on, but were even in the ascendant, having expelled their adversaries. The pope admired the outstanding qualities of these men, and reckoning their loyalty to be of great military importance, he accepted their offer gratefully and said he would personally undertake to recommend them. He then exhorted them to continue in the path of virtue and, to attach them to himself and his party more closely, gave them a standard displaying the arms of his own family for them to bear in perpetuity. The device represented a red eagle holding a blue dragon in its claws. The exiles carried the standard they received from the pope in that war, and today it is carried by the leaders of the Guelf Party, a college founded as public institution in Florence after the return of the exiles.[56] So both of their own accord and at the urging of the pontiff, they began to prepare themselves admirably for war, choosing as their commander Guido Guerra, a man outstanding both for his physical strength and his good judgment. And as soon as it was learned that the king's troops were approaching, the Tuscans set out to meet them in Mantuan territory. Their fine appearance attracted the attention of the French, beautifully equipped as they were with arms and horses and all the other gear that bestows distinction on military men. Even among the French they were a striking sight.[57]

So they were kindly received by the king's commanders and 87 asked to join their march. Since Tuscany was being defended by strong enemy forces, and since they had no intention of involving themselves in a war there, they headed for Rome via the Flaminian Way and Umbria. Charles was exceedingly pleased by the arrival of the Tuscans, as they were the first Italians to join him. Added to this was the weighty recommendation of the pope as well as the testimonials to their loyalty and prowess given by the commanders

iunxerant, et accedebat pontificis commendatio gravis et ducum qui cum illis iter fecerant fidei simul virtutisque testimonium. Itaque benigne eos allocutus rex amplissimis verbis gratias egit, quod suos per ignota loca et impacatas regiones iter facientes egregia virtute industriaque adiuverint; enim vero magna ab se praemia expectare eos debere, modo felicitas adsit, quam pietas et iustitia et profecto vires suae amicorumque certissimam pollicentur; se quidem ita animatum domo venisse, ut nomine dumtaxat regio contentus esse velit; ceterum opes ac victoriae praemia iis qui secum militaverint partiturum.

88 His atque huiusmodi verbis cum tandem finem rex fecisset, Guido, quem sibi praefecisse Etruscos diximus, in hunc modum locutus est. "Etsi nostrum erat, o rex, tibi potius gratias agere quam te nobis, tamen et humanitatem tuam libenter agnovimus et eam cum fortitudine ac ceterarum virtutum tuarum cumulo adiunctam esse gaudemus. Nos quidem saevitia Manfredi patriis pulsi sedibus, non quanta ardor est[81] exhibere in medium possumus; et haec ipsa quae restant corpora et lacertos praestare magis, cum tempus poscet, quam nunc intempestive ostentare iuvabit. Tibi autem gratias agere et habere nos convenit, quod vagis errantibusque tamquam salutare sidus nobis caelitus affulgens viam ac spem remeandi domum, quam primo non cernebamus, aperuisti. Tua enim summa virtus stragem hostium nostrorum ac per eorum ruinam reditum nobis in patriam certissimum pollicetur. Pro te igitur, nedum quod paucorum dierum iter duces tuos prosecuti qualemcumque operam impendimus, sed ne cum in vulnera quidem ac ferrum ruerimus, satisfecisse tibi ac tuis in nos meritis aestimabimus.

89 "Atqui duae, uti nos putamus, res ad fidem belli plurimum valent: commune hostis odium et expetita victoriae praemia utrinque accommoda. Haec duo Florentinis ceterisque Tuscis qui tua signa in hoc bello secuturi sunt convenire videmus. Neque enim fuit nec esse debuit adversus ullum unquam maius et arden-

who had accompanied them on the march. So the king addressed them warmly, thanking them in most liberal terms: that by travelling through unknown places and troubled regions they were supporting their friends with extraordinary courage and zeal; that they could expect great rewards from him if things turned out happily, as promised most certainly to be the case given their piety and justice and indeed their strength and that of their friends. For himself, he was disposed to return home[58] and so would be content with the mere title of king, but riches and the prizes of victory would be allotted to all who fought alongside him.[59]

When the king had at length finished a speech along these 88 lines, Guido, the Tuscan commander, spoke after this manner: "Although, O King, we ought rather to be giving you thanks than receiving it, we nevertheless gladly acknowledge your kindness and rejoice that it is joined to courage and a host of other virtues. It is impossible for us, whom Manfred's rage has expelled from our ancestral estates, to express publicly the extent of our commitment, and it will be better to reveal it when the time is ripe, with the bodies and sinews that remain to us, rather than boast of it unseasonably now. Yet it is appropriate for us to be thankful and to give you thanks because, like the star of salvation shining on us from the heavens, you have opened up a way and a hope of returning home which we had not glimpsed before on our uncertain wanderings. For your high courage promises the slaughter of our enemies, and through their ruin, our own most certain return to our country. We believe that we shall have repaid you what we owe, not when we have performed a few day's indifferent service following your commanders on their march, but when we shall have risked wounds and cold steel on your behalf.

"Two things, we believe, greatly strengthen loyalty in time of 89 war: a common hatred of the enemy, and an expectation that the rewards of victory shall be appropriate to both sides. We see these two conditions coming together in the case of the Florentines and

tius odium quam nobis est in Manfredum: quippe non solum has recentes quas nuper ab eo perpessi sumus clades, sed damnatam invisamque stirpem et patris avique et proavi iniurias in filio persequimur. Haec enim scelesta nefandaque familia, ab extrema Germanorum barbarie exurgens, fortunatos tranquillosque per id tempus Etruriae populos ad vulnera et sanguinem ac vastitatem urbium perpulit; nec ullas iam multos annos calamitates vidimus quarum hinc non fuerit semen et causa. Verum haec communia mala et ab utraque factione, si modo non funditus desipiant, pariter deploranda. Illud proprium nostrarum partium, quod numquam pontifices romanos haec familia persecuta est, quin nobis quoque, qui eadem sectabamur, fuerint ab eisdem persecutoribus clades inflictae. Federicus huius proavus, qui Svevorum primus nomen romani principis falso indutus est, quam nefaria molitus sit non ignorare te credimus. Sensit Italia non romanum imperatorem, quem ille falso mentiebatur, sed novum Hannibalem adventasse. Qui cum Mediolanum, urbem inclitam ac maximum romani imperii ornamentum, hostis et barbarus evertisset, sparsit per Etruriam venenata malorum semina, cum civili discidio per singulas urbes facto malos foveret, bonos persequeretur. Secutus est huius acerbitatem Herricus filius, qui ad scelus paternum summam ipse ingratitudinem addidit, post regni munus liberalissimum persecutor acerrimus factus. Successit in haereditatem scelerum alter Federicus, huius Manfredi pater. Is quid adversus pontifices molitus sit, memorare quid attinet? Narrant enim et narrabunt, quamdiu memoria hominum manebit, concilia adversus illius vesaniam Lugduni celebrata, cum pontifex Italia profugus

other Tuscans who are going to follow your banners in this war. Our hatred of Manfred is fiercer than any that has ever been, or ever should be, against anyone. Indeed we are avenging not only the recent defeats we have suffered at his hands, we are avenging in the son the injuries done us by his father, grandfather, and great-grandfather; we are persecuting his whole accursed and hateful stock. This wicked and impious family, sprung from the barbarous depths of Germany, has driven the once happy and peaceful peoples of Tuscany to blows, to bloodshed and to the devastation of their cities, nor have we seen for many a year any calamities that have not had their seed and cause in this source. But these are common evils, to be deplored equally by both sides, if they are not utter fools. Our party has the special distinction of having had defeat inflicted on us, as well, whenever this family was persecuting the Roman pontiffs whose lead we follow. We believe you are well aware of the abominable plots laid by Frederick, Manfred's great-grandfather, who was the first of the Hohenstaufen to assume falsely the name 'Emperor of the Romans.'[60] Italy learned that it was not a new Roman emperor who had come to her, as he falsely claimed, but a new Hannibal. Like the enemy and barbarian he was, he destroyed Milan, a famous city and the greatest ornament of the Roman empire, then spread poisonous seeds of evil throughout Tuscany, fostering the wicked, persecuting the good, and creating civil discord in every city. His cruelty was imitated by his son Henry, who added the height of ingratitude to his father's wickedness, becoming the most bitter persecutor of the very King-dom that had been given him as the most generous of gifts. A second Frederick, the father of Manfred, then succeeded to this patrimony of wickedness. Is there any point in recalling his plots against the popes? Stories are told, and shall be told as long as human memory lasts, how councils were held at Lyon in opposition to his raving fury;[61] how the pontiff, in flight from Italy, was no

vix ultra flumen Rhodani tutum ad damnandam huius perfidiam locum invenerit.

90 "Haec tibi nota sunt, rex, et cum tuae domus laude coniuncta. Sed quid adversus nostrarum partium homines putas illam saevitiam per haec ipsa tempora edidisse, cum quanto magis irritaretur, tanto adversus pontificis fautores illius rabies atrocius insaeviret? Pulsi tunc urbibus nostri[82] exularunt; castellis et arcibus quibus se receperant obsessi sunt; qui vel fortuna aliqua belli vel longa obsidione in eius manum pervenerunt, barbaram illius crudelitatem experti per varia et inaudita supplicia vitam amisere. Sunt multi in hoc coetu quem vides, quorum ille parentes aut fratres aut agnatos necarit, qui nunc arma tecum ferentes eadem illa in filio supplicia deposcunt.

91 "Affulserat tandem post huius mortem parumper fortuna nobis. Restitutos in patriam Manfredus iterum dissipavit. Itaque illud satis certum exploratumque est, nos numquam quietem habituros, nisi haec familia funditus deleatur. Quare et veteri odio et praesenti spe quietis ita nos ardere in Manfredum puta, ut omnis[83] acceleratio ad eius perniciem segnis ac tarda nobis videatur.

92 "Solet vero nonnumquam mentes hominum sollicitas reddere praemiorum suspicio, quotiens is qui plus potest, sine gravi iactura exsolvere promissa non valet. Absunt haec a desiderio praemiorum nostrorum. Nos ea sequimur praemia, quae nihil commoditati, nihil potentiae tuae detractura sint, sed vim ac robur allatura. Non enim agri neque urbes hostium bello captae, sed reditus in patriam nobis praemium sit. Sic autem statuimus: et tua in regno potentia nos in Etruria servabit et ipse velut murum habebis ad vim, si qua unquam regno tuo immineat, ab ea parte propulsandam. Summa

sooner safely across the Rhone than he found an occasion to condemn Frederick's perfidy.

"These things are known to you, O King, connected as they are 90 with the glory of your house. But surely it was Frederick II who gave birth to this ferocity against our party at the present time, this madness that rages the more terribly against the pope's supporters the more it is provoked? Expelled from their cities, our partisans lived in exile; the castles and citadels that received them were besieged; those who fell into his hands after long sieges or by the fortune of war experienced his barbaric cruelty and died after suffering strange and varied forms of torture. There are many in this band before you whose parents, brothers or relations he put to death, and many who now bear arms alongside you are demanding those same tortures be visited on the son.

"Finally, after Frederick's death, fortune shone on us for a little 91 while. But Manfred has once again scattered those who had been restored to their country. So this truth is well established and confirmed by experience: that we shall never have peace until this family is entirely blotted out. Believe, then, that our ancient hatred and our present hope of peace have kindled in us such passionate zeal against Manfred that, however quickly the man is hastened to his destruction, it will seem to us sluggish and dilatory.

"Men tend sometimes to become anxious about the possibility 92 of reward whenever [they see that] powerful persons are unable to redeem their promises without grave loss to themselves. But our desire for prizes suffers from no such anxiety. We are in pursuit of prizes that will detract nothing from your prerogative or power, but will add to your force and strength. Let our reward be not territory or cities captured from the enemy in war, but restoration to our country—for thus we have decided. Your power in the Kingdom will keep us safe in Tuscany, and you yourself will have a kind of wall to repel attacks from that direction, should any ever threaten your kingdom. So be persuaded that these Tuscan men

igitur erga te fide hos fore homines persuade, quos et commune hostis[84] odium et communis utilitas tibi coniungit. Illud vero tamquam summam addidisse volumus, ut tanti finito bello nos feceris, quantum in ipso bello promereri conspexeris. Devotos certe et addictos tibi utcumque habebis."

93 Haec oratio magis acceptos regi exules fecit ac maiori fiducia in familiaritatem admisit. Paratis omnibus quae ad bellum opportuna fuerunt, cum his copiis quas e Gallia duxerat, item cum tuscis exulibus ac aliis latini nominis qui aut spe praemiorum aut partium studio sequebantur, fines regni secus Casinum ingreditur, custodia aditus, quo facile arceri ab ingressu poterat, ignavia hostium neglecta. Germanum deinde oppidum expugnare aggressus, magna virtute militum id cepit. Eo in loco Tuscorum virtus primum conspicua fuit: suo namque conatu, per fossas et aggerem evadentes, imprimis causa oppidi capiendi fuere.

94 Expugnatione huius oppidi conterritis ceteris finitimae quaedam urbes ad victorem defecerunt. At Manfredus contractis undique copiis statuit in Samnio hosti occurrere. Quod postquam intellexit Carolus, dimicandi cupidus Samnium petit. Nec ulla inde mora: simul atque in conspectum venit, in aciem primus eduxit. Nec detrectavit pugnam Manfredus, sed eductis et ipse in aciem suis fortunae se obtulit.

95 Antequam pugnari coeptum esset, speculanti hostium agmina Manfredo una seorsum acies prospecta est equis et armis egregie structa. Erat huic suus dux suumque vexillum; signa pontificis haud sibi iam incognita discernebat. Signifer ea die fuisse traditur

have the utmost loyalty to you, joined to you as they are by common interests and a common hatred of the enemy. Let me add this by way of summing up: when the war is over, reward us in proportion to the merit we have won in that war, as you see it. In any case you will find us pledged devotedly to your service."

This oration made the exiles more welcome to the king, and he admitted them with greater confidence to his friendship. Everything needed for war was now ready. With the troops he had brought from France and with the Tuscan exiles and others of the Latin name who were following him from partisanship or hope of reward, he entered the borders of the Kingdom near Monte Cassino. This promontory is the watchtower guarding the gateway to the Kingdom; it could easily have blocked his entry had it not been neglected through the lethargy of the enemy. He proceeded to storm the town of San Germano[62] which he took, thanks to the great courage of his troops. It was there that the courage of the Tuscans was first conspicuous, for it was through their efforts that the moats and ramparts were crossed. They were thus a primary reason for the town's capture.[63]

The capture of the town terrified the rest of the region, and certain towns on the border defected to the victor. But Manfred, having assembled his forces, decided to meet the enemy in the Sannio.[64] When Charles learned of this he left for the Sannio, spoiling for a fight. As soon as he came in sight of the enemy he immediately deployed his troops in battle array. Nor did Manfred evade the fight; he, too, drew up his forces in combat order and entrusted his fortunes to battle.

Before the fighting began, Manfred, gazing out over the ranks of his enemies, saw one company in particular that stood out for the excellence of its horses and equipment. It had its own commander and its own standard: the pontifical standard Manfred knew so well. It is said that the standard-bearer that day was Corrado da Montemagno, a Pistoian knight, a man unquestion-

93

94

95

Corradus Magnimontanus eques pistoriensis, vir procul dubio pace belloque egregius; dux autem Guido cognomento Guerra, celsi vir animi ac prope singularis. Perquirenti ergo a suis quorumnam virorum id agmen esset, Florentinorum Tuscorumque reliquorum qui diversa sectentur esse respondent. "Enim vero, ubi sunt," inquit, "alterius factionis homines ex eadem Etruria in quos ego tanta beneficia dudum contuli?" Cum adesse negarentur, permotus ingratitudine simul ac ignavia hominum, "Illa," inquit, "acies," tuscos exules ostentans, "nisi victrix hodie esse non potest. Nam, si ipse vicero, illos quam adversarios eorum mihi coniunctos malim." Ad suos inde reversus signum proelio tuba dari iussit.

96   Concursum est acriter ab utraque parte pugnaque diu anceps fuit, Germanis pro Manfredo, Gallis Tuscisque pro Carolo enixe dimicantibus. Nec milites solum, verum etiam reges ipsi comminus pugnantes plurima eo die discrimina pro victoria subiere.[85] Post longum certamen Caroli fortuna et militum virtus superavit, profligatisque Germanis Manfredus pugnans occiditur. Hanc pugnam non longe a Benevento commissam constat, quinto ferme anno postquam apud Arbiam pugnatum fuerat. Praeter magnam caedem multi nobiles ignobilesque captivi in victoris manum devenere. Inter quos Iordanus, qui bello etrusco dux fuerat et Petrus Ubertus eques florentinus, qui ambo in Provinciam a Carolo missi longo carcere vitam finiere. Reliqua Caroli expeditio redigendis urbibus regni in potestatem fuit, quas circumferendo bello, nullo iam obsistente brevi perdomuit.

97   Dum florentini exules Carolum secuti circa hoc tempus militiae terunt, Novellus ac ceteri diversae factionis principes qui Florentiam tenebant, Caroli victoria maiorem in modum conterriti iamque adversariorum potentiam formidantes, contrahere sese ac de

ably outstanding in peace and war. The commander was Guido Guerra, a remarkable man of lofty spirit. When Manfred inquired of his companions what this company was, they replied that it contained the Florentine and other Tuscan Guelfs. "Well, then," said Manfred, "where are the Tuscan Ghibellines whom I have helped so much for so long?" When told they were not present, he was angered by their ingratitude and sloth. "That company," said he, pointing to the Tuscan exiles, "cannot but triumph today, since if I win I shall prefer to have them on my side rather than their adversaries." Turning then to his troops, he ordered the trumpeter to give the signal for battle.[65]

There was bitter fighting on both sides and for a long time the outcome was in doubt, with the Germans fighting strenuously for Manfred, the French and the Tuscans for Charles. Not only the soldiers but even the kings themselves fought hand to hand, undergoing much peril that day in the cause of victory. After a long struggle Charles' good fortune and the courage of his troops won out. The Germans were put to flight and Manfred fell in combat. This battle was joined, as is known, not far from Benevento in roughly the fifth year after the battle of the Arbia.[66] Aside from the great slaughter, many captives, noble and non-noble, came into the hands of the victors. Among them was Giordano, who had been the commander in the Tuscan war, and Piero degli Uberti, a Florentine knight. Charles sent both of them to Provence, where they died after many years in prison. The rest of Charles' expedition was devoted to bringing the cities of the Kingdom under his control. Having established a military presence, he subdued them in a short time without resistance.[67]

While the Florentine exiles were spending their time to this purpose in military service with Charles, Novello and the other Ghibelline leaders who controlled Florence were terrified by Charles' victory. Being now fearful of their adversaries' power, they began to restrain themselves and their normally fiery partisanship

96

1265

97

solito partium ardore multum in dies remittere coeperunt, et simul exulum quidam, qui per agros ac propinqua degebant[86] loca, in spem erecti, convenire in unum ac novis rebus animum intendere. Plebs sollicita et propter crebra tributorum onera dominantibus infensa motum aliquem rerum affectabat. Liberae iam multitudinis voces praesentia incusantis vulgo iactabantur.

98   Quae cum in dies augescerent, placuit Novello ceterisque eius factionis principibus gliscentem populi motum consilio praevenire, ac sub specie pacis concordiaeque civilis imminentibus malis iam inde[87] occurrere. Re igitur ad populum delata conformandum civitatis statum et homines diversae factionis, qui nullius mali suspecti in urbe remanserant, in partem rei publicae recipiendos censent. Ita triginta sex viris ex utraque factione delectis negotium datur, ut quae pro optimo civitatis statu agenda forent, ea statuere providereque curarent. Insuper quo magis aequitas appareret,[88] potestas atque iurisdictio in urbe ad duos simul praesides, viros religiosae militiae, Catalanum et Lodoringum, defertur, quorum alter Novello suisque, alter diversis partibus haud dubius habebatur fautor. His Florentiam accitis potestas iurisdictioque populi nomine commissa est, et una cum triginta sex viris (quos supra delectos ostendimus) deposito partium studio communi tranquillitati studere sunt iussi.

99   Crebrae ab his consultationes habitae et quaedam non inutiliter constituta, quorum illud praecipuum, ut artium quibusdam honestioribus collegia essent, utque vexilla signaque haberent, ac novi quotiens quid in urbe oriretur, populares cuiusque collegii in unum concurrerent. Ea res quamquam parva primo visa, tamen

cooled day by day. Meanwhile, certain of the exiles who dwelt in the countryside and in nearby places became hopeful and began to meet together to plan a coup. The commons, anxious and hostile to their rulers owing to heavy taxation, were showing signs of restlessness. Free voices among the populace were now openly ventilating their criticisms.

As such behavior was increasing daily, Novello and the other 98 Ghibelline leaders decided to head off the burgeoning popular unrest by holding a meeting, and to put a stop to the threatening evils with a show of peace and civic concord. So the matter was 1266 laid before the people, and it was decided that the city should be harmonized and that those Guelfs who had remained in the city and were above suspicion should be restored to membership in the commune. The job was given to thirty-six men chosen from both factions whose remit was to oversee and decide what should be done to ensure the optimal condition of the city. Moreover, to create a greater appearance of fairness, power and jurisdiction in the city were handed over to two chief legal officers to serve simultaneously, Catalano and Lodoringo, who were members of religious orders. One of them was regarded as a reliable supporter of Novello and his party, the other of the opposition party. The two were summoned to Florence and power and jurisdiction was entrusted to them in the name of the people. Together with the Thirty-Six, whose election we described above, they were bidden to put aside partisan feeling and strive for the common tranquillity.[68]

These men held frequent consultations and established some 99 useful customs. Of these the most important was that certain of the more honorable guilds should form clubs with standards and devices, and that popolani belonging to each club should rally quickly whenever some attempt at a coup arose in the city.[69] This practice, although it seems a small thing at first sight, nevertheless

populum a dominantibus ad libertatem traducebat, arma capere et ad suum quemque locum convenire iubens.

100   Itaque, haec ubi deprehensa sunt, nobilitatem urere coeperunt, nec deerant iam qui aperta murmura suspicionesque iactarent. Accessit insuper illud, quod stipendia equitum publice a Novello petita non ita, ut mos erat, statim promerentur. Quibus rebus maiorem in suspicionem adductus principes familiarum nobilium quae suarum partium erant, ne sub umbra pacis maiora quaedam se adversus moliri paterentur, commonefacere coepit. Ipse auxilia amicorum propere arcessivit; Germanos paratos armatosque circa se esse iussit. Ex his coorta seditione, nobilitas iam pridem infensa prior arma corripere ac pulsis triginta sex viris rem publicam in suam potestatem redigere statuit.

101   Initium motus a Lambertis factus.[89] Hi enim e proximis aedibus cum armatorum manu egressi in forum novum (ibi namque triginta sex viri tractandis rebus conveniebant) primi impetum fecerunt. Eorum clamore dissipato collegio, cum alius alio perfugisset, civitas repente in armis fuit. Plebs quidem ac multitudo omnis urbana ad Trinitatis convenit; Novellus autem cum omni fere nobilitate suae factionis ac Germanorum equitatu auxiliaribusque amicorum ad Martis aedem. Ibi cum aliquanto constitisset plebemque ad Trinitatis esse audiret, profectus inde recto itinere adversus populum aciem direxit. Nec plebs quidem detrectavit certamen, sed obviam impigre se obtulit. Verum multitudo lapidum, quae instar grandinis e turribus aedibusque pluebat, coeptam inhi-

helped lead the People out of lordship into liberty, as it encouraged them to take up arms and meet in prearranged places.

Hence when the nobles found out what was going on, they 100 were incensed, and some already were murmuring openly and ventilating their suspicions. Furthermore, the knights' salaries that Novello was requesting from public sources were not being paid in a timely fashion, as had been the practice. This circumstance increased his suspicions, and he began to warn the leaders of the Ghibelline noble families that they should not tolerate conspiracies against themselves under the cover of peace. He himself hastily summoned his friends' auxiliaries and ordered the Germans to attend him, armed and ready. As a result of these actions an uprising began, and the nobility, which had for some time been acting in an aggressive manner, were the first to seize arms. They expelled the Thirty-Six and decided to restore the commonwealth to their control.

The coup attempt began with a rising of the Lamberti. They 101 left their dwellings nearby with a force of armed men and struck the first blow in the Mercato Nuovo (that being where the Thirty-Six met to conduct business). That body was scattered by the uproar they caused, and after they had taken refuge one from the other, the city suddenly sprang to arms. The commons and the whole urban populace met in the church of San Trínita, while Novello, with nearly all the Ghibelline nobility, the German knights, and his friends' auxiliaries, met at the Baptistery.[70] After waiting there for some time, Novello learned that the commoners were at San Trínita. He made his way straight to the church, drawing up his troops in formation against the People. The commons for its part did not shrink from combat, going out smartly to meet him. But the mass of stones that rained down like hail from the towers stopped the incipient battle. Novello was shaken by the peril and recalled his forces, withdrawing to the Baptistery by the same route he had come. There, having considered the

buit pugnam. Eo namque periculo commotus, suos Novellus revocavit ac per eandem qua venerat viam ad Martis aedem reduxit. Ibi cum singula reputaret, minime sibi tutum arbitratus est irritata ac inimica multitudine, nonnullis etiam nobilium abalienatis intra eadem moenia noctem operiri. Itaque inde rursus movens signa, ad eas aedes in quibus Catalanus et Lodoringus erant profectus claves portarum, quoad egrederetur urbe, postulavit. Praesides e fenestris clamitantes hortabantur eum urbe nequaquam excedere ac se motum illum populi sedaturos promittebant. Verum tanta suspicio invaserat animum ut cuncta ad suam suorumque perniciem interpretaretur. Clavium igitur potestas ubi facta est, praeconem alta voce percontari iussit, an Germani omnes adessent, cumque responsum esset adesse, rursus an auxiliares omnes; cumque id quoque responsum fuisset, signiferum incedere iussit. Ita profectus ab aedibus praesidum pone theatrum vetus et Scheradii templum ad portam bovariam, qua primum Arnus influebat urbem, cum omni suorum multitudine ac pleraque nobilitate suae factionis egreditur. Mox laevum tenens iter circumdata urbe in viam pratensem descendit, nec quicquam commoratus eadem die Pratum se contulit.

102 Ibi sublato iam metu errorem suum recognoscens iamque consilium damnans, quod ipse suique magnis praesidiis suffulti urbem nullo pellente reliquissent, sera paenitentia, si qua posset, emendare aggressus est. Quare postridie[90] omnibus copiis ad urbem revertitur. Hesterno tumultu concussa civitate portae adhuc clausae erant. Cives quibus id muneris iniunctum desuper excubabant. Qui cum adventum Novelli suorumque ad populum detulissent, multitudo statim armata ad eam portam cucurrit. Ab his repulsus Novellus, cum neque vi neque precibus regredi in urbem posset, frustra aliquot horis circa moenia consumptis Pratum copias reduxit. At populus iam sui iuris gubernationem rei publicae haud

whole situation carefully, he decided it was extremely unsafe to spend the night within the walls with an excited and hostile populace and with some of the nobility alienated from him as well. So bringing forward the standards once again he set out for the buildings where Catalano and Lodoringo were and demanded the keys to the gates so that he could leave the city. The rectors, shouting from the windows, urged him not to leave the city, and promised that they would quell the popular uprising. But Novello had grown so suspicious that he interpreted everything they said as aimed at the destruction of himself and his followers. So when he got control of the keys, he bade the herald cry in a loud voice, "Are the Germans here?" And when they replied that they were, again he cried, "Are all the auxiliaries here?" When they too answered yes, he ordered the standardbearer to advance. So they left the Palace of the Podestà, went behind the old theater and the church of San Piero Scheraggio to the Porta dei Buoi where the Arno first flows into the city, and exited with all his forces and most of the Ghibelline nobles. Then, turning left, he marched round the city and came down into the Via Pratese. Without delay he decamped that same day for Prato.

Once there, his fears abated and he recognized his mistake. 102 Now he cursed his decision to leave the city with his forces before anyone had ejected him and when he still had a sizeable guard to support him. Repenting too late, he set out to correct his error if possible. So the following day he returned to the city with all his forces. The previous day's uproar had shaken the city and the gates were still shut. The citizens in charge of this duty were keeping watch from above, and when they reported the arrival of Novello and his men to the People, the multitude immediately armed itself and ran to the gate. Novello, thus checked, could gain reentry into the city by neither force nor entreaty, and after wasting a few vain hours near the walls, he marched his troops back to Prato.[71] But the People, having now in no uncertain terms taken

ambigue nactus, civitatem in antiquum popularem morem stabilire constituit. Eius rei gratia de duodecim viris creandis loco veterum Antianorum tunc primum institutum est et opportuna consilia ad res graviores decernendas constituta. Nec duo posthac praesides, quasi divisa[91] rei publicae cura, sed unus dumtaxat potestatem dictionemque iuris populi nomine exequebatur.

103 Firmato iam rei publicae statu et in antiquum popularem modum restituto, quod nobilitas ferme tota aberat, maximum profecto civitatis ornamentum, ad decorandam illustrandamque civitatem revocare omnis exules et in sua quemque restituere placuit. Id ad tranquillitatem quoque pertinere visum, ne forte exclusi per vim aliquid molirentur. Lege itaque ad populum lata, omnibus civibus qui vel dudum post arbiensis pugnae casum vel nuper cum Novello abscesserant, remeandi in urbem est potestas permissa.

104 Redierunt hi qui Carolum secuti fuerant sexto postquam exulaverant anno, magna fortium virorum manus ac multis bellis exercitata, plaudente admodum populo et equos armaque[92] ac cetera militaria in iuventute reduce quasi robur quoddam rei publicae intuente. Cupiens autem populus discordias inimicitiasque nobilitatis, si qua posset, omnino sedare (sic enim non praesenti modo, sed futuro etiam tempore putavit tranquillae civitati esse licere) crebra providit matrimonia inter factionum principes ad vinciendam necessitudinem contrahi. Itaque et Novello comiti Foresius Adimar gener est datus et Donati cum Ubertis affinitate coniuncti. Multae praeterea in ceteras familias necessitudines inductae, quo discordiae illarum in perpetuum sopirentur.

over the governance of the commonwealth in their own right, decided to order the city government after the old popular fashion.
With this end in view, they established then for the first time, in
place of the old college of Anziani, a board of Twelve Men,[72] and
set up councils charged with deciding weightier matters. After this
time, instead of two legal officers dividing responsibility for the
commonwealth between them, only one podestà exercised power
and jurisdiction in the name of the People.

The condition of the commonwealth was now stabilized and   103
the old popular ways restored. Since nearly all the nobility were
gone—who, surely, are a city's greatest ornament—it was decided,
in order to bring honor and fame to the city, to recall all the exiles
and restore each one to his place. The decision also had regard to
public order in that those excluded might organize violent conspiracies. The law was passed in the presence of the People,[73] and permission was granted to all citizens who had left some time ago after the disaster at the Arbia, or more recently with Novello, to
return to the city.

Those who followed Charles returned in the sixth year after   104
their exile. They were a great band of powerful men, hardened in   1266
numerous wars. The People cheered enthusiastically when they
caught sight the horses and arms and other military gear of the
youths who had returned, regarding them as a bulwark of the
commonwealth. But the People, taking thought not only for the
present but for the future tranquillity of the city, wanted to put to
rest entirely, if possible, the quarrels and enmities of the nobility.
So they arranged numerous marriages between the leaders of the
factions with a view to linking them in bonds of mutual obliga-
tion. Thus Foresi de'Adimari became the son-in-law of Count
Guido Novello; the Donati intermarried with the Uberti; and
many further bonds of this nature were sanctioned between the
other families so as permanently to put to rest their quarrels.

105   Id autem quo magis faceret populus, eo inductus est quod olim
per nuptiarum repulsam initia fuerant malorum in civitate coorta.
Licet enim antea quoque studia partium ob favorem, ut supra docuimus, imperatorum pontificumque et divisiones civium inde iam
coeperant, tamen addidit his impetum quendam et quasi procellam nuptiarum infausta repudiatio. Id autem (ut pro notitia rerum
superiora quaedam repetamus) tale aliquid fuisse traditur.

106   Bondelmontes fuit eques florentinus per eam tempestatem, ut
videtur, in primis splendidus. Huic inimicitiae graviores fuere cum
Ottone Arrigi filio Fifanti, e familia item nobili. Otto validis propinquitatibus subnixus, praecipue Ubertorum Lambertorumque,
potentissimarum per id tempus familiarum, iuvabatur; Bondel-
monti vero et ipsi per se valido quidam insuper potentium favebant. Cum has inimicitias longius demum progressuras palam esset, insurgentibus bonis viris pax tandem recipitur. Quin etiam
quo stabilior esset, affinitate nuptiisque firmatur, sponsa Bon-
delmonti receptaque nepte Ottonis ex sorore. Res una cum pace
vulgata fuerat et iam pro confecta opinione omnium habebatur;
diesque dicta erat ad nuptiarum solemnia apparatusque ad eam
rem propalam facti.

107   Enim vero hanc affinitatem coniunctionemque fautores quidam
iuvenis nequaquam probabant. Itaque per eos ipsos dies matrona
quaedam e Donatorum aedibus, cum forte domesticorum sermone
affinitatem carpentium ea cognovisset, iuvenem familiarius com-
pellatum obiurgare coepit, quod longe nobilis imparem sibi genere
formaque uxorem accepisset inconsulte nimium atque investigato.

The People were led to this course of action the more readily as   105
it had been a rejected marriage that, once upon a time, had first
given rise to the city's sufferings. Although, owing to prejudices in
favor of emperors and popes, partisanship and civic discord had
begun even before that time, as I have shown above, nevertheless
an inauspicious repudiation of a marriage had added a stormy impetus, as it were, to the existing causes of division.[74] The story, of
which I shall repeat certain details so as to clarify the foregoing
events, goes something like this.[75]   1215

Buondelmonte was, it seems, among the most splendid Floren-   106
tine knights of his time. He nursed an enmity towards Oddo di
Arrigi de' Fifanti, who was also of a noble family. Oddo was supported by powerful kin, especially the Uberti and the Lamberti,
the mightiest clans of the time, while Buondelmonti was strong in
his own right and also had the backing of certain powerful individuals. When it became obvious that these enmities were just going
to get worse, men of good will finally rose up and imposed a
peace. And to make it more lasting, it was strengthened with a tie
of marriage: Buondelmonte was betrothed to a female descendent
of Oddo on his sister's side. The engagement was announced together with the peace, and everyone believed the matter was settled. A date had been announced for the wedding, and wedding
arrangements were being made in public.

To be sure, certain supporters of the young man did not ap-   107
prove at all of the connection he was forming. Thus it happened
during this time that a certain lady of the house of Donati, having
chanced to hear members of her household criticizing the match,
took the young man aside and began to chide him in a friendly
way that he, a nobleman, had thoughtlessly and without careful
inquiry accepted as a wife a person much his inferior in birth and
physical appearance. "Forsooth", said she, "most willingly shall I
save this one for your wedding," pointing to her nubile daughter,
who was a great beauty. The kindly admonition of the woman and

"Nempe ego tibi," inquit, "vel cupientissime hanc tuis asservabam nuptiis," filiam ostendens aetate nubilem,[93] forma egregiam. Percussere illico iuvenis pectus celsioris puellae vultus et admonitio mulieris. Itaque ceu furiis quibusdam agitatus, cum ea secum reputaret ac formam formae familiamque familiae conferret, posteriora oblata constituit praeferenda.[94] Reversus itaque postridie ad mulierem, "Adhuc tempus, o matrona," inquit, "est perperam facta corrigendi. Ego enim divertens ab illa cui nihil praeter iacturam poenae me astringit, tuam, si ita vis, rite suscipiam."

108   Nec mora audaci coepto: muliere adnuente, eo ipso tempore quo primae futurae erant nuptiae, secundae parantur. Otto igitur et repulsae parentes agnatis necessariisque in unum vocatis facinus indignum contumeliamque enarrant: ab se quidem neque verbo neque facto quicquam admissum quod illius mentem vel leviter modo abalienare potuerit; id totum superbiam atque contemptum esse. Ea cum prope lacrimabundi exponerent fidemque propinquorum implorarent, permoti maiorem in modum qui aderant vindicandam esse contumeliam statuerunt. Erant sane hi permulti nobiles, a quibus cum de vindictae modo agitaretur, Lambertus Musca occidendum censuit, rem factam, ut vulgari habetur proverbio, caput habere dictitans. Eo ab aliis quoque per indignationem consilio sumpto, dies et locus ad caedem memorabiles quaerebantur. Pascha potissimum visum est in tempore; aedes vero puellae cuius spreverat nuptias pro loco delectae. Itaque paschatis die, cum e veteri ponte albo equo albaque, ut traditur, amictus veste iuvenis descenderet, egressi coniurati ab aedibus Amideorum (ibi namque ex constituto paulo ante convenerant) illum circumsistunt, abiectumque ex equo multis vulneribus conficiunt. Inter-

the face of the young noblewomen struck the youth instantly to the heart. Like a man possessed by the Furies, he turned the matter over in his mind incessantly, comparing the two girls in terms of their appearance and the prominence of their families. Finally he decided on the second girl. So he went back the next day to the woman and said, "There is still time, Signora, to correct mistakes. I shall break off my understanding with her, to whom I am bound by nothing but fear of penalties,[76] and take your daughter, if you so wish, with all due ceremony."

Buondelmonte lost no time putting into action his bold design. 108 With the woman's assent, he arranged a second nuptial ceremony for the very same date that the first was to have been held. So Oddo and the rejected parents called together their relatives and friends and described the dishonorable deed and insult. They ascribed Buondelmonte's behavior entirely to his own pride and contempt, and refused to admit to any word or action on their own part that might have alienated him even in the slightest. They were practically in tears as they told their tale and asked for the loyalty of their connections. Those who were present were profoundly affected and decided that the insult must be avenged. Many of these were nobles, and while they were debating about the manner of their revenge, Mosca Lamberti gave it as his view that Buondelmonte should be killed, repeating the Italian proverb, *Cosa fatta, capo ha*.[77] In their anger the others, too, accepted Mosca's advice, and they set about finding a memorable place and time for the killing. Easter seemed to them the best time, and for the place they chose the house of the girl who had been spurned. Thus on Easter Day, when the youth was coming down off the Ponte Vecchio, dressed in white and riding a white horse according to report, the conspirators came out the house of the Amidei (where, by agreement, they had met shortly before), surrounded him, pulled him off his horse and dispatched him with repeated blows. Present at the killing were certain members of the Uberti

fuerunt huic caedi Uberti et Lamberti quidam et alii puellae propinqui; plurimum tamen ipsius Ottonis manu⁹⁵ perpetrata est. Cecidit vero non longe a Martis signo, quod e veteri sublatum templo ad pontem collocatum extabat, idque in calamitate civitatis quidam notarunt.

109   Percussores statim post caedem globo facto in Amideorum aedes se receperunt. Rumor vero per urbem diffusus pro diei solemnitate et hominum superbia populum commovit. Nam etsi error fuerat deserendis nuptiis, poena legibus constituta erat pecuniarum promissarum iactura; caedi vero ex coniurato homines, incivile videbatur. Denique occisi cognati affinesque in unum coeunt, nec nobilitas solum, verum etiam plebs incerto scinditur favore. Hinc odia civium irritata vehementius exarsere, ut non iam civili modestia, sed vulneribus et sanguine summa perdendi pereundique cupidine certaretur.

110   Haec igitur in civitate discidia ex nuptiarum repulsa considerans orta, florentinus populus contrariis remediis curare tentavit. Itaque restitutis nuper in urbem civibus auctor extitit novarum affinitatum inducendarum. Enim vero maior erat morbus quam ut ex huiusmodi medicamento sanitas illi posset afferri. Licet enim ab initio magnam spem laetitiamque praeberent, tamen paulo post irrito conatu provisa apparuere. Neque concordia diu stetit, nam praevalentibus longe his qui cum Carolo vicerant aliamque factionem non secus ac victam despicientibus, formido simul et indignatio adversarios agitabat, praesertim cum plebs quoque, memor ar-

and Lamberti clans and other relatives of the girl, but most of the killing was done by the hand of Oddo himself. Buondelmonte fell not far from a symbol of Mars which had been taken from the old temple and placed by the bridge, a circumstance which some took to be a sign of the calamity that would fall upon the city.

After the killing the assassins immediately formed themselves 109 into a band and sought refuge in the house of the Amidei. The story spread through the city, and the men's arrogant deed, on so holy a day, shocked the populace deeply. For while it was certainly wrong of Buondelmonte to have broken off his marriage, the penalty established by law for his action was the loss of monies he had promised. That these men had conspired to murder him seemed behavior unbefitting a republic. In due course the blood relations and connections by marriage of the young man came together as a united body, and even the commoners, not just the nobles, were divided by shifting loyalties. Soon the enmities among the citizens began to kindle and catch fire, and so the struggle was carried on, not with civil restraint, but with knives and blows, in a fever of death and destruction.[78]

Thus the Florentine People, taking into account that the pres- 110 ent civil discords had had their origin in a rejected marriage, tried to cure them with a remedy of opposites. So it became the spon- 1266 sor of new relationships by marriage among the citizens it had just restored to the city. But in fact the disease was too serious to be cured by such medicine. For while at the start it offered hope and joy, the policy was soon revealed as a wasted effort. Harmony did not last long. Those who had conquered with Charles were by far the stronger party and they despised the other faction as beaten men. The Ghibellines were harassed by fear and hatred, especially when even the commoners, remembering the battle of the Arbia and the blow the commonwealth had then suffered, began to attack them with curses and frank expressions of abhorrence as the authors of the great disaster and as deserters who had betrayed the

biensis pugnae ac vulneris rei publicae tunc accepti, auctores tantae cladis ac transfugas cives, qui decus patriae Senensibus prodidissent, liberis iam detestationibus maledictisque lacesseret. Accessit his suspicio ingens, quod crebra fama haud ambigue vulgabat, Corradinum Corradi filium, Federici nepotem ingentes copias in Germania parare, regni pro recuperatione paterni in Italiam transiturum. Ad cuius spem adventus Pisani Senensesque ac ceteri eius factionis modo[96] Caroli victoria fracti haud segniter erexerant animos, et sollicitatum ab his Corradinum circumferebant eorumque fiducia opum inniti. Itaque quasi novarentur antiqua partium vulnera, neutra factio satis alteri confidebat.

III   Interea Carolus regni iam compositis rebus, cum ad securitatem suam plurimum pertinere iudicaret Pisanos Senensesque ante Corradini adventum in suam potestatem traducere, praefectum quendam e suis cum equitatu in Etruriam misit. Postulatum hoc a florentinis civibus regis amicis quidam auctores sunt eorumque precibus adductum regem copias suas in haec loca misisse. Equidem vel Florentinos vel alios contendisse id ab rege non infitias eo:[97] ceterum utilitatis rationem, ne Suevis regnum Siciliae velut hereditarium repetentibus favor aliquis in Etruria resideret, regem permovisse magis crediderim.

112   Erat illa quidem communis suspicio, nec regis modo, verum etiam pontificis. Cum enim permagni rerum motus ab Etruria provenire[98] consuevissent, nequaquam negligendas eas partes romano pontifici visum est. Itaque ad comprimendum omnem exinde motum, novo quidem exemplo, sed admodum necessario gubernationem Etruriae, quasi ab imperio recisam, sibi ac romanae sedi pontifex reservavit. Id autem eo tolerabilius fuit, quod nemo per id tempus praesidebat imperio et ex auctoritate romanae sedis factum non ambitiose constabat, sed rebus ipsis vehementer flagi-

honor of their country to the Sienese. Moreover, there was a great deal of distrust because of the frequent, unambiguous reports that Conradin, son of Conrad, grandson of Frederick, was readying large forces in Germany with the intention of coming to Italy and recovering his father's kingdom. The Pisans and the Sienese and the rest of that faction, though only recently shattered by Charles' victory, were quickly regaining their spirits in expectation of Conradin's coming, and they put it about that Conradin was coming at their instigation and that he was relying on their loyal aid. Thus the ancient wounds of party were opened anew, and each party mistrusted the other.

Meanwhile Charles had settled the affairs of his kingdom, and, deciding that it would add greatly to his security to bring the Pisans and Sienese under his control before Conradin arrived, he sent one of his commanders with a cavalry force into Tuscany. Some authorities claim that the king did this at the request of Florentine citizens friendly to the king, and that it was their prayers that led the king to send his forces to those places. But one needn't draw the conclusion that it was the Florentines or others who pressed this course of action on the king. For my part I prefer to believe that the king was motivated by his own interest in preventing Tuscany from becoming a haven for the Hohenstaufen in their bid to recover the Kingdom of Sicily as their inheritance.

Indeed the pope had the same idea. Since great uprisings so often broke out in Tuscany, it seemed inadvisable for the Roman pontiff to neglect that region. Thus, in order to quell any unrest from that source, the pope, in an unprecedented but necessary step, rescinded the Empire's governance of Tuscany and reserved it for himself and the Roman See. His action was the more tolerable as no one at that time was presiding over the Empire, and it was evident that the Roman See had exercised its authority not out of self-interest but because the circumstances themselves required it. Tuscany was thus reserved to the governance of the pontiff and

III

1267

112

tantibus. Reservata igitur Etruria eiusque gubernatione pontifici, Carolus tamquam vicarius illi praeficitur. Atque ob has causas permotus rex quasi iusto quodam imperii titulo equitatum primo in Etruriam misit.

113 Adventantibus itaque regiis copiis, cives qui nuper sub rege militaverant ducem ipsum atque Gallos militiae cognitos, una cum tota factione quae ob victoriam regis in patriam ac rem publicam redierat, gratulabundi recipere parant. Contra vero adversarii conterriti, pridie quam hae copiae Florentiam intrarent, sponte sua egressi abiere, tertio fere postquam exules redierant mense. Hoc itaque discidio cum partium renovata studia essent rursusque certamen futurum appareret, cives qui in urbe remanserant, eximia in regem benevolentia accensi, quem auctorem reditus sui et protectorem salutis haud falso praedicabant, plenum civitatis arbitrium illi permiserunt. Malatestam Verruchianum, principem eius familiae quae postea plurimum floruit, a rege praefectum Florentiae per ea tempora comperio. Summae tamen hic praeerat rei ac regio nomine dominatum exercebat, nam iuri quidem dicendo vindicandisque delictis minores praeerant magistratus. Bellum mox a civibus qui exierant adversus urbem inferri coeptum et quidem pluribus locis; tumultuosius tamen ab Hillaro circumque ea loca hostis imminebat, nec latrocinia modo clandestina, sed praedae quoque palam abactae; augebaturque concursu multitudo, ut iam paene iusti exercitus instar haberetur.

114 Adversus hanc crescentem in dies manum et iam usque ad moenia urbis infestantem populus florentinus egressus, cum hostis

Charles was appointed his vicar, as it were. And it was for these reasons, as someone holding what was, in a certain sense, a just title to power, that the king was first spurred on to send a force of cavalry to Tuscany.

When the royal forces arrived, the citizens who had lately 113 fought under the king, together with the whole party that, thanks to the king's victory, had returned to their country and commonwealth, prepared to receive with joy and thanks the commander and the Frenchmen whom they recognized from their military service together. Their adversaries, on the other hand, were terrified and left town of their own accord the day before the French troops arrived in Florence, just about three months after they had returned from exile. Thanks to this rupture, party strife began anew, and it was evident that there would once again be a struggle for power. The citizens who stayed behind in the city glowed with exceptional benevolence towards the king, whom they acclaimed (quite rightly) as the author of their restoration, their savior and protector, and granted him full authority over the city. I have ascertained that it was Malatesta dal Verrucchio, the head of a family which afterwards enjoyed great success, whom the king placed in charge of Florence during that period. He took the lead in the most important affairs, exercizing lordship in the king's name, while lesser magistrates were in charge of dispensing justice and punishing crimes. The Ghibelline citizens who had left soon began to make war against the city from many different bases, but the greatest uproar came from Sant' Ellero. The enemy menaced these places not only with clandestine acts of thievery, but also with open plunder, and their numbers increased daily from these encounters until they began to be thought of, almost, as a real army.[79]

Against this ever growing force, which was now harrassing 114 them right up to the walls of the city, the Florentine People marched out and compelled their enemies by force of arms to take

intra munimenta vi et armis compulisset, castellum subinde ipsum expugnare aggreditur. Quod etsi erat munitissimum, tamen annitentibus civibus qui militiae gloriam sibi vindicabant ac virtutem ostentantibus, summa vi capitur. Ingens exulum manus in eo castello oppressa est; maxima vero eorum pars in ipso expugnationis ardore per iram caesa, sed praesertim in nobilitatem saevitum. Alia insuper castella, priusquam Florentiam rediretur, exulibus[99] extorta et captivi quidam abducti. E quibus Gerius Volonianus, cum quibusdam agnatorum in parte publicarum aedium trusus, diuturna captivitate maceratus est. Inde carceri nomen inditum,[100] non a conditore, ut tulliano Romae carceri, sed ab eo qui captivus asservatus est Voloniano dicto.

115   Reverso in urbem exercitu ac diversae factionis hominibus, qui nuper ante copiarum regis adventum demigraverant, hostibus iudicatis exorta est inter cives haud parva contentio. Hi enim, qui dudum post arbiensem pugnam exulaverant, adversariorum sibi bona postulabant. Fuerant enim tunc eorum domus in urbe simul agroque dirutae praediaque vastata, in quorum compensationem nunc eorum ipsorum bona, qui tunc vastandi diruendique auctores fuerant, deposcebant. Qua in re nulla cum modestia esset, sed qui plus poterat, plus habere niteretur, placuit ad regis arbitrium rem deferri. Causa cognita statuisse regem perhibent, ut e bonis eorum qui hostes iudicati essent, civibus quorum olim domos villasque evertissent, pro cuiusque existimatione damnorum satisfactio esset. Ea de causa duodecim viri ad eam rem creati cuncta examinarunt et in libellos redegerunt. Ita restitutio petita est. Quod reliquum erat bonorum exulum, partim in rem publicam versum, partim collegio guelfarum partium attributum.

refuge behind fortifications, then set about attacking the Ghibellines' castle. Although it was very well fortified, it was stormed and captured by citizens striving to win military glory for themselves and to show their courage. A great band of exiles was crushed in that castle. The greater part of them were slaughtered in anger at the crisis of the siege, but the nobles were attacked with particular ferocity. Other castles, too, were seized from the exiles before they returned to Florence, and certain persons were taken captive. Among these was Geri da Volognano, who was confined in part of the city hall with certain of his relatives until he was worn down by his long incarceration. Thereafter the prison was named 'Volognano', not from its founder, like the Tullian Prison in Rome, but from a man who was held captive there.[80]

The army returned to the city and the Ghibellines who had recently emigrated before the arrival of the king's troops were legally declared enemies. This gave rise to no small strife among the citizens. Those who had gone into exile shortly after the battle of the Arbia demanded for themselves the property of their adversaries. For at that time their homes in the city had been demolished and their estates in the countryside plundered. In compensation they now demanded the property of the very men who had been the authors of that earlier demolition and plundering. Since in this matter there was no sense of fairness — the more powerful sought to have more — it was decided to defer the matter to the king's judgment. The case was heard, and it was announced that the king had determined to give satisfaction to the citizens whose homes and country estates had earlier been destroyed, in accordance with the valuation of each man's losses, from the goods of those who had been declared enemies. A board of Twelve Men chosen for this purpose looked into the whole business and drew up records. Thus was restitution claimed. What remained of the exiles' property was allotted partly to the commonwealth and partly to the Guelf Party.

116   Videntur autem et pontifex et rex non sine causa augendae ex-
tollendaeque huiusce factionis studiosi fuisse. Quippe romanus
pontifex a Manfredo suisque multifariam iniurias olim perpessus
et tunc maxime Corradini formidans adventum, hos homines,
quorum fidele obsequium et constantem erga se romanamque
ecclesiam animum experimento cognoverat, cunctis temporibus
praevalere cupiebat; et rex fortitudinem fidemque eorum militiae
expertus pro veteri amicitia et quod diversam factionem in Etruria
obrutam volebat, immodico complectebatur favore.

117   Itaque illud primo per haec ipsa tempora constitutum quidam
putant, ut ea civium pars collegium gubernatoresque publice delectos haberet, ut essent quibus commodorum eius praecipua semper cura diligentiaque incumberet. Ego vero et diu ante hoc tempus fuisse duces partium in civitate comperio, idque publicis
annalibus multis extat locis. Et quidem aliquandiu observatum est,
ut non cives, sed peregrini duces eligerentur, viri nobiles domi et
qui easdem in suis civitatibus sectarentur partes. Itaque Lucam Sa-
bellum, Bertuldum Ursinum, Thomam Severinianum suo
quemque anno ducem guelfarum partium Florentiae fuisse legimus. His cives a factione delecti in consilium dabantur. Sed postea
ad cives negotium rediit et plures simul duces creari coepti sunt,
cum antea unus dumtaxat dux singulis annis esse consuesset. Id
collegium maximam in urbe habet auctoritatem et velut censuram
quandam in cives exercet, ut qui notatus fuerit, alienus ab omni
honore publico habeatur. Sed haec suis temporibus narrabuntur;
nunc hactenus dixisse abunde sit.

118   Eodem anno bellum adversus Senenses renovatum est, properantibus Florentinis arbiensem cladem ulcisci. Itaque praefectum
regis secuti cuncta circum[101] Senas infestius popularunt. Cum vero

It appears that the pope and the king had good reason for their zeal in enriching and exalting this faction. For the Roman pontiff had suffered injuries in many places at the hands of Manfred and his supporters, and at that moment he was afraid of Conradin's coming, so he wanted those men to enjoy permanent superiority whose faithful service and firm loyalty to himself and the Roman Church he had tested. And the king, knowing their courage and loyalty in military service, showed them overweening love and favor out of old friendship and because he wished to overthrow the Ghibelline faction in Tuscany. 116

Thus for the first time, as some think, there was established a college for the Guelf Party with publicly chosen captains, so that there should be individuals specially entrusted in perpetuity to oversee its interests. But I have discovered that there were leaders of the Party in the city long before that time, and this fact is visible in the public records in many places. Indeed it was for some time the practice to choose not citizens, but foreigners as captains, men who were noble in their homelands and who adhered to the Guelf cause in their own cities. Thus we read that Lucas Sabellus, Bertuldus Ursinus, and Thomas Severinianus were each in their own years captains of the Guelf Party in Florence. These men were provided with counselors chosen by the party. But at a later time the job came back to the citizens, and they began to create multiple captains to hold office simultaneously, whereas formerly the custom was to have only one captain each year. This college enjoys the greatest authority in the city and exercises a kind of moral censorship[81] over the citizens; any man who is censured is considered ineligible for any public honor. However, these matters will be narrated in their due order; what has been said so far is more than enough.[82] 117

In the same year a new war against the Sienese was begun, the Florentines being in haste to avenge the defeat on the Arbia. So following the royal lieutenant, they laid waste with great ferocity 118
1267

maximus pugnandi ardor esset, hostem ne populationibus quidem atque incendiis, quae passim ante oculos ostentabantur, ad pugnam pellicere valuerunt. Sed cum iis esset in locis exercitus, nunciatum est exules magna manu ad Bonitium convenisse. Itaque eo confestim versa est totius belli moles. Nam praefectus regis et Florentini retro ad Bonitium moverunt castra, et Pisani Senensesque ita demum a se pestem aversuros existimantes si alibi hostis destinaretur, defendere Bonitium tota vi ac exules qui intus erant omni ratione statuerunt confovere. Ita iuxta pertinaciter atque impigre utrinque incumbentibus, ut in eo appareret totius belli discrimen versari. Praefectus quidem et Florentini primo ac subitaneo impetu expugnare Bonitium adorti, cum et natura loci egregie muniti et structura hostium facile repulsi essent, stativis ante oppidum positis obsidere perrexerunt. Exules autem et suo ipsi robore et magnis Pisanorum Senensiumque adhortationibus confirmati non minus alacriter resistebant, praesertim cum per crebros internuncios certiores fierent a Senensibus Pisanisque opis ferendae gratia copias ingentes parari. Is rumor per castra quoque diffusus effecit, ut ex civitatibus quae erant in tutela regis (iam enim frequentes sese illi coniunxerant) auxilia vocarentur. Rex quoque ipse tractus eo certamine in Etruriam venit. Iter eius ex Viterbio Arretium primo, inde Florentiam fuit. In utraque civitate summo applausu civium nec ullo genere honoris non impenso receptus, in castra inde se contulit. Primo regis adventu oppidani legatione ad eum missa lenire mentem regis nitebantur. Postquam vero alieniorem

to the lands around Siena. Yet at the moment when their ardor for battle was at its height, they were unable to coax the enemy to a fight despite the fire and devastation being enacted everywhere before his eyes. But while the army was near Siena, the news came that the exiles had gathered a great force at Poggibonsi. So at once the weight of the whole war came to bear on that place. The royal lieutenant and the Florentines moved their encampment back to Poggibonsi, and the Pisans and Sienese, thinking it would deflect the plague from themselves if their enemy was headed elsewhere, decided to defend Poggibonsi with all their strength and to bring comfort in any way they could to the exiles within. With both sides concentrating their efforts there with equal vigor and tenacity, it appeared that the crisis of the whole war would take place in the town. The royal lieutenant and the Florentines launched a surprise attack to capture the city but were easily repelled by the extraordinary natural defenses of the place and by their enemies' fortifications. So they pitched camp in front of the town and laid out a siege. The exiles, for their part, steadied by their own strength and by the encouragement of the Pisans and Sienese, fought back with no less ardor, especially as they were informed via frequent messengers that the Sienese and the Pisans were readying large forces to help them. The rumor spread, too, through the Florentine camp that auxiliary forces were being summoned from the cities under the king's protection (for they were already joining him in great numbers). The king himself was also drawn into the battle and came to Tuscany. He journeyed from Viterbo to Florence via Arezzo. In both cities he was greeted with great enthusiasm by the citizens and shown every kind of honor. Then he made his way to the camp. When the king first arrived the townsmen sent him a legation to try to soften his determination. Then, when they realized he was unsympathetic and the affair was going to be settled entirely by violent means, they brought up their siege defenses

senserunt ac rem penitus ad vim spectare, machinas adduci, praesidia circa oppidum communiri, ex formula sic egerunt.

119 "Iniuriaris, o rex. Sive enim tuo nomine vim affers, imperium romanum, cuius possessio sumus, indigne offendis: sive imperii, cuius te vices gerere in Etruria asseris, fidos et bene meritos iniuria lacessis."

120 Responsum: "Postquam ex formula disceptare placet, imperii nomine ista gerimus. Proinde, si possessio imperii estis, nos exercitumque nostrum intra moenia suscipite; sin pactionibus tergiversamini, ut rebelles iure ulciscimur."

121 Ita dirempta colloquia sunt, et oppugnatio incepta. Regi apprime rei militaris perito et[102] vel eximiis ducibus comparando nullum oppugnandarum urbium genus fuisse ignotum crediderim. Sed repugnabat natura ipsa loci, qui vel de industria ad omnem vim arcendam factus videbatur. Sublimi atque praeciso undique fere aditu oppidum imminebat; qua vero collis ad oppidum iungebatur, contra eum locum non turres modo, verum etiam stationes armatorum oppositae omnem vim hostium perfacile dimovebant. Irrito igitur conatu cum oppugnatio languesceret, rex diuturna incubatione domitare hostem constituit, nec prius abscedere quam Bonitium caperetur. Quare obsidione vehementius intentata, ex amicis civitatibus magna multitudine confluente oppidum undique cinxit et praesidia pluribus locis communivit. Tandem cum omnis spes obsessis adempta esset ac iam necessaria deficerent, Bonitium regi deditur quarto postquam rex advenerat mense, his qui intus erant incolumibus abire pactis.

and strengthened their guardposts around the town, declaring, according to legal form, as follows:

"O King, you are committing an unjust act. If you are threatening violence in your own name, you are committing a dishonorable offense against the Roman Empire, whose possession we are. If you are acting in the name of the Empire, whose representative in Tuscany you claim to be, you are unjustly attacking trusty and deserving subjects." 119

His response was: "Since it pleases you to make the matter a legal issue, We are acting in the name of the Empire. Wherefore, if you are a possession of the Empire, receive Us and our army within your walls. If you are going to turn your backs on treaties, We have the right to punish you as rebels." 120

Thus the colloquy was cut off, and the siege began. My belief is that a king outstanding for his military experience, a man to be compared with the greatest commanders, would know every way to besiege a city. But the place was naturally impregnable, seemingly fashioned on purpose to repel force of any kind. The town commanded steep, sharp approaches on almost every side, and the place where the hill joined the town was defended not only by towers but by detachments of armed men who with great ease would drive off any enemy force. An assault being therefore useless, the king decided, when the siege had begun to go slack, to subdue the enemy by a long blockade and not to leave until he had captured Poggibonsi. So he settled down to the siege with great determination, and surrounded the city on all sides with a multitude of reinforcements from friendly cities, strengthening his guardposts in many places. Finally, when the besieged had lost all hope and were running out of necessities, they surrendered Poggibonsi to the king. This occurred in the fourth month after the king's arrival. It was stipulated that those within the town could leave without molestation.[83] 121

122   Inde per mediam hiemem movens rex cum Florentinis ac ceteris amicis pisanos ingreditur fines. Capta ab eo in his locis aliquot
castella,[103] portus etiam expugnatus et turres quae portui imminebant eversae. Populato deinde circa Pisas agro Lucam (ea tunc civitas amicissima regis erat) se recepit. Refecto paucis diebus exercitu postulantibus Lucensibus Mutrone[104] obsedit. Id castellum
non vi, sed astu captum a rege est. Simulatis enim cuniculis quasi
moenia eversuris, noctu magna vis ruderum importata ante oculos
obsessorum per dies egerebatur. Quare illi conterriti, cum iam nu-
tare moenia falso decepti metu existimarent, arbitrio regis se permiserunt. Per hunc modum rex munitissimum castellum recepit;
receptum autem Lucensibus tradidit.

The king then set out in the middle of winter with the Floren- 122
tines and other allies and crossed into Pisan territory. He captured
several castles there, and also took the port, destroying the towers that commanded it. Next, having laid waste to the territory
around Pisa, he betook himself to Lucca (that town being then
very friendly to him). There his army refreshed itself for a few
days, then, at the request of the Lucchesi, laid siege to Mutrone.
The king took this castle by a ruse rather than by force. Great
piles of dirt and rubbish were carried there by night to support the
pretence that tunnels were being dug to undermine the walls. The
besieged, watching this day after day, grew terrified and were deceived by false fear into thinking that the walls had begun to fall
over. So they surrendered themselves to the king's authority. In
this way the king acquired a well-fortified castle, which he then
turned over to the Lucchesi.[84]

LIBER TERTIUS

1   Is qui secutus est annus turbulentos habuit motus. Cum enim esset in Etruria rex ac omnes civitates quae prius Federici, mox et Manfredi sectatae fuerant partes, praeter Senenses et Pisanos, in suam fidem voluntatemque traduxisset et hos[1] ipsos domitare pararet, duo sub idem fere tempus afferuntur nuntii. Altero Corradinus Italiam Tridentumque iam pervenisse, altero in urbe Roma atque Sicilia motus rerum haudquaquam contemnendi et civitatum procerumque defectus nuntiabantur. Rerum novarum causa haec fuerat.

2   Hispani erant duo regii generis, Arrigus et Federicus. Hi adversus fratrem regnum in Hispania obtinentem infensi, tandem extorres patria exularunt, collectaque virorum manu, quando adversus fratrem se nihil proficere existimabant posse, in Africam transgressi Tunetae apud regem longo tempore meruerunt. Ibi praeda simul stipendiisque ditati, cum de communibus tandem fortunis consultarent, placuit ut Arrigus (is enim maior erat natu) cum omni pecunia ac cetera gaza in Italiam traiiceret, Sardiniae regnum a pontifice maximo petiturus.

3   Delatus igitur e Carthaginis portu, cum secundum consilium Italiam pontificemque adiisset, fautore utitur Carolo, qui nuper victo Manfredo flagrantissima apud pontificem gratia praevalebat. Et erant sane Arrigus fratresque arctissimo consanguinitatis gradu materna Carolo stirpe coniuncti. Quamobrem et necessitudinis iure et procurationis beneficio inductus petenti Carolo magnam pecuniae vim Arrigus mutuat. Sed dum pontifex de regno deliberat et regis gratia concedere parat, ortis in urbe Roma seditionibus

BOOK III

The following year was marked by considerable political turbu-   1
lence. The king[1] was in Tuscany and had rendered obedient to   *1267*
himself all the cities formerly loyal to Frederick and Manfred with
the exception of Siena and Pisa, over whom he was preparing to
establish his lordship. Then, at about the same time, two messengers arrived. One brought news that Conradin had already entered
Italy via Trent; the other told of serious uprisings in the city of
Rome and of rebellions by cities and princes in Sicily. The cause
of the revolutions I shall now explain.

There were two Spaniards of royal lineage, Arrigo and Fede-   2
rigo. Both were enemies of a third man, their brother, who had
obtained for himself the throne of Spain. Eventually the two were
banished from their country and went into exile. They collected a
band of men and, reckoning that resistance to their brother was
useless, crossed the sea to Africa where they spent a long time in
the service of the king of Tunis. There they grew rich from plunder and from their wages. Finally they met to discuss their common fortunes, and it was decided that Arrigo (who was the older)
should cross over to Italy with all their money and other treasure
and seek to obtain the kingdom of Sardinia from the pope.

Leaving the port of Carthage, Arrigo went to Italy and applied   3
to the pontiff in accordance with the plan. He used Charles as his
backer, who, thanks to his victory over Manfred, enjoyed above all
others the pope's warmest favor. Arrigo and his brothers were, to
be sure, very near blood-relations of Charles on Charles' mother's
side. Because of this kinship and because of Charles' helpfulness to
him Arrigo lent Charles a vast sum of money at the latter's request. But while the pope was considering the Sardinian question
and was on the point of granting Arrigo's request for the king's
sake, sedition arose in the city of Rome. The citizens had taken to

civibusque ad arma ruentibus, ad sedandas eas tempestates ab Romanis Arrigus deposcitur, ac ex Viterbio (ibi nam tunc pontifex
degebat) Romam vocatur, senatusque potestas volente populo illi
tribuitur.

4   Pacata itaque[2] urbe, cum veluti dominatum iure partum nullo
respectu pontificis exerceret ac maiora quaedam moliri videretur,
pontifici simul atque regi in suspicionem venit. Ob id intermissum
Sardiniae negotium est a pontifice et Carolus repetenti mox pecunias, ne maiores ad nocendum facultates illi adessent, bono consilio haudquaquam reddebat. Coeperat Arrigus iam inde ab initio
contrariam pontifici Caroloque factionem magis fovere;[3] utramque
tamen intra urbem aequitatis simulatione continebat. Ut vero suspicionem pontificis Carolique advertit, alienus extemplo[4] factus,
Pisanos et Senenses ac ceteros eius factionis homines occulte soli-
citare coepit; ad Corradinum item mittere, favorem suum fra-
trisque ac romanam urbem, si adveniat, polliceri. Magnum hostes
momentum in utroque reponebant. Itaque ad Federicum Corradus
Capitius neapolitanus, regni tunc exul, cum una Pisanorum navi
missus est, litteras ferens ab Arrigo fratre, ut cunctis posthabitis ex
Africa in Siciliam ad res novandas traiiceret. A Corradino etiam
frequentes ad Siciliae populos et ad paternos amicos litteras regio
nomine scriptas detulit.

5   Maturata igitur re Federicus et Capitius in Siciliam transeunt.
Ducentos milites hispani generis, totidem Germanos, quadringentos vero Tuscos secum traduxere. Ibi spargendis Corradini litteris
et maioribus quam attulerant profitendis, brevi admodum tempore
Siciliam fere totam praeter Syracusas et Messanam et Panormum
ad defectionem compulerunt. Et simul Romae, ubi de Siciliae

arms and Arrigo was asked by the Romans to calm their dissensions. He was summoned from Viterbo (where the pope was then staying) and by the will of the people was granted senatorial power.[2]

Once Arrigo had pacified the city, he exercised lordship over it 4 without any regard to the pontiff, as though he had acquired it himself by right, and he also appeared to be hatching even greater plans. This made both king and pontiff suspicious. So the pope broke off the negotiation about Sardinia and Charles wisely would not repay Arrigo's money when he asked for it, lest the latter should have greater resources for doing harm. From the start Arrigo had displayed partiality towards the faction hostile to the pope and to Charles, but he had retained both factions within the city in a show of evenhandedness. Once he became aware of the suspicions of the pope and Charles, however, he immediately became estranged and began secretly to seek help from the Pisans, the Sienese and other Ghibellines. He also sent word to Conradin promising him the city of Rome, as well as his own support and that of his brother, if Conradin would come. The enemy set great store by both these promises. Thus Corrado Capizio, a Neapolitan and an exile from the Kingdom, was sent on a Pisan vessel to Federigo with letters from Federigo's brother Arrigo stating that he should drop everything, leave Africa, and come to Sicily to start a revolution. From Conradin Capizio also brought many letters written in the king's name to the peoples of Sicily and to friends of his father.[3]

When the time was ripe Federigo and Capizio crossed to Sicily, 5 bringing with them two hundred Spanish knights, an equal number of Germans, and four hundred Tuscans. There they circulated Conradin's letters, and, claiming to have larger forces than they had in fact brought, they drove to revolt within a short time practically all of Sicily, save Syracuse, Messina and Palermo. Once Arrigo in Rome had heard of the Sicilian rebellion, at around the

motu auditum est, Arrigus non ultra cunctandum ratus, viros amplissimos principes civitatis qui guelfarum partium erant, ad se in capitolium evocatos corona armatorum circumdat. Ex his Napoleonem et Matthaeum Ursinos, summa gratia homines summaque nobilitate, confestim, ne quis motus in urbe suscitetur, extra urbem captivos delegat; Iohannem vero et Lucam Sabellos in capitolii carcere asservat; diversae autem factionis hominibus licentiam impunitatemque permittit.

6   Ita repente mutatis rebus eodem paene tempore de Corradini adventu ac de romanae urbis motu Siciliaeque defectu rex certior factus, ancipitique perculsus malo, Senensium Pisanorumque curam omittere ac veluti ad domesticum extinguendum incendium properare coactus est. Relicta igitur parte equitatus in Etruria, ne Corradino veniente civitates quae in fide erant praesidio vacuae forent, reliquae omnes copiae a rege contrahuntur, et per Brutios atque Lucanos itemque per Siciliam ad inhibendas defectiones praesidia submittuntur.

7   Per idem fere tempus Pisani viginti quatuor naves longas ad populandam maritimam oram solicitandasque civitates adversus Carolum dimisere, edictumque erat, ut cum litus Italiae satis lustrassent exulesque (magna illorum vis ea in classe vehebatur) suis locis exposuissent, in Siciliam ad Federicum et Capitium pervaderent, auxilio partium, si quid expediret, futurae. Corradinum in Italiam venientem supra decem Germanorum millia usque Tridentum prosecuta sunt. Inde, seu pecuniarum inopia, seu quod satis virium sibi adfore in Italia propter studia partium existimabat, ad tria millia delectorum equitum retentis, ceteram multitudinem domum remisit. Ipse Tridento profectus secus Athesim fluvium Veronam pervenit; inde ad dexteram[5] flectens in Ligures duxit. Nam recto quidem itinere haudquaquam petere Etruriam tam exiguis

same time, he decided to delay no longer. Summoning the most distinguished leaders of the Guelf Party to appear before him on the Campidoglio, he had them surrounded by men at arms. At once he caused Napoleone and Matteo degli Orsini, two popular members of the nobility, to be held as hostages outside the city so as to prevent uprisings within it. Giovanni and Luca de' Savelli he kept in the prison of the Campidoglio, while the Ghibellines were allowed to commit every act of license with impunity.

Thus the situation had changed rapidly. The king was informed 6 at practically the same time about Conradin's coming, the uprising in Rome and the rebellions in Sicily. Caught between twin evils, he was compelled to abandon his concerns with the Sienese and Pisans and to rush back to put out the fire, as it were, in his own house. So he left behind in Tuscany part of his cavalry, lest the cities allied to him should be without defense when Conradin came, and mustered all the rest of his troops, sending detachments through Basilicata, Calabria and Sicily to check the rebellions.

Around the same time the Pisans sent twenty-four galleys to 7 pillage the coastline of the Kingdom and to encourage its cities to rise up against Charles. They had been ordered, after they had finished scouring the shoreline of Italy, and put ashore in their native places the large number of exiles they had brought with them in the fleet, to join Federigo and Capizio in Sicily and bring their partisans whatever help they could. Conradin, meanwhile, had come to Italy, escorting over ten thousand Germans as far as Trent. There, whether from lack of money or because he thought the force, in view of the Italians' partisan zeal, would be sufficient, he kept with him about three thousand picked knights and sent the rest of the host home. Leaving Trent, he followed the river Adige and came to Verona; from there he turned west and led his men to Liguria. He didn't dare make straight for Tuscany with so small a force: Bologna, Reggio, Modena and certain other cities were sympathetic to Charles and the pope, while the peoples of

copiis ausus est, Bononiensibus et Reginis et Mutinensibus et aliis
quibusdam civitatibus cum Carolo et pontifice sentientibus, popu-
lisque Etruriae Apennini iuga obsidere paratis et transitu Germanos arcere. Quare Ligures petens, cum ad litus inferi maris descendisset, ipse quidem cum paucis mari delatus, copiae vero per
lunensem agrum pedestri itinere Pisas venere. Paucis hinc diebus
ad quietem sumptis, cum Pisanis ac ceteris suae factionis qui ad
eum ex omni Etruria quantum ad neminem unquam gratulabundi
convenerant, Lucensium ingreditur fines. Erant Lucae regii equites, quos in Etruria ob hoc ipsum supra ostendimus a rege relictos,
et praeterea Florentinorum ceterarumque civitatum ingentes equitum peditumque copiae. Hi omnes obviam hostibus egressi ad
duo fere passuum millia quasi pugnaturi constiterunt. At Germani
et ceteri qui cum Corradino erant, adversam aciem intuentes, se ad
pugnam compararunt. Flumen e proxima fluens palude acies diri-
mebat. Hoc dum utrique ut alteri prius transeant expectant, spatio
diei frustra consumpto, cum nihil aliud quam sese invicem conspexissent, irrita mora demum abscessere.

8   Corradinus haud multo post Pisis movens per florentinum
agrum Bonitium pervenit, paucisque diebus circum[6] ea loca moratus, cum omnibus copiis Senas contendit. At regiis equitibus,
quos praesidii causa relictos in Etruria diximus, hoc propositum
erat, ut aequis fere itineribus cum hoste per amica vadentes oppida
suis facerent animos et hostes a populationibus cohiberent. Itaque,
ut Senas pervenisse Corradinum intellexere, ex florentino agro
Arretium (nam ea tunc civitas in regiis partibus vel fidissima erat)
transire pergunt, cumque Varicum pervenissent, Florentinorum
equitatu comitante praefectus regis, quasi satis virium in se esset,
dimissis florentinis equitibus et offerentium ultra prosequi repu-
diata opera cum suis Arretium versus ire perrexit.

Tuscany stood ready to fortify the Apennine passes and block the Germans' crossing. So Conradin made for Liguria. Having come down to the shore of the Tyrrhenian Sea, he himself went by sea with a few men to Pisa, while his troops arrived there by the land route through the Lunigiana. After a few days' rest in Pisa, he crossed the border into Lucca with the Pisans and the rest of his partisans who had come to greet him from all over Tuscany in unprecedented numbers. At Lucca were King Charles' knights (whom as we said he had left in Tuscany for this purpose) as well as large numbers of horse and foot from Florence and other cities. All these forces came out to meet the enemy, drawing themselves up as though for battle about two miles out of the city. The Germans and the rest of Conradin's men, eyeing the enemy formation, prepared for battle. A river flowing from a nearby swamp separated the two lines. Both sides stood waiting for the other to cross the river first, and wasted a whole day doing nothing but watching the other army opposite. Finally, after this unprofitable delay, both armies left.[4]

Shortly afterwards Conradin went from Pisa through Florentine territory to Poggibonsi, and after spending a few days nearby, headed for Siena with all his troops. But the royal cavalry (whom as we said had been left behind to guard Tuscany) had orders to shadow the enemy's march, and to pass through friendly towns, giving heart to the Guelfs and containing the enemy's acts of plunder. Hence, having heard that Conradin had arrived in Siena, they made plans to pass through Florentine territory to Arezzo (for at that time the latter city was extremely devoted to the royal cause). But when they reached Montevarchi, the king's captain, apparently believing his own forces sufficient, dismissed the Florentine knights who had accompanied him thus far on his journey. They offered to accompany him farther, but he rejected their assistance and struck out with his men on the road for Arezzo.

9   At hostes id futurum suspicati, ducibus florentinis exulibus, decem fere passuum millibus ab Arretio insidias locant. Iter est perangustum inter sinistros montes atque Arni ripas varioque connexu vallium aptissima insidiis loca. Eo cum regii equites neque explorato neque satis composito agmine descendissent, hostes repente signo dato a fronte et a tergo simul invadunt. Occupatur pons a Germanis, et quod facile erat transitu, regii arcentur; alii simul terga premunt; alii desuper tela convolvunt. Ita in medio circumventi, cum nusquam perrumpere valerent nec ullus ad ostentandam virtutem locus esset, brevi opprimuntur. Toto[7] ex equitatu regio parva admodum pars, quae ante detectas insidias pontem transierat, evasit; reliqui omnes aut eo in loco caesi sunt aut captivi Senas abducti.

10   Hanc victoriam hostis magnificentius extollendo, cum id late fama litterisque vulgasset, multos mortales quasi quodam futuri eventus[8] praesagio a regis favore ad hostem deflexit. In regno tamen magis quam in Etruria rebelliones secutae, sive quod hi constantiores sunt populi sive quod praesentes victoriae non pluris eam putabant quam esset. Ceterum nec imminens Corradini terror nec oppressio regiarum copiarum aliquas Etruriae civitates a fide regis avertit. Quin etiam Arretini ipsi, quorum in oculis paene facta caedes et profligatio erat, in partibus regis constantissime perseverarunt.

11   Inter haec, Pisanorum viginti quatuor naves, quas dimissas supra ostendimus, omnia circa Caietam ac reliquam maritimam oram populatae, cum multis in locis exules ut commodum erat exposuissent multaque ad rebellionem concitassent, tandem in Sici-

The enemy got wind of what was happening and, guided by the 9
Florentine exiles, laid a trap about ten miles out of Arezzo. The
road there was extremely narrow, passing along the banks of the
Arno through looming mountains and labyrinthine valleys, an
ideal spot for a trap. The royal knights were riding down to that
place, having neither reconnoitred the road ahead nor established
any tight formation, when suddenly a signal was given and the enemy attacked simultaneously from ahead and behind. The bridge
was occupied by the Germans, who in this way blocked the royal
forces from making an easy escape. Other forces pressed upon
them from the rear, while still others shot darts at them from
above. Being thus surrounded and unable to break out in any direction, in a place ill-suited for the display of courage, they were
quickly crushed. Of all the royal cavalry only a small part escaped,
the part that had crossed the bridge before the trap was sprung.
The rest were either slaughtered there or were taken as prisoners
to Siena.[5]

The enemy praised their own victory to the skies, and after 10
news of it had been carried abroad by tongue and pen, many
souls, thinking it a presage of future events, transferred their loyalties from the king to the enemy. Yet the rebellions that followed
were more serious in the Kingdom than in Tuscany, either because
the Tuscan peoples are more steadfast, or because they had made a
more realistic estimate of the enemy's victory, being nearer to it. In
any case, neither the threat of Conradin's presence nor the destruction of the king's troops turned the cities of Tuscany from
their allegiance to the king. Indeed, even the Aretines themselves,
under whose very eyes, almost, the slaughter and defeat had taken
place, persevered with great constancy as partisans of the king.

Meanwhile, the twenty-four Pisan ships (whose mission we de- 11
scribed above) at last sailed to Sicily after plundering the whole lit-
toral around Gaeta and elsewhere, putting ashore exiles in as many
places as seemed useful, and inciting numerous local rebellions.

liam navigarunt. Corradinus aliquot dies Senis commoratus, demum inde movens per rusellanum et viterbiensem et sutrinum
agrum ante faciem pontificis, qui per id tempus Viterbii erat, Romam pervenit. Atqui praemiserat ad eum pontifex monens ac sub
gravium comminatione censurarum edicens, ne regnum Siciliae,
quod ad romanam spectaret sedem, neve Carolum ab eadem sede
appellatum regem impeteret; satis superque esse, quod pontifices
romani pro sua dudum beneficentia a maioribus eius ingratissime
perpessi essent. In ipsum tandem pontificis mandata spernentem
latae erant censurae, quas adolescens sublimi animo usque adeo
contempsit, ut ante pontificis oculos exercitum ducere et hostilia
cuncta ostentare non dubitarit.

12   Romae appropinquantem populus romanus armatus obviam
progressus summa omnium ordinum gratulatione imperatoria
transvectum pompa in capitolium perduxit. Ibi, cum non modo
principes, verum etiam omnes cuiusque generis studiis partium incensi ex Etruria et Umbria ac reliqua Italia convenissent, paratis
omnibus quae ad bellum opportuna erant, quod per Casinum aditus in regnum Caroli praesidio teneri nuntiabatur, per tiburtinum
albanumque agrum fines regni ingressus est. In his autem locis
Carolum suis copiis, licet admodum disparibus, obviam habuit.
Nam Corradinum quidem, praeter tria Germanorum millia de-
lecta, insuper magna procerum manus ex Liguribus et Tuscis,
praeterea ex Umbris et Picentibus et Sabinis, non principes modo
eius factionis, verum etiam multitudo ingens studio partium incensa, item romani cives earundem partium, sequebantur. His
accedebat Arrigus hispanus cum haud contemnenda manu magnoque militum numero mercede conductorum.

13   Carolus vero et apud Messanam, quae per id tempus mari terraque oppugnabatur, et per maritimam regni oram multis in locis
copias necessario disperserat; in Etruriam quoque partem equita-

Conradin spent several days in Siena and then set out, under the very eyes of the pontiff (who was then in Viterbo), through the territories of Roselle, Viterbo and Sutri, arriving finally in Rome. The pope had sent ahead warnings and menaces of grave ecclesiastical censure[6] if Conradin should attack the kingdom of Sicily, which pertained to the Roman See, or Charles, whom the same See regarded as Sicily's king. It was enough and more than enough that the Roman pontiffs, in return for their long benevolence, had been most ungratefully made to suffer by Conradin's ancestors. Conradin spurned the pontiff's commands and the censures were duly handed down. The young man treated them with such sublime contempt that he did not hesitate to march his army under the pope's very eyes and flaunt all his hostile intentions.

As he approached Rome the Roman people came out in arms 12
to meet him and to the great joy of all the orders he was conveyed with imperial pomp to the Campidoglio. To Rome came not only the imperialist barons but also fervent Ghibelline partisans of every description from Tuscany, Umbria and the rest of Italy. Having made all his preparations for war, Conradin entered the Kingdom through the territory of Tivoli and Albano, as he had been told that the approach to the Kingdom by way of Monte Cassino was being guarded by Charles. But Charles met him in the former lands, although with markedly inferior forces. For Conradin, in addition to his three thousand picked German knights, commanded a great force of noblemen from Liguria and Tuscany and also from Umbria, the Marche and Sabina; they included not only the leading men of the imperial party but also a huge host of fervent Ghibellines as well as Roman citizens of the same party. In addition there was Arrigo the Spaniard with a respectable force as well as a large number of mercenaries.[7]

Charles, on the other hand, had of necessity dispersed his 13
forces both at Messina, which at that moment was being besieged by land and sea, and in many places along the coast of the King-

tus amiserat.[9] Magna tamen animi fiducia iis quas habebat copiis
ad hostem ductis, non procul ab eo castrametatus est. Ibi cum
multitudinem ac robur hostium viresque examinaret suas, artis et
ingenii opus fore statuit; nam aperto quidem certamine non superare modo, sed ne resistere quidem hosti se posse confidebat. Consilio maxime ad eam rem usus dicitur Alardi cuiusdam senis, viri
nobilis, domi ac in re militari apprime docti, cuius hortatu rex ex
omni suorum exercitu octingentos equites delectos insciis hostibus
proximo sub colle continuit; reliquam vero multitudinem in planitiem dimisit, praefecto quodam e suis regio ornatu sic, ut rex ille
crederetur. Ipse non longe ab his quos post collem reservarat,
paulo sublimiori de loco pugnam spectaturus constitit. Corradini
duces cum aciem struerent, Ligures et Tuscos et Hispanos in
fronte collocarunt; Germanos circa signa in subsidiis posuerunt.
Ut igitur pugnari coeptum est, Tusci et Hispani et Ligures ingenti
ardore regias turmas aggressi, magnam stragem ediderunt. Nec
longo tempore illorum impetus sustineri potuit, sed postquam an-
tesignanis reiectis ventum est ad intima regis agmina et praefectus
regiis ornatus insignibus ad terram prostratus, clamantibus cunctis regem esse captum, Germani quoque et hi qui in subsidio
erant, ne expertes victoriae forent, sese pugnae admiscuerunt. Ita
profligatis hostibus, cum passim fuga effusissima fieret, victor
quoque in sequendo propellendoque dissipatur. Nullum iam in
campis densum agmen, nullum in subsidiis robur manserat; vagus
miles et praedae intentus quasi certissimus victor exultabat. Maxima[10] pars fugientes insecuta sese a conspectu longe abstulerat.
Tum rex circumducta repente delectorum acie in campum descen-

dom; he had also sent part of his cavalry into Tuscany. But he had great confidence in the forces he had brought with him and pitched camp not far from the enemy. There, having scrutinized the numbers and strength of the enemy and his own resources, he decided that he would have to use craft and ingenuity, since he was sure that in an open fight he would not be able even to resist the enemy, let alone defeat him. It is said that in this affair Charles followed the advice of a certain old man named Alardo, a nobleman and an expert in domestic and military matters. At his urging the king selected from his entire army eight hundred knights and kept them in reserve, without the enemy's knowledge, at the foot of a nearby hill. The rest of the host he sent down into the plain under one of his commanders dressed in royal attire so that the latter might be mistaken for the king. He stationed himself to watch the battle on an eminence not far from the hill behind which he had placed his reserves. Conradin's commanders placed the Ligurians, Tuscans and Spaniards in the van of their battle-order, and kept the Germans in reserve near the standards. So, as the battle began, the Tuscans, Spanish and Ligurians attacked the royal squadrons with great spirit and caused enormous slaughter. Their charge could not long be sustained, and after they had driven back the van and had been carried to the very heart of the royal battle-line, they threw down the captain who had been dressed up with the royal insignia. They all began shouting that the king was captured. The Germans and the other reserves, wanting to be present at the victory, threw themselves into the fight. Having beaten their enemy and scattered him hither and yon in flight, the victor's forces too began to spread out in pursuit. Now there remained no solid formation in the camps, no bulwark in the reserves; the soldiers were wandering about intent on plunder, exulting as though certain of victory. The greater part of the army, in pursuit of the fugitives, was now out of sight. It was at this point that the king, surrounding himself suddenly with his battalion of picked men, fell

dit; structo ipse ac denso agmine sparsos invadit; multis subita vi oppressis aut in fugam versis in ipsa signa Corradini fertur ac uno momento dissipat. Corradinus, ceu miraculo attonitus, cum e victore victus inopinato factus esset, cum paucis inde comitibus aufugit. Rex suos ab insequendo continuit, sed densum conglobatumque tenens agmen redeuntes ab insectatione suorum hostes, integer fessos et structus incompositos, excipiebat. Per hunc modum oppressis hostibus, plena tandem victoria potitus est.

14   Corradinus die noctuque continuata fuga Romam pervenit, et a Guidone Feretrano, quem proficiscens ad bellum Romae in praesidio reliquerat, exceptus est. Populus quoque romanus non invitus illum recepit, inscia adhuc plebe cladium receptarum. Sed mox adventantibus romanis civibus diversae factionis, qui ab Arrigo dudum pulsi cum rege in pugna fuerant, ducibus Ursinis et Sabellis civitas confestim in armis fuit. Quamobrem metuens Corradinus relicta urbe Asturam incognitus petiit, eo consilio ut inde Pisas navigaret. Circum ea captus loca regi deditur. Nec multo post Neapolim ductus ex sententia civitatum, quarum syndicos ad iudicium de captivo statuendum Carolus toto ex regno contraxerat, securi percussus est, primo adhuc[11] aetatis flore et adolescens potius quam vir. Percussi sunt item cum eo dux Austriae eiusdem fere aetatis et Gerardus pisanus qui Tuscorum dux in proelio fuerat. Arrigus vero hispanus cum e proelio aufugisset, in agro reatino captus ac regi traditus iure quodam consanguinitatis et pactione eius qui tradiderat vitam retinuit, perpetua tamen captivitate dam-

upon Conradin's camp. Attacking scattered forces with a solid and well-disciplined formation, the king destroyed or put to flight many of the enemy with his sudden blow. He was carried right up to Conradin's own guard and destroyed it in a single moment. Conradin was thunderstruck as though by a miracle, having unexpectedly been changed from victor to vanquished, and fled with a few companions. The king prevented his troops from following him, but kept them in a close and solid formation. Hence his force was sound and disciplined when it met the tired and disordered enemy, returning from its pursuit of the royal host. In this way the enemy was destroyed and a complete victory was at last attained. 1268

After a day and a night of continuous flight, Conradin arrived 14 in Rome and was received by Guido da Montefeltro whom he had left in charge of Rome when he set out for the war. The Roman People, too, were not unwilling to receive him, ignorant as they still were of the disaster he had suffered. But shortly thereafter the city was suddenly in arms thanks to the arrival of the Roman citizens of the Guelf party who had been expelled by Arrigo and who had fought on the king's side in the battle; the uprising was led by the Orsini and the Savelli. As a result Conradin took fright and left the city, going incognito to Astura, with the intention of sailing thence to Pisa. But he was captured near Astura and handed over to the king. Shortly thereafter he was taken to Naples and beheaded by sentence of the cities whose representatives Charles had assembled from the whole Kingdom to judge the prisoner. He was still in the first flower of his age, more a boy than a man. Beheaded with him also was the duke of Austria, who was about the same age, and Gherardo Pisano, who had commanded the Tuscans in the battle. Arrigo the Spaniard, who had fled the battle, was taken in the territory of Rieti and handed over to the king. Because of his blood-relationship with the king and because of an agreement he had made with his captor, he was not executed, but condemned to life imprisonment. After these events Sicily and

natam. Post haec in Sicilia ceterisque regni locis omnia in potestatem Caroli rediere.

15   Dum ea gerebantur apud regem, Etruria quievit, magna praesi-
diorum parte absente et animis in eventum proelii omnium versis.
Verum, ut peracta res est et Corradinus oppressus, ad bellum domesticum versae mentes, copias parare ac redintegrare certamina
perrexerunt. Itaque proxima post proelium aestate Senenses exulesque florentini qui Senis erant omnibus copiis profecti, Colle oppidum iuxta Elsam fluvium obsederunt. Id cum Florentiae nuntia-
tum esset, confestim equites peditesque eo properare ac sociis
opem ferre iussi sunt. Cum aliquanto ante solis occasum ad ea loca
equites pervenissent diversa ab hostibus regione, oppidi intra moenia recepti, peditum agmen, quod tardius incedens, non prius
quam altera die adfuturum erat expectare constituerant. At hostes
ob hoc ipsum conterriti prima luce retro moverunt castra. Id vero
cum trepidantius agerent, spem rei bene gerendae praebuerunt
equitibus. Itaque capta repente sunt arma nec ultra peditem expectare placuit, sed egressi magno ardore, hostem trepidum ceden-
temque invadunt. Oppidani quoque prosecuti et specie multitudinis et clamore iuvarunt. Ab his versi in fugam Senenses
profligantur; nec dubitatur, si pedes adfuisset, quin acerbissima illa
clades Senensium numeraretur. Equites tamen ipsi, quantum
maxima potuerunt edita caede, neminem fere captivum servavere.

16   Eodem anno Ostina a Florentinis obsessa. Occupaverant id castellum exules qui e proelio aufugerant. Mox, cum arctius preme-
rentur, noctu deserto loco evadere tentantes, cum incaute id face-

all the other lands of the Kingdom renewed their obedience to Charles.[8]

While these events were taking place under the king's command, Tuscany was quiet, since a large part of its garrisons were away and all eyes were trained on the outcome of the battle. But once the matter was settled and Conradin beaten, the Tuscans turned their attention to the war at home and bestirred themselves to raise troops and renew their struggles. Thus, during the next summer after the battle, the Sienese and the Florentine exiles in Siena set out with all their troops and laid siege to Colle Val d'Elsa. When the news arrived in Florence, the cavalry and infantry were ordered to march there at once and help their allies. The cavalry arrived a little before sundown on the side of the town opposite the enemy and were brought inside. They decided to wait for the infantry which travelled more slowly and so would not arrive until the next day. But the enemy were terrified at the prospect of further Florentine reinforcements and at dawn moved their encampment farther back. This revealed the enemy's fear, and gave hope to the Florentine cavalry that they might accomplish great deeds. So, seizing their weapons, they decided not to wait any longer for the infantry, but went out with high spirit and attacked the timorous and retreating enemy. The townsmen too went out and made themselves useful by the clamor they made and by giving the appearance of numbers. The Sienese took to their heels and were overwhelmed. If the infantry had been present, this would undoubtedly have counted as the worst of all Sienese defeats, but the cavalry were able to take few prisoners despite the great slaughter they had caused among the enemy.[9]

The same year the Florentines besieged Ostina, a castle that had been occupied by the exiles who had fled from the battle. Soon the latter were closely beset and tried to get out by leaving the place at night. But they did this so carelessly that the watch-

rent, non fefellerunt custodes; itaque insurgente clamore magna ex parte aut capti aut interfecti sunt.

17   Haud multo post reductas ab Ostina copias, Lucensibus postulantibus, quoniam adversus Pisanos ducere parabant, equites peditesque auxilio missi, usque ad Pisarum moenia cuncta popularunt et castella quaedam circa Auserim fluvium ceperunt.

18   Pax deinde cum Senensibus ex diutino bello recepta. Illi enim, cum spes nulla iam amplius superesset, ad Caroli gratiam conversi praefectum eius intra urbem acceperunt pacemque fecerunt cum florentino populo. Inter ceteras conditiones pacis illa fuit, uti Senenses florentinorum exulum neminem Senis senensive in agro esse morarive paterentur. Ea de causa quidam exulum Senis abeuntes casentinatem cum sese in agrum conferrent, capti per media loca et Florentiam ducti sunt, moxque de illis supplicium sumptum. Inter hos fuit Actiolinus Farinatae filius, eques florentinus, patre genereque illustris.

19   Eodem anno circiter Kalendas octobres duabus noctibus et luce media continuatis imbribus flumina mirandum in modum supra solitam magnitudinem excreverunt, pleraque egressa alveis circumiacentia inundarunt loca. Fluvius Arni factus auctior, cum magnam vim materiae trabesque exsectas et arbores revulsas radicitus[12] turbulento vertice deferret ad pontem, qui est ad Trinitatis aedem, transversus impegit; tumentibus mox aquis et, quia eo tenebantur obice, per urbem redundantibus instar diluvii cuiusdam omnia complevit. Tandem maiori aquarum vi disiecto ponte, impetus in alterum inde pontem delatus simili ruina illum quoque subvertit. Ita e quatuor pontibus, qui ripas Arni intra urbem iungebant, duobus eversis purgato demum alveo aquae cesserunt.

20   Annum insignem multis rebus insigniorem fecit pontificis mors, et contentio mox inter patres secuta, quae tanta obstinatione

men were alerted; so the alarm went up and a large proportion of the exiles were either captured or killed.

Soon after they returned from Ostina, the Florentine cavalry and infantry were sent out to Lucca. The Lucchesi had requested their aid as they were getting ready to march out against the Pisans. The Florentines laid waste to everything right up to the walls of Pisa and captured some castles near the river Serchio.

Peace then brought an end to the long war with the Sienese. The latter, now deprived of further hope, besought Charles' favor, accepted into their city one of his commanders, and made peace with the Florentines. Among the conditions of peace was one stating that the Sienese would allow no Florentine exile to remain either in Siena or in Sienese territory. That was how certain exiles, leaving Siena to take refuge in the Casentino, were arrested on the road, brought to Florence and then put to death. Among these men was Azzolino, the son of Farinata, a Florentine knight famous for his father and his lineage.[10]

In the same year, around the fifteenth of October, after two nights and a day of continuous rain, the rivers rose in an astonishing way above the normal depth, and many overflowed their beds and flooded the adjacent land. The Arno, growing ever greater, carried a huge mass of timber, broken beams and uprooted trees, swirling turbulently, down to the Ponte San Trínita where it dashed against the piles. The river's waters, blocked there, soon swelled up and washed over the city like a flood, filling all the streets. Finally the increasing violence of the waters knocked over the bridge, and it was borne down to the next bridge[11] with such force that it too was pulled under and collapsed. Thus of the four bridges which joined the banks of the Arno within the city, two had been wrecked. Eventually the river bed was purged and its waters ceased their destructive course.[12]

A year notable for many events was made more notable still by the death of the pontiff and the contention among the cardinals

17

18

19

1269

20

agitata est ut prope biennium trusi pertinaciter obdurarent. Ob eas partium discordias, adversa factio rursus in spem erecta, multa per Etruriam moliri dicebatur, Pisisque et apud Bonitium magnam vim hominum diversa sentientium convenisse. Ne apud Senenses quidem quietas esse res, multos enim spe novarum rerum aperte iam fremere. Accedebat ad hunc metum absentia regis necessario futura, quoniam Ludovicus Francorum rex, Caroli frater, magna parata classe, qua in Africam traiiceret, Carolum rogaverat, ne communi Christianorum causae deesset.

21 Harum itaque suspicio rerum ad curam Etruriae regem pertraxit, conantem, priusquam proficisceretur, impendentes rerum motus consilio praevenire. Quare Romam petens auctoritatem senatus iam pridem sibi demandatam, sed quodam tempore intermissam resumens Gebellinos in ipsa urbe primum afflixit. Mox in Pisanos conversus quibus infensissimus credebatur: quod per superiora tempora inimicissimo in regem fuerant animo, quod naves ad procurandas defectiones civitatum miserant, quod pecuniis et militibus Corradinum foverant. Ob ea cum putarent omnes ne eversione quidem Pisarum satiari regis animum posse, Florentinique et Lucenses, perpetui Pisanorum hostes, quasi ad certissimum illorum exitium secuturi regem se alacriter comparassent, contra spem ac vota hominum facile pax est a rege Pisanis concessa. Nam simul atque tetigit Etruriam rex, legati Pisanorum praesto adfuerunt mandatis sese obtemperaturos offerentes, mari etiam, quo per id tempus praevalebant, benigne operam polliciti. Sic obviam eundo et prompte offerendo, regis flexere mentem ut

that followed it. The succession was debated with such obstinacy that they remained shut up for nearly two years.[13] Thanks to these discords among the Guelfs, the Ghibellines took heart once again and were said to be hatching numerous plots throughout Tuscany. At Pisa and near Poggibonsi a large group of Ghibellines were meeting, and even among the Sienese there was some unrest, for already the expectation of a coup had brought into the open numerous rumblings there. What added to this apprehension was the coming absence of the king for necessary reasons. His brother, King Louis of France, had prepared a great fleet to sail to Africa and had called upon Charles not to abandon the common cause of all Christians.[14]

These suspicious circumstances led the king to turn his atten-   21
tion to Tuscany in a prudent effort, before he set out for Africa, to prevent impending coups. So he went to Rome and took up the senatorial power which had been entrusted to him long ago but which he had laid aside for a certain period, and he crushed the Ghibelline party in that city for the first time. Then he turned to the Pisans. He was thought to be extremely hostile to them, as they had in former times displayed great animosity towards him, sending ships to incite revolt in his cities and aiding Conradin with money and troops. So everyone thought that the king's desire for revenge could not be satiated even by the destruction of Pisa, and the Florentines and Lucchesi, perpetual enemies of the Pisans, had joyfully prepared themselves to follow the king, fully expecting Pisa's downfall.[15] But against all desire and hope the king readily granted the Pisans peace. For as soon as the king reached Tuscany, Pisan ambassadors at once appeared before him, offering to subject the city to his authority and promising generously to help him on the seas, where at the time they enjoyed preeminence. By going out to meet him and making an immediate offer they so changed the king's attitude that not only did he not persecute them at that moment, but he even formed an alliance

non solum non persequeretur eos in praesentia, verum etiam foedus in futurum coiret. Id regis factum multorum animos offendit, neque latuit regem ab omnibus fere amicis improbatam eius lenitatem erga tam saevos quondam hostes fuisse.

22 Proximo anno, vere primo, pax inter Florentinos et Pisanos facta est praesentibus ac iubentibus regis legatis. Fuerat enim bellum cum his post Corradini adventum, nec sane conditiones multae dictae nec libentibus animis pax recepta, sed ne regis auctoritati refragari viderentur. Quare properans contrario aliquo facinore[13] querelas amicorum tollere, Bonitium, praecipuam adversariorum sedem (quod in oppidum tota ex Etruria homines diversae factionis vel civitatibus eiecti vel regis adventum formidantes se recipere consuerant) per Guidonem praefectum suum obsidendum evertendumque curavit. Neque tamen ita gratuito, ut non pecunias ob eam rem praefectus exigeret. Promiserunt florentini populi nomine Rogerius Malespina et Clericus Pactius, equites florentini; ea post eversum oppidum praefecto flagitante persoluta est. Incolis autem (magna enim pars illorum voluntaria remanserat) sub ipso monte locus ad inhabitandum concessus.

23 Ex illo iam tempore mutatam rerum conditionem reperio apud Senenses, ac diversa factione succumbente in societatem amicitiamque florentini populi non dissimili partium studio devenisse. Pacatis igitur civitatibus quamdiu sedes romana vacavit, quieta omnia per Etruriam fuere.

24 Rex autem post Ludovicum fratrem in Africam profectus bellum una gessit, prosperos certe habiturum successus, ni mors immatura Ludovicum oppressisset. Illius interitu coepta tandem ex-

with them for the future. This action of the king offended many people, and he was well aware that his mildness towards those who had once been fierce enemies was condemned by nearly all his friends.[16]

The following year, in early spring, peace was made between the Florentines and the Pisans in the presence, and at the bidding, of the king's legates. For there had been a war between the two peoples after Conradin's coming. The treaty contained relatively few conditions, but the king's authority was not to be gainsaid, so the Florentines accepted the peace without pleasure. For this reason the king made haste to silence his friends' complaints by performing a great deed that would be in their interest. So he saw to it that his commander Guido besieged and destroyed Poggibonsi, an important Ghibelline base, where the men of that party used to take refuge from all over Tuscany when exiled from their cities or fearful of the king's arrival. Still, this did not take place free of charge: the commander demanded to be paid for it. Ruggieri Malaspini and Chirico de' Pazzi, Florentine knights, pledged the amount in the name of the Florentine People, and after the city had been destroyed the amount was paid on the general's demand. The inhabitants of Poggibonsi, most of whom had decided voluntarily to remain, were allowed to settle on a new site at the foot of the hill.[17]

I find that from that time forward Florentine relations with the Sienese changed. The Ghibellines were put down and the Sienese entered into alliance and friendship with the Florentine people thanks to a partisan spirit not dissimilar to their own. So the cities were at peace, and tranquillity reigned throughout Tuscany for as long as the pontifical see was vacant.[18]

The king set out for Africa after his brother Louis and made war there in concert with him. The war would certainly have enjoyed a prosperous outcome had not Louis suffered an untimely death. At his demise the expedition, so long in the planning, re-

22

1270

23

24

peditio ad irritum rediit; pactiones tantum et tributa quaedam, quo honestior esset pax, a barbaris extorta. Reversio inde Caroli in Italiam fuit et quidem cum omni procerum manu, nam et Philippus Ludovici filius, qui post obitum patris regium nomen susceperat, et alia procerum multitudo Carolum secuta per Italiam transiit. Hi etiam tunc discordes patrum animos et sedem vacuam offenderunt: tanta siquidem erat pervicacia, ut eos neque dei metus neque hominum preces neque christianorum querelae ab obstinatione et certamine dimoverent. Ad extremum vero post longas expectationes, quia inter se convenire non poterant, extra collegium respicientes Theodaldum placentinum, per id tempus in Syria commorantem, romanum pontificem designarunt, qui mox Gregorius decimus nominatus est. Is per litteras e Syria arcessitus ac summa omnium gratulatione Viterbii inunctus, cum haud multo post Hierosolymae recuperandae gratia concilium apud Lugdunium Galliae urbem indixisset, constituto tempore Viterbio movens comitante rege ac magna procerum manu Florentiam venit. Susceptus summa laetitia nec minori veneratione, cum amoenitate urbis delectatus in illa resedisset, amor coepit, si qua fieri posset, studia partium ac discordias civium sedare eiectosque dudum, cum bona venia illorum qui urbem tenebant, reducere. Id suopte ingenio a pontifice optatum incenderant[14] insuper exulum preces, qui se in pontificis auctoritate reponentes illius ad pacem invocabant clementiam. Suscepto igitur negotio pontifex ante omnia de hoc ipso cum Carolo egit, ac ubi regem non repugnaturum intellexit, magistratus principesque civitatis magno numero ad se vocatos in hunc modum traditur allocutus:

25 "Cum ad curandas hominum infirmitates discipulos suos magister ille supremus dimitteret, in quamcumque domum intrarent, pacem ei domui dicere praecepit. Et nos igitur quamquam imme-

turned empty-handed, having extorted only certain agreements and tributes from the barbarians so that the peace would be more honorable. Charles then returned to Italy, and with all his lords too; indeed, both Philip, Louis' son, who had assumed the royal title after his father's death,[19] and a second throng of barons passed through Italy following Charles. They too encountered the discordant cardinals and the empty papal see. For so obstinate were the prelates that neither the fear of God nor the prayers of men nor the protests of Christians would budge them from their stubborn rivalries. At last, after long suspense, they looked outside their own college — since they could not agree among themselves — and chose Theodald of Piacenza (who at that time dwelt in Syria) as the Roman pontiff. He took the name of Gregory X.[20] He was summoned from Syria by letter and anointed at Viterbo to universal applause. Shortly thereafter he called a council at Lyons, a city of Gaul, for the recovery of Jerusalem; once the date was set, he left Viterbo and came to Florence, accompanied by the king and many of his barons, where he was received with great joy and no less veneration.[21] He dwelt in the city, delighted by its amenities, and out of love for it began to seek ways of quieting its discords and partisan passions and restoring its exiles with the approval of those who controlled the city. It was the pope's own natural disposition to wish for this outcome, but the entreaties of the exiles also moved him. They had placed themselves under his authority and called upon his clemency to restore peace. The pope took up their case, consulting first with Charles about the matter. When he had ascertained that the king would not be opposed, he summoned a great number of the magistrates and civic leaders before him and spoke to them, it is said, in the following manner:[22]

"When our Supreme Master sent out his disciples to cure the infirmities of mankind, he taught them, whenever they entered a house, to say *peace unto this house*.[23] We, therefore, though called unworthily to succeed Him in this office, believe We shall have

1273

25

riti ad huius muneris successionem vocati, sic in mandatis ambulasse credemus, sic praeceptum domini, cui non parere nefas est, adimplesse si hanc vestram urbem ingressi pacem illi edicamus. Nam quid agat quis vel ad obedientiam maius vel ad utilitatem hominum conducentius? Constat enim nec domum nec civitatem salvam esse ullam posse, si pax exulet, discordia insit. Unde ex eodem sacrario illa quoque sunt prompta: Omne regnum in se ipsum[15] divisum desolabitur, et domus supra domum cadet.

26   "Equidem iam antea discordias et seditiones huius populi audiens mecum ipse horrebam, et nunc, cum hanc urbem vestram inspexi ac propius[16] morbo admovi manum, vehementius horreo misereorque vos prudentes quondam homines in tantam amentiam esse prolapsos. Etenim, per immortalem illum et ineffabilem Deum! quid sibi volunt haec partium studia? quid contentiones istae civiles? quid inextinguibile odium ac paene vesanus malevolentiae ardor in proximos, in cives, in consanguineos vestros? Est hominum quidem puerilis stultitiae annos supergressorum consilii sui, praesertim in re maiori et seria, rationem aliquam probabilem reddere. Vos, quaeso, utra tandem ratione factum vestrum defendere potestis, divinane an humana? Atqui, si divina inspicitis praecepta, nihil est fere quod[17] diligere magis debeatis quam proximos. Vos capitaliter eos odistis. Si humana, nihil magis quam patriam. Vos impie illam evertitis. Neque enim patria quicquam est aliud quam civitas, neque civitas aliud quam cives ipsi, quos qui pellit, qui necat, qui persequitur, proximos odit, patriam vastat.

27   "At unde ista vesania? unde hic tantus manat furor? Causam profecto non levem, non contemnendam, sed gravissimam urgentissimamque subesse oportet, quae ad tam nefariam mentem voluntatemque perpellat. Quaenam est igitur haec tam praepotens

walked in His precepts and fulfilled the Lord's command (which it is wicked not to obey) if We say peace to this city of yours after entering it. Indeed, what act could be either more obedient or more useful to mankind? For it is evident that neither any house nor any city can be saved once peace is exiled and discord enters. Wherefore let these words also be set forth from the same holy treasury: *Every kingdom divided against itself shall be laid waste, and house shall fall upon house.*[24]

"Yea, long before now have I heard of the discords and unrest 26 of this people, and I have shuddered within Me. Now, when I have gazed myself upon this city of yours and placed mine hand near unto the patient, I am deeply shocked and saddened that you, once prudent men, have fallen prey to such madness. By that immortal and ineffable God, I ask: what means this partisanship? Why these civic rivalries? Whence this inexhaustible hatred, this nearly uncontrollable spirit of malevolence against your neighbors, your fellow-citizens, your own blood-relatives? It is the mark of men who have passed the years of youthful foolishness to be able to give some good reason for their course of action, especially in great and serious matters. But you! With what reasons human or divine, pray, can you defend your actions? Indeed, if you have regard for divine commands, there is almost nothing you ought more to do than love your neighbor. Yet you hate them with a murderous hatred. If you have regard to human laws, you ought to love nothing more than your country. Yet you ruin it with your impiety. Your country is nothing other than your city; your city nothing other than its citizens. He who exiles, kills, and persecutes his fellow-citizen hates his neighbor and destroys his country.

"But what is the source of this uncontrollable fury, of this ter- 27 rible rage? Surely a cause that creates in you so wicked a state of mind and will ought not to be trivial or unworthy, but something very serious and compelling indeed. What, pray, is this

tamque perurgens causa? Iuvat enim audire, immo doleo audivisse. Quod guelfus est, inquit, aut gebellinus: nomina ne ipsis quidem qui illa proferunt nota. In his non nobilitas modo, verum etiam fatua plebs, cuius nec interesse quicquam potest, insanit, ac prout huius vel illius factionis est, ita alterius nomen in opprobrium iactat et capitali persequitur odio. Ea nimirum causa est cur cives necantur, domus incenduntur, evertitur patria, sititur proximi sanguis. O puerilem stultitiam! o amentiam non ferendam! Gebellinus est: at christianus, at civis, at proximus, at consanguineus! Ergo haec tot et tam valida coniunctionis nomina gebellino succumbent, et id unum atque inane nomen (quod quid significet nemo intelligit) plus valebit ad odium quam ista omnia tam praeclara ac tam solida et expressa ad caritatem? Neque vero magis ego vos quam illos reprehendo, nam utrisque idem est error et querelae ratio par. Utraque enim factio dum potuit, cives pepulit, domos incendit, proximorumque sanguinem concupivit; altera alteram saepius ulta est et ab irato Deo quasi flagellum quoddam ad affligendum alterutros vicissim traditum.

28   "Cum igitur in his quae superiori tempore a vobis factitata sunt insignis stultitia, vesanus error, eversio patriae, ac divinae simul humanaeque legis contemptus non cernatur modo, verum etiam palpetur, quid est iam tandem hominum non ad extremum perditorum? Nonne contraria facere velle quam adhuc fecistis? Resipiscite igitur aliquando et haec partium studia pestifera quidem ac detestanda oblivione sempiterna delete. Sit pro odio caritas, pro malevolentia dilectio, pro eversione status, pro pernicie salus. Ecce

overwhelming and urgent cause? I should like to hear it; or rather I should grieve to hear it. The answer? 'He is a Guelf' or 'He is a Ghibelline' — names understood not even by those who utter them. Not only the nobility but even the silly plebs, who can have no interest in such matters, go mad over them. Whoever belongs to one or the other faction curses the name of the opposite party and persecutes it with murderous hatred. Such, evidently, is the reason why citizens are murdered, homes burnt down, the country ruined, the blood of one's neighbor thirsted for. What childish stupidity! What insupportable madness! He is a Ghibelline: yes, but he is also a Christian, a citizen, a neighbor, a blood-relative! Shall names describing connections so many and so strong fall before the name of Ghibelline? Shall this single, empty name, whose meaning no one knows, weigh more on the side of hatred than all of these important, real and explicit titles of affection weigh on the side of charity? I do not censure you more than them: both of you are in error and there are equally good grounds to lament the behavior of you both. Both factions, when they could, expelled citizens, burned houses, lusted for the blood of neighbors; each party avenged itself on the other; each was handed over in turn to the other for punishment as though it were being chastised by an angry God.

"Since, then, in your prior behavior one may not only see, but 28 even feel the egregious stupidity, the irrational error, the ruin of your country and the simultaneous contempt for laws human and divine, is there any of you so lost in depravity that you would not rather do the opposite of what you have thus far done? So come to your senses, now, and wipe forever from your memories this accursed plague of partisanship. Let there be love in place of hatred, affection in place of malevolence, stability in place of ruin, salvation in place of your souls' undoing. For behold, those whom you have expelled from the city come before you seeking peace and wish to live in harmony with you, putting aside the brutal fury of

enim illi ipsi quos urbe eiecistis praevenientes pacem petunt ac deposito immani partium furore memoriaque omni praeteritorum deleta concordibus vobiscum animis vivere cupiunt. Id illi nuntiant; id ultro suppliciter exposcunt. Quomodo igitur pax etiam ad mundi huius inanem fastum gloriosior et honorificentior esse potest quam vobis rem publicam obtinentibus pacem ab illis peti ac vestro beneficio in urbem reduci? Nempe in alterutris iniuriis extrema quaeque acerbissima est. Si itaque illi accepti recens vulneris memoriam deponere parati sunt, quid vos, qui id vulnus intulistis, facere decet? Nonne multo[18] proclivius memoriam omnem iniuriarum obrutam velle?

29   "Denique, quoniam haec vestra partium studia pro romanis pontificibus contra eorum inimicos suscepisse asseveratis, ego romanus pontifex hos vestros cives, etsi hactenus offenderint, redeuntes tamen ad gremium recepi ac remissis iniuriis pro filiis habeo. Et vos ergo in nostra causa non plus quam nos ipsos velle par est. Quare, si bellum pro nobis suscepistis, pro nobis etiam pacem suscipiatis."

30   Haec pontificis oratio, etsi multitudini grata, praestantibus tamen viris, quibus tunc res publica nitebatur, onerosa fuit. Itaque placuit, quando perardua videbatur res, non protinus ad eam e vestigio respondere, sed dictis sententiis et in consilio re discussa. Igitur mature ex placito civium ad haec se responsuros affirmantes ex auditorio abierunt, coactoque postridie consilio, in quo optimus quisque ex nobilitate plebeque haud cunctanter affuit, de hoc ipso refertur. Dura sane omnibus ac minime tuta videbatur exulum reductio, et indignabantur plerique conturbata paene natura rerum et in contrarium versa id patrocinium pro inimicis adversus amicos a pontifice susceptum. Denique et negare postulata et conqueri

partisanship, blotting out all memory of the past. This is what they are telling you; this is what they beseech you on bended knee. What peace, even according to the vain pride of this world, could be more glorious and honorable than a peace entreated of you, while you are rulers of the commonwealth, by those who would be restored to the city through your grace and favor? Surely in a case of mutual injury the last injury is thought the most bitter. If therefore *they* are prepared to forget the injuries they have lately received, what is appropriate for *you* to do, who have inflicted that injury? Shouldn't you be much more inclined to wish that all these injuries be forgotten?

"Finally, since you claim to have adopted this partisan zeal for   29
the sake of the Roman pontiffs in opposition to their enemies, I, the Roman pontiff, consider these your fellow-citizens to be my sons. Even though hitherto they have offended Me, they have returned now to my bosom, and I have received them, forgiving the injuries they have done Me. It is not right for you to demand more in my cause than I do myself. So as you have undertaken war on my behalf, accept now peace on my behalf as well."

The pontiff's oration, though it pleased the multitude, was a   30
burden to the great men upon whom the commonwealth relied. So they decided, as the matter seemed extremely awkward, not to respond to it immediately, but to canvass views and discuss the matter in council. Thus, having told the pope they would respond to his remarks in due course in accordance with the will of the citizens, they left the audience chamber. The following day a meeting was called, eagerly attended by leading representatives of the nobility and the common people, to deal with the pope's proposal. Everyone felt the restoration of the exiles would be quite difficult and unsafe, and many were angry that in contravention of the natural order the pope had undertaken to protect his enemies against his friends. At length it was decided to reject his proposals and protest them openly. Thereupon a great throng of citizens came

aperte placuit. Reversi ergo ad pontificem magna civium frequentia, cum ante illius faciem maesti procubuissent, unus ex his, cui mandatum fuerat, in hunc modum locutus est:

31 "Postulatio tua, gloriosissime pontifex, eo nobis onerosior fuit, quo tibi magis obtemperare optamus. Quidquid a nobis refragabitur, in eo vis reverentiam superabit, magnitudo periculi voluntatem. Oramus vero eadem ut aequitate nos fideles devotosque aures audiant tuae, qua adversarios persecutoresque audierunt. Porro, etsi magna laus est parcere hosti, nunquam tamen aequum fuerit eos qui adversus te arma tulerint infesta et eos qui pro te pugnantes proprium fuderint sanguinem in eodem gradu meriti collocare. Denique nihil indignius aut perversius esset quam sic inimicos protegere ut amicos impugnes.

32 "Multa igitur in oratione tua admirari, eo vel maxime[19] stupore commoti sumus, quod, quasi tibi ignotum esset, quid sibi vellent haec partium studia flagitasti et quasi damnatam rem ac nomina ne ipsis quidem qui illa proferunt nota insectatus es. Nempe, si pugnare pro romana ecclesia, si defendere pontifices adversum persecutores furor ac dementia vocitanda sit, nihil est quod dicamus. Sin autem pium et gloriosum omnibus ac praecipue tibi videri debet, quo ore, quaesumus, Pater, studia partium nostrarum, quae semper hoc egerunt, pestifera detestandaque appellas?

33 "Utrum partes nostras non pro romana ecclesia contra imperii assertores stetisse dices vel favorem ecclesiae impendisse stultum simul ac damnatum esse? Atqui stetisse nos pro ecclesia, praeterquam facta, litterae quoque pontificum, quarum[20] infinitus paene numerus in publicis servatur archiviis, cohortationum et commen-

back to the pontiff and prostrated themselves sorrowfully in his presence. One of their number had been assigned to speak, which he did as follows:

"Your request, most glorious pontiff, is the more burdensome 31 to us as we should very much like to comply with it. If we must to some extent act counter to it, it is because the power and scale of the danger therein overcomes our reverence and good will towards You. But we ask that your ears hear us, your faithful and devoted followers, with the same spirit of fairness that You have listened to our adversaries and persecutors. Furthermore, though to spare an enemy deserves great praise, it is still unfair to assign the same degree of merit to those who have borne hostile arms against you as to those who have poured out their blood fighting for you. Finally, there can be nothing more inappropriate and misguided than to protect one's enemies in such as way as to injure one's friends.

"There was much that was surprising in your speech, but what 32 absolutely stunned us was your question—as though You didn't know the answer—'What means this partisanship?' and your attack on the 'names not understood even by those who utter them', as though they were things accursed. To be sure, if to fight for the Roman Church, if to defend popes against their persecutors are actions to be defined as madness and fury, we shall have nothing to say. But if these are actions that all (and You in particular) would agree were pious and glorious, how can You, Father, dare label our partisan zeal, which has always acted in this way, an 'accursed plague'?

"Are You saying that our party has not always stood for the Ro- 33 man Church against the champions of the Empire? Or that favoring the Church is something foolish and deserving of condemnation? That we have in fact stood for the Church is documented not only by deeds, but by papal letters, too, full of exhortations and commendations, of which an almost infinite number are preserved in public archives. Nor, indeed, are the merits of our ances-

dationum plenae testantur. Nec sane tam exigua fuerunt merita nostrorum, ut quae acerbissimis illis temporibus contra Federicum et Manfredum gessimus quaeque ab illis ob favorem ecclesiae passi sumus, tam facile debuerint memoria excidisse. An igitur favorem ecclesiae impendisse nefarium est ac eodem gradu nos, qui pro illa contra persecutores arma tulimus, et adversarii nostri, qui impia ecclesiae intulerunt arma, collocandi sumus atque eodem crimine (quod non sine gemitu te dicentem audivimus) partes nostrae illorumque damnandae?

34   "Nam quod quaeris divinane an humana ratione factum nostrum defendere possimus, nos et divina, quod pastori caelitus nobis praefecto obtemperavimus eiusque persecutoribus restitimus, et humana, quod vim vi repulimus et quod nefarios cives e civitate deiecimus. At proximos odisse contra praeceptum est. Noli, quaeso, nos ad hanc scrupulosam vivendi normam vocare; aliter enim caelum, aliter terra regitur. Porro ne praedecessores quidem tui, quamquam sanctissimi, percutientibus maxillam unam, iuxta praeceptum Domini, alteram porrexerunt, sed restiterunt viriliter adversus Federici Manfredique plagas, et cum resistere amplius desperarent posse, ne in altera percuterentur, trans Alpes usque aufugerunt. Nam de patria quidem satis legibus exemplisque maiorum cautum est malos cives in numero civium non esse habendos.

35   "Sed nomina videlicet et ea ipsa inania nos commovent? Non sumus ita leves neque tam ignari rerum, ut de verbo digladiandum putemus. Quin immo id ipsum, quod tu magni facere videbaris, unde nomina ipsa factionum dicantur, parvi admodum momenti apud nos est. Quid enim refert, unde quidque dicatur? Res plane

tors so slight that their deeds against Frederick and Manfred in those bitterest of times, their sufferings on behalf of the Church, deserve to be excised so easily from memory. And is it a wicked thing to devote oneself to the cause of the Church? Are we who bore arms for it against its persecutors, and our adversaries who impiously bore arms against the Church, to be placed on the same level? Is our party and theirs to be condemned for the same crime? This was something we couldn't hear You say without groaning to ourselves.

"You asked whether we could justify our actions either by divine or human law. We can appeal to divine law in that we have obeyed the Heavenly Shepherd as our commander and have resisted his persecutors; to human law in that we have repelled violence with violence and thrown wicked citizens out of the city. Yes, to hate one's neighbors is contrary to the divine command. But please don't hold us to this scrupulous moral norm: it is one thing to rule heaven; another, earth. Furthermore, not even your predecessors, holy men though they were, offered their other cheek, in accordance with the Lord's command,[25] to those who had struck them on the one cheek; they resisted manfully Frederick's and Manfred's blows, and when they despaired of being able to resist any longer, they fled across the Alps rather than be struck on the other cheek. As far as our country is concerned, we are sufficiently cautioned by the laws and examples of our ancestors not to reckon wicked citizens among the citizen body.

"But is it really just empty names that motivate us? We are not so shallow or inexperienced as to believe that one need fight over words. The source of the factions' names, which you seem to make so much of, really matters very little to us. What difference does it make where the names come from or what they mean? What alarms us are deeds and the facts themselves. Our ancestors long ago were expelled from the city and went into exile. They suffered harsh punishments at the hands of the Ghibellines: some were

271

ipsae ac facta nos commovent.²¹ Pulsi dudum urbe maiores nostri exularunt. Dura supplicia de illis sumpta; lacerati alii duris poenis, alii effossis oculis longo et implacabili carcere vitam amisere. Nobis deinde per scelus ac proditionem fractis dirutae domus, villae incensae, vastati agri, necati quicumque in potestatem adversariorum viri pervenerunt. An hoc de verbo cuiquam certamen videri potest ac non potius de vita et sanguine? Voca hos ut libet: rem ipsam attendimus. Nec, si nomen ipsum ignotum est, facta quoque illorum nobis²² sunt ignota et quae dudum fecerint et quae facturi sint, si potestatem nanciscantur.

36   "Nam quod praevenientes pacem petunt quodque memoria praeteritorum deleta concordibus nobiscum animis vivere ultro et suppliciter exposcunt, una atque eadem respondendi vera et simplex ratio est. Errat profecto bonitas tua, beatissime Pater, si illorum verbis credendum existimat. Fortuna quidem illis mutata est, animus vero idem permanet. Credamus vero²³ illorum verbis, si non alias ipsi nos credentes fidentesque apud Arbiam simul cum patria prodiderunt. Pacem petentibus annuamus et intra moenia recipiamus, si non isti ipsi intra moenia retenti tempus nocendi contra fidem observarunt. An vero quod tunc nullo impellente praeter insitam acerbitatem fecerunt, nunc extrema plaga exulceratos quam, ut a te disserebatur, acerbissimam esse constat, non existimabimus esse facturos? Non est ita. Plerique enim plus quam oportet infensionis memoriam servant, nec quisquam inimico et laeso non stulte se credit, quoniam hominum voluntates obscurae sunt, verba et frons persaepe mentiuntur.

37   "Itaque non tam huius inanis, ut tu modo vocitabas, fastus nobis est cura quam salutis nostrae, nec tam gloriam affectamus illo-

tortured, others were blinded and lost their lives after long and hopeless imprisonment. Then, after we had been brought down by wickedness and betrayal our houses were knocked down, our country estates burned, our fields devastated, and whoever of us came into the hands of our adversaries was murdered. Is there anyone who would call this a struggle over a mere word? Is it not rather about life and blood? Call it what you will, we look to the facts. We may not know what the name 'Ghibelline' means, but we know what they have done to us, what they did long ago and what they are planning to do if given the chance.

"But 'they come before us seeking peace and beseech us on   36 bended knee to live hereafter in harmony with us, blotting out all memory of the past.' There is one true and simple answer to this, Holy Father. Your goodness is certainly mistaken if You think their words are to be believed. Their fortune has changed, but their intentions remain the same. We might believe their words if on another occasion when we believed and trusted them, by the river Arbia, they had not betrayed us together with their country. We might consent to their appeal for peace and receive them back within our walls if it had not been these very men who, inside our walls, watched for a chance to break their faith and harm us. Should we believe that they will not do what they did before, when they had no motive beyond their native bitterness, now that they have been goaded to it by this last blow, which (as You Yourself say) is agreed to be the bitterest? Surely not. Many men nurse the memory of an offense longer than they ought, and no one is so foolish as to entrust himself to an enemy or to someone he has injured. The will of man is dark, and his words and countenance often lie.

"Thus, our concern is not so much for this 'empty pride', as   37 You call it, as for our security; we are attracted less by the glory of restoring them than by the feeling of safety we enjoy from keeping them out. The argument You put last in your oration, as though it

rum ex reductione quam ex reiectione securitatem. Quod autem
extremo in loco tua quasi validissimum habuit oratio, si bellum
pro vobis suscepimus, pro vobis quoque pacem suscipere debere,
quamquam in eo auctoritas tua nos admodum frangit, tamen vide
ne aequum sit, cum in extrema odia et gravissimas inimicitias con-
ieceritis, tunc pacem nobis periculosam indicere ac illis ipsis quos
offendimus salutem nostram, ut credamus, postulare.

38   "Quare, si pax dumtaxat petitur, ut pro vobis bellum suscepimus, sic etiam pacem suscipere non abnuimus; sin, ut in urbem
quoque recipiantur, curam salutis nostrae nimium abiecisti. Neque
enim par fuerit te illos ad gratiam et nos intra moenia recepisse.
Nam tibi quidem quid periculi receptio illa afferre potest? Nobis
vero quid non potest intra una moenia futuris? Sed quid nos aut
de aequitate causae aut de meritis nostris disseramus, quos tu resi-
piscere iubes et contraria facere quam adhuc fecerimus? O incredi-
bilem temporum mutationem! O spem fatuam nostram! An, cum
Innocentius, cum Urbanus, cum Clemens, romani pontifices ante-
cessores tui, nos adhortationibus et litteris ad persecutionem adversariorum impellebant, cum signa dabant quae armati sequere-
mur, cum opera nostra non solum gloriosa mundo, verum etiam
Deo accepta praedicabant, laudibus extollebant, quisquam putas-
set fore aliquando, ut romanus pontifex nos pro his factis resipis-
cere et[24] contraria facere quam adhuc fecimus commoneret? Non
possumus dicere non eandem esse sedem (est enim una et perpetua), sed illud dicimus: nos ab romana sede in fraudem compulsos,
quod ad quae instanter hortata fuerit, ea nunc acriter reprehen-
dit et damnat. Tu autem, Pater, vide etiam atque etiam quid

were the strongest—that if we have undertaken war on your behalf, we ought to undertake peace on your behalf as well—this
does have force with us, thanks to your authority. But look: is it
fair, when You have intermeddled amongst violent hatreds and the
most serious possible hostilities, to then declare a peace which is
dangerous to us and which puts our security, as we believe, at the
mercy of men who hate us?

"So if You are merely seeking peace, we won't refuse to accept   38
peace, just as we have accepted war on your behalf. But if this
peace includes taking them back into the city, You are recklessly
throwing away concern for our security. For us to accept them
back into the city, and for You to accept them into your favor, are
two quite different propositions. What risk does such an accep-
tance pose to You? But what might they not do to us once we are
all together inside the walls? And why are You speaking to us of
the justice of our cause and our merits when You are bidding us to
come to our senses and act differently from the way we have hitherto acted? It is unbelievable how times have changed! How foolish were our hopes! When Innocent, Urban, and Clement, your
predecessors as Roman pontiffs, were urging us on by letter and
exhortation to persecute their adversaries, when they gave us bat-
tle-standards that our men-at-arms were to follow, when they
praised our deeds and proclaimed that not only were such deeds
glorious in this world but that they were welcome in the sight of
God as well, who would have thought that there would come a
time when a Roman pontiff would advise us to come to our senses
about such deeds and do the opposite of what we had hitherto
done? We cannot say that the Roman See has altered (for it is one
and eternal), but we can say that we have been forced into fraud
by the Roman See, since things we were once urged vehemently to
do are now bitterly reproached and condemned. Consider very
carefully what you are doing, Father. Time brings many changes,
and human affairs coil back and forth like a snake. If the Church

agas. Multa quidem tempus affert variaeque vicissitudines rerum serpunt, nec, si nunc persecutoribus caret ecclesia, in futurum quoque carituram exploratum habes. Veniet profecto tempus in quo studia faventium improbasse nequaquam conducet ac resipiscent forsan plures quam tua levitas[25] debeat optare."

39 Magistratus quidem et cives qui ad pontificem venerant ita dixere. Pontifex autem nihilominus in proposito permansit. Denique urgere atque monere non prius destitit quam ipse[26] arbiter sumptus ad res componendas pacem pronuntiavit inter cives, gravissimis in eius pacis trangressores constitutis poenis. Ad tollendam vero suspicionem eorum qui urbem tenebant, complures ab exulibus iussit fidei servandae gratia obsides tradi. Ea cum perfecisset, basilicam dedicavit Gregorianam quae est trans Arnum iuxta supremum pontem. Nam et ipse, quamdiu Florentiae diversatus est, aedibus resederat Mozianis ei basilicae finitimis; laetatusque sua tandem opera pacem esse factam, litteras in pariete eius basilicae, huius pacis memorationem continentes, incidi non abnuit, quae hodie quoque in eo loco extant.

40 Haec tamen omnia plus in praesentia spei quam in posterum successus habuere. Cives enim qui graviter tulerant adversariorum in urbem reditum, haud multo post haec suspiciones fingere, rumorem spargere, occulte quaedam machinari; denique tantum terrorem illis qui per foedus redierant incussere, ut consistere non ausi sponte sua demigrarent. Ita longos pontificis in pacanda civitate labores brevis adversatio irritos fecit. Quae cum postea resciret, usque adeo indigne tulit, ut non solum obsides ab exulibus traditos e vestigio restitui iuberet, verum etiam transgressores graviter multaret populoque et urbi interdiceret sacris. Huic interdicto fere per triennium civitas obnoxia fuit. Nec facile dixerim maior obstinatio in pontifice, an contumacia fuerit in civibus.

has no persecutors at the moment, you cannot be sure that it will not in the future. The time will surely come when it will no longer be advantageous for Her to have condemned the zeal of Her supporters, and then, perhaps, more of them will 'come to their senses' than your fickle behavior should wish."

Such was the response of the magistrates and citizens who went to the pontiff. But the pope persisted in his design. In the end he did not abandon his bully pulpit until he had made himself arbiter of their differences and was making peace between citizens, assigning grave penalties to those who violated his truce. In order to remove the suspicions of those who controlled the city, he ordered a number of the exiles to be handed over as hostages in order to oblige the rest to keep their word. After he had done this, he dedicated the church of San Gregorio in Oltr'arno, near the last bridge. He himself dwelt while in Florence at the Palazzo de' Mozzi next to the church. He took pleasure in the fact that peace had been made thanks to his efforts and consented to have an inscription cut in the wall of this basilica commemorating the event. The inscription still exists there today.[26]

All this, while a hopeful sign at the time, was less effective with respect to the future. The citizens who were upset at the return to the city of their adversaries, soon thereafter began to fabricate suspicions, spread rumors, and plot in secret. In the end they struck such terror into those whom the peace had permitted to return that the latter did not dare remain, but emigrated of their own accord. Thus the long efforts of the pope to pacify the city were brought to nothing by a short campaign of opposition. When afterwards the pope came to hear of this, he was so enraged that he not only ordered the hostages the exiles had handed over to be immediately released, but he also laid a heavy fine on the culprits and an interdict on the People and the City. The city was subject to the interdict for nearly three years. It would be difficult to say which was greater: the obstinacy of the pope or the contumacy of

Neque enim pontifex, quamvis multum rogatus, interdictum sustulit, neque praestantes in re publica cives eo conterriti mutaverunt sententiam.

41   Altero dehinc anno Bononiae seditionibus exortis diversa factio urbe depellitur. Eo studio partium equites profecti, cum iam appropinquarent, egressi contra Bononienses nec sibi esse opus auxilio dixerunt pulsis adversariis nec in urbem recipere Florentinos velle, ne maioris turbationis materia oriretur. Ita palam spreto civitatis subsidio non sine indignatione Florentiam rediere.

42   Diversa eodem anno apud Pisanos fortuna fuit. Illi enim iisdem seditionibus agitati Iohannem Gallurae iudicem cum parte civium pepulerunt. Is ad Florentinos Lucensesque confugiens studio partium in societatem susceptus copiisque adiutus acre bellum intulit Pisanis. Sed hic haud multo post morbo interiit.

43   Postero dehinc anno Ugolinus comes, cum omni reliqua factione Pisis per seditionem pulsus, et ipse quoque ad Lucenses Florentinosque confugit et in societatem receptus est. Magnus hic rerum motus Pisanis fuit, propterea quod non in urbe modo, verum etiam per agrum magna multitudo Ugolinum sectabatur. Itaque Florentini et Lucenses in spem erecti exercitum parare ac exules Pisanos fovere statuerunt. Cum omnia parassent, magnis equitum peditumque copiis fines Pisanorum ingressi, non solum populaverunt agrum, verum etiam castella quaedam Pisanorum ceperunt; quod indignationem pontificis auxit. Nam ille paulo ante praeceperat civitatibus nihil inter se hostile moliri, sed ad suum arbitrium controversias referre. Itaque dolens poenas a se dictas contemni,[27] multo vehementius irritatus est.

the citizens. For the pope would not remove the interdict, though frequently implored to do so, nor were the republic's leading citizens so frightened by it that they changed their minds.

In the following year there was an uprising in Bologna and the Ghibellines were thrown out. The Florentine cavalry set out for Bologna out of partisan loyalty, but when they approached the city, the Bolognese came out to say that they had expelled their adversaries and had no need of Florentine assistance. They did not want to receive the Florentines in their city, they said, lest they provide fuel for a larger conflagration. So the cavalry returned to Florence with some indignation that the Bolognese had openly spurned their help.   41   1274

In the same year the Pisans experienced a different fortune. They were wracked by the same civil strife and expelled Giovanni, Judge of Gallura,[27] with his party. He fled to the Florentines and the Lucchesi where, owing to partisan loyalties, he was received as an ally and given military aid. He waged war bitterly against the Pisans, but died of disease shortly thereafter.   42

In the following year Count Ugolino with the rest of the Guelfs was expelled from Pisa for sedition, and he too fled to the Lucchesi and the Florentines and was received as an ally. This caused great instability in Pisa as Ugolino had a great following not only in the city but also in the countryside. Thus encouraged, the Florentines and Lucchesi decided to raise an army to support the Pisan exiles. When all was ready, they crossed into Pisan territory with large numbers of horse and foot. Not only did they lay waste to the land, but they also captured certain Pisan castles. This only increased the pope's anger. For he but a short while before had instructed the cities that they should not engage in hostilities with each other but should refer their disagreements to him as their arbiter. It vexed him that they had disregarded the penalties he had laid down, and he became still more strongly provoked.   43   1275

44   Per haec ipsa tempora synodus apud Lugdunium celebrata multaque a pontifice provisa ad propositum illud suum recuperationis
Hierosolymae pertinentia. Nam et cum Graecis quibusdam foedus
est ictum et quidam eius gentis errores improbante concilio sublati
et Rodulphus iam pridem ad romanum delectus imperium sub ea
conditione receptus, ut proximo inde anno in Italiam transiret.

45   Secuta est post haec pontificis reversio, qui eodem fere itinere
quo profectus erat, repetivit Italiam. Ergo superatis Alpibus, cum
in citeriorem Galliam primo, mox in Etruriam descendisset et iam
Florentiae appropinquaret, etsi non deerat suspicio ingens apud
principes civitatis ob superiorem indignationem, tamen reverentiae
magnitudo et sanctitatis opinio usque adeo praevaluit ut, omissis
ceteris respectibus, omnis multitudo urbana obviam profunde-
retur. At pontifici erat propositum ab ingressu urbis abstinere.
Itaque non longe a porta deflectens iter ex via bononiensi, qua
tunc adventabat, in arretinam viam contendit. Forte Arnus per eos
dies factus auctior maiorem sese obiecit quam uti vado transmitti
posset. Ea vi coactus est pontifex contra propositum animi per
pontem iter facere urbisque partem transitu attingere, nec quicquam moratus, continuo egreditur, duobusque passuum millibus
ab urbe via arretina diversatus est. De interdicto autem tollendo
nihil abeo impetrari potuit. Tantum, dum per urbem iter fecit,
gratiam et benedictionem civibus exhibuit; egressus vero iisdem
quibus prius censuris obnoxiam reliquit civitatem.

46   Inde postridie movens Arretium petiit. Eo cum pervenisset,
haud multos post dies morbo correptus gravi e vita migravit tertio
Idus ianuarii, quarto fere anno postquam sedere inceperat. Fuit
autem vir optimus et procul dubio sanctissimus, ingentis quidem
animi contra christiani nominis inimicos et qui sacrae recuperatio-
nem terrae semper meditaretur, ad eamque unam rem Christianos
omnes positis inter se contentionibus intendere debere censebat.

During this same period a synod was held at Lyons where the 44
pope passed numerous measures relating to his plan to recover 1274
Jerusalem.[28] He made a treaty with some of the Greeks and
caused the council to condemn certain errors of that nation.
Rudolf's election as Roman emperor, which had taken place some
time before, was approved on condition that he come to Italy the
following year.[29]

After the Council the pope returned to Italy by almost the 45
same route he had left it. Thus, having crossed the Alps, he came
down first into Lombardy, then to Tuscany, and at last approached
Florence. Although the city's leaders still regarded him with great
suspicion owing to the indignation he had displayed earlier, reverence and his reputation for sanctity prevailed to the point that the
whole urban multitude cast aside other considerations and poured
out to meet him. But the pontiff's intention was to avoid entering
the city. So not far from the gate he turned off the Via Bolognese
by which he had come and made for the Via Aretina. By chance
the Arno at that moment was higher than usual, and it was impossible to ford it. So the pope was compelled against his will to
make his journey by bridge and pass through a part of the city in
transit. He did this without stopping but exited immediately and
found lodging two miles from the city on the Via Aretina. All attempts to get him to lift the interdict failed. Only when making
his way through the city did he give grace and blessing to the citizens. Once he had departed, however, he left the city subject to
the same censures as before.

The next day he went on and made for Arezzo. Arriving there, 46
he was taken with a severe illness only a few days later, and died
on 11 January just about four years from the beginning of his 1276
pontificate. He was an excellent man and unquestionably very
holy, extremely hostile to the infidel, and obsessed the recovery of
the Holy Land. He believed that all Christians, putting aside their
own quarrels, should concentrate on this one goal. That was why

Ea de causa fiebat, ut studia partium, quae plerique romani pontifices ante foverant, ipse quidem propellere longe detestarique videretur. Sepultus est Arretii summa cum veneratione multaque circum illius corpus miracula postmodum subsecuta fidem eius sanctitatis indubiam praebuere.

47 Post novendiale sacrum inclusi patres Innocentium quintum pontificem creaverunt. Hic inter primas gratulationes interdictum gregorianum contra Florentinos positum benigne sustulit civitatemque ad sedis apostolicae gratiam recepit.

48 Proxima dehinc aestate Florentini et Lucenses magnis equitum peditumque copiis fines Pisanorum ingressi sunt. Fossa erat interim munitionis causa manufacta, quae regionem secans in Arnum procurrebat. Hanc Pisani crebris per eam propugnaculis ad vim hostium propellendam excitatis tutabantur. Cum ad eam ventum esset ac saepius tentata incassum transitio foret, quoniam lata et profunda fossa desuper tutelis firmata hostes facile repellebat, una tandem pervadendi via animadversa est per ipsum fluvii alveum secus fossae caput. Itaque contractis eo repente copiis equites primo, mox pedites transiere. Inde ad laevam conversi Pisanos pluribus locis sparsos ad tutelam fossae repentino impetu pervadunt. Turpis fuga hostium passim fuit, nec prius finis insequendi factus quam ad ipsa Pisarum moenia pervenerunt. Florentini et Lucenses post victoriam longo captivorum agmine multaque praeda, victricibus copiis ad ipsam fossam unde Pisanos deiecerant reductis, stativa posuere, nihil inde non hostile contra Pisanos molientes.

49 Dum his esset in locis Florentinorum exercitus, Valascus quidam hispanus a pontifice missus in castra pervenit indutiasque indixit ex pontificis auctoritate. Idem quoque apud Pisanos ab

he hated and rejected the partisanship which many Roman pontiffs before him had fostered. He was buried at Arezzo with great reverence, and the many subsequent miracles associated with his physical remains rendered unquestionable the belief in his sanctity.[30]

After the novena the cardinals in conclave elected Innocent V 47 as pontiff. Among his first acts of thanksgiving he graciously lifted Gregory's interdict against the Florentines and received the city back into the favor of the Apostolic See.[31]

The following summer the Florentines and Lucchesi entered 48 Pisan territory with a large body of horse and foot. In the mean- 1276 time a dike had been constructed as a defense-work; it ran from the Arno, cutting the region in two. The Pisans guarded it all along its length with numerous bastions erected to repel enemy forces. When the latter arrived and had tried repeatedly, but without success, to cross it—for the dike, being wide and deep and protected from above, easily repelled invaders—they at last discovered that the one way to get across was through the river bed itself near the head of the dike. So, suddenly massing their forces there, the cavalry first, then the infantry made the crossing. Then wheeling to the left, they broke through and attacked suddenly the Pisans who were spread out in numerous places to protect the dike. The enemy disgraced themselves, fleeing en masse, and were pursued to the very walls of Pisa. After their victory, the Florentines and Lucchesi, accompanied by a long line of prisoners and much plunder, brought their victorious troops back to the very dike from which they had dislodged the Pisans and set up garrisons there. Thereafter they made no more hostile moves against the Pisans.

While the Florentine army was in that area, a certain Spaniard 49 named Valasco, an envoy of the pope, arrived in the camp and declared an armistice by papal authority. He had done the same in Pisa. Then, having established himself as an intermediary, he ex-

eo factum. Post haec, medium se cum interposuisset, castigando atque monendo pacem extorsit. Conditiones in ea dictae ut Pisani Ugolinum comitem ceterosque exules in urbem reciperent; bona quae[28] ante exilium possederant integra[29] redderent. De aliis vero omnibus quibus de controversia esset in pontificis arbitrium consenserunt. Ita ab armis tunc discessum est.

50   Per hos ipsos dies Innocentius pontifex romanus, qui apud Arretium nuper assumptus fuerat, Romae decessit, sexto fere[30] postquam sedere inceperat mense. Eo defuncto apud Lateranum inclusi patres Adrianum creaverunt. Is fuit genere Italus, patria Genuensis. Hoc etiam intra paucos dies Viterbii defuncto, Iohannes xxi creatur, genere hispanus, qui et ipse sexto post coronationem mense apud Viterbium casu testudinis periit.

51   Ita quatuor pontificibus intra biennium defunctis, tandem Nicolaus tertius ad pontificatum assumitur, vir praestantissimus ex gente Ursina. Hic, etsi familia studio partium vel praecipua ortus, regi tamen privatim infensus erat quod nuper mortuo Romae Innocentio, cum ad deligendum pontificem inclusi de more patres convenissent, praesidens conclavi rex gallicos patres contra Italos vel impudenter foverat, ex quo magna nostrorum in se contraxerat odia. Ea igitur indignatione accensus pontifex et simul quia[31] maiorem potentioremque esse putabat quam libertati expediret, multa in suo pontificatu molitus est, quo regiam amplitudinem nimis elatam deprimeret. Nam et vicariatum Etruriae, quem ecclesia regi commiserat, exinanivit, et senatoriam urbis potestatem, quam ad eam diem continuarat rex, coegit dimittere; constitutione insuper edita, ne cuiquam regi aut regia stirpe oriundo senatoriam aliamve dignitatem Romae habere liceret, per quam nota inureba-

torted a peace agreement using threats and reprimands. The terms laid down were that the Pisans should receive Count Ugolino and the rest of the exiles back into the city, and that the property the latter had possessed before their exile should be fully restored to them. It was agreed to submit the rest of their disputes to papal arbitration. Thus it was that they laid down their arms.[32]

It was at that very time that Innocent, who had been assumed to the Roman pontificate not long since in Arezzo, died in Rome, hardly six months after he had begun his reign. With his death, the cardinals were confined to the Lateran and elected Hadrian. He was an Italian from Genoa. He too died a few days later at Viterbo. John XXI was then created pope, who also died in Viterbo six months after his coronation when a ceiling collapsed on him.

Thus, four popes had died within two years. But at last Nicholas III was elevated to the papacy, an outstanding man from the house of the Orsini.[33] Although from a family that was extremely Guelf in its political sympathies, he had a private quarrel with the king. This was because, after the recent death of Innocent at Rome, when the cardinals had gathered as usual in seclusion to elect the next pope, the French king, who was guarding the conclave, shamelessly favored the French over the Italian cardinals, thus drawing upon himself the hatred of our Italian cardinals. The pope was angry with the king for this reason, but also because he believed that Charles had become mightier and more important than was consistent with the liberty of the Church. So he made repeated efforts during his pontificate to reduce the king's inflated prestige. He stripped him of the vicariate of Tuscany that the Church had committed to him and forced him to give up the senatorial power that he had continued to hold up until that moment. He published a constitution, moreover, prohibiting a king or anyone of royal lineage from holding senatorial or other rank in Rome; through this constitution both Charles and Arrigo the Spaniard, who had lately been made senators, were stigmatized.

50

1276
1277

51

tur Carolo et Arrigo hispano, qui proximi fuerant senatores. Quoque[32] romana sedes minus opera indigeret regis, Bertuldum Ursinum propinquum suum turmas equitum alere iussit sub praetextu
urbium recuperandarum, quae per id tempus a Guidone Feretrano
principe diversarum partium in Umbria occupabantur. Discordias
quoque et simultates Etruriae civitatum, per quas fautores partium
et infinitam pecuniarum materiam rex captare solebat, tollendas
sopiendasque curavit per Latinum legatum, virum religiosum ac
praecipuae auctoritatis.

52   Igitur tertio anno pontificatus Nicolai Latinus Florentiam veniens magno honore a civitate receptus est. Mittebat illum pontifex gratia inimicitiarum publice privatimque tollendarum. Praeter industriam legati, quae in prensandis hominibus hortandisque
plurima fuit, illa quoque res non mediocriter suffragata creditur ad
pacem, quod nobilitas per id tempus acerbis inter se inimicitiis
conflictabatur armataeque familiae per urbem longis agminibus in-
cedebant pugnaeque et vulnera crebro committebantur, non sine
trepidatione tumultuque civitatis. Itaque hac deformitate rerum
fastiditi cives ac plane fatigati a desiderio reducendorum exulum
non penitus abhorrebant, nec porro nobilitas resistere poterat,
cum integra non esset, et quod alteri renuerent, id alteri sequen-
dum vel de industria suaderent.

53   His de causis factum est ut longe faciliorem viam ad res componendas Latinus[33] haberet quam dudum eadem in causa atque re
Gregorius habuisset. Exhortatus ergo homines, cum auctoritatem
pontificis publice privatimque interponeret, tandem civium pacem
ac reductionem exulum fieri obtinuit. Quo autem maior firmitas
paci inesset, advocata concione, cum multitudo omnia complesset, ipse sublimi de loco profatus longa oratione commoda pacis
explicuit eamque velut salutarem acceptandam servandamque sua-

So that the Roman see would have less need of the king's help, he commanded his kinsman Bertoldo Orsini to raise a force of cavalry under the pretext of recovering the Umbrian cities that the Ghibelline leader Guido of Montefeltro had occupied at that time.[34] The feuds and quarrels of the Tuscan cities, which were wont to supply the king with supporters and great sums of money, the pope took steps to calm through his legate, Latino, a holy man of great authority.[35]

Thus it was that in the third year of Nicholas' pontificate, Latino came to Florence and was received in the city with great honor. His mandate was to eliminate public and private causes of hostility. In addition to the legate's great industry in canvassing and persuading people, it is believed that he was helped in no small degree by the circumstance that the nobility at that time were at each other's throats. Families marched in long, armed cavalcades through the streets and were constantly involved in bloody fights, causing fear and disturbance throughout the city. The citizens had thus become disgusted and weary of this wretched state of affairs and so were not entirely averse to the desire to bring back the exiles. And the nobility was unable to resist, divided as it was: if one party refused to do something, that was reason enough for the other party to endorse it as a sound course of action.

For these reasons Latino had a much easier time settling local affairs than Gregory had had a little while before in regard to the very same issues. He exhorted the people, therefore, interposing pontifical authority in matters public and private, and at last succeeded in bringing about a civil truce and the return of the exiles. In order to strengthen the truce he called a meeting, and when the crowd had filled the area he himself addressed them from a lofty place, explaining to them at great length the advantages of the peace, and persuading them that they would be more secure if they accepted and preserved it. The terms of the arbitration were then announced, and he bade the representatives of the exiles to

sit. Conditionibus deinde ex arbitrio pronuntiatis, syndicos exulum assurgere iussit publiceque inspectante populo in mutuos amplexus civium devenire. Ad tollendas vero suspiciones multos utrinque[34] vades ultro citroque dari iussit. Forma quoque rei publicae gubernandae ab eo noviter instituta est, creato magistratu quatuordecim virum[35] mixtorum ex utraque factione, qui pro tempore praeesset[36] civitati.

54 Publicis compositis negotiis privatas subinde inimicitias tollendas curavit, pacatis familiis tam eiusdem factionis inter se quam diversarum, ubicumque privata odia ob caedes aut vulnera subessent. Ea quo magis rata forent, affinitatibus ultro citroque contractis homines censuit obligandos. Monumenta vero damnationum in publicis archiviis contra exules per superiora tempora reposita non cancellanda modo, verum etiam una cum libris tollenda providit, quo penitus earum rerum deleretur memoria. Bona quoque exulum, quae vel a fisco ex publicatione vel a privatis per potentiam tenebantur, illis quorum fuerant uti restituerentur effecit. Ex hoc iam tempore diversa factio magna multitudine in urbem rediit praeter quosdam principes, quibus concordiae gratia reditus est ad tempus aliquod dilatus. Fuerunt autem hi circiter sexaginta ex praecipuis familiis diversae factionis quibus circa urbem Romam exilii locus pro voluntate pontificis destinatus est. Illud praeterea additum, ut castella quaedam circa urbem in pontificis custodia essent utque magistratus Florentiae pontifex ad biennium ex arbitrio daret. Ea cum perfecisset legatus, ingenti prudentiae fama non immerito parta abiit, relicta civitate pacata et concordi quam impacatam discordemque susceperat.

rise and publicly embrace their fellow citizens in full view of the populace. To remove suspicion, he ordered the parties to exchange a number of persons to stand surety for both sides. He also established the constitution of the commonwealth in a new form, creating a magistracy of Fourteen Men, representing both factions, who would temporarily rule the city.

Having settled public business, he then saw to the removal of 54 private hostilities. He made peace among families of the same faction as well as between families of different factions, wherever private hatreds were festering as a result of murders or bloodshed. To strengthen these acts of reconciliation, he decreed that the people concerned should bind themselves reciprocally by ties of marriage. He saw to it that records from earlier times condemning the exiles which had been placed in public archives were not only crossed out but that the books containing them were removed, so that the memory of those events should be entirely blotted out. The exiles' goods and property that had been confiscated by the public fisc or usurped by private individuals he caused to be restored to their former owners.[36] It was from this moment that the Ghibellines now began to return to the city in great numbers, aside from certain leaders whose return had been put off for a fixed period for the sake of preserving concord. The latter constituted about sixty men from the leading Ghibelline families, for whom a place of exile near Rome was designated in accordance with the will of the pope. In addition, certain castles near Florence were to be placed in the custody of the pontiff, and the pope was to appoint the magistrates of the city at his pleasure for a period of two years. After he had accomplished these things the legate departed, having won, not undeservedly, a great reputation for practical wisdom. The city he had taken in hand when it had been disturbed and inharmonious he left behind him in a state of peace and concord.[37]

55   Ceterum ex hac providentia legati et simul ex revocatione vica-
riatus, de quo supra mentionem fecimus, rex dominatum Florentiae omnino dimisit, liberaque iam civitas et sui iuris facta a
quatuordecim viris gubernabatur. Hic rerum status fere biennium
duravit. Nec dubitatur,[37] si is pontifex vixisset diutius, quin longe
magis ea forma rei publicae fuerit duratura. Igitur quatuordecim
viris ex utraque factione rem publicam gubernantibus primo quidem anno quieta omnia domi forisque fuerunt, nec quicquam memoria dignum per id tempus accidit. Secundo quoque anno quies
domi viguit; foris autem multa, ceu nubila in sereno coorta, futurae tempestatis formidinem incussere. Causae vero turbationum
hae suberant.

56   Nicolaus, de cuius animo erga regem supra diximus, proximo
autumno apud Suriani arcem septem millibus passuum a Viterbio,
cum reficiendi sui gratia eo secessisset, subito apoplexiae morbo
correptus et officio linguae destitutus paucos post dies migravit e
vita. Quo sublato, cum de successore deligendo inter patres agitaretur, assumpti nuper a Nicolao cardinales italicum; altera vero
factio et ipsa per se potens et ab rege sublevata atque impulsa galli-
cum cupiebat. Aliquot menses cum eo modo concertassent neque
de pontifice convenire possent, Viterbienses infensi Ursino generi
ex superiori dominatu seditione facta ad arma ierunt novosque sibi
magistratus pulsis veteribus creaverunt. Inde caeco amentique furore conclave quo patres inclusi erant irruentes, duos Ursinos cardinales per vim detractos non sine contumelia abduxerunt. Abdu-
ctus est etiam cum his Latinus ille quem legatum nuper
florentinae pacis auctorem fuisse supra monstravimus. Sed hic
postmodum conclavi redditus est: duo autem Ursini privato car-

Now, thanks to the legate's foresight and to the revocation of   55
the royal vicariate (which we mentioned earlier) the king had lost
entirely any signorial powers in Florence, and the city was free and
under its own jurisdiction, governed by the Fourteen Men. This
state of affairs lasted almost two years, and that constitutional
form would undoubtedly have lasted much longer had the pontiff
lived. With the commonwealth ruled by the Fourteen Men chosen
from both factions, all was quiet at home and abroad for the first
year, and nothing worthy of record happened during that time. In
the second year, too, domestic tranquillity flourished, but abroad a   1282
number of clouds appeared in the clear sky, causing fear about
storms to come. The underlying causes of the disturbance were as
follows.

Pope Nicholas, whose attitude to the king we have described   56
above, withdrew for a rest the following autumn to Soriano, a castle seven miles outside Viterbo. There he was suddenly seized
with apoplexy and lost the use of his tongue; he died a few days
later. With him gone, the prelates began to discuss the choice of
his successor. The cardinals Nicholas had recently created wanted
an Italian, while the opposing faction, which was both powerful in
itself and also supported and manipulated by the king, wanted a
Frenchman. When they had argued in this way for several months
without agreeing on a pontiff, the people of Viterbo, who were
hostile to the rule of the Orsini clan, rose in arms, expelled their
old magistrates and appointed new ones. Then in blind and sense-
less fury they broke into the conclave where the prelates were immured and seized violently two Orsini cardinals whom they then
abducted in an insulting way. Abducted along with them was the
same Cardinal Latino who (as we showed above) had been responsible for the recent pacification of Florence. He was later returned
to the conclave, but the two Orsini were held in the dungeon of a
private individual. As a result, the French faction among the cardi-

cere detenti. Quo facto altera patrum factio praepotens ac plane victrix quem cupiebat pontificem habuit.

57 Creatus est igitur Martinus quartus, natione gallicus. Hic usque adeo regi coniunctissimus fuit, ut omnia sibi debere videretur. Ex hac itaque coniunctione et praesentia regis, qui paulo post gratulatum ad pontificem decucurrerat, civitates Etruriae, quae dudum in partibus fuerant, rursus ad regem inclinari coeperunt eiusque nutum in cunctis respicere. Quare praefecto Rodulphi imperatoris, quem ille post ablatum regi vicariatum volente pontifice quasi redditam imperio in Etruriam miserat, Florentini et Lucenses parere amplius noluerunt. Ob eam rem comminari ille primo et multas proferre. Mox ubi cognovit parvipendi, collecta manu quadam germanorum equitum Miniate ex oppido, quam veniens in Etruriam sibi arcem sedemque delegerat, bellum adversus Florentinos Lucensesque commovit. Haec res studia partium, quae iam extincta videbantur, iterato incendit. Itaque non multo post in suspicionem conversi Pisciam, oppidum lucensis agri, cuius incolae ad diversas partes inclinare videbantur, Lucenses Florentinique simul iunctis copiis obsederunt. Cum obsessi de conditionibus agerent Florentinique mitiorem partem amplexi recipiendas suaderent, obiurgati sunt a Lucensibus quod mixti ex utraque factione pristinam illam vim animi in tuendis partibus amisissent. Ita sublata reconciliationis spe Piscia oppugnatur; captaque tandem, ad solum evertitur.

58 Per hoc ipsum tempus Sicilia tota a rege defecit, et simul per Flaminiam atque Umbriam Guido Feretranus princeps diversae

nals acquired the upper hand and triumphantly elected the pontiff they wanted.[38]

Thus did Martin IV, a Frenchman, become pope.[39] He was extremely close to the king and was obviously his creature. So thanks to this alliance and to the presence of the king, who shortly thereafter hastened to the pope to congratulate him, the cities of Tuscany that had long been the king's partisans began once again to lean in his direction and to follow his lead in everything. That was why the Florentines and the Lucchesi were no longer willing to obey the lieutenant whom the Emperor Rudolf had sent into Tuscany after Charles had been removed as vicar. (Rudolf had done this with the pope's[40] approval, as though the region were being turned over to the Empire.) The lieutenant first began issuing threats, then fines. When he realized he was being ignored, he collected a force of German knights stationed in the town of San Miniato (which he had chosen as his citadel and base when he had come to Tuscany) and started a war against the Florentines and Lucchesi. This caused partisan passions, which had seemingly died out, to burst into flame once more. Thus, shortly thereafter, their suspicions aroused, the Florentines and Lucchesi joined forces and besieged the town of Pescia in Lucchese territory whose inhabitants seemed to favor the Ghibellines. When the besieged began discussing terms, the Florentines embraced the more pliant party and persuaded them to accept terms, but the Florentines were then upbraided by the Lucchesi for having lost, through contact with Ghibellines, their old zeal for protecting partisan interests. Thus all hope of reconciliation was lost. Pescia was besieged, captured, and razed to the ground.[41]

During this very period all Sicily rebelled against the king and at the same time Guido of Montefeltro, the leader of the Ghibellines, was reported to be planning a number of adventures in Umbria and the Marche. For all these reasons, and since now a renewal of partisanship was plainly visible and the city was awash

57
1281

58

factionis multa audere molirique ferebatur. Ob haec omnia, cum iam plane studia renovari partium cernerentur cunctaque suspicionibus redundarent, Florentini consortium diversae factionis hominum, qui in administranda re publica dudum recepti fuerant,[38] amovendum censuerunt. Quare quatuordecim virorum officio, qui mixti ex utroque genere civitatem regebant, antiquato, priores artium creavere. Tres ab initio creatos constat, postea sex, inde duodecim, mox octo, quod suis quidem temporibus apparebit. Nec tamen huius magistratus nomen tunc primo in re publica repertum est: constat enim annalibus octoginta ferme annis ante id tempus priores artium in re publica fuisse, sed postea omissum ac paene obliteratum. Tandem hoc tempore amplificata potestate resumptum est.

59   Populare autem maxime id genus administrandi esse vel ex nomine ipso intueri licet. Quod enim potentes quidam plus nimio turbationes optare videbantur, ad pacatum tranquillumque genus hominum, non tam bellis et contentionibus quam negotiis in pace gerundis intentum, civitatis translata est gubernatio, atque ob id priores artium dicti, quia non ex rapacibus neque seditiosis, sed ex frugali pacatoque hominum genere, ut cuiusque exercitia erant, suffragiis populi anteferebantur (nam qui inertes sunt, ex aliorum bonis nutriantur oportet). Hunc magistratum nomenque hodie quoque in civitate durare trigesimo atque octavo supra centesimum anno signum fuerit non absque optima ratione excogitatum fuisse. Nam quae damnosa sunt, et si non homines at tempus experientiaque, rerum magistra, redarguit, nec diuturna fore permittit. Primi tunc omnium priores artium creati fuerunt Bartolus Bardius Iacobi equitis filius, ex familia nobili et in primis locuplete,

with distrust and suspicion, the Florentines decided to get rid of the power-sharing arrangement with the Ghibellines who had previously taken part in the government of the commonwealth. Thus the magistracy of the Fourteen — the representatives of the two parties who had been ruling the city — was done away with, and the Priors of the Guilds were appointed. At first, as is known, three were appointed, then six, then twelve, and after that eight: this will all be shown in the appropriate place. Then was not the first time a magistracy of this name had existed in the commonwealth. According to the annals there were evidently Priors of the Guilds in the commonwealth some eighty years before this time, but the office afterwards fell into disuse and was nearly forgotten. After a long interval the magistracy was resumed with broader powers in the period under discussion.

This form of administration was populist to the highest degree, as can be seen from its very name. Because there were certain powerful individuals who seemed inordinately given to civil discord, the government of the city was handed over to a quiet and peace-loving sort of person who was more inclined to carrying on business in peacetime than to engaging in war and strife. That is why they were called Priors of the Guilds: they enjoyed popular approval and preference because they were neither predatory nor seditious, but frugal and peace-loving persons each exercising his own métier (for the lazy have to feed off the goods of others). That this magistracy under the same name has lasted in the city up to the present day, one hundred and thirty-eight years later, is a sign that it was excellently designed. Even when human beings cannot do so, time and Experience, the mistress of nature, show harmful things to be wrong-headed and do not allow them to enjoy long life. At that time, the very first Priors of the Guilds to be created were Bartolo di messer Jacopo de'Bardi, from a noble and extremely rich family, Rosso Bacherelli, and Salvi del Chiaro Girolami. These men were immured in the palazzo of the commune,

1282

59

Rossus Bacarelli, Salvius Clari Hieronymi. Hi publicis aedibus inclusi nec aliud quicquam quam de re publica cogitare[39] iussi sunt et sumptus ex publico eis praebiti, cum ceteri omnes ante id tempus magistratus domum suam redire post negotia consuessent. Duodecim apparitores illis a populo dati, sex viatores ad convocandos cives, totidem ad[40] cetera obeunda ministeria. Tempus autem huius magistratus bimestre constitutum est, quod hodie quoque servatur. Post hos duplicatus est numerus et sex pro tribus suffragio civium suffecti; in sex enim regiones divisa civitate singulos ex singulis ad prioratum sumi placuit.

60   Eodem anno imbres assidui circiter Idus decembres compluris[41] dies noctesque continuati omnia paene urbis loca inundarunt. Ab his cum sementes dilutae ac solo abrasae interiissent, confestim adempta spe futurarum messium annonae caritas est consecuta.

61   Per idem tempus Caroli regis filius, novis rebus Siciliae excitus, ad patrem ex Gallia properans cum quadam manu equitum Florentiam venit, nec minori applausu receptus est quam si pater urbi dominaretur. Eodem quoque anno Caroli auxilio missi equites urbani sexcenti apparatu insigni, qui regi in Siciliam traiicere festinanti circa Regium Calabriae oppidum sese coniunxerunt et in obsidione Messanae aliisque subinde locis fideliter simul strenueque suam operam navarunt.

62   Res postulare videtur ut de rebellione Siciliae ac de ceteris quae eidem acciderunt regi, discursu brevissimo referamus, praesertim cum eius res adeo sint cum civitatis rebus connexae ut magnopere intersit illas cognoscere, et auxilia eo missa quibus ex causis evocata, quibusve locis obsecuta fuerint, non aliter quam per eorum explicationem queat[42] intelligi.

63   Post victum Corradinum recuperatamque Siciliam, cum civitates quae dudum Capitii et Federici ductu rebellaverant in regis

forbidden to deliberate about anything except public business, and maintained at public expense; previous officials had all been allowed to return to their own homes after work. The people gave them twelve clerks, six runners to assemble the citizens, and six servants to take care of their other needs. The term of the magistracy was established at two months, just as it is today. After the first priorate the number was doubled and by a vote of the citizens six priors were appointed instead of three. The city being divided into six regions, it was agreed that each region would choose one person for the priorate.

In the same year, around the Ides of December, there were many days of continuous heavy rain which flooded nearly the whole city. As a result the crops were washed away and destroyed, immediately removing all hope of future harvests, and in consequence there was famine and want.[42]

At this time the son of King Charles, disturbed by the rebellions in Sicily, hastened from France to join his father and came to Florence with a troop of cavalry. He was received with no less applause than if his father had been lord of the city. Also in that year the city sent six hundred well-equipped knights to help Charles. They joined the king near the town of Reggio Calabria as he was making haste to cross over into Sicily. They acquitted themselves with great energy as well as loyalty at the siege of Messina and thereafter in other places.[43]

It seems appropriate to give a brief account here of the rebellion in Sicily[44] and the other events relating to the king, especially as these matters are so interconnected with the affairs of our city that an explanation of the former contributes greatly to the comprehension of the latter. Indeed, one cannot otherwise understand why the expeditionary force was summoned there or why they served in the places they did.

After the defeat of Conradin and the recovery of Sicily, those cities that had previously rebelled under the leadership of Capizio

60

61

62

63

fidem potestatemque rediissent, praefecti ad eas gubernandas viri gallici, feroces natura atque superbi, innumeras Siculis inferebant clades, tantaque erat gubernatorum petulantia ut non iam liberorum hominum, sed mancipiorum loco Siculi haberentur. Pro levissimis rebus ac saepe pro verbo liberius emisso supplicia aderant crudelissima. Delatorum plenae erant urbes; laquei et secures in levissimis habebantur poenis. Ad haec avaritia Gallorum inexhausta et auri cupido insatiabilis nocentes pariter innocentesque pervadebat, nec ullus rapinarum erat modus. Divitiae pro crimine maiestatis lesae habebantur, ut quisque amplissimo erat patrimonio, ita in periculum acerrime vocabatur: id genus hominum rebellionis auctor fuisse, id maledixisse regi, id Corradini imaginem domi habuisse accusabatur. Iacturae fortunarum iam in consuetudinem venerant; optabiles quidem, modo supplicia excarnificationesque cessarent. His accedebant libidines non maiorum modo, verum etiam ministrorum in uxores et filias Siculorum sine ullo respectu aut verecundia, ut quidquam placitum fuerat.

64   Hanc durissimam servitutem aliquot annis perpessae civitates, tandem superante patientiam magnitudine iniuriarum in furorem vertuntur. Initium rerum novarum a Panormitanis factum. Hi enim diem festum extra urbem agentes, cum a Gallis eo profectis arma explorarentur ac eo praetextu sinus mulierum papillasque[43] obtrectarent, concita ob eam foeditatem seditione Gallos lapidibus primo, mox armis persecuti omnes interfecerunt. Rumor deinde Panormo in alias civitates delatus eodem exemplo ad arma et caedem populos excivit. Ita per totam Siciliam trucidati Galli, cum ardor eorum petulantiae proprio sanguine extinctus esset, non so-

and Federico became loyal once more to the power of the king. The Frenchmen sent out to govern them, who were by nature fierce and proud, caused innumerable sufferings among the Sicilians. In their insolence they treated the Sicilians like slaves rather than like the free men they had once been. The latter were subjected to the cruelest punishments for the lightest of causes — often for a word spoken a little too freely. The cities were full of informers, and the noose and the executioner's axe replaced lighter punishments. Moreover, the inexhaustible avarice of the French and their insatiable lust for gold embraced the innocent as well as the guilty, and their acts of plunder were beyond measure. To be rich was to be guilty of treason, and the larger one's patrimony, the keener the danger one invited. It was the rich man who was accused of having fomented rebellion, of having cursed the king, of keeping images of Conradin in his house. The loss of one's fortune now became commonplace; indeed it became desirable so long as it brought a stop to punishments and torture. To these crimes were added acts of lust — not only on the part of the great men, but even of their ministers — perpetrated arbitrarily, without respect or shame, against the wives and daughters of the Sicilians.

The cities endured this hard slavery for several years, but at 64 last, the magnitude of their sufferings overcame their patience and was transformed into rage. The rebellion started in Palermo. The Palermitans were holding a festival outside the city when the French came up to check them for weapons, and on that pretext began fondling the breasts of their women. The repulsive nature of this act started a riot, and the French were attacked first with rocks, then weapons, and every one of them was killed. The tale then spread from Palermo to the other cities, and stirred up the peoples there to arms and slaughter. Thus the French were cut to pieces throughout Sicily. By the time the furious anger at their insolence had drunk its fill of their blood, the French had given up

lum divitias male coacervatas, sed corpora insuper Siculis relinquere.

65   Rex per id tempus in Etruria erat, qui audita Siculorum defe-
ctione magnis itineribus in regnum contendit. Eo cum pervenisset,
copias undique contrahit; Florentinos ac ceteras amicas civitates
auxilia rogat. Ipse apud Regium, qua proxime est transmissio in
Siciliam, constitit. Ibi copias venientes excipit, quaeque opportuna
sunt ad transitum parat. Erat perdifficilis transmissio, propterea
quod omnes ferme regis naves in Siciliae portibus navalibusque as-
servabantur, quae tunc rebelles cuncta tenebant. Itaque, contractis
ex omni maritima Italiae ora navibus, Messanam (quae proxima
erat) traductis copiis obsidere incepit. Vehemens eius urbis oppugnatio fuit, nec remissior sane eorum qui obsidebantur in resis-
tendo audacia. Nam et rex in hac una urbe, quam primo cir-
cumsteterat, iudicium de se fieri apud alios Siciliae populos haud
falso existimabat, utque res ea successisset, ita ab aliis quoque aut
formidari se aut contemni. Et Mamertini contra victoris iram per-
timescebant; Gallorum superbia crudelitasque ante oculos versabatur, cui foeditati honestam profecto mortem censebant praeferendam. Rege circa Messanam habente castra bellicumque terrorem
Siculis ostentante, civitates crebris legationibus ad Petrum Arragonum regem missis sibi ut subveniret precabantur. Regnum Siciliae
ad illum pertinere docebant, quoniam uxor eius Constantia Manfredi quondam Siciliae regis filia esset, ad quam consumpta virili
prole haud dubie regni pertineret successio; possessionem vero civitates unanimiter et cupientissime offerre. Iam vero Manfredi
mortem ulcisci, ad quem magis quam ad generum nepotesque[44]
spectare? Praesertim cum idem sit interfector, idem occupator re-

to the Sicilians not only their ill-gotten riches, but their lives as well.[45]

The king was at that moment in Tuscany. When he heard of 65 the Sicilian revolt, he marched quickly to the Kingdom and upon his arrival assembled forces from every quarter. The Florentines and other friendly cities were asked to help. The king himself stayed in Reggio, where one crosses over to Sicily, and welcomed the troops there as they arrived while making suitable preparations for the crossing. The crossing to Sicily was particularly difficult because almost all the king's ships were docked in Sicilian ports and naval facilities, which were all controlled by the rebels. So, after scouring the coasts of Italy for ships, he began the siege of Messina, on the shore opposite, with the forces he had assembled. His attack on that city was vigorous, and the resistance of the besieged was no less brave. For the king rightly believed that the other Sicilian peoples would form their judgment of him from his performance at this one city, the first he had besieged, and that they would fear or despise him to the extent he succeeded there. The inhabitants of Messina, on the other hand, were terrified of the victor's wrath; they had witnessed with their own eyes the arrogance and cruelty of the French, and they believed an honorable death preferable to such infamous treatment. The king ringed Messina with encampments to impress the Sicilians with the terrors of war, while the cities sent a string of ambassadors to King Peter of Aragon[46] to beg for his aid. They informed him that the Kingdom of Sicily belonged to him, since his wife Constance was the daughter of Manfred, the late king of Sicily; the male line having died out, the succession of the kingdom undoubtedly had fallen to her; the cities with one accord and with the greatest eagerness offered him possession of the kingdom. And indeed, whose duty was it to avenge Manfred if not that of his son-in-law and grandsons? This was even more the case as it was the same man who had killed Manfred, occupied his kingdom and perse-

gni, idem civitatum vexator; quae pati ut ludibrio habeantur,[45] contra decus sit regii nominis.

66   His tandem vocibus permotus rex Siciliam capessere constituit. Et adiuvabat celeritatem eius coepti, quod ipse paulo ante magna parata classe in Africam traiecerat afflictisque magna strage Barbaris et oppido in litore expugnato, non longe a Sicilia victorem exercitum classemque habebat. Profectus igitur ex litoribus Africae, cum Panormo applicuisset, receptus summa gratulatione a Panormitanis rexque Siciliae appellatus, structis de cetero navibus Messanam petere contendit. Carolus, quod praevalere hostem classe intelligebat ac periculosum arbitrabatur tota Sicilia adversante in illa includi et commeatus penuria urgeri, dissolvendam obsidionem ac in Italiam[46] remeandum statuit. Id regis consilium ubi per castra innotuit, tantus repente concursus ad mare factus est (properantibus cunctis ne in postremis traiicerent), ut non multum a fuga et desperatione res illa distare videretur; tentoria et machinas et apparatum omnem in castris relinquerent;[47] vixdum traducto exercitu hostium classis advenit. Carolus autem quia non decertandum in praesentia, sed alia ratione gerendum existimabat bellum, copias dissolvit et auxilia amicorum[48] domum remisit. Sed classis, dum[49] abiret, per speculatores hostium conspecta ab Arragonibus invaditur. Ex ea aliquot naves in quibus Pisanorum triremes fuerunt quatuor ex foedere nuper ad Carolum missae capiuntur et Messanam ducuntur. Equites vero florentini a rege dimissi domum rediere, incolumes quidem, praeterquam quod tentorium publicum ex more duci eorum traditum in illa fuga in castris apud Messanam amiserant. Quod a Mamertinis captum, diu inter spolia asservatum est.

67   Altero dehinc anno domi quies fuit, nec lacessitis bello nec lacessentibus. Nam et praefectus Rodulphi nuper in Etruriam mis-

cuted his cities. It was contrary to his royal honor that they should become objects of derision.

The king was strongly moved by these arguments, and he de- 66 cided to set out for Sicily. His enterprise was all the more swiftly undertaken in that he had a little while before set up a fleet, crossed to Africa, and inflicted great slaughter on Barbary; and having taken a town on the coast he possessed a victorious army and fleet not far from Sicily. So he set out from the coast of Africa and on his arrival in Palermo was received with great joy by the populace and hailed as king of Sicily. He then assembled a fleet and set sail for Messina. Charles, recognizing the superiority of the enemy fleet and thinking it risky, with all Sicily against him, to be trapped there and beset by lack of provisions, decided to abandon the siege and turn back to Italy. When the king's decision became known in the camps, there was such a sudden rush down to the sea (for nobody wanted to be the last to cross) that the operation was hardly distinguishable from a hopeless rout. The tents and siege-engines and all the equipment were left behind in the camps, and scarcely had the army withdrawn when the enemy fleet arrived. Charles, however, having decided not to fight at that moment but to wage war in another way, dissolved his forces and sent his friends' auxiliaries home. But when he was on the point of leaving, his fleet was discovered by enemy scouts and attacked by the Aragonese. Several of his ships were captured and brought to Messina, including four Pisan triremes that had recently been sent to Charles in accordance with the treaty. The Florentine knights dismissed by the king came home unharmed, although in their flight they lost the city's great field-pavilion, which had in accordance with custom been entrusted to their leader. It was captured by the men of Messina and long preserved among their spoils.[47]

The next year was tranquil domestically, and the Florentines 67 neither made war nor had war made against them. The lieutenant 1283 Rudolf had recently sent to Tuscany, the one who had begun to

sus qui Miniate ex oppido bellum coeperat inferre, non conse-
quentibus viribus ab incepto destiterat, et missi ad Carolum
equites domum remearant. Itaque ad laetitiam conversis animis
ludi quidam insignes eo anno per urbem dati et apparatus magnifici vicatim prope exhibiti; viri unum in morem vestes plerique
albas induti, mulieres quoque omni sumptuositate ornatus Compitalia exercuere.

68   Sequitur post hunc annus insignis multis rebus. Eo anno foedus ictum est[50] cum Genuensibus. Superaverant enim[51] illi paulo
ante Pisanos navali proelio et reliquias belli persequebantur.
Quamobrem credebatur Pisanorum nomen omne posse deleri, si
Genuenses quidem mari, Florentini autem et socii terra adorirentur. Et profecto causae suberant legitimae ad bellum, quod illi post
pacem non satis pacate in Lucenses[52] finitimos se habuisse,[53] Ro-
dulphique praefecto bellum nuper inferenti cohaesisse arguaban-
tur. Ad hoc igitur icto foedere, Florentini et Lucenses ceterique socii constituto tempore profecti ad ipsa prope Pisarum moenia
posuerunt castra; Genuenses autem mari aderant quadraginta longis navibus. Hae terrestres maritimaeque copiae cuncta igne ferroque populatae sunt. Post multiplices illatas clades exercitus dis-
cessere eo proposito, ut proxima dehinc aestate maiori apparatu
marique terraque rursus coirent ad Pisas obsidendas.

69   Cum itaque salus nulla Pisanis superesse videretur, Ugolinus
comes, qui florentina ex pace nuper redierat Pisas, locum adversarios criminandi nactus, quod obstinata quadam perversitate Florentinos Lucensesque sibi inimicos infestosque reddidissent, quibuscum amice erat vivendum, "Quid," inquit, "profuit haec

make war from the town of San Miniato, abandoned his enterprise from lack of resources. The knights that had been sent to help Charles returned home. So the citizens turned their minds to festivity, and gave some famous shows in that year throughout the city, with magnificent displays in nearly every neighborhood. Many men, dressed up in white clothing of a uniform cut, and women too, sumptuously arrayed, celebrated street-festivals.[48]

The year that followed was distinguished by numerous events. 68
In that year a treaty was signed with the Genoese. They had re-   1284
cently beaten the Pisans in a naval battle and were hunting down
the remnants of their fleet. On this account it was believed that
the Pisans could be entirely wiped out if the Genoese attacked by
sea and the Florentines and their allies by land. There were, to be
sure, legitimate grounds for the war, as the Pisans were accused of
not treating their neighbors, the Luccchesi, in a peaceful manner
after the truce, and of having aligned themselves with Rudolf's
lieutenant in the lately-threatened war. Having formed a league on
this account, the Florentines, the Lucchesi and other allies set out
at the appointed time and pitched camp by the very walls of Pisa,
while the Genoese brought up forty galleys by sea. These land and
sea forces laid waste to everything with fire and sword. After they
had inflicted great damage, the armies departed with the intention
of coming again by land and sea to besiege Pisa the following summer with still more apparatus of war.

Thus the Pisans seemed to be in a hopeless situation, and this 69
gave Count Ugolino, who had recently returned to Pisa after the
Florentine peace, the opportunity to denounce his opponents.
Thanks to an obstinate perversity, he charged, they had made enemies of the Florentines and Lucchesi, with whom they ought to be
living on a friendly basis. "What profit is there," said he, "in this
stubborn desire to take sides against nearly all our neighbors? In
my view, the empire of the Pisan people should be extended by
sea, while on land we should embrace our neighboring cities in

pervicacia, ut prope omnium finitimorum diversas tam cupide ar-
riperemus partes? Ego quidem ut mari propagandum populi pisani imperium, sic terra vicinas civitates benevolentia et caritate
putabam continendas. Id profecto maioribus nostris sapientissimis
viris placuisse video, qui Corsicam, qui Sardiniam, qui Baleares in-
sulas procul sitas imperio subiicientes suo, Lucam in vestibulo
paene urbis nostrae positam intactam reliquerunt. Hi vero contra
praeclari gubernatores nostri molestissimas simultates domi paran-
tes nulla probabili ratione perpetuos nobis hostes a terra imminere
procurarunt. Et nunc quoque mea sententia est Florentinos esse
pacandos. Nec sane id videtur difficile, si eius rei naturam penitus
discernamus. Etenim quibus de rebus nobis atque illis contentio
est? De Sardiniae dominatu, an de insularum aliarum possessione? At id ne in cogitationem quidem eorum unquam venit. An
certare nobiscum volunt de rerum maritimarum potentia? At id
quidem curae illis nunquam fuit. An quod agro nostro indigent
quem colant ex quove alantur? Satis ipsi quidem superque habent
agri, neque nostrum requirunt neque exposcunt. Quid est ergo
quod nos cum illis in contentionem deduxerit, praeter inane quoddam partium studium leviter corrigendum, si paucorum rabiem,
qui hac inimicitia nos superfluo onerarunt, comprimamus?"

70   Haec ab illo haud falso iactata metus imminens comprobabat.
Septuaginta quidem naves longas parare Genuenses ferebantur; a
terra vero magnos dilectus equitum peditumque haberi ut proxima
aestate Pisas obsiderent. Id formidantes Pisani, cum una salus videretur si Florentini a societate Genuensium averterentur, Ugolino
comiti, quod is Florentinorum sociorumque amicus et studio partium similis habebatur, adhaeserunt. Ille ubi mentes civium ad se

charity and good will. This, I see, is certainly what our ancestors, those wisest of men, decided to do when they subjected far-off Corsica, Sardinia, and the Balearic Islands to their empire, while leaving Lucca untouched, though the latter was situated practically on the doorstep of our own city. Our present distinguished governors, on the contrary, have kept us supplied with noxious domestic quarrels while seeing to it, for no good reason, that we are perpetually threatened by enemies on land. I am now, still, of the opinion that we should make peace with the Florentines. It will not seem difficult once we grasp fully the nature of the situation. After all, what is it that our two cities are fighting over? The control of Sardinia or the possession of the other islands? Such a thing has never entered their heads. Is it their desire to fight with us for control of the sea? That is something they have never cared about. Do they need our land to cultivate or to support their population? They have land enough and more; they neither need nor seek our own. What is it, then, that has brought us into contention with them, aside from this inane partisanship — a partisanship that could easily be neutralized if we would suppress the rabid passion of a few men who burden the rest of us with this needless hostility?"

These words, uttered by Ugolino forcefully and with no little 70 truth, were rendered persuasive by the imminence of the danger. The Genoese were reported to be readying seventy galleys; on land there were large numbers of horse and foot being levied to besiege Pisa the next summer. This put fear into the hearts of the Pisans, whose only salvation seemed to lie in detaching the Florentines from their alliance with the Genoese. Thus they aligned themselves with Count Ugolino because, being of their same party, he was considered a friend of the Florentines and their allies. When he saw that he had won his fellow-citizens over to his way of thinking, Ugolino toppled the leaders of the Ghibelline party and now began governing the city in his own name; to do this, he im-

traductas vidit, diversae factionis capita deturbat ac suo iam nomine civitatem gubernat; ad hoc ipsum auxilia florentini populi
implorat. Ea mutatio rerum Florentinos deflexit. Itaque reliquo
bello, quod proxima aestate ad Pisas gestum est, nequaquam interfuerunt, contenti mutatione rerum et amica factione pro inimica
urbi praefecta. Quare a Genuensibus tantum, qui cum septuaginta
navibus longis constituto tempore affuerunt, et a Lucensibus, qui
perseverarunt in foedere, bellum est postea illatum. Nec dubitatur,
si Florentinus in foedere permansisset, extremam fuisse perniciem
illam Pisanis futuram.

71   Eodem anno producta urbis pomeria sunt et nova subinde
moenia longe maiori ambitu designata celeberrimisque viis–
Casentinati, Bononiensi, Pratensi, Pistoriensi–opera portarum
egregie instituta. Ea vero secunda an tertia productio fuerit, haud
equidem certissimum[54] dixerim. Plurimi tamen existimant secun-
dam fuisse, cum prima de templo Martis ad thermas publicas ac
theatrum vetus complecterentur moenia. Inde productum constat
pomerium hinc ad ripas fluminis, illinc ultra sacras Laurentii aedes. Tertio longe progressum est, ut supradiximus, quibus in locis
nunc moenia portaeque existunt. Trans Arnum vero prima aedifi-
catio fuit circa vetustum pontem, suburbana aedificia et villae
hortis permixtae. Inde mox vici tres facti: duo secus Arnum supra
infraque pontem, tertius recta a ponte via. Hi vici diu absque mu-
nimento publico fuerunt, ac propterea frequentes in his locis turres privatim factae quo tuto habitari in illis posset. Tandem et hi
moenibus cincti collesque superne munimentis[55] apprehensi. His
quoque in locis mox crescentibus incolis aedificiisque subinde
adiunctis, pomerium productum est longe maiori ambitu quam

plored the aid of the Florentine People. This political change altered the Florentine attitude. Thus they took no part in the rest of the war which was fought in Pisa the following summer, as they were happy with the political changes and the governance of the city by a friendly rather than an unfriendly faction. So after that date the war was prosecuted by the Genoese alone, who had 1284 brought their seventy galleys at the appointed time, and by the Lucchesi, who had remained in the league. There is no doubt that if the Florentines had continued as members of the alliance, the Pisans would have been totally exterminated.[49]

In the same year the city limits were enlarged and new walls of 71 much greater extent were laid out, with gates placed prominently on the most famous roads, those to the Casentino, to Bologna, to Prato and to Pistoia. I cannot say with certainty whether this was the second or third time the walls had been extended. Many think it was the second time, since the first walls ran from the temple of Mars to the public baths and the ancient theater. The next circuit was evidently expanded from the south side to the bank of the river and from the north beyond the church of San Lorenzo. The third circuit went far beyond that (as we have already said) to the place where the walls and gates now stand. In Oltr'arno the first building took place around the Ponte Vecchio, consisting of suburban structures and villas with gardens. Soon thereafter three districts were formed, two along the Arno east and west from the bridge, and the third on the road running directly south from the bridge. These districts existed for a long time without any public defenses, and for this reason numerous private towers were erected in these places to protect the inhabitants. At length these districts too were surrounded by walls, and the hills above them covered with defense works. These places too soon filled up with inhabitants and dwellings. The circuit was expanded to a far greater extent than formerly, and three magnificent gates were constructed

prius, portaeque magnifici operis tres factae celeberrimis trans Arnum viis: Pisana, Senensi, Arretina.

72   Eodem anno Carolus rex moritur, vir procul dubio egregius, longe tamen belli artibus quam pacis insignior. Res siquidem a se praeclaras armis gestas impunita suorum licentia in pace foedavit ac nimio despectu ad rebellionem coegit. Duabus praecipuis in Italia victoriis auctus: altera qua Manfredum, altera qua Corradinum superavit. Sed utrasque secutae rebelliones minus esse laetas permiserunt. Ad extremum capto filio Siciliaque amissa in medio turbationum maximarum interiit apud Foggiam, Calabriae oppidum.

73   Altero dehinc anno Guillielminus Arretinorum praesul castrum Caeciliae, admodum natura munitum, in finibus arretini agri Senas versus occupavit, praesidioque militum imposito novis rebus Senenses conterruit. Itaque contractae eo propere Senensium copiae et a Florentinis missi equites peditesque castrum circumsedere. Varia dehinc oppugnatio et usque in mensem quintum protracta obsidio, quae tam valida fuit affluentibus undique auxiliaribus turmis ut praesul Arretinorum, etsi coactas ipse[56] quoque ostentaret copias, tamen apparatus magnitudine absterritus ferre suis auxilium non sit ausus. Fame tandem expugnati[57] qui intus erant, deserto per noctem castro fuga sibi consuluerunt, sed ea cognita per hostes, magna pars intercipitur. Ipsum vero castrum, ne quando propter egregiam eius loci opportunitatem similia tentarentur, ad solum usque Senenses everterunt.

74   Per hoc ipsum tempus Princivallis Fuscanus ab Rodulpho in Etruriam missus parere sibi civitates postulabat. Consensisse eius missioni Honorium pontificem romanum, qui nuper Martino suc-

on the three most famous streets of Oltr'arno, the Via Pisana, the Via Senese and the Via Aretina.[50]

In the same year King Charles died. He was unquestionably a distinguished man, but far more able in the arts of war than in those of peace. Indeed, the unrestrained license of his followers in peacetime marred his famous feats of arms and caused men to despise and rebel against him. He won glory especially with his two victories in Italy: the one in which he beat Manfred, and the other in which he overcame Conradin. But the rebellions which followed both victories made them less felicitous. In the end, with his son in captivity and Sicily lost, he died near Foggia, a town of Calabria, in the midst of extreme turmoil.[51]

The following year, Guglielmino, the bishop of Arezzo, occupied the castle of Cecilia, a naturally fortified place in Aretine territory near the border of Siena. He established a garrison there and frightened the Sienese with threats of rebellion. So the Sienese hastened to assemble their troops there and the Florentines sent troops of foot and horse to surround the castle. Various attacks followed and the siege lasted as long as five months. The castle was held in so tight a grip, with auxiliary troops flooding in from all sides, that the bishop of Arezzo, although he too could boast a concentration of forces, nevertheless was deterred by the size of the war machine arrayed against him and dared not reinforce his troops. At length the garrison was overcome by hunger and fled, abandoning the castle by night, every man for himself. But the enemy found this out, and a large number of them were intercepted. The castle itself was razed to the ground by the Sienese lest it ever be employed for similar purposes thanks to its strategic position.

It was at this time, too, that Princivalle dal Fiesco was sent by the Emperor Rudolf to Tuscany to demand the submission of the cities in the emperor's name. It was widely reported that Pope Honorius, who had recently succeeded Martin, had consented to

72
1284

73
1285

74
1286

cesserat, vulgo ferebatur, et dedita opera quo minus abhorrerent animi, ut Italus genere et studio partium non alienus legaretur. Is cum Florentiam intrasset et prece magis quam auctoritate niteretur, plus valuit respectus causae publicae quam privati generis. Itaque, ut aliis, ita et huic parere civitas noluit. Quare post paucos dies Florentia egressus Arretium petiit. Ibi quoque cum eadem postulasset, neque alteram factionem trahere in sententiam potuit, quod a nomine imperii abhorrebat, neque alteram, quoniam nomen familiae Fliscanae ex qua ipse ortum ducebat, suspectum partibus habebatur. Ita ab utrisque spretus tandem abivit.

75   Proximo post hunc anno semina gravissimarum turbationum Arretii coorta finitimas civitates in suspicionem primo, mox in apertum bellum compulere. Haud multo quidem ante id tempus Arretini exemplo Florentinorum permoti, priorem artium sibi creaverant, virum quendam popularem ac nobilitati maxime infestum. Guelfo huic nomen fuit. Is armata multitudine castella quaedam Arretinorum per nobilitatem prius occupata repetere; mox quia dicto non parebatur, obsidere coepit. Nonnulla vero ex his pertinacius resistentia, tandem vi capta expugnataque ad solum aequavit. Praecipue tamen Pactiorum et Ubertinorum potentiae infestus, quorum castella pluribus locis cum evertisset, tandem Civitellam obsedit in qua Guillielminus praesul, homo diversarum partium et arretini populi inimicus, residebat. Eo in loco dum exercitus esset, principes nobilitatis, qui primo ob studia partium varie inter se dissidebant, veriti ne, si id oppidum ductu auspicioque prioris expugnaretur, in nimiam plebs evaderet potentiam

his mission. Princivalle had been chosen on purpose since he was an Italian and a Guelf sympathizer and as such his ambassadorship would cause less resentment. Having entered Florence he attempted to compass his end through entreaty rather than command; but respect for the common cause outweighed respect for the house of a private individual. Thus the city would no more submit to him than to the others who had demanded her obedience. So a few days later he left Florence and went to Arezzo, where he made the same demand. But he could bring neither faction over to his way of thinking, the one because the imperial name was repugnant to it, the other because it harbored a partisan suspicion of the house of the Fieschi from which he sprang. He was thus spurned by both parties and finally left.[52]

The following year the seeds of very serious tumults began to germinate in Arezzo, driving the nearby cities first to distrust her, then to open war against her. Not long before this time the Aretines, inspired by the Florentine example, had created as Prior of the Guilds a man of popolano status who was extremely hostile to the nobility. His name was Guelfo.[53] Having armed the multitude, he tried to recover certain Aretine castles that had been occupied earlier by the nobility. Soon, since the nobility would not obey his orders, he began to lay siege to their castles, and the few that resisted more tenaciously he stormed and captured by force, then razed to the ground. He was particularly hostile to the power of the Pazzi and Uberti families, many of whose castles he destroyed. Finally he besieged Civitella, where dwelt Bishop Guglielmino, a Ghibelline and a man hostile to the Aretine people. While the Aretine army was there, the leaders of the nobility, who had at first been divided amongst themselves by partisan feeling, grew fearful lest the town be captured under the leadership and auspices of the Prior, causing the commons to become overmighty and to demand back what they, the nobility, had usurped. Stimulated by anxious fear and at the same time by hatred of the common peo-

75
1287

ac[58] se quoque usurpata reposceret, eo metu anxii et simul invidia plebis commoti, reconciliatis inter se animis ac seditione in exercitu facta, duce Rainaldo Bostole, ad hostes[59] transfugerunt. Ob eam rem obsidio statim soluta est ac exercitus domum reductus.

76 Nec multo post omnis nobilitas una cum praesule contractis undique suis amicorumque viribus Arretium intravit,[60] impetuque in priorem artium facto, cum illum fracta ac[61] depulsa plebe corripuisset,[62] avulsis per contumeliam oculis foedum spectaculum suis civibus dimiserit.[63] Urbem vero ac publicarum rerum curam inter se partiti gubernabant; bonos et graves e plebe viros urbe deiecerant. Nec tamen hic status rerum diuturnus fuit. Nam peculiare nobilitatis malum, superbia et ambitio, conflictare dominantis[64] coepit. Itaque suspicionibus coortis Guillielminus praesul una cum Ubertinis et Pactiis, ex quibus ipse oriundus erat, ceterisque Arretinorum familiis eius factionis, impigre raptis praeveniens armis nobilitatem ceteram urbe deturbat. Ipse per gentilium agnatorumque favorem sublevatus tyrannidem invasit.

77 Erant duae factiones Arretio pulsae: una ex plebeis, qui priorem artium secuti fuerant; altera ex nobilitate, per fraudem postmodum eiecta. Hi omnes in unum coeuntes castella Rondine, Sabinum et alia quaedam circa urbem munita loca occuparunt bellumque ex his Arretio intulerunt. Mox, quia non satis per sese existimabant posse, ad Florentinos legatione missa, cuius princeps fuit Domitianus quidam e familia vetere, opem supplices precabantur. Addiderunt et orationem precibus ex vetustate amicitiarum ac simili studio partium collectam: nullam esse florentino populo, si antiqua repetantur, neque vetustiorem neque diuturniorem

ple, they were reconciled to each other and, having begun a rebellion in the army, fled under the leadership of Rinaldo Bostoli to the enemy. For this reason the siege was immediately abandoned and the army returned home.

Shortly thereafter the whole of the nobility, together with the 76 bishop, collected their forces and those of their friends everywhere and entered Arezzo. They attacked the Prior of the Guilds and seized him, having shoved their way through the common people. To humiliate him they plucked out his eyes, leaving behind a revolting spectacle for their fellow-citizens. They then divided up the city and the administration of public affairs among themselves and took control of the government, ejecting from the city good and weighty citizens who sprang from the common people. Yet this state of affairs did not last long: the characteristic vices of the nobility, arrogance and ambition, began to create conflicts among the rulers. Thus mistrust arose, and Bishop Guglielmino, together with the Ubertini and the Pazzi (to whose families he himself belonged) and the other Aretine clans of Ghibelline sympathies, preemptively seized arms and with great vigor expelled the rest of the nobility from the city. With the assistance of his relatives and blood-relations the bishop then made himself tyrant.[54]

There were two factions that had been expelled from Arezzo, a 77 plebeian one that had followed the Prior of the Guilds, and a noble faction that had later been expelled through deceit. They joined together and occupied the castles at Rondine, Monte San Savino, and certain other fortified places around the city, making war from them against Arezzo.[55] Soon, realizing their own power was not sufficient, they sent a legation to the Florentines led by a certain Domiziano, from an old family, to beg for aid. To supplement their pleas they made a speech whose topics were the antiquity of their friendship and their common political sympathies. If one went back to ancient times (they said) the Florentine People had had no older nor more long-lasting alliance than the one they

societatem quam cum ea parte Arretinorum quae nunc a communibus inimicis eiecta, supplex in eius fidem patrociniumque confugit; cum hac enim parte statim post Federici mortem foedus societatemque initam esse a Florentinis, tunc primum ex longa servitute sese in libertatem vindicantibus; hac eadem parte rei publicae gubernacula tenente, quo quidem anno pugnatum[65] apud Arbiam, bis equites peditesque Arretinorum senensem agrum cum Florentinis ingressos; in ipsa vero arbiensi pugna plures prope caesos fuisse Arretinorum acervos quam ullius sociae civitatis; post longum deinde exilium ac fractas opes Carolum regem, subsidio partium caelitus dimissum, vix ab ulla per Etruriam civitate receptum esse priusquam ab Arretinis; copias inde suas et Corradino venienti opposuisse et in tanta trepidatione cunctorum, cum prope in oculis suis caedi exercitum regis conspexissent, tamen in fide una cum Florentinis constantissime perseverasse; neque postea obsidendo Bonitio neque aliis locis ubi de studio partium ageretur suam aut operam aut praesentiam defuisse; nunc eosdem se Arretio pulsos, non tam vi contrariae factionis civium quam exterorum; Guillielminum siquidem potentiam omnem ex clientelis ac finitimis tyrannis diversarum partium coegisse seque domestica seditione plebis nobilitatisque laborantes, partim vi, partim perfidia pepulisse; orare uti pro vetere amicitia proque diuturna coniunctione non patiantur eos ab se frustra auxilium petere. Nam utilitatis quidem rationem minime se explicare velle, cum apud homines loquantur prudentissimos et qui probe norint quantum intersit diversam factionem an amicam urbi illi praeesse, praesertim cum Pactii et Ubertini et huiusmodi homines quietis simul libertatisque hostes in ea dominentur, quibuscum haud dubium sit bel-

enjoyed with that very party of Aretines who had now been expelled by their common enemies and who, as suppliants, were seeking refuge in Florentine protection and loyalty. The Florentines, asserting their liberty for the first time after long slavery, had entered into a league and alliance with this party after the death of Frederick; this party had been in control of the Aretine government in the very year the battle of the Arbia was fought, and twice had the Aretine foot and horse entered Sienese territory with the Florentines; in that same battle of the Arbia masses of Aretine troops had been slaughtered, more than any other allied city; then, after a long exile and the destruction of their resources, King Charles was sent by heaven to aid their party, and the Aretines had been almost the first to welcome him to Tuscany; their forces had thereafter also opposed the coming of Conradin despite the universal terror when they had seen him slaughter the king's army practically before their eyes; yet they had persevered with great constancy in their loyalty to the Florentines, and neither at the siege of Poggibonsi nor anywhere else that partisan zeal had been called for had their presence or efforts been lacking. Now these same men had been expelled from Arezzo by the violence of a Ghibelline faction consisting less of citizens than of foreigners; Guglielmino had acquired all his power from clients and nearby tyrants of the Ghibelline faction; he had expelled the Guelfs, partly by force and partly by betrayal, when they had been struggling against domestic rebellions of the common people and the nobility. They were pleading, in the name of their old friendship and long association, that the Florentines should not suffer them to seek aid in vain. They had no need to explain the argument from utility since they were addressing men of great prudence, who well understood the difference between a friendly and a hostile faction ruling that city, especially since it was the Pazzi and Ubertini and men of that sort, enemies of tranquillity and liberty, who were ruling it and could be counted on eventually to make

lum tandem florentino populo esse futurum; ceterum referre, utrum nunc tenentibus amicis circa urbem castra et opportunitatem maximam praestare valentibus, an postea illis iam perditis bellum sit suscipiendum.

78   Movit oratio mentes, quippe vera esse constabat quae ab legatis dicebantur. Itaque responsum illis datum est: populum quidem florentinum bono esse animo, verum et sociorum sententiam illis esse expectandam, quos ad hoc ipsum e vestigio convocarent. Accitis deinde sociorum legatis reque in consilio discussa, constituerunt arretinos exules, utpote vetustos amicos, in communem societatem suscipere iisque opem ferre quoad in urbem atque in sua restituerentur. Ad hoc ipsum renovato foedere octingentos equites illis decrevere, horum quingentis e vestigio traditis, reliquos sese, cum res exigeret, missuros polliciti. Recepto igitur sociorum equitatu arretini exules, cum ipsi quoque equitem peditemque satis magno numero armassent, per singulos fere dies usque ad Arretii moenia crebris incursionibus infestabant. Quare et hi qui urbem tenebant diversarum item partium auxilia postulare coacti sunt. Ob eam causam omnes florentini exules qui ubicumque terrarum erant eo concurrerunt; praeter hos quoque ex Umbria et Picentibus studio partium insignes complurimi. Ita certamen atque bellum ex integro nascitur.

79   Eodem anno bis incendia Florentiae coorta:[66] primum in Cerretanorum aedibus, deinde aliud longe maius quo Circulorum domus crematae sunt ingenti cum iactura praedivitis familiae. Honorius quoque pontifex romanus per hoc ipsum tempus decessit, biennio fere postquam sedere inceperat.

80   Proximo dehinc anno cura in arretinum versa bellum. Nam auxilia diversae factionis eo contracta florentinum ac senensem agrum subitis incursionibus reddebant infestum. Tandem pro-

war on the Florentine People; but they *would* raise the question whether the war should be undertaken now, when their friends held encampments around the city and were able to offer them great advantages, or later, when these advantages had been lost.

The oration was effective since what the ambassadors were say- 78 ing was obviously true. So they received this response: the Florentine People were well disposed to them but they would have to wait upon the views of their allies, whom they would meet with immediately for this purpose. Representatives of the allies were then summoned and the matter was discussed in council. It was decided to accept the Aretine exiles as old friends into their common alliance and to help them until such time as they should be restored to their city and their property. The league was renewed for this purpose. They were allotted eight hundred knights, of whom five hundred were turned over to them immediately, while the rest they promised to send when circumstances should require them. When they had received the allied cavalry, therefore, the Aretine exiles — who themselves had armed a considerable number of horse and foot — began almost every day making frequent raids up to the walls of Arezzo. Hence those who controlled the city were compelled in their turn to request aid from the Ghibellines. So all the Florentine exiles everywhere in the world hastened there, as well as many famous partisans from Umbria and the Marches. Thus did the battle and the war begin anew.[56]

In the same year fires broke out twice in Florence, the first in 79 the dwellings of the Cerretani, then a much bigger one in which 1287 the Palazzo Cerchi was consumed with great loss to that exceptionally rich family. Pope Honorius also died around that time, about two years after he had begun his pontificate.[57]

In the following year attention turned to the Aretine war. The 80 Ghibelline auxiliaries who had assembled there were making Flor- 1288 entine and Sienese territory unsafe with their sudden incursions. Finally the Florentines decided to set out with all their forces to

ficisci totis viribus et simul exules Arretinorum in societatem receptos fovere, simul eorum qui intra urbem erant petulantiam retundere placuit. Ea de causa magni delectus Florentiae habiti sunt;
Senensium vero ac sociorum aliorum copiae ingentes arcessitae.
Ex his omnibus confectus est ingens equitum peditumque numerus. Signa militaria aliquot dies ante extra urbem prompta tempusque profectioni constitutum pridie Kalendas iunias. Quae[67] ubi
advenit,[68] signa moventes Arretium versus per superiorem Arnum
contenderunt. Nec insignior apparatiorve exercitus nec omnibus
rebus instructior post arbiensem pugnam emissus ferebatur. Cum
in fines Arretinorum pervenissent, Leonam et alia pleraque circa
Ambram fluvium castella ceperunt; eorum plurima in deditionem
accepta, nonnulla etiam vi expugnata. Inde copiae Laterino ad-
motae. Id oppidum Arno supereminet octo passuum millibus ab
Arretio, natura loci satis munitum. Circa illud stativis positis, cum
circumvallare oppidum coepissent et appareret pertinacius incuba-
turos, Lupus quidam exul florentinus, qui cum aliqua manu in
praesidio erat, conterritus magnitudine apparatus paciscitur uti
cum suis abire incolumis liceat. Ita deducto praesidio oppidum
tradit. Florentini ergo et socii post Laterinum captum inde iam
structi ad hostem duxerunt, proximeque contra Arretium positis
castris crebra proelia in portis ipsis commiserunt, omniaque circa
urbem igne ferroque hostilem in modum vastarunt.

81   Ad viii Kalendas sextiles non procul a porta ludicrum equorum cursu certantium praemiumque de more, ut domi ea die
fieri[69] consuevit, ab illis editum est. Inter eos vero ludos procella

support the Aretine exiles whom they had accepted as allies, and at the same time to blunt the insolence of those inside the city. For this reason there was a great levy of troops in Florence, and the Sienese and other allies also called up great numbers of troops. From all these sources an enormous army of horse and foot was assembled. The military standards were brought outside the city several days before and a date of 31 May was set for the expedition. When that day arrived, the standards advanced towards Arezzo and drove through the upper Arno. It was said that there had not been such a notable or well-equipped or well-trained army sent out since the battle of the Arbia. When they arrived at the Aretine border, they took Leona and a number of other castles near the river Ambra; most of them surrendered, but a few were taken by force. Then the troops advanced on Laterina. This town overlooked the Arno about eight miles out of Arezzo and was naturally well fortified. They pitched camp nearby and began to invest the town. It seemed as though they were going to be nesting there indefinitely when a certain Lupus, a Florentine exile in command of the garrison, grew terrified at the size of the Guelf war machine and made an agreement permitting him to leave unharmed with his troops. So the garrison made its exit and he handed over the town. Then the Florentines and their allies, having captured Laterina, brought the army up to the enemy in battle formation and having encamped right across from Arezzo, engaged in numerous skirmishes before its very gates, laying waste in hostile fashion to everything around the city with fire and sword.

On 25 July, not far from the gate, they held a horse-race with 81 the customary prizes, as they usually did at home on that day. During these games a storm suddenly arose and blew so violently in the part of the encampment where the Sienese troops were staying that a great number of their pavilions were thrown into a heap by the furious blowing and whistling of the wind. This was a presage of the future disaster to the Sienese, whose meaning was

subito coorta, praesertim[70] in ea parte castrorum ubi Senensium tendebant copiae, sic vehementer inflavit, ut magnam partem tabernaculorum vesano quodam impetu stridoreque glomeraret. Id praesagium futurae cladis Senensium fuit, quod paulo post ex re ipsa intellectum est. Nam confectis his rebus, cum abire placuisset, Florentini eodem quo prius venerant itinere, Senenses autem diversa regione, via Senensi remeabant. Eorum itaque discessum conspicientes Arretini qui intra urbem erant, invadere Senensium agmen statuerunt. Itaque post eos quam citatissime[71] egressi quatuor fere passuum millibus ab urbe consequuntur. Ibi vertere signa retro ac decertare invitos compellunt. Sed ubi manus conserere coeperunt, et eques equiti, pedes pediti congressus rem comminus gerere, pugna erat atrox et clamor ingens variaeque fluctuationes et caedes adnitentibus utrinque edebantur. Tandem superati Senenses omissa resistendi spe in fugam vertuntur. Magna eorum strages per iram et indignationem superioris vastationis a victoribus[72] edita est. Qui vero eorum a caede superfuerunt, maxima ex parte capti sunt et Arretium ducti.

82 Florentini vero nihil penitus eorum sentientes nec urbi intermisso itinere Laterinum pervenerunt. Ibi cum paulo post deletas Senensium copias cognovissent, quamquam graviter eos angebat sociorum casus et iactabant quidam ad comprimendam Arretinorum insolentiam exercitum esse reducendum, tamen vicit eorum sententia qui tuta magis quam speciosa suadebant. Itaque parte equitatus Laterini relicta quae Arretinorum cohiberet impetum, reliquas omnes copias Florentiam reduxere.

83 Dum ea geruntur in Arretinis, alia insuper bellorum[73] materies apud Pisanos exoritur. Ugolinus enim comes, cuius mentionem supra fecimus, Ugolinum Gallurae iudicem, hominem et studio partium et consanguinitate sibi coniunctum, Pisis pepulit. Ipse malo consilio cum diversarum partium hominibus in gratiam re-

grasped shortly thereafter with the help of the event itself. For after these accomplishments, when it had been decided to leave, the Florentines went back the way they came, but the Sienese returned home through different country on the Via Senese. Observing their departure, the Aretines inside the city decided to attack the Sienese column. So exiting as swiftly as possible after them, they caught up with them four miles from the city, and forced them, despite their reluctance, to reverse their order of march and engage in battle. Then they began to join in close combat and fight hand to hand, knight against knight, foot-soldier against foot-soldier. The fighting was dreadful and the clamor unbearable. The tides of battle changed constantly with both sides striving to butcher the other. At last the Sienese were overwhelmed and, having lost all hope of resistance, turned to flight. The victors inflicted enormous slaughter, spurred on by their anger at the devastation they had suffered earlier. Most of those who survived the massacre were taken prisoner and brought back to Arezzo.

The Florentines heard nothing at all of these events and did 82 not break their journey home until they came to Laterina. There they learned, shortly after the event, that the Sienese troops had been wiped out. Although the misfortune of their allies caused them great pain, and some demanded that the army should return and teach the Aretines a lesson, nevertheless the dominant view was that safety was preferable to a specious bravery. Thus, part of the cavalry was left behind at Laterina to contain the Aretine attack, while all the rest of the allied forces returned to Florence.[58]

While this was happening in Aretine territory, fuel for yet more 83 wars appeared in Pisa. Count Ugolino (whom we have mentioned above) expelled from Pisa Judge Ugolino of Gallura,[59] a man who was of his own party and a blood-relation. The former was ill advised to seek the favor of the Ghibellines again, since shortly thereafter they captured him and threw him into prison. On the

diit, a quibus non multo postea captus in carcerem truditur. At Ugolinus Gallurae iudex ceterique pisani cives per factionem eiecti ad Lucensium Florentinorumque opes confugientes causa fuerunt foederis inter civitates renovandi. Itaque eodem anno auxilia equitum peditumque a Florentinis missa, una cum Lucensibus agrum pisanum intrarunt. Ibi coniunctis Pisanorum exulibus bellum Pisis intulerunt.

84   Eodem anno Florentiae exaltata est circa baptisterium area et latericio opere constrata caementis de industria congestis, quo reliquae urbis superficiei par esset; pecunia ad eam rem perficiendam ex aerario prompta. Pontis etiam ad Heram fluvium (id enim castellum in florentini populi dicionem paulo ante pervenerat) arx et turres insigni opere communitae civesque ad eius loci custodiam bini cum militari praesidio destinati.

85   Inter haec Arretini ob victoriam de Senensibus habitam maiorem in modum elati, castella quae ab exulibus tenebantur magnis copiis oppugnabant. Cum itaque Carcianum circumsedissent atque id castellum omni apparatu urgerent, ceteris quoque castellis eadem vis immineret, exules Arretini difficultate rerum commoti Florentiam oratum mittunt, ne se[74] extremo in periculo constitutos in hostium manus pervenire patiantur. Commota ob id civitas mittendas iterum copias in agrum arretinum decrevit, non tamen tanti apparatus quanti priore expeditione facti. Quod enim obsessi aegre sustinere oppugnationem credebantur, ob id magis properare, nec auxilia sociorum expectare placuit. Itaque urbani equites ad octingentos, mercede conducti ad ducentos, peditum vero ad quatuor millia in hoc subitaneo exercitu fuere. Has copias cum adventare sensissent Arretini, obsidionem dissolverunt, revocatisque in urbem copiis et multitudine confestim armata certissimo dimicandi proposito obviam hostibus progressi sunt; atque ubi in conspectu fuerunt, aciem struunt potestatemque pugnandi faciunt. Florentini quia praevalere illos multitudine intelligebant, Laterini

other hand, Ugolino, Judge of Gallura, and the other Pisan citizens driven out because of factionalism, took refuge with the Lucchese and Florentine forces, and became the cause of a renewed league between the two cities. Hence in the same year auxiliary troops, horse and foot, were sent out by the Florentines and, linking up with the Lucchesi, invaded Pisan territory. There they made war against the Pisans in company with the Pisan exiles.[60]

In the same year the area around the baptistery was raised and paved with solid brickwork; it was built up with the aim of making it equal to the level of the rest of the city. The funds to accomplish the work were supplied by the public treasury.[61] Another remarkable public work was the citadel and towers built at Pontedera (this was a castle that had shortly before come under Florentine authority). Two citizens were appointed to guard the place with a military garrison.[62] 84
1288

Meanwhile, the Aretines, highly elated with their victory over the Sienese, made an attack in force on the castles held by the exiles. They invested the castle of Carciano and were attacking it by every means possible, and the same forces threatened the rest of the castles as well. In desperation, the Aretine exiles implored Florence not to to allow them to fall into enemy hands in their hour of need. This stimulated the city to decree once again an expedition into Aretine territory. But it was not so large an expedition as the previous one. Since it was believed that the besieged could not hold out long, they decided to hurry up and not wait for the help of their allies. So there were eight hundred of the city's knights, two hundred mercenary knights and four thousand foot in this impromptu army. When the Aretines heard this army was coming, they abandoned the siege, recalled their troops to the city, and hastily armed the populace. Then, grimly determined to fight, they went out to meet the enemy. When the latter came in sight, the Aretines drew up their battle lines and challenged them to battle. The Florentines, in view of the Aretines' numerical superiority, 85

copias continebant; tantum militem de superiori loco coniunctum paene moenibus oppidi ostentabant, in planitiem vero non descendebant. Itaque irrita tandem expectatione absque ulla pugna discessum est. Sed Arretini, postquam abscesserunt, parte copiarum Bibienam transmissa Casentinati via usque ad Sevam fluvium tumultuosius profecti, tantum terrorem incusserunt ut Florentiae intra moenia trepidaretur. Ob eam rem copiae sunt confestim revocatae.

86   Eodem anno circiter idus Decembris continuis imbribus auctum flumen Arni totam fere inundavit urbem; quaedam etiam adiacentia aedificia eius impetu corruerunt.

87   Nec multo post Arretini magnis copiis profecti ad Varicum, fecerunt castra oppidumque oppugnarunt. Inde pars copiarum tumultuosius delata Collinam ad usque praedabunda pervenit. Eo de loco (neque enim plus quam septem passuum millibus Florentia abest) quam magna possunt incendia ostentant. Hoc tumultu in suspicionem versae mentes, praesertim cum⁷⁵ manus quaedam exulum florentinorum cum Arretinis venisse diceretur, verentibus principibus civitatis ne quid arcani subesset mali, iuventutem obviam exire cupidam intra⁷⁶ moenia continuere. Quare hostes licentius vagati, post magnas demum illatas clades praedamque abunde captam, ad suos qui circa Varicum erant revertuntur.

88   Per idem tempus Pisani studio partium inducti Guidonem Feretranum, iussu pontificis in Gallia exulantem, crebris arcessitum litteris sibi ducem praefecerunt, quo Lucensibus ceterisque eius factionis Ugolinoque Gallurae iudici exulibusque aliis nuper eiectis, a quibus lacessebantur bello, resisterent. Ugolinum vero comitem, quem supra captum et in carcerem trusum ostendimus, cum duobus filiis totidemque nepotibus una in turri simul clausos subtracto protinus cibo fame necaverunt, ad eam immanitatem nihil

kept their forces inside Laterina, and paraded their soldiery only on higher ground near the walls of the town; they did not come down to the plain. Then, unexpectedly, the Florentines left without giving battle. After their departure the Aretines sent part of their troops to Bibbiena while the rest went marauding along the via Casentina as far as the river Sieve. They caused so much terror that Florence trembled inside its walls, and in response, instantly recalled its troops.[63]

In the same year, around 13 December, continuous rains caused the Arno to swell up and inundate the city. Certain buildings near its banks collapsed under the impact of the waters.[64] 86 / 1288

Shortly thereafter the Aretines set out in force for Montevarchi, and encamping there, assaulted the town. Then they sent part of their troops marauding and causing a tremendous uproar as far as San Donato in Collina. From this place (which is no more than seven miles from Florence) they drew attention to themselves by lighting the largest fires they could. This uproar began to excite suspicions, especially in view of the band of Florentine exiles that was said to have come with the Aretines. The city's leaders feared that some wicked plot was afoot, and kept the young men, who wanted to go out, inside the walls. So the enemy roamed about at will, and after causing immense damage and taking vast amounts of plunder they returned to their forces near Montevarchi. 87

In this same period the Pisans, under the influence of partisan passion, summoned, after a campaign of letter-writing, Guido of Montefeltro, who had been exiled to Lombardy by papal command, and made him their captain. They did this so as to resist the Lucchesi, the rest of the Guelfs, Judge Ugolino of Gallura and the other recently-expelled exiles, who were harassing them in the war. Count Ugolino (who as we showed above had been thrown into prison) and the two sons and two grandsons who had been shut up with him in the tower were starved to death; the Pisans' only motive for this heinous act was partisan passion. However, 88

ob aliud quam ob studia partium impulsi. Ceterum ea res Lucensium sociorumque suspicionem adauxit et parare vires animumque in futurum certamen coegit. Ita cuncta vicissim Etruria studiis partium erecta conflictabatur.

this deed increased the mistrust of the Lucchesi and their allies, and they began to prepare their strength and their spirit for a future battle. Thus all of Tuscany was aroused to conflict by successive acts of partisanship.[65]

LIBER QUARTUS

1   Iam appetebat ver, et una omnium cura in Arretinum versa erat
bellum. Florentini quidem pro crebris incursionibus ostentatisque
nuper urbi incendiis, Senenses vero pro calamitate proelio accepta
properabant ulcisci; Lucenses antiqua partium voluntate Florentinis coniuncti; ad hoc Pistorienses, Volaterrani, Pratenses aliique
socii sequebantur; cives praeterea eiusdem factionis Arretio pulsi,
qui frequentia circum[1] urbem castella occuparant et in societatem
Florentinorum recepti erant: hi omnes inter se foederati bellum
inferre properabant.

2   Contra vero Arretini diversae factionis qui intus erant, quibus
Guillielminus praesul fere dominabatur, ad hoc Pactii, Ubertini,
Tarlati, praepotentes Arretinorum familiae, cumque his Bonus Feretranus, multique praeterea[2] nobiles ex Umbria et Picentibus studio partium tracti, omnesque florentini exules Arretii convenerant,
bellum et ipsi ex diverso gesturi.

3   Apparatus fere omnium civitatum ad id bellum factos, demora-
tus est Caroli filii adventus. Is enim, fervente nuper inter Carolum
patrem ac Petrum Arragonum regem qui Siciliam invaserat bello,
captus navali proelio apud Neapolim fuerat a Roggerio classis hostium praefecto. A quo cum in Siciliam devectus esset, Constantia
quondam Manfredi regis filia, accitis singularum civitatum sindicis
ad sententiam de captivo ferendam, cum omnes poenam capitis
adversus eum decrevissent, ipsa quasi beneficio suo morti ereptum

BOOK IV

Summer was already upon them, and all eyes had turned anx- 1
iously towards the war in Arezzo. The Florentines and the Sienese 1289
were hastening to take their revenge, the former because of the numerous incursions and ostentatious burnings that had recently
taken place near their city; the latter because of the defeat they
had suffered in battle. The Lucchesi joined the Florentines willingly out of the old party spirit, and Pistoia, Volterra, Prato and
other allies followed them. In addition there were the citizens of
the Guelf party who had been expelled from Arezzo and had occupied a string of castles around the city; they, too, had joined the
Florentine alliance. The entire confederation was in a fever of
preparation for war.

On the other side were the Aretines of the Ghibelline faction 2
inside the city, whose lord, for all practical purposes, was Bishop
Guglielmino. Party spirit had drawn there also the Pazzi, Uber-
tini, and Tarlati, those powerful Aretine families, and Buono of
Montefeltro along with them, as well as numerous noblemen from
Umbria and the Marche. The Florentine exiles all gathered at
Arezzo, and they, too, were ready to make war on the side of the
enemy.

Nearly all the cities were mobilized for war when a delay was 3
caused by the arrival of Charles's son.¹ Amidst the agitations of
the late war between his father Charles and Peter of Aragon, who
had invaded Sicily, the younger Charles had been captured in a naval battle off Naples by Roger, admiral of the enemy fleet, and
brought to Sicily. There, representatives of each city were summoned to pass sentence on the captive, and they handed down the
death penalty against him. At this point, Costanza, daughter of
the late King Manfred, snatched him from the jaws of death, and
in a show of generosity sent him to honorable confinement in

in Hispaniam misit et honesto carcere asservavit. Ita callido consilio civitatum odia in Carolo accendit ob damnationem filii, et ipsa sibi humanitatis clementiaeque laudem insignius comparavit.

4   Mortuo deinde patre Carolo, iuvenis e carcere certa pactione dimissus in Galliam transiit. Inde mox Italiam adventare nunciabatur, pontificem aditurus et regni paterni gubernacula suscepturus. Huius adventus expectatio Florentinos Senensesque et alios socios detinuit, cupientissima nobilitate, cum ille advenisset, praesenti obsequium exhibere. Venit ille tandem circiter Kalendas maias, Florentiamque ingredienti magnifice sunt honores impensi. Inde cum, paucos dies commoratus, Senas versus abiret, fama ingens fuit Arretinos magnas equitum peditumque copias paravisse, ut iter facientem in agro senensi adorirentur. Quod postquam Florentiae auditum est, etsi Carolus ipse turma suorum equitum confisus, nihil pro sua tutela postulasset, tamen equites urbani extemplo arma capere iussi, usque ad extremos Senensium fines grato obsequio prosecuti fuere.

5   Inde mox reversis, confestim in Arretinos expeditio indicitur, et socii certiores facti convocantur. Signa vero militaria, quo maturius conveniret miles, extra urbem deprompta apud Ripolim via arretina aliquot dies continuere. Cum vero iam convenissent copiae et cuncta ad iter parata forent, consilio duces habito, contra omnium expectationem transire Arnum, et Casentinati via ad hostem ducere statuerunt. Praeerat autem copiis Amerigus Narbonensis, quem Carolus ut expertum[3] bello Florentinis sociisque ducem reliquerat, et cum eo sex cives egregii ad hoc ipsum delecti. Superato monte, cum circa Puppium descendissent, quoniam id

Spain. Thus she cleverly stoked the fires of the elder Charles' hatred towards the cities who had condemned his son, and won for herself a reputation for kindness and mercy.

Then the elder Charles died, and after negotiations his young 4 son was let out of prison and went to France. Afterwards news came that he was coming to Italy to have an audience with the pope and to take the helm of his father's kingdom. The Florentines and the Sienese and other allies held back [from the Aretine war] in expectation of his coming, the nobility being particularly anxious to place themselves at his service when he came. He finally arrived around the first of May, and there were magnificent 1289 ceremonies laid on for his entry into Florence. After staying a few days, he set out for Siena. There was a widespread rumor that the Aretines had readied a large force of cavalry and infantry to ambush him on the road to Siena. When the rumor was heard in Florence, though Charles himself had confidence in his own troop of horse and had not asked for a guard, the urban knights were immediately commanded to arm themselves, and they provided the young king with a welcome escort as far as the borders of Siena.[2]

As soon they had returned, the expedition against Arezzo was 5 announced and the allies were notified and assembled. The military standards were brought outside the city to Ripoli on the Via Aretina for several days so that the soldiery would have more time to come together. Once the forces were assembled and everything was ready for the march, the commanders held a meeting and decided, contrary to expectation, to cross the Arno and march towards the enemy over the Casentino. Amerigo of Narbonne was in command. Charles had left him behind to help the Florentines and their allies as he was an experienced war leader, and six distinguished citizens were chosen to serve with him for this same purpose. They climbed up the mountain and came down on the other side near Poppi. This was the castle of Count Guido Novello, an

erat oppidum Novelli comitis, quem in hostium semper fuisse numero constabat, et tunc etiam apud Arretinos eodem studio partium versabatur, sub ipso oppido castris positis, longe lateque ut maxime possunt regionem populantur. Arretini primum recta via copiarum adventum expectabant, sed postquam ex fuga et trepidatione hominum pecorumque in Casentinati hostes adesse cognovere, et circa Puppium cuncta ferro igneque vastari, confestim omnibus equitum peditumque copiis Arretio profecti, Bibienam venerunt. Fuisse autem traduntur Arretinorum octo millia peditum, equitum vero non amplius nongentis. Ducebat autem Guillielminus praesul et Bonus Feretranus et alii quidam praestantes diversarum partium viri, qui per id tempus rei militaris peritissimi habebantur.

6   Cum in conspectum venissent, nec fere plus mille quingentis passibus inter se castra distarent, Arretini, etsi longe impares numero copiarum, tamen confisi virtute suorum, primi flagitarunt pugnam. Nec Florentini quidem detrectarunt certamen, sed proelio se impigre obtulerunt. Cum ergo pugna decernere statuissent in proxima planitie (Campaldinum incolae vocant), sese ex composito compararunt, et acies utrimque struxerunt. Florentini prima fronte equitatum omnem, quo admodum praevalebant; post hunc peditum robur collocarunt, extenso longius utroque cornu, ut, si opus foret, equitatum complecterentur; scutatos vero et sagittarios per cornua ipsa ab utraque parte disposuere. Praeter has duas, subsidiariam aciem extra ordinem unam ex Pistoriensibus et aliis sociis, quibus Cursius Donatus eques florentinus praeerat. Arretini vero eodem modo tres et ipsi acies fecerunt: primam equites; mox aliquo intervallo pedites; insuper extraordinariam aciem, cui Novellus praeerat comes.

inveterate enemy, who on this occasion, too, had taken the side of the Aretines owing to party spirit. The allies pitched camp under his very walls and devastated as much of the region as they could. The Aretines at first expected the troops to come by the direct route, but once they learned, from the terrified flight of men and beasts, that the enemy had gone to the Casentino and were devastating everything near Poppi with fire and sword, they set out immediately with their entire army, both horse and foot. Leaving Arezzo, they came to Bibbiena. It is said that the Aretine forces numbered eight thousand infantry but not more than nine hundred cavalry. However, Bishop Guglielmino led them, along with Buono of Montefeltro and certain other distinguished Ghibellines who were considered the most experienced warriors of their day.

When they had come into view, and there was hardly more 6 than a mile and a half between the camps, the Aretines, though far inferior in numbers, were nevertheless the first to challenge battle, confident as they were in their own strength and courage. The Florentines for their part did not hold back from the fray, but threw themselves energetically into battle. When they had agreed to decide the battle on the nearby plain, which the locals called Campaldino, they placed themselves in battle-order and drew up their lines on either side. Since their mounted forces were markedly superior, the Florentines placed all their cavalry in the van, and behind them the cream of the infantry, spread out wide on both flanks so that they could close in to cover the cavalry if necessary. The shieldsmen and archers were stationed in the midst of the flanking forces on either side. In addition to these two main forces, there was one subsidiary force outside the regular order of battle, consisting of Pistoians and other allies led by Corso Donati, a Florentine knight. The Aretines, too, drew up three battle lines: first, the cavalry; then, at some distance, the infantry; and finally an extraordinary force led by Count Guido Novello.

7   Erat inter duces exercitus florentini populi Verius Circulus, e
familia nobili, et ipse summis divitiis magnaque prudentiae virtutisque fama. Is, cum suae tribus antesignanos equites, qui primi
hostem pervasuri essent, legere ex officio cogeretur, sese primum
legit, etsi tunc ex crure aegrotantem, insuper filium et nepotem.
Ceterorum autem neminem se lecturum esse dixit, verum qui patriam amarent, eos sponte sua profiteri debere. Eius viri eximium
praestantemque in rem publicam animum admirati cives, plerique
verecundia adducti, id sibi munus ultro depoposcerunt, cum prius
multi, ut grave periculosumque, detrectare niterentur. Ita, ad centum quinquaginta antesignani equites facti, et in his viginti ad
equestris ordinis dignitatem tunc primum assumpti.

8   Ut igitur sonuere tubae et clamor ad coelum tolli coeptus est,
antesignani equites, qui ab utraque parte aciem praecedebant,
concitis infestius equis veluti procella quaedam sese mutuo pervasere. Atque primo statim congressu tanta fuit hostium vis tantusque ardor, ut magna pars florentinorum equitum prosternere-
tur, reliqui vero in fugam versi, recipere se ad maiorem aciem
coacti sint.[4] Hoc igitur prosperum antesignanorum certamen magno clamore prosecutus reliquus Arretinorum equitatus, in ipsam
maiorem aciem delatus est tanto quidem ardore ut impetus eius
sustineri nequiverit, pulsusque campo florentinus equitatus com-
pelleretur ad peditem refugere. Ea res metum primo, mox victoriam peperit Florentinis. Dum enim cedentes persequitur Arretinorum equitatus, peditem suum longe dimisit. Itaque evenit
posthac ut Arretinus nullo in loco integer pugnaret, sed alibi
eques, alibi pedes, cum integro hoste congrederetur. Sustinuit
enim[5] florentinum[6] equitatum acies peditum, quae dextro sinis-

The leaders of the army of the Florentine People included Vieri 7
de'Cerchi, a nobleman famous for his great wealth as well as his
courage and practical wisdom. Compelled by duty to pick three
knightly champions who would go out first to meet the enemy, he
chose himself first, although he was suffering from a bad leg, then
his son and grandson. He declared that he would choose none except those who loved their country, and that such persons ought
to volunteer of their own accord. His fellow citizens admired the
man's quite exceptional patriotic spirit, and many were shamed
into demanding this duty for themselves, too, although they had
earlier held back from it as something onerous and beset with
danger. In this way up to one hundred and fifty knights became
champions, and twenty of these were newly raised to the eques-
trian order at that very moment.

So as the trumpets sounded and the shouts began to rise 8
heavenwards, the knightly champions who had ridden out in front
of their lines on either side spurred their horses furiously and
charged at each other like a whirlwind. And in that first clash,
such was the force and ardor of the enemy that a large part of the
Florentine cavalry was unhorsed, while the rest turned tail and
were compelled to return to the main body. The rest of the
Aretine cavalry followed upon this successful clash of champions
with a great cry and bore down on the main body with such ardor
that the Florentine cavalry were unable to sustain the impact but
were driven from the field and forced to fall back to the infantry
line. This retreat at first made the Florentines afraid, but afterwards brought them victory. For the Aretine cavalry, while in pursuit of the retreating Florentines, left their own infantry far behind
them. Thus it transpired that, after this point in the battle, the
Aretine army nowhere fought as a unit, but attacked a united enemy with their cavalry joining battle in one place, their infantry in
another. The Florentine infantry line supported their cavalry because, as we showed above, it was spread out on the left and right

troque, ut supra monstravimus, cornu refugientem equitem complexa, sagittis et hastis et omnifariam telorum genere apertis lateribus incessebat hostis.[7] Acerrimum itaque certamen eo in loco excitatum est. Arretini enim primo in impetu[8] victoriam reposuerant; quare, summa vi annixi, dissipare Florentinorum agmen nitebantur. Sed tutabatur pedes ad quem sese equitatus receperat, eratque fluctuatio quaedam et motus incertus prementium simul ac renitentium.

9 Et iam pedestris Arretinorum superveniebat acies, quae relicta ab equitibus suis, cum illi cedentis[9] persequerentur, nondum sese pugnae miscuerat. Ea si equitibus suis coniungeretur, inclinare ad Arretinos victoria haud dubie videbatur. Inter haec Cursius Donatus, qui extraordinariae praeerat aciei, intellecto suorum periculo, etsi praeceptum fuerat ne iniussu ducis proelium iniret, tamen perniciosum ratus ultra differre, "Adoriamur," inquit, "commilitones, hostium equitatum, priusquam pedes eorum se immisceat pugnae. Neque vero me in tanto discrimine civium meorum aut praeceptum ducis aut poena deterret. Si enim vincimur in acie illa, morituro non ultra formidanda est poena. Sin,[10] ut spero, vicerimus, tunc Pistorium veniat qui supplicium de nobis sumere volet."

10 His dictis, cum aciem concitasset, ex transverso hostem invadit. Ab hac maxime acie victoria parta creditur Florentinis. Nam hostes a tergo violentius percussi, retro iam respicere coacti sunt; et qui primo aegre resistebant, remisso hostium impetu in illos incu-

wings to cover the retreating cavalry; it harried the advancing enemy on its exposed flanks with spears and arrows and every sort of missile. So the bitterest fighting broke out in that place. The Aretines had placed their hope of victory in that first assault; hence, attacking with all their might they had attempted to shatter the Florentine line. But the infantry line absorbed and protected the cavalry, and there was a kind of wavering and uncertain motion of men simultaneously pressing forwards and resisting.

Now the Aretine infantry was arriving on the scene. It had 9 been left behind by the cavalry when the latter went in pursuit of the retreating Florentines, and had not yet joined the fray. And if they had joined up with the cavalry, there seems little doubt but that the victory would have gone to the Aretines. At that moment, however, Corso Donati, who was leading the irregulars, grasped the parlous situation of his side. Although he had been instructed not to enter the battle unless ordered to do so by the commander, he nevertheless decided it would be disastrous if he held back any longer. He said: "Let us attack the enemy knights, fellow soldiers, before their infantry joins the battle. For my part I shall let neither the orders of my commander nor fear of punishment deter me when my fellow citizens are in danger. If we in this force are conquered, then as dying men we shall have no punishment to fear. If, as I hope, we shall win, then let the man who wants to inflict punishment on us come to Pistoia."

With these words he spurred on his force and attacked the en- 10 emy at a right angle to their line of advance. That force is given the most credit for the Florentine victory. For they struck the enemy with great violence from behind and forced them to pay attention to their rear; and those elements of the allied forces who had been bitterly resisting the Ghibellines, once the pressure was lifted, were able to fall upon them. Once surrounded by the Florentine infantry, the enemy cavalry were easily overpowered. Count Guido Novello did not in like fashion bring up the force he com-

buere, et interclusus a suo peditatu equitatus hostium perfacile opprimebatur. Novellus autem comes aciem cui praeerat non item in auxilium suorum adduxit, sed ubi implicatum vidit equitum agmen, princeps fugam arripuit. At Guillielminus praesul, cum ante peditum staret aciem multique suaderent ut, profligatis iam equitibus ac victoria ad hostes inclinante, ipse Bibienam se reciperet vitamque a periculo tutaretur, interrogasse dicitur num et peditem reducere tuto posset. Cum negaretur peditem servari posse, "Mors," inquit, "communis mihi et pediti sit. Ego quos in periculum duxi, nunquam destituam." Ita redintegrata pugna hostes acriter invadit, nec multo post proelians occiditur; peditesque nudati equitum praesidio tandem superantur, ac multa caede opprimuntur. Ceciderunt in ea pugna Arretinorum supra tria millia, et in his Guillielminus praesul et Bonus Feretranus et alii quidam insignes diversarum partium viri; capti insuper ad duo millia. In Florentinorum quoque exercitu insignes quidam viri, qui primo illo equestri certamine corruerant,[11] desiderati sunt. Dantes Alagherii poeta in epistola quadam scribit se in hoc proelio iuvenem fuisse in armis, et ab initio quidem pugnae hostem longe superiorem fuisse, adeo ut a Florentinis multum admodum timeretur; ad extremum autem victoriam partam esse, tantamque inimicorum stragem in eo proelio factam ut paene eorum nomen ad internecionem deleretur.

11   Constat autem tertio Idus iunias pugnatum fuisse apud Campaldinum, eademque die atque hora Florentiae[12] nunciatam esse[13] victoriam. Cum enim priores, curis ac vigiliis anxii, per meridiem indulgerent somno, fores maiori vi pulsatae crepuerunt et vox festinantis audita: "Surgite: nam hostibus superatis victoriam habuistis." Ad eam vocem cum se laeti extulissent, apertis foribus gratu-

manded to help his own side, but was the first to flee when he saw
the cavalry become entangled. On the other hand, Bishop Guglielmino, stationed in front of the infantry, when many were urging
him to take refuge at Bibiena and protect his life from danger, in
view of the fact that their cavalry had been shattered and the victory was passing to the enemy — Bishop Guglielmino is said to
have asked whether he could lead the infantry back safely. When
told the infantry could not be saved, he said, "Then let me die
with the infantry. I shall never abandon the men I have led into
danger." Thus he entered the fray with renewed force, attacking
the enemy bitterly, and shortly thereafter died in battle. The infantry, stripped of mounted protection, were finally overwhelmed and
defeated with great slaughter. More than three thousand Aretines
fell in that battle, among them Bishop Guglielmino, Buono of
Montefeltro and certain other nobles of the Ghibelline party; as
many as two thousand were captured. The Florentine army also
lost certain distinguished men who fell in the initial knightly encounter. The poet Dante Alighieri writes in a certain letter that he
was present at the battle as a youth in arms, and that the enemy
was far superior at the beginning of the fight, so much so that the
Florentines were very frightened indeed, but in the end victory
was achieved, and the slaughter of the enemy in that battle was so
great that their reputation was almost totally destroyed.[3]

It is established that the battle of Campaldino took place on 11
June, and that news of the victory arrived in Florence on the same
day and hour. It was mid-day, and the priors, exhausted from anxiety and sleepless nights, were taking a nap, when there came a
great pounding on the doors and a messenger's voice was heard:
"Get up! The enemy is beaten; you have won!" The priors sprang
up joyfully at the voice, and opened the doors with gladness and
thanksgiving. The news flew through the streets, and there were
throngs of rejoicing citizens running to and fro, filling the piazzas.
But when the author of the tale was sought for, no one came for-

labantur. It fama confestim per urbem, et concursus fit civium gratulantium; turbae atria publica compleverunt. Sed quaerebatur auctor, nec ullus extabat. Quare is rumor quasi vanus nulloque probatus auctore, tunc quidem concidit. Nocte vero insequenti cum ab exercitu veri tandem nuncii advenissent, modumque et tempus commissi proelii enarrarent, compertum est victoriam fuisse partam eadem illa hora, qua prioribus quiescentibus fuerat nunciata. Quod etsi mirabile videtur, tamen alias quoque legimus contigisse. Nec sane alienum est credere divinum numen, qua benignitate victoriam praestat, eadem per famam ocissimam favore propitio illis ipsis quibus faverit nunciare. Nam et Macedonico quidem bello, Persa rege pugna superato, pari miraculo victoriam Romae nunciatam legimus. Et per Domitiani tempora in grandi suspicione civitatis partam apud Germanos victoriam, Romae eo ipso die fama certissima divulgavit. Multa sunt praeterea huiuscemodi tradita, si forte in eo genere verbositatem consectari libeat, et exempla nostrorum simul externorumque colligere.

12 Florentini post victoriam profligatos fugientesque persecuti, Bibienam Arretinorum oppidum eodem impetu ceperunt. Finitimis deinde castellis partim vi, partim voluntate in potestatem redactis, eversisque Bibienae moenibus, octavo post victoriam die Arretium versus copias duxere. Ea tarditas causa fuit ne urbe potirentur. Nam si protinus, victoria parta, eo copias traduxissent, capi profecto Arretium potuit, nullis firmis praesidiis et magna trepidatione urbem premente. Sed mora interposita confirmavit animos pavoremque ademit, et simul delapsi proelio milites variis itineribus domum redierant, ut iam urbem tutari valerent. Cum ergo Arretium pervenissent, castris apud Veterem Domum positis, oppugnare urbem aggrediuntur ab ea parte qua nondum moenibus cincta, sed vallo tantum et fossis munita erat. Eius rei gratia, cum

ward, so the story collapsed as an empty and unproven rumor. Yet on the following night when the true report at last arrived from the army, and the manner and time when the battle took place was told, it was discovered that victory was achieved in the very same hour it was announced to the sleeping priors. This seems marvellous, but we have read of this happening in other places, too. And it is by no means inappropriate to believe that the divine power by whose generosity victory was won, with an equal generosity announced his propitious favor instantaneously to the very persons he had favored. During the Macedonian War, when the Persian king was defeated in battle, we read that the news was announced in Rome by means of a similar miracle. And in the time of Domitian, when Rome was full of apprehension, an extremely positive report was spread in the city on the very day that a victory was won over the Germans.[4] There are many other traditions of this kind, if one cares to indulge in this prolix sort of research and collect domestic and foreign examples of the phenomenon.[5]

After their victory the Florentines pursued the shattered and 12 fleeing enemy, taking the Aretine town of Bibbiena in the same action. Then, partly by force and partly through voluntary means they brought the neighboring castles under their control, threw down the walls of Bibbiena, then, on the eighth day following the victory, marched their troops towards Arezzo. This delay was the reason they failed to bring the city under their control, for if they had marched there immediately after the victory had been won, they could certainly have taken Arezzo, gripped as that city was by terror and lacking a strong garrison. But the delay strengthened their spirits and lessened their fear, and, at the same time, soldiers who had escaped the battle had been returning home by various routes, so that now they were able to defend the city. Thus when the Guelf forces arrived in Arezzo, they pitched camp at Casa Vecchia and began to batter the city on the side that was not yet girt with walls, but was only defended by a palisaded earthwork

turres ligneas pluribus locis confecissent, magnum terrorem intulerunt hostibus, tantaque fuit potiundi spes ut duo ex prioribus,
novo quidem exemplo, ad urgendam oppugnationem in castra
proficiscerentur. Ab his adhortati milites ac plane[14] incensi, per
singulos ferme dies impetu facto, fossas complere, vallum rescin-
dere conabantur. Tandem, cum augesceret periculum aegreque iam
resisteretur, Arretini noctem obscuram atque ventosam nacti,
eruptionem subito fecerunt, facibusque in turres ac machinas con-
iectis, omnes cremaverunt. Quare, desperata expugnatione, cuncta
prius circa urbem populati, castellisque frequentia (namque ad eos
defecerant) praesidio militum communitis, Florentiam copias reduxere.

13   Redeunti exercitui obviam effusa civitas nullum genus honoris
praetermisit ducibus militibusque tribuere. Denique, triumphali
pompa per urbem transmissi, parmam et galeam Guillielmini
praesulis spectaculo civium praelatas, in antiquo Martis templo
quasi opima spolia suspenderunt; quae hodie quoque visuntur. In
publicis autem eius victoriae monumentis ita scriptum est, quod
Gibellinos apud Campaldinum profligassent. Id ex eo adscriptum
est, quod Arretini exules foederati et socii in eo bello adfuerant.
Qua de causa honestius visum est Gibellinos superatos scribere
quam Arretinos, ne pars quoque illa Arretinorum, quae socia et
amica et studio partium coniuncta fuerat, notaretur.[15]

14   Non multo post reductas Arretio copias, Lucensibus exulibusque pisanis auxilia rogantibus missa peditum duo millia, equites quadringenti. Lucenses cum his et aliis sociorum auxiliis fines
Pisanorum ingressi, cuncta igne ferroque popularunt; castella insuper quaedam vi capta ad solum everterunt. Inde Vicum Pisanorum expugnare adorti, cum magnos impetus ad moenia eius

and a moat. That was why they so terrified the enemy when they began to build wooden siege-towers in many places. So great was their hope of capturing the city that two of the priors, in an unprecedented step, set out for the camp to urge on the attackers. They harangued the soldiers to the point of raging fury, so that they attacked day after day, trying to fill the moat and cut through the earthwork. Finally, as the danger increased and resistance grew bitter, the Aretines took advantage of a dark and windy night to make a sudden sally, setting fire to the siege-towers and war machines, burning them all. This made the Guelf army despair of the siege, and they marched their troops back to Florence after devastating everything around the city and supplying garrisons for the network of castles (for these had defected to them).[6]

13 The city poured out to meet the returning army and rewarded the soldiers and their commanders with every conceivable kind of honor. Finally, they were carried in triumphal pomp through the city, and the helm and shield of Bishop Guglielmino were born before them as a spectacle for the citizenry before being hung up in the old temple of Mars[7] as spoils of victory, where they can still be seen today. In public records the victory was described as the defeat of the Ghibellines at Campaldino. It was so described because Aretine exiles were present at the battle as allies and confederates. That was why it seemed more honorable to say "the Ghibellines were defeated" and not "the Aretines": it avoided stigmatizing those Aretines who had been loyally attached to the Guelf cause in friendship and alliance.[8]

14 Not long after the troops returned from Arezzo, the Lucchesi and Pisan exiles asked for help, and two thousand foot and four hundred horse were sent. The Lucchesi with the help of these and other allies crossed the Pisan border and caused general devastation with fire and sword; they also captured certain castles by force and razed them to the ground. Then they set about besieging Vicopisano, and made some large-scale assaults against the walls

oppidi fecissent, oppidanis egregie repugnantibus ab incepto destiterunt.

15 Eodem anno extremum fere per autumnum rursus in agrum
Arretinum copiae reductae sunt ex huiusmodi causa. Post afflictas
opes vastatosque hostiliter agros, Tarlatus quidam Arretinus, vir et
genere et divitiis clarus, gubernationem susceperat civitatis. Eius
potentiam, ut fit, perosi quidam in illum coniurarunt, et per oc-
culta colloquia reducere in urbem exules ac Florentinorum auxilia
recipere intra moenia constituerunt.[16] His arcane solideque compositis, cum dies constituta iam adesset, subitanea profectio a magistratu indicitur, et candela ad portam accensa, ante illius consu-
mationem equites gravi sub multa iubentur exisse. Igitur, propere
exeuntibus copiis, cum inclinante iam sole proficiscerentur, Varicum de prima vigilia pervenerunt. Ibi, quod reliquum erat noctis
ad quietem sumpto, postera die Civitellam (id enim castellum
Arretini exules tenebant) se citato agmine contulerunt, ut proxima
nocte, quemadmodum constitutum erat, urbem intrarent. Rem
mature compositam effectumque habituram inopinatus turbaverat
casus. Ex coniuratis siquidem unus, proiecto aedium ruente, con-
fractus graviter corpus, extremo vitae tempore totam rem atque
ordinem sacerdoti nudaverat. Sacerdos vero periculosum sibi ratus
rem tam atrocem silere, patefecit eam principibus civitatis. Ita, coni-
uratione oppressa, res ad irritum recidit, et urbs, cognito florentinorum equitum adventu, solertius est custodita. Quamobrem,
paucis diebus Civitellae commorati equites, irrito labore domum
rediere.

16 Domi quoque eodem anno res innovatae, ac vexillifer iustitiae
tunc primum creari coeptus. Qua de re altius ordientes pro cogni-

of the town, but the townsmen defended themselves well, and the undertaking was abandoned.[9]

Almost at the end of the autumn of the same year the troops were marched back again into Aretine territory. The reason was as follows. After the depletion of its resources and the devastation of its fields through enemy activity, Arezzo had handed over the reigns of power to a certain Tarlato, a wealthy Aretine of distinguished ancestry. As usually happens, his power aroused the hatred of certain persons who conspired against him, and they decided to hold secret talks with a view to restoring the exiles and bringing a Florentine garrison inside the city. The plot was laid with the utmost care and secrecy, and when the appointed day had arrived, the Florentine magistrates announced an immediate expedition. Lighting a candle by the doorway, they commanded the knights, under grave penalties, to exit the city before the candle should burn down. So the troops departed with great speed. They left at sundown and had reached Montevarchi sometime after midnight. Spending the rest of the night in sleep, they went the next day in a flying column to Civitella, a castle held by Aretine exiles. The plan was to enter Arezzo the following night. The affair was well planned and would have worked, but it was spoiled by an unexpected mischance. Part of a building fell down on one of the conspirators, injuring him gravely, and being on the point of death, he revealed the whole plot to a priest. The priest decided it would be dangerous for him if he concealed so frightful a thing, and told the Aretine authorities. Thus the conspiracy was put down and the affair came to nothing. The city, learning of the arrival of the Florentine knights, looked to its defenses with particular care. So the knights, having spent a few days at Civitella, returned home after their fruitless efforts.[10]

In the same year there were innovations domestically as well. It was then that the first Standard-Bearer of Justice was chosen. To explain this office, we shall need briefly to go back a little way and

15

16
1289

tione rei, pauca superius repetemus. Nam, cum duae sint historiae partes et quasi membra, foris gesta et domi, non minoris sane putandum fuerit domesticos status quam externa bella cognoscere.

17   Florentiae igitur admodum vetusta atque, ut ita dixerim, primaeva videtur nobilitatem inter plebemque contentio. Fuit haec eadem, credo, aliis civitatibus, sed hic, nescio quomodo robustiores vigentioresque familiarum stirpes, tamquam fecundissimo in agro satae, altius increverunt; et plebs animis erecta potentioribusque infensa id unum habuit concordiae vinculum, nobilitatis metum. Cum enim inferioris potentiae homines magnitudini illorum pares esse non possent, ac saepe iniuriae contumeliaeque imbecillioribus inferrentur, unica prospecta est resistendi via, si populus una sentiret, neminis iniuriam pateretur, privatim inflictas contumelias publice vindicaret. Studia rei publicae capessendae hinc nimirum sunt populo coorta; hinc nobilitatis depressio. Ita demum enim populus se salvum esse posse existimavit, si ipse rem publicam gubernaret, ne nobilitas, supra potentiam propriam, rei publicae quoque abuteretur potentia, vel ad inferendas clades vel ad inflictas quominus ulcisceretur prohibendum. Hoc certamen diu incerto exitu conflictavit civitatem, utque est humanarum vicissitudo rerum, hi modo, illi quandoque¹⁷ praevalebant. Nonnunquam etiam mixti ex nobilitate et plebe magistratus sumebantur usque ad priores artium. Priores maxime gubernandi genus populare fuit, neque tamen ab initio merum: lex enim inertes tantum repellebat, nobilem vero non inertem esse non vetabat. Una fere simul cum prioribus, ad tutandum rei publicae statum, artium signa conventusque sunt restituta, quo armati cives, cum opus foret, concurrerent, ac praesentem civitatis statum, si res exigeret, tutarentur. Iuri autem dicundo in civitate duo praeerant magistratus: alter cum potestate

begin at an earlier point in time. For history has two parts or
limbs, as it were — foreign and domestic affairs — and it should be
understood that domestic conditions are as important to compre-
hend as foreign wars.

Well, then, in Florence there seems to have been an ancient, 17
even primeval struggle between the nobility and the common people. It was the same in other cities, I believe, but here somehow
the family stocks, being stronger and more vigorous, grew to a
greater height, as though planted in the most fertile ground. The
common people were high-spirited and hostile towards the powerful; fear of the nobility their one bond of harmony. Since the men
of lesser power could not equal the greatness of the nobility and
often suffered injury and insult, the one avenue of resistance they
saw was for the People to share a common purpose, suffer injury
to none of their own, and exact public vengeance for private offenses. Hence, no doubt, arose the People's desire to take control
of the commonwealth; hence came the levelling of the nobility.
The People for a long time had believed it could be secure if it
ruled the commonwealth itself, and thus prevented the nobility
from abusing public powers, in addition to its own power, in such
a way as to cause havoc and prevent injuries from being punished.
This struggle long afflicted the city, and its issue was uncertain, as
is the way of human affairs: now one side would prevail, now another. Sometimes also, down to the time of the priorate, the magistracies would contain a mixture of noble and common people.
Even the priorate, which was the most popular kind of government, was not purely popular in the beginning: the law only prohibited persons without a trade [from holding office]; it did not
forbid the nobility from practicing a trade.[11] Guild levies and standards were re-established at almost the same time as the priorate
in order to protect the commonwealth. Thus, armed citizens in
time of need would assemble to protect the regime if circumstances demanded it. The chief jurisdiction in the city was exer-

legitima ad causas et iudicia, alter populi defensor. Quia vero contingebat maleficia per nobilitatem committi, ad quorum punitionem magistratus accedere non audebat, quoniam stipati catervis suorum nobiles ab ipso quoque magistratu formidabantur et vexati pulsatique apparitores frequenter redibant, sicque iustitia impediebatur. Ad eam rem tollendam corrigendamque vexilliferum iustitiae creare[18] placuit.

18   Creatus est igitur primum septem annis postquam priores artium fuerant constituti. Eius electio prioribus commissa, tempusque vexillifero iustitiae definitum est mensium duorum. Additum est in lege, ut de plebe dumtaxat legere eum liceret, utque consiliarios haberet quatuor, praefectos duos peditesque armatos mille, e tota plebe vicissim descriptos: ex tribu videlicet Scradiana ducentos, totidem ex Transarnina, ex reliquis autem quatuor tribubus singulis centum quinquaginta. Horum descriptio annua erat, et quotiens vocarentur,[19] armati adesse ac vexillum iustitiae sequi iubebantur.[20] Additum est praeterea[21] in lege, ne quis ex nobilitate inter mille pedites legeretur, ne impediret, ne verbis minacibus uteretur, adversus transgredientem poena graviter constituta. Vexillifer promere vexillum per legem non poterat nisi iussu magistratus, nec una cum prioribus tunc habitabat nec quicquam fere aliud auctoritatis habebat, nisi quod princeps mille armatorum erat ad iustitiam in potentiores, si illi parere magistratui recusarent,[22] exequendam.

19   Eodem quoque anno primum in civitate constitutum est, ne quisquam qui prior fuisset foretve, intra triennium ab eo tempore quo magistratu abierit, sumi ad prioratum rursus posset, cum ante quidem nulla lex vetaret, sed pudor tantum homines a petitione

cised by two magistrates: one[12] had legitimate power to hear cases and administer the courts, the other[13] was the defender of the people. But there was a tendency for malfeasances committed by the nobility to go unpunished by cowed magistrates. The latter went in fear of the nobles with their retinues, who would often harass and beat their clerks, and so prevent justice from being done. To stop this abuse and correct the situation, it was decided to create the office of Standard-Bearer of Justice.

The office was created, therefore, seven years after the priorate 18 was established. Election of the Standard-Bearer was entrusted to the priors, and the term of office was fixed at two months. The law specified that he could only be chosen from the common people, and that he was to have four counselors, two lieutenants and a thousand armed foot-soldiers. These were all to be enrolled from the common people by turns; thus two hundred from San Piero Scheraggio, the same number from Oltrarno, and one hundred fifty each from the other four parts of the city.[14] These men were enrolled for a year's term, and were commanded to present themselves armed and to follow the Standard-Bearer whenever they were summoned. The law also specified that no nobleman should be chosen as one of the thousand foot-soldiers, and that no nobleman should interfere with them or threaten them verbally, and heavy penalties were fixed for anyone who should break this law. The Standard-Bearer was forbidden to raise the standard except by command of the magistrates, nor at that time did he live with the priors, nor exercise any other sort of authority.[15] He was merely the leader of a thousand armed men, charged with enforcing justice against the powerful, should they refuse to obey the magistrates.

In that year, too, it was first laid down in the city that no one 19 who had been or would be a prior could be chosen for the priorate again within a three-year period from the time when he had left office. No law had forbidden this before; only shame held men

compesceret. Id interim tempus quoniam lege vetatur, vetitum vulgo nuncupatum est. Causa vero legis fuit, ut pluribus ad honores pateret via, neque ob gratiam aut potentiam continuarentur.[23] Ea tamen lex magis necessaria fuit sortitionibus magistratuum quam petitionibus. Haec domi forisque eo anno gesta sunt.

20   Proxima deinde aestate Florentini, ante maturationem segetum, suas sociorumque contractas copias rursus in Arretinos duxere, sperantes longis belli calamitatibus ac terna iam frumenti amissione fatigatos, manus tandem esse daturos. Hac igitur intentione profecti, Arretio copias admoverunt. Sub ipsas urbis portas crebris proeliis commissis, nihil cum ad extremum profecissent, nec ullus intra urbem motus ad res novandas suscitaretur, ad vastationem agrorum conversi, omnia circa urbem hostiliter populati sunt; nec segetes modo, verum etiam vites et arbores. Demum, vastatis omnibus atque incensis, Casentinati via remeantes, castella quaedam Novelli comitis expugnare adorti, pleraque everterunt. Inde Florentiam exercitus reductus.

21   Eodem anno Florentini et Lucenses et aliae sociae civitates, renovato genuensi foedere, contra Pisanos copias duxere. Genuenses mari aderant, classem habentes navium longarum quadraginta. Ab his innumerae prope clades terra marique sunt illatae Pisanis. Cum enim hi terra, illi mari convenissent, nihil resistere poterat. Itaque, et Liburnum, proximum portui oppidum, ab his captum est atque incensum, et portum ingressi, turres eius everterunt. Onerarias insuper naves lapidibus gravatas in ipsis faucibus portus dimisere, quo illius usus receptusque impediretur. Inde, cum in

back from seeking such a distinction. Since one was legally forbidden to hold office during this interim period, it came to be called the 'forbidden' in the vulgar speech.[16] The reason for the law was to allow more men to hold public office, and to prevent magistrates from remaining in office through power and influence. Still, this law was more necessary in the case of magistrates chosen by lot than it was for those seeking office by election.

These were the events at home and abroad during that year. In the following summer, before harvest-time, the Florentines assembled their own and their allies' troops and once again marched to Arezzo, hoping that the long calamities of war and the loss of their harvest for the third time would wear the Aretines down and finally make them surrender. They set out with this intention and brought the troops to Arezzo. They engaged in frequent battles beneath the very walls of the city, but were not able to achieve any decisive victory nor did they start a coup inside the city to bring about political change. So they turned their efforts to devastating the fields, and ravaged the whole area around the city, not just the crops, but even the vines and the trees. Then, having destroyed and burnt everything, they returned through the Casentino, attacking certain castles of Count Guido Novello, most of which they sacked. Then the army returned to Florence.[17]

In the same year the Florentines, the Lucchesi, and other allied cities renewed the league with the Genoese and marched their troops against the Pisans. The Genoese came by sea with a fleet of forty galleys; these had wrought inestimable damage by land and sea upon the Pisans. When these land and sea forces had been combined, they were irresistible. Thus they captured and burned the nearby town of Livorno, whose port they entered, destroying its towers. They also sank cargo ships loaded with rocks in the very mouth of the port to hinder its operations and prevent its recovery. Then, when each army had gone its separate way, the Florentines, returning along the river Era, took certain castles in that

20

1290

21

sua quique discessissent, Florentini secus Heram fluvium redeuntes castella quaedam per ea loca Pisanis ademerunt, et praesidio militum munierunt. His peractis rebus, cum Florentiam exercitus rediisset, Guido Feretranus, qui per ea tempora dux Pisanorum erat, castella ipsa improviso impetu adortus, pari facilitate qua amissa fuerant pleraque recuperavit. Quod postquam Florentiae auditum est, equites peditesque rursus egressi Volaterras usque rapto agmine contenderunt. Ibi, cognita amissione castellorum et hostium recessu, non ultra profecti, rediere.

22   Altero mox anno Pisani, duce Guidone Feretrano, Pontem ad Heram fluvium, quem Florentini per superiora bella occupatum egregio munierant opere, arcemque super imposuerant turribus fossisque inexpugnabilem, nocturna ceperunt fraude. Cum enim praefecti castello (cives duo hi erant), partim avaritia, partim ignavia, vix tertiam partem militum sub vexillis haberent; et hi ipsi qui aderant, confisi munitionibus, negligenter obirent munera vigiliarum, ea res per hostem cognita ad tentandam fraudem invitavit. Itaque, Guido Feretranus ea spe tractus, per silentium illo copias duxit ad[24] octavum[25] Kalendas ianuarias,[26] nactus ex industria ventosam et gelidam noctem, quo minus vigiles intente custodirent. Ubi vero ad fossas quibus arx circumdabatur, latas quidem et aquarum plenas, devenit, lintre (quam ea de causa iumentis advexerat) in aquam demissa, milites ad ulteriorem aggerem traiecit. Inde scalis in proximam evadentes turrim, nemine penitus sentiente, cum satis magnus numerus introisset, custodes somno graves praefectosque ipsos, nil tale suspicantes, invaserunt; magna parte eorum interfecta, reliquis vero captis, ponte et castello munitissimo potiuntur.

area from the Pisans and garrisoned them. This done, the army returned to Florence. But Guido of Montefeltro, who was at that time the Pisan commander, made a surprise attack on these castles, and recovered them with the same ease with which they had been lost. When news of this came to Florence, the cavalry and infantry went out again as far as Volterra, pressing on quickly in a flying column. There, having learned that the castles had been lost and the enemy had returned, they went no further, but turned back.[18]

The following year the Pisans, led by Guido of Montefeltro, captured Pontedera at night in a sneak attack. During earlier wars the Florentines had occupied this town and provided it with exceptionally good defenses, building an impregnable citadel over it with towers and moats. The two citizens who served as its castellans, partly through avarice and partly through negligence, had scarcely a third of the garrison under their banners, and those soldiers who were present, relying on the defenses of the place, were neglectful of their guard duties. The enemy learned of the situation, which tempted them to try a strategem. Thus Guido of Montefeltro became hopeful and quietly brought his troops up on 25 December. He intentionally chose a blustery and freezing night when the guards would be less vigilant. Arriving at the moat surrounding the citadel, which was broad and full of water, he had a raft (which they had carried by draft animals for the purpose) lowered into the water, and threw soldiers across the moat to the opposite bank. Then the soldiers climbed ladders placed against the nearest tower without anyone hearing them. When a sufficiently large number had entered, they attacked the guards, fast asleep, and the castellans themselves, who suspected nothing. A large proportion of the garrison was killed and the rest were captured; and the enemy seized control of the bridge and its well-fortified castle.[19]

22

1291

23   Huius amissionem loci, cum ob eximiam opportunitatem ad
bellum, tum ob verecundiam sociorum, florentinus populus gravis-
sime[27] tulit. Itaque, ira et indignatione accensus, bellum contra Pisanos veluti proprium suscepit, cum antea Lucensium magis id
bellum auspiciis gereretur; Florentinus tantum submittere auxilia
solitus esset. Sed tunc, quasi ad eos vindicta spectaret, Florentini
ipsi per se immaturo adhuc anno fines Pisanorum cum exercitu ingrediuntur. Ibi, vastando per iram agro expugnandisque infestius
castellis, dum minabundi contendunt, tanti subinde imbres multos
dies continuarunt ut, superantibus aquis, vi ipsa ducibus militibusque abeundi retro exprimeretur necessitas. Reductis igitur copiis, expectare placuit maturitatem segetum, ac tunc demum in
hostes reverti. Itaque, omnibus edictum est tunc ab armis discederent, Kalendis vero iuniis rursus adessent.

24   Interea apparatus insignes facti atque dux ad id bellum delectus
Gentilis Ursinus, vir egregius bello ac studio partium eximius.
Is Florentiam cum aliqua manu equitum romanorum campano-
rumque adveniens, copias omnes Florentinorum duxit in Pisanos;
sociae quoque civitates ob studium Florentinorum auxilia misere.
Ingressi Pisanorum fines, cum hostis nusquam prodiret, quam
proxime Pisis[28] admoverunt copias. Nec usquam tanta pugnandi
aviditas Florentinis fuit; quippe sic ardebant animi ob foedam
amissionem munitissimi loci ut etiam in ipsis hostium portis discrimen pugnae subituri vel cupientissime deposcerent.

25   Erat intra urbem Guido Feretranus, vir ut calliditate quidem et
astu profundissimus[29] artifex, sic ad aperta certamina parum au-

The Florentine People took very seriously the loss of this place,   23
both because of its strategic position in wartime and because it
was an embarrassment for the allies. Thus, in anger and indignation the People took on this war against the Pisans as their own
affair. Previously, the war had been carried on more under the
auspices of the Lucchesi, while the Florentines were accustomed
merely to supply auxiliaries. But now, as though the vendetta had
become their own, the Florentines themselves of their own accord
entered Pisan territory with their army in the early part of the
year. Angrily they laid waste to the fields, and castles were sacked
with great ferocity. But while they were pressing ahead menacingly,
great rainstorms arose and continued for many days, so that the
violence of the superabundant waters compelled the commanders
and their men to turn back. So the troops marched back, and it
was decided to wait for the harvest-time, and then return to fight
the enemy. All the soldiers were told to stand down for the moment, but to present themselves again for service on the first of
June.

Meanwhile, they assembled an impressive supply of military   24
equipment and chose as their commander Gentile Orsini, a distinguished warrior and Guelf partisan. He arrived in Florence with a
band of Roman and Campanian knights, and led all the Florentine forces against the Pisans. The allied cities also send auxiliaries out of loyalty to the Florentines. They entered Pisan territory
and when no enemy advanced to meet them, they marched their
troops right up to Pisa. The Florentines had never been so keen to
fight. Indeed, they were so passionate about the shameful loss of
their highly fortified position that they eagerly challenged the
enemy to meet them in a decisive battle before the very gates of
the city.

Inside the city was Guido of Montefeltro, a deep and crafty fel-   25
low when it came to strategems, but reserved in the face of open
battle. Although he had plenty of knights and foot soldiers (for he

dax. Is, quamquam equitatu peditatuque abundaret (nam, praeter urbanos, ad octingentos equites mercede conducti intra moenia erant, populi vero multitudo ingens), tamen nedum in aciem prodire, sed ne eruptionem quidem ullam facere tentavit. Quare, aliquot dies circa Pisas commorati, quando etiam confessione hostium apparebat detrectare eos pugnam, nec dimicandi potestatem facere velle, omnia circa urbem ferro igneque populati, retro moverunt castra. Post haec, pervagati licentius agros, cunctisque hostiliter vastatis atque incensis, tandem copias reduxere, proelio quidem nullo contra Pisanos commisso, ceterum ea opinione et alacritate hominum ut hostes pro victis haberentur ob apertam detrectationem pugnae ac patientiam foedissimae vastitatis.

26   Circa finem eius anni fundamenta primum iacta sunt infinitarum domi novitatum, ac forma rei publicae, qua iam trigesimo supra centesimum utimur anno, tunc primum instituta. Arretino enim, ut supra diximus, bello cum prosper finis esset impositus, ac victoria inde parta maiorem in modum auxisset civitatem, mox et pisano bello haud dubie superior Florentinus haberetur, maiora de se populus sapere coepit, ac ab externis bellis ad intestinam libertatem respicere. Nobilitas enim, quae ad eam diem princeps in civitate fuerat, non satis aequam societatem cum populo exercebat; praepotens siquidem opibus et animis, plus quam liberae civitati conveniret elata, haud facile temperabat ab iniuriis inferendis. Homines longis stipati clientelis et multis, ut par erat, propinquitatibus subnixi, imbecillos honesta veluti[30] servitute premebant; frequentes ab his pulsatos mediocris fortunae homines, frequentes bonis spoliatos, praediis eiectos fuisse constabat. Quae etsi inter-

had eight hundred mercenary knights in addition to the urban knights, as well as a huge number of ordinary citizens), he nevertheless refused to make even a sally of any sort, to say nothing of engaging in pitched battle. So after the Florentines had spent several days near the city, when it became clear that, by the enemy's own admission, the Pisans were holding back from battle and were not going to take the risk of fighting, they withdrew their forces, laying waste to everything near the city with fire and sword. Then they wandered at will through the fields, plundering and burning everything, and finally marched back to Florence without engaging the Pisans in battle. But their actions had been keenly admired by everyone, while the Pisans were considered to be the losers, as they had refused open battle and had allowed a shameful degree of devastation to their territory.[20]

Towards the end of the year the foundations were first laid for 26 an infinite number of domestic innovations, and the constitutional form that we have used in the commonwealth now for more than 130 years was first instituted. For after a happy ending was brought to the Aretine war, as we have related, and the victory there achieved had greatly advanced the city's position, and then when the Florentine people were considered to be the undoubted winners of the Pisan war, the People began to grow conscious of its own power, and to turn its attention from foreign wars to domestic liberty. The nobility, which up to that time had been the leading force in the city, had never acted as an equal partner with respect to the People. Superior in wealth and arrogant in manner, its haughtiness was unsuited to a free city, and it could be restrained from committing unjust acts only with the greatest difficulty. Supported by their vast cliéntèles and assisted by their numerous family connections, they reduced the weak to a state resembling honorable servitude. Many were the men of modest fortune whom they attacked physically; and many were despoiled of their goods or expelled from their estates. Although the city tried from time to

dum vindicare pergebat civitas, tamen et favore propinquorum immodico sustentabantur, et horrebant homines eorum iniurias deferre, veriti potentiam familiarum et caedes ac vulnera plus quam iacturam patrimonii formidantes. Nec sane plenam ad servitutem plebis quicquam aliud obstare videbatur quam quod nobilitas ipsa, inter sese varie divisa, aemulatione et invidia concertabat.

27   Hanc igitur deformitatem et labem rei publicae tollere aggressus est vir unus, per eam tempestatem magnitudine animi et consilio pollens, Ianus Labella, claris quidem maioribus ortus, sed ipse modicus civis et apprime popularis. Is, seorsum primo cum singulis questus de potentia nobilitatis, segnitiem patientiamque populi increpabat, quod singulorum iniurias tolerando, non intelligeret universis simul turpissimam servitutem impendere; perstultum quidem putare ad se quoque vim non esse perventuram, cum domitis quibusque primis, ad alteros subinde vis tamquam incendium transeat; at enim occurrendum esse iam, nec uti plus crescat patiendum; adolevisse id certe malum, nondum tamen ita roboratum, ut medicari non possit; quod si ultra negligant, ac alteros alteri respiciant, frustra tandem auxilium contra inveteratam pestem optaturos.[31] Haec et istiusmodi iactando atque iterando, studia hominum incendit, mentesque erexit ad rem publicam capessendam. Assurgentibus ergo popularibus ac eius coepto faventibus, rem ad magistratum detulere, tandemque, multitudine plebis advocata, cum de hoc ipso consultaretur ac variae sententiae pro cuiusque ingenio dicerentur, assurgens ipse, in hunc maxime modum proposita de re coram disseruit:

time to punish these offenses, the nobility were upheld by the shameless favoritism of their relations, and men shrank from denouncing their unjust acts, fearing the power of their families and dreading wounds and death more than the loss of their patrimonies. Indeed, it seemed that the only obstacle to the complete servitude of the common people was the nobility's own internal divisions, riven as it was by envy and competitive rivalries.

One man tried to stop the corruption and decline of the commonwealth: Giano della Bella, who showed greatness and wisdom during that stormy time. He was descended from distinguished ancestors, but was himself a man of moderation and strongly populist in his sympathies. This leader first complained privately with individual citizens about the power of the nobility and criticized the inertia and passivity of the People, how they kept letting individuals suffer injustice, how they failed to realize that they were all as a group being threatened by shameful servitude. He said it was the height of stupidity to believe that violence would not affect one personally, as once the first people were brought to heel, violence would then strike others too, spreading like fire. Resistance was necessary now; the evil must not be allowed to grow. For though the disease had been allowed to spread, it had not yet so taken root that it could not be healed. But if they neglected the situation further and everyone waited for someone else to act, in the end they would find themselves hoping in vain for help against an endemic plague. By raising these issues over and over he fired up men's spirits and stiffened their resolution to take the commonwealth in hand. The popular classes arose and supported the effort, going forth to take the matter to the magistrates. And finally, when the people had been summoned,[21] and different opinions were being canvassed and expressed concerning the issue in accordance with each man's temper, Giano della Bella arose and addressed the crowd on the issue in the following general terms:

27
1292

28   "Semper eiusdem mentis sum, o cives; et quanto magis de re publica mecum ipse cogito, tanto in hac magis firmor sententia, necessarium fore aut[32] superbiam praepotentium familiarum retundere, aut libertatem omnino amittere. Eo quidem res deductas cerno, ut patientia vestra et libertas stare simul non possint; utram vero ex his retinere debeatis, neminem sanae mentis dubitaturum crediderim. Nec porro me praeterit quanto cum periculo meo sim ista dicturus, verum boni civis esse nequaquam arbitror, dum patria consilium poscit, in propriam utilitatem intuitum retorquere ac ex suo privato commodo publicis consiliis moderari. Dicam igitur libere quod sentio. Mihi quidem videtur libertas populi duabus rebus contineri: legibus scilicet atque[33] iudiciis. Quotiens enim illa duo plus possunt in civitate quam singuli cives, libertas servatur; quotiens autem reperiuntur quibus leges et iudicia contemnere liceat impune, actum esse quidem putandum est de libertate. Quid enim tibi liberum fuerit ab iis qui, si modo libeat, possunt absque iudiciorum metu in te atque in tua[34] violentas manus iniicere? Considerate nunc demum condicionem vestram, ac nobilitatis facinora vobiscum percurrite. Tunc mihi dicat aliquis, liberane civitas sit, vel iam pridem oppressa. Id vero facilius respondebit, si vel in urbe vel in agro vicinum aliquem ex illo potentium globo habuerit. Quid enim usque adeo nostrum est quod illi non concupiverint? Aut quid concupiverunt, quod non mox prosequantur? Aut quid prosequuntur, quod non per fas et nefas se debere consequi putent? Ne corpora quidem nobis,[35] si vera fateri volumus, iam libera sunt. Pulsatos cives, possessionibus eiectos, incendia, rapinas, vulnera denique et caedes complurium per hosce annos commissa a potentioribus meministis. Horum vero facinorum auctores patratoresque, partim sic aperti ut infitiari non curent,

"I have always been of the same mind, fellow citizens, and the   28
more I consider public affairs, the more I am convinced that we
must either check the arrogance of the powerful families or lose
our liberty altogether. Things have reached the point, I think,
where your tolerance and your liberty are no longer compatible. I
think too that no one of sound judgment can be in doubt which of
the two is to be preferred. It does not escape me that it is dangerous for me to speak of these things. But a good citizen, I think,
puts aside his own interests when his country needs his advice,
and he does not cut down his public statements to suit his private
convenience. Therefore I shall speak my mind freely. It seems to
me that the liberty of the people consists in two things: its laws
and its courts. Whenever the power of these two things prevails in
the city over the power of any individual citizen, then liberty is
preserved. But when some people are permitted to scorn the laws
and the courts with impunity, then one has to conclude that liberty is gone. For in what sense are you free when there are people
who, with no fear of judgment, can lay violent hands on you and
your property whenever they please? Therefore consider now what
your condition has come to, and review the crimes of the nobility.
Then tell me, any one of you, whether you think the city is free or
whether it has long existed in a state of oppression. The answer
will be easier for those who have a neighbor in the city or the
countryside who is one of this mob of powerful men. Is there anything we possess that escapes their greed? And what objects of
their greed have they not immediately claimed for themselves?
And what have they claimed for themselves that they don't feel
justified in taking, whether by fair means or foul? Our very bodies, if we will only admit it, are no longer free: just remember the
citizens who have been beaten or chased from their property, and
the numerous examples of arson, plunder, bloodshed and killing in
these last years. Some perpetrators of these evil deeds do them so
openly that they don't bother to deny them, while others have

partim sic manifesti ut nequeant infitiari, ante oculos versantur nostros, et quos carcer ac supplicium coercuisse debuerat, hos catervis armatorum stipatos magnifice per urbem incedere videmus, et nobis iam et magistratui longe formidandos. Hanc igitur mihi libertatem quisquam vocabit? Et qua alia condicione tyranni utuntur quam ut occidant, ut pellant, ut auferant quae libitum est, sine iudiciorum metu? Quod si unus eiuscemodi in singulis civitatibus libertatem perimit, quid in nostra a tot simul evenire existimandum est? Oppressi, credite mihi, iam pridem sumus, et libertatem speciosam inani verbo, servitutem revera turpissimam sustinemus.

29   "Sed haec ita esse, dicet quispiam, nemo ambigit; at remedium te, non deplorationem flagitamus. Huius ergo tam foedae servitutis depulsio, unde sumenda sit, non admodum cognitu difficile reor. Ut enim ex legum iudiciorumque lapsu interiisse libertatem videmus, sic ex eorum ipsorum erectione vobis illa reviviscet. Quare, si libertatem cupitis (cupere autem pariter ac vitam omnes debemus), illa duo vobis in suam auctoritatem restituenda sunt, et omni nixu diligentiaque firmanda. Et leges quidem vobis multae sunt de vi, de caede, de latrociniis, de iniuriis, de ceteris denique maleficiis coercendis. Has itaque leges singulari nota contra potentioris[36] innovandas censeo, et alias insuper adiungendas. Cum enim malignitas hominum dietim crescat, nova insuper prospicientia opus esse quis ignorat?

30   "Sed illud in primis necessarium puto, ut delictorum poenae contra potentioris[37] augeantur. Ut enim, si quis gigantem ac pusillum hominem ligare velit, non eodem, credo, vinculo uteretur, sed gigantem quidem non nisi catenis aut rudentibus, alterum vero chorda vel loro putaret compescendum, sic poenae, quae legum vincula sunt, longe fortiores contra grandes istos et potentes constituendae[38] videntur, nam quae nunc[39] sunt in legibus, eos non

been caught in the act and are unable to deny them. So they remain at large: we see men who deserve prison and punishment strutting like lords around the city with crowds of armed retainers, terrifying us and the magistrates. Is anyone going to tell me that this is liberty? How is this condition different from tyrants who kill, expropriate, take whatever they want without fear of judgment? And if one man of this sort can destroy liberty in one city, what shall we think of our city where it happens simultaneously at the hands of so many? We have certainly been oppressed for some time, believe me, and we keep up the appearance of liberty with empty words, while in reality we suffer the most shameful servitude.

"Someone may object, however, and say: no one doubts that 29 that is the case, but we want solutions, not hand-wringing. To this I say: we can find a way to shake this shameful servitude from our backs with no great difficulty. For if the corruption of the laws and the courts has caused the death of liberty, the rebuilding of those institutions will bring liberty back to life. If you wish to be free, therefore — and we should all desire freedom as much as we do life — restore those two things to their proper authority, and be strenuous and strict in keeping them in force. You have many laws restraining violence, killing, theft, assault, and other crimes. These laws must be renewed to take particular notice of the powerful, I say, and new measures must be added. For who can ignore the need for new, additional precautions given the daily increase in human wickedness?

"The most necessary step, I think, is for criminal punishments 30 to be increased in the case of the powerful. Surely if you want to tie up both a giant and a midget, you don't use the same kind of bonds. You tie the giant with chains and cables, the midget with ropes and thongs. Punishments are the bonds of law, and likewise must be made stronger for great and powerful men. The punishments we have on the books now don't hold them. I would add

tenent. Unum praeterea his adiungo, ut proximi atque familia eisdem poenis obligentur. Semper enim participes maleficiis gentiles agnatosque fuisse putandum est, quorum fiducia quis elatus maleficia commiserit. Iudiciorum autem vim duo maxime impedire solent: probationum difficultas et exequendi defectus. Nam et testes formidant contra potentioris[40] deponere, quo uno metu cuncta paene iudicia subvertuntur; et si quando probatur, magistratus exequi horret. His nisi provideritis, scitote vos nullam rem publicam habituros. Nam, quid prodest leges vel optimas in civitate esse, si iudicia irritentur? Primum igitur testium difficultatem resecandam censeo, ac famam ipsam contra potentioris[41] admittendam. Cum enim maleficium esse patratum constet, et publica vox hominum finitimorum, agri denique ipsi et saltus a potentiori aliquo factum clament, non mihi anxias probationes quaerat iudex quas novit metu potentiae deterreri, sed[42] fama ipsa illi satis esto.

31 "Ad exequendi vero difficultatem, quaeso, animos advertite. Quippe, maius quiddam esse cerno quam homines opinentur, nec tam a magistratu, quam a populi robore dependere. Si enim populus, quemadmodum decet, praestantiam in re publica retinere volet, executio iudiciorum etiam contra potentissimos facillima erit; sin alios admirabitur et supra se putabit, magistratus simul rostraque tepescent. Ea nimirum res dudum animadversa deprehensaque effecit ut vexillifer iustitiae crearetur, cuius ego vim tam brevi antiquatam esse admiror. Sed stultum est, ut arbitror, cum populus ipse remissus ac negligens fuerit, vicarios eius conqueri non acres[43] fuisse. Et simul tam multa tunc omissa fuerunt, ut in-

the further stipulation that family and kin are to be included in punishments. We should consider clan and kinsmen as complicit in the crime, for it is his reliance on them that encourages the nobleman to commit crimes. Two things usually hinder the effectiveness of our courts: the difficulty of proving cases and the failure to execute sentences. Witnesses are afraid of testifying against powerful men, and nearly all judicial procedures are subverted by this single fear; and even if the case is proven, the magistrate shrinks from executing sentence. If you do not change these things, you will have no republic. What good are even the finest laws in a state if legal proceedings are made void? So you must first of all, I think, curtail the problem of witnesses; in the case of powerful men, public notoriety must be admissible as evidence. Thus when some malfeasance has been committed, and there has been a public outcry of the neighbors, when the very fields and woodlands cry out that it was done by some powerful man, in my view let the judge not seek scrupulous proofs, which he knows will not be forthcoming owing to fear of power; but let notoriety alone suffice for him.

"As to the difficulty of executing sentence, please pay careful at- 31 tention, for I think this is a greater matter than people realize, depending less on the magistrates than on the strength of the people. For if the People really wants, as it should, to keep its predominance in the commonwealth, the sentences of the courts, even against powerful persons, will readily be carried out. But if the people is dazzled by the nobility and defers to it, this will make both the magistrates and the courts lukewarm in their efforts. All this was noted and understood a while back when the Standard-Bearer of Justice was created, but I marvel that his power has so rapidly fallen into abeyance. But it is stupid to complain, I think, when the People itself is spiritless and negligent, that the People's agents lack keenness. Yet at that time so many things were passed over that the matter seems to have been left in an uncompleted

choata potius res quam perfecta videretur. Ego igitur vexilliferi auctoritatem censeo maiorem in modum esse roborandam. Itaque, primum illud decerno, ut non mille armati, ut ante, sed quater mille toto vicissim e populo descripti vexillifero tribuantur. Deinde vexilliferum ipsum una cum prioribus publicis aedibus collocandum esse dico, ut praesens querelas civium intueatur et sentiat, praestoque sit rei publicae necessitatibus ne, si domi degat, aut non mature intelligat aut privatorum intercessionibus, quod hactenus factum scimus, illius opera retardetur.

32   "Tertium insuper et hoc ipsum tunc praetermissum adiungo, ne quisquam e potentioribus, etiamsi artificio se contexerit, ad prioratum sumi possit, ne favendi reis impediendique iustitiam habeat facultatem. Satis enim superque illorum potentia per se ipsa onerosa est, nisi insuper publica potestate armetur. Ita, legibus quae passim iacebant erectis poenisque acrioribus adversus potentes constitutis iudiciisque roboratis, cessare illos a tyrannide compelletis, vel certe, si effrenes esse pergent, tamquam pestiferam corporis partem ac sanitatem minime recepturam, ferro igneque exterminabitis, posita hac nimia superfluaque patientia, quae videntes sentientesque vos in servitutem perducit.

33   "Dixi fere quae salutaria rei publicae et simul vobis[44] necessaria puto ad libertatem. Quae, si difficillima factu essent ac magno labore magnisque sumptibus comparanda, tamen propter utilitatem suaderem capessenda. Nunc autem, cum sint facilia et in manibus reposita vestris, quis usque adeo dissolutus erit, ut malit per iniuriam turpiter servire, quam per ius et honestatem par ceteris fore? Maiores nostri ne imperatoribus quidem romanis servire sustinuerunt, quamquam et titulum praetendentibus et dignitate hominum servitutem honestante. Vos vilissimis hominum servire sus-

state. So I believe the authority of the Standard-Bearer of Justice needs very much to be strengthened. In my view he should, first of all, have at his command, not a thousand armed men as heretofore, but four thousand, to be recruited from the whole people by turns. I also think that the Standard-Bearer himself should reside in the public palace together with the priors, so that he will personally hear and understand the complaints of the citizens and provide for the needs of the commonwealth. If he remains at home he will either lack full knowledge of the situation or he will be slow to act because of interventions from private individuals, such as we know to have happened hitherto.

"I should add a third provision which was overlooked at that time: that no powerful man, even if he pretends to be a tradesman, can be raised to become a prior, and thus put into a position to help criminals and to impede justice. Their existing power is sufficiently burdensome to us, without adding the armor of public authority. In this way, if you resuscitate the laws, establish severer punishments against the powerful, and strengthen the courts, you will force them to stop their tyrannous behavior. Certainly, if they continued unchecked, you will have to root them out with iron and fire as you would incurably sick limbs, putting aside that excessive patience of yours which is leading you with open eyes and ears into slavery. 32

"I have said what I think are the measures that will save the commonwealth and are necessary for our liberty. If they were difficult and expensive and involved great labor, I would tell you that they had to be carried out anyway because of their usefulness. As they are easy, however, and lie within your power, who is so corrupt that he would rather serve in humiliation and injustice than be equal to others in rights and honor? Our ancestors forebore to serve even Roman emperors, although the title to which the emperors pretended and their rank made the servitude less dishonorable. Shall you continue serving the vilest of men? Our ancestors 33

tinebitis? Illi caedes ac vulnera et patrimoniorum iacturas ac infinitas paene contentiones pro dignitate et praestantia subierunt. Vos prae metu et ignavia, quos vobis subesse decet, eos sponte vestra tyrannos vobis superponetis? Nec pudet populum unum, id est multitudinem tantam fortium virorum, quae omnes finitimos virtute bellica superavit et mille hostium perfregit cuneos, eam domi reversam huius vel illius familiae potentiam pertimescere, ac despectum superbiamque illorum, qua veluti mancipia iam premimini, tam ignave perferre? Dicendi finem faciam, ne me longius abripiat impetus; nam et obiurgare populum reverentia praepedior, et hanc degenerem patientiam vestram reminiscens, aequo animo praeterire non valeo. Vos tantum quaeso iam, ut libertati vestrae salutique consulatis."

34 Magno cum assensu audita est oratio, et laudarunt omnes celsam viri praestantiam. Ita, inflammatis cunctorum animis, lex perfertur contra potentiores familias, quae ordinamenta iustitiae vocitarunt, propterea quod quemadmodum illae subderentur iustitiae certa via et ordine constitutum est. Quae vero forent potentiores familiae adversus quas ferebatur lex, subinde exprimitur. Fuerunt intra urbem duodequadraginta familiae per eam legem annotatae; extra urbem vero complures, quae praediis suis consistentes haud aequam vicinitatem cum imbecillioribus exercebant. Potestas etiam prioribus tradita alios quoque, si eis videretur, annotandi. Ita, perculsa nobilitate, potestas et arbitrium rei publicae ad populum rediit. Proximis deinde comitiis Ianus ipse legis auctor, iubente populo, ad prioratum assumitur. Is una cum collegiis vexilliferum iustitiae creavit et in consessum recepit. Primus omnium post hanc legem vexillifer iustitiae fuit Baldus Ruffulus, vir nequaquam segnis, sed qualem prima illa[45] tempora flagitabant, ad reprimendos potentiores auctoritatemque populi afferendam. Hic,

bore death and wounds and the loss of their patrimonies and endless strife for the sake of their dignity and preeminence. Shall you, out of fear and baseness, place over yourselves, of your own free will, tyrants who ought to be subject to you? Should a whole people, that is, a vast multitude of strong men, who have conquered by their warlike valor all their neighbors and have smashed a thousand enemy legions, not be ashamed, returning home, to fear the power of this or that family and basely suffer the nobility's pride and contempt to make us slaves? I shall stop now, so that I do not become carried away by my own vehemence. The respect I feel for the People prevents me from chiding them, yet when I call to mind this degenerate passivity of yours I cannot remain silent and calm. I am asking you only to take thought for your own liberty and welfare."

The oration met with wide approval, and everyone praised the 34 man's elevated and outstanding character. In this way the People were fired up to pass a law against the powerful families. It was called the Ordinances of Justice because it ordained ways and means to subject those families to justice. The powerful families that were the target of the law will be given below. There were thirty-eight families from within the city proscribed by the law, while outside the city there were many other families living on their estates who were in the habit of behaving unjustly towards their weaker neighbors. The priors were given the power to proscribe other individuals as well if they saw fit. Thus the nobility were dealt a hard blow, and power and authority in the commonwealth returned to the people. In the assemblies that followed, Giano himself, the author of the law, was raised to the priorate at the behest of the People. He and his colleagues elected the Standard-Bearer of Justice and admitted this official to their counsels. The first Standard-Bearer of Justice after passage of the Ordinances was Baldo Ruffoli, an active man such as those early times required, vigilant in restraining the powerful and asserting the

nunciata caede plebei hominis a quodam ex his familiis quae no-
tatae fuerant[46] perpetrata, confestim prodiens cum vexillo, populares in arma excivit, secutaque multitudine aedes Gallorum (ex ea
namque familia erat qui caedem fecerat) circumstetit, gentilesque
et agnatos homicidae persecutus, extorres patria egit, aedes diruit,
praedia vastavit. Ex eo tantus terror iniectus est nobilitati, ut non
minus iam formidarent populares, quam ipsi[47] quondam fuerant a
popularibus formidati.

35   Constituta per hunc modum re publica domi, externam ad
quietem versae mentes, de pace cum Pisanis agere coeperunt. Fuerant enim Pisani longo iam bello plus quam dici queat afflicti,
atque ita vires eorum contritae ut diutius resistere posse nequaquam viderentur. Sed ne nobilitas, quae bello clarescere solebat,
per occasionem militiae aliquid moliretur, et plebs nusquam a rei
publicae custodia abscederet, pacem potius visum est quam bellum
expedire, teneris adhuc legibus et rei publicae statu nondum solide
stabilito.

36   Legati duo ea de causa missi, Melior Guadagnius[48] et Arrigus
Paradisius, cum Pisanorum legatis Pistorii convenerunt. Difficilior
eius pacis conventio fuit, quia socii omnes, in primisque Lucenses
et Ugolinus Gallurae iudex, pacem longe improbabant, victoriam
in manibus esse putantes. Sed pervicit Florentinorum voluntas;
paxque tandem proximo dehinc anno perfecta est, sociis quoque
omnibus eam pacem recipientibus, ne sine Florentinis cogerentur bellum supra vires proprias[49] sufferre. Condiciones huiusmodi
dictae receptaeque: ut Pisani Ugolinum Gallurae iudicem ceterosque pisanos cives eius factionis, qui per id tempus exulantes

People's authority. When informed of the murder of a common citizen by a member of one of the proscribed families, he immediately went forth with the standard, roused the People to arms, led a crowd to the house of the Galli family (to which family the murderer belonged) and surrounded it. He hunted down the murderer's clan and kinsman, drove them into exile, destroyed their houses, and laid waste to their estates. The nobility was filled with such terror at this treatment that they now began to fear the People as much as the People had once feared them.[22]

Public affairs having thus been put in order at home, the People 35 turned their attention to tranquillity abroad, and began to negotiate a peace with the Pisans. The Pisans had by then undergone unspeakable sufferings on account of the long war, and their strength was so worn down that it seemed they could resist no longer. Nevertheless, it seemed the better course to make peace rather than continue the war. The nobility, which generally distinguishes itself in wartime, might use the occasion of military service to begin some plot, and the common people were not about to relax their vigilance in protecting the commonwealth, seeing that the new laws had just begun to take root and the condition of the commonwealth was still fragile.

Two ambassadors were sent out for this purpose, Migliore 36 Guadagni and Arrigo Paradisi, who met with the Pisan representatives at Pistoia. It was the more difficult to agree on peace as all the allies, especially the Lucchesi and Judge Ugolino of Gallura, were highly critical of the negotiations, believing victory to be within their grasp. But the will of the Florentines triumphed, and peace was finally made the following year. The allies all accepted 1293 the peace as well: to do otherwise would have compelled them to make war without the Florentines, a task beyond their powers. The conditions announced and adopted were as follows. The Pisans were to restore to the city and to their possessions Judge Ugolino of Gallura and all other Pisan citizens of his faction who

Lucensibus se Florentinisque coniunxerant, in urbem atque in sua omnia reciperent; captivos eius factionis quotcumque haberent ex civibus aut clientibus, libere dimitterent, ac esse in urbe morarive paterentur aequo iure cum aliis civibus; moenia et arcem Pontis ad Heram fluvium, quam[50] nuper[51] Florentinis abstulerant, funditus everterent; Guidonem Feretranum eiusque commilitones et socios Pisis dimitterent; magistratum, qui urbi iustitiaeque praeesset, biennio Pisani deligerent non ex aliis civitatibus oppidisve quam quae in societate Florentinorum Lucensiumque fuissent ad bellum Pisis inferendum; additum praeterea est, ne ex his locis damnatum exulem eiectumve quemquam deligerent; Florentinis perpetua apud Pisanos importandis exportandisque rebus mari terraque immunitas foret; si Guelfus et Lottus Ugolini comitis filii, quem Pisani fame necaverant, eo in foedere adscribi vellent, licere[52] illis intra sextum mensem; id si facerent, eandem illis condicionem fore quae Ugolino Gallurae iudici ceterisque eius factionis circa restitutionem in urbem liberationemque captivorum, ut supra expressum est. Hae Pisanis condiciones dictae. Florentini Pecciolae castellum reddere Pisanis promiserunt.

37 　　Pax certe fuit honorificentissima omnium, et tamquam victis impositae leges. Sed evenit Pisanis quod in ancipiti malo evenire plerumque solet. Ante foedus enim pericula belli prospicientes eaque formidantes, pacem facere properarunt. Post foedus autem ictum, cessantibus iam belli periculis, pacis pericula solum intuebantur. Redire exules in urbem, magistratum ex hostibus praeesse sibi, periculosum existimabant. Crudelitas nuper in Ugolinum comitem expressa et filiorum reditus ac potentia ante oculos versa-

had been exiled during this period and who had allied themselves with the Lucchesi and the Florentines. They were to free all the hostages of that faction, both citizens and their clients, and the freed hostages were to be allowed to live in the city on an equal basis with the other citizens. The walls and the citadel of Pontedera which they had recently taken from the Florentines were to be demolished. Guido of Montefeltro and his soldiers and allies were to leave Pisa. The Pisans' chief judicial magistrate[23] was to be chosen, for a period of two years, only from among those cities or towns that had been allied with the Florentines and Lucchesi in the late war against Pisa; and it was further specified that this magistrate was not to be someone who had been condemned, exiled or expelled from one of these cities or towns. The Florentines were to enjoy perpetual immunity [from taxation[24]] when importing and exporting goods by land and sea through Pisa. If Guelfo and Lotto, the sons of Count Ugolino (the man the Pisans had starved to death) wished to enter into this pact, they were to be allowed to do so for a period of six months; if they did so, they were to be granted the same terms as Judge Ugolino of Gallura and the members of his faction with respect to restoration to the city and to the freeing of hostages, as specified above. These were the terms on the Pisan side. The Florentines agreed to return the castle of Pecciole.[25]

No peace treaty could have been more honorable than this one; it was imposed on the Pisans like laws on a conquered people. But there transpired in the case of the Pisans what usually happens when evils are double-edged. Before the treaty, they had looked fearfully on the dangers of war and had hastened to make peace. Once the treaty had been made and the dangers of war had receded, all they could see were the dangers of the peace. They considered perilous the return of the exiles and the rule of a magistrate chosen from among their enemies. The cruelty they had used against Count Ugolino and the return to power of his sons were

37

batur.[53] Hoc igitur metu anxii, nec Feretranum dimittebant, ut convenerant[54] in foedere, neque captivos liberabant. Turres solum et moenia ad Heram fluvium diruere coeperant, verum ita segniter et otiose ut appareret eos de pace simul belloque cogitare. Ea cunctatio cum longius traheretur, Ugolinus Gallurae iudex per literas Florentiam missas querebatur neque captivos dimitti, neque sibi aliisque exulibus facultatem remeandi Pisas fieri, neque impleri cetera quae Pisani spopondissent: itaque videret florentinus populus ne circumveniri socios ac derisui fore adversariis patiatur.

38   Ob eam suspicionem oratores missi duo, Rogerius Ugonis Albici et Cambius Ildebrandini Bellincionis, hisque mandatum est uti se Pisas conferrent peterentque conventa ex foedere adimpleri. Cum illa essent perfecta, tunc Pecciolae illis traderent, promissione ab his recepta erga incolas eius castri se benigne amiceque habituros, nec illis in fraudem versuros quod Florentinorum sociorumque in eo bello favissent partibus. Profecti oratores, cum apud Pisanos mandata peregissent, moverunt studia hominum ad ea quae in foedere convenerant adimplenda. Itaque, paulo post per literas renunciarunt proclamatum esse Pisis reditum exulibus patere; moenia et turres ad Heram fluvium magna ex parte eversa fuisse et quod superest assiduo iam opere demoliri, ac cetera esse impleta omnia, praeter captivos, qui nondum liberati forent; convenisse autem, ut illis positis apud Heram traditisque, ipsi Pecciolae redderent intra dies octo vel captivos eodem in loco restituerent. Ita, demum recepti sunt captivi ex foedere et Pecciolae reddi-

constantly before their eyes. Made anxious by these fears, they did not dismiss Guido of Montefeltro, as they had agreed to do in the treaty, nor did they free the hostages. They began to dismantle the towers and walls at Pontedera, but in such a desultory fashion that it looked like they were thinking about war as well as peace. After they had been dragging their feet in this way for some time, Judge Ugolino of Gallura wrote to Florence complaining that the hostages had not been released, that neither he nor the other exiles been given the opportunity to return to Pisa, and that other conditions to which the Pisans had agreed were not being fulfilled. The Florentine People (he wrote) should not allow its allies to be circumvented and mocked by its adversaries.

Thus two ambassadors were sent out, Ruggeri d'Ugo degli 38 Albizzi and Cambio d'Aldobrandino Bellincioni. They were instructed to go to Pisa and request that the terms of the treaty be fulfilled. Only when they had been fully carried out would Pecciole be turned over to them. They should also extract a promise from the Pisans that the inhabitants of that castle should be well treated and not suffer mischief because they had favored the cause of the Florentines and their allies in the late war. The ambassadors, having gone to Pisa and presented their commission, were able to convince the Pisans to fulfill the terms of the treaty. Thus, shortly thereafter, they reported back by letter that there had been a proclamation opening Pisa to the exiles; that the walls and towers at Pontedera had mostly been demolished, and that the rest of the demolition work was proceeding apace; and that all the other conditions had been fulfilled, except that the hostages had not yet been released; but it had been agreed that once the hostages had been moved to Pontedera and handed over, the Florentines themselves would turn over Pecciole within eight days, or the hostages would be released at Pecciole.[26] Thus, the hostages were finally turned over in accordance with the treaty and Pecciole was returned to Pisa. The Pisans then chose a magistrate from

tum Pisanis. Magistratum autem ex Colle oppido foederato Pisani tunc delegere, ut convenerant[55] in pace. Per hunc modum finis bello pisano tunc[56] impositus est.

39   Altero dehinc anno nihil dignum memoria foris gestum reperio. Nam et Arretini exules, conspecta Florentinorum voluntate, pactiones quasdam, duras sane et asperas, cum his qui urbem tenebant inierant, ac redditis quibusdam castellis,[57] ipsi in exilio, sub reductionis spe irrita, remanserunt. Itaque, neque contra Pisanos propter recentem pacem, neque contra Arretinos ob exulum desperationem, eo anno quicquam gestum est. Annus tamen insignis fuit duobus pontificibus romanis subinde creatis: Caelestino Perusiae a patribus supra biennium iam inclusis, mox sexto fere post mense eo se abdicante; Bonifacio octavo apud Neapolim a cardinalibus in pontificem assumpto. Per idem fere tempus basilica Sanctae Crucis in ea qua nunc est forma aedificari Florentiae coepta est, cum prius breve admodum eo in loco sacellum foret, longe dispar ab illa quam nunc videmus magnificentia.

40   Externam mox pacem intestinae discordiae secutae civitatem concussere. Ianus enim Labella, post legem contra nobilitatem latam, malevolentia potentiorum et invidia parium agitatus, tandem in exilium pulsus est, non dissimili exemplo ac ceterorum hominum qui beneficiis ingratorum populorum fundamenta suae stabilitatis collocarunt. Gesta vero est res in hunc modum. Rixa inter agnatos familiae nobilis coorta, quidam e minima plebe homo, dum alterutri favet, excepto lethali vulnere oppetierat. Hic etsi non satis constabat cuius manu cecidisset, tamen eius delicti fama in auctorem certum iactabatur. Cum igitur hic, seu gratiae seu innocentiae fiducia, ad magistratum venisset ac se praesens purgaret, tandem absolvitur. At plebs, quae iam erecta vindictam caedis ex-

Colle Val d'Elsa, a town in the Florentine federation, as they had agreed to do in the peace. In this way an end was brought to the Pisan war.[27]

I have found nothing worth recording in foreign affairs for the following year. The Aretine exiles, having seen what the intentions of the Florentines were, entered into certain highly unfavorable agreements with the men who controlled their city. They turned over certain castles to these men, but themselves remained in exile, disappointed in their hope of return.[28] Thus nothing was done this year either against the Pisans, because of the recent peace, or against the Aretines, because of the despair of the exiles. Nevertheless, the year was distinguished by the election of two popes. Pope Celestine was elected by the cardinals after they had been immured for more than two years, but the man abdicated about six months later.[29] The conclave then elevated Boniface VIII to the pontificate.[30] Around the same time the church of Santa Croce in Florence began to be built in its present form. Before that time there had only been a narrow little chapel, very different indeed from the magnificent structure we see today.[31]

So peace reigned abroad, but the city was soon shaken by discord from within. Giano della Bella, after the law against the nobility had been passed, aroused such ill-will among the powerful and such envy among his peers, that he was finally cast into exile. His was a case not dissimilar to that of other men who have founded their estate on helping ungrateful peoples. It happened in the following way. A riot arose between branches of a noble family, and a certain person of the lowest condition, having favored one or the other side, died as the result of a mortal wound. Although it was not clear by whose hand the man had fallen, a certain individual was believed without question to be responsible for the crime. This man, trusting either in his innocence or in his influence, came before the magistrate, defended himself, and was finally acquitted. But the common people, who had been waiting in expec-

39
1293

40

379

pectabat, ubi absolutum sensit, iram a reo in iudicem vertit; raptis-
que[58] confestim armis, ad aedes Iani Labellae multitudo convenit,
cum videlicet patronum libertatis, auctorem legis, vindicem tyrannorum, succurrere adversus potentiam nobilium sordesque corrupti magistratus clamitabat. Ianus hunc motum plebis neque
comprimere studuit, cum facile id posset, nec rursus sese ducem
illis praebuit, sed ad priores ire monuit, ac vexillum iustitiae sequi.
Non tamen paruit multitudo, sed protinus a Iani aedibus ad praetorium oppugnandum perrexit. Ibi, incensis refractisque foribus,
non prius destitit quam violentia et rapinis, foedo quidem exemplo, sese contaminavit. Hic populi furor, quoniam ibi ab initio
convenerat, ex aedibus Iani Labellae manasse videbatur, et move-
bat plerosque invidia quod esset ad hunc potissimum urbanae
multitudinis facta concursio, quodque patronus libertatis fuerat
appellatus. Denique, carpere potentiam hominis criminarique non
nobilitas modo, verum etiam plebei quidam coeperunt, et quamquam in ceteris adversi, in hoc tamen uno pari voluntate conspi-
rantes. Ceterum diversis rationibus nobilitas quidem, ob leges in
se promulgatas, hominem male oderat; populares autem, etsi periculum rei publicae simulabant, nulla tamen alia re quam invidia
torquebantur. Igitur, proximis comitiis ferocissimo quoque ad
prioratum assumpto, Ianus ipse de vi publica accusatur, quod multitudinem armatam privato consilio domi habuisset, quodque eadem multitudo illius iussu praetorium oppugnasset.

41   Ob eam accusationem civitas confestim erecta atque solicita
animis, pro tanto rerum motu in diversum[59] abiit. Nam plebs quidem ac omnis multitudo urbana rem pergraviter ferebat, et

tation that the crime would be punished, when they found out he had been acquitted, transferred their anger from the defendant to the judge. The multitude immediately took to arms and assembled at the house of Giano della Bella, calling upon him as the patron of liberty, the author of the Ordinances, and the avenger of tyrants, to come to their aid against the power of the nobles and of greedy, corrupt magistrates. Giano had no desire to quell this uprising of the commons, though he might easily have done so, but he also did not want once more to become their leader. Instead, he told them to go to the priors and follow the Standard of Justice. But the multitude ignored him and went immediately to attack the palace of the Podestà. There they set fire to and broke down the doors, not stopping before they had stained themselves with violence and plunder, setting a disgraceful example. This mad outburst of the people seemingly could be traced to the house of Giano della Bella, since it was there they had first assembled. Many were envious because the urban multitude had run to him, singling him out and hailing him as the patron of liberty. Finally, not only the nobility began to criticize and denounce the man's power, but even some of the common people; and although they disagreed on other matters, in this conspiracy they were of one mind. They had different motives, to be sure. The nobility nourished an evil hatred of the man because of the laws he had promulgated against them; the popolani pretended the commonwealth was at risk, but in reality were tormented by envy. Thus, at the next assembly a particularly ferocious set of priors was chosen, and Giano himself was accused of criminal violence in that he had harbored an armed multitude at his house by his private, deliberate choice, and this multitude had attacked the Palace of the Podestà on his command.

This accusation immediately set the city on edge and it became 41 sharply divided over this important turn of events. The common people and the whole urban multitude took the matter very badly

concurrebat frequens ad Iani aedes, parata pro illius salute ferro decernere; hortabaturque uti bono esset animo, nec inimicos invidosque metueret: tantum enim vis tantumque potentiae florentina plebe inesse ut ea sibi coniuncta, terrori ipse potius inimicis esse debeat quam ab illis terreri. At nobilitas contra implacabili odio in illum exarserat, venisseque tempus vindictae existimabat, quae cum per se multum posset, addita popularium manu priorumque auctoritate, inexpugnabilis videbatur.

42   Certamen procul dubio futurum erat maximum, si ad manus ventum esset, sed non permisit Ianus civile bellum sui causa moveri. "Cedamus," inquit, "potius inimicorum calumniis, et locum invidiae permittamus. Me quidem, iudiciorum auctorem assertoremque, nemo unquam dixerit vim contra iudicia paravisse; nec meo quisquam exemplo civis adversus publicam auctoritatem capiet arma. Innocentia mea et beneficia in populum collata bene de reditu sperare iubent." Ita amicissimum quemque complexus, urbe excessit; absensque capitis damnatus est. Damnati sunt item cum eo Taldus frater et Rainerius nepos, aedesque et praedia eorum vastata. Ex huius viri exilio quanto populus, in se ipso divisus, factus est imbecillior, tantum nobilitati spes et animi creverunt, quod non multo post dare ostendit.

43   Tertius iam intrarat annus post rem publicam in arbitrium populi redactam. Nobilitas vero, indigne ferens leges contra se latas, praesertim cum in dies magis experiretur se potentia simul auctoritateque spoliari premique ab iis, quos ipsa paulo ante premere exagitareque consuesset, tandem sibi prospicere coepit. Quae cum intelligeret vulnus acceptum ex propriis discordiis initium fomen-

indeed, and crowds converged on Giano's house, ready to defend him with the sword and urging him to be of good cheer, and not to fear his enemies and those who envied him; the Florentine commons (they said) had so much strength and power that when they joined him, his enemies would have to be more afraid of him than he of them. The nobility, on the other hand, were consumed with an implacable hatred of him, and believed the time had come for their revenge; it seemed to them they were unbeatable, since to their own considerable power they had added numbers of popolani and the authority of the priors.

There would undoubtedly have been a great struggle if matters 42 had come to blows, but Giano would not allow a civil war to start on his account. "I prefer to give way," said he, "to the calumnies and jealousy of my enemies. For my part, I am an advocate and defender of the courts, and no one shall ever say of me that I have intended violence against the courts, nor shall it be by my example that any citizen takes up arms against the public authorities. My innocence and the benefits I have conferred upon the People bid me be of good hope that I shall return." With these words he embraced his closest friends, then left the city. In his absence he was condemned to death. Condemned with him also were his brother Taldo and his nephew Ranieri, and their houses and estates were destroyed. The exile of this man made the People weaker, as it became divided within itself, just as it nourished the hope and spirits of the nobility, as we shall shortly see.

It was now the third year since the commonwealth had come 43 under the control of the People. But the nobility was angry about 1295 the laws passed against them, especially as every day they felt themselves to be stripped little by little of their power and authority and to be kept down by those whom but a little while before they used themselves to oppress and attack. Finally they began to look out for themselves. They understood that the blow they had suffered had its cause in their own discords, and they decided first

383

taque sumpsisse, redintegrare animos primo, inde communi consilio rebus suis mederi statuit. Itaque, sublatis inter se quibus iam
perierant[60] odiis, in gratiam redierunt[61] principes familiarum, pacemque fecerunt ex diuturnis certationibus. Inde mox de communi
salute consultantes, decreverunt magistratum adire et palam
conqueri de legis iniquitate; ad extremum autem quoquo modo
adniti. Coetu igitur sui ordinis facto, cum priores adiissent, tolli
contra se durius constituta postularunt. Plebs autem simul atque
nobilitatem coetus agere conspexit, studio retinendi iuris erecta
perstabat, rata (id quod erat) nobilitatem ad extremum vi esse co-
naturam. Suspicionibus igitur et certaminibus coortis, quando his
quidem obtinere, illis vero negare propositum erat, tandem itur ad
arma, et magno tumultu per urbem discurritur. Nobilitas equis insignibus stragula veste ornatis ut eius temporis magnificentia et
dedita gloriae belli aetas consueverat, suarum quisque familiarum
insignibus, magna multitudine convenerat; e praediis quoque et
clientelis evocata peditum ingens manus, facinorosorum insuper et
audacium hominum turba, militare simul consueta. Cum his copiis nobilitas tribus urbis[62] locis constitit, rata per hunc modum
facilius urbem discurrere, et plebem, ne se moveret,[63] distinere
posse. Una stetit acies apud Martis templum; altera apud forum
novum; tertia trans Arnum, apud superiorem pontem. Plebs autem et ipsa raptis armis in unum convenerat, et frequentia per vias
ad prohibendam equitum vim impedimenta coniecerat; saxis insuper telisque domos communiverat;[64] tantusque fuit apparatus populi ut nobilitas spe vincendi dubia invadere non auderet, sed in illis ipsis quibus convenerat locis armata structaque perstaret.
Tandem, intercedentibus bonis viris pacemque suadentibus, arma
deposita sunt a nobilitate, paucis admodum eorum quae prius sta-

to come to agreement, then mend their fortunes by following a common plan. So they abandoned the mutual hatreds that had been ruining them; the heads of families were reconciled to each other and made peace, putting an end to their daily quarrels. They then took thought for their common welfare, and decided—as a way, finally, of exerting themselves—to go before the magistrates and complain in person about the iniquity of the laws. So assembling a group of their order, they went before the priors and requested that the severer measures against themselves be lifted. The common people, as soon as it saw the nobility assemble, became vigilant to hold on to their rightful authority, thinking (as in fact turned out to be the case) that the nobility would in the end not stick at violence. Thus mutual suspicion and quarreling arose, it being the purpose of the nobility to obtain, and of the common people to oppose, changes in the law. Finally, they had recourse to arms, and great tumult spread through the city. The nobility came together in large numbers, each bearing his family crest, riding fine horses, richly caparisoned, as was the custom in that age so devoted to magnificence and the glory of war. They summoned also a large band of infantry from their clientage and from their estates, a crowd of reckless criminals who were used to fighting. With these forces the nobility established three bases within the city, thinking they could in this way move more easily through the city and block the movements of the common people. One force was set up at the Baptistery, another in the Mercato Nuovo, and a third in Oltrarno, by the first bridge.[32] The commons for its part seized arms and assembled together; it set up numerous barricades in the streets to check the force of the knights; and it also stockpiled rocks and missiles in its homes. So impressive were the military preparations of the People that the nobility grew doubtful that it could win and did not dare attack, but remained armed and ready in the urban bases where it had gathered. Finally, men of good will intervened and persuaded them to make peace. The no-

tuta fuerant abrogatis, et ea magis ex auctoritate priorum quam ex populi voluntate. Tunc igitur ab armis discessum est, ceterum animi civium armati manserunt, nec unquam posthac cessatum vel a popularibus nobilitatem deprimere vel a nobilitate conari pro recuperanda dignitate. Prioribus qui tunc erant populus succensuit, quod nobilitati favissent. Itaque, in abeuntes magistratu convicia sunt dicta, et illa ipsa pauca quae nobilitati condonarant, paulo post in pristinam normam revocata sunt.

44 Agitatum praeterea est, plebe annitente, de Iano Labella in urbem revocando, quod is solus civis ad conterendam nobilitatis vim unice natus videbatur, et fecerat plane desiderium eius conspecta nuper in nobilitate audacia et attemptata legum abrogatio. Cum igitur de illo revocando agitaretur, adversarii ad Bonifacium pontificem confugerunt. Ille per litteras magistratui populoque praecepit ne Ianum Labellam neve Taldum fratrem aut Rainerium nepotem ab exilio revocarent, neve ad dignitatem aliquam vel honorem admitterent, neu in urbem reciperent; ea si contra fieret, auctores adiutoresque, civitatem denique totam gravissimis obligavit poenis. Causa autem[65] in litteris exprimitur, quoniam ille sator discordiarum inter cives fuisset. Eas ob litteras reductio Iani impedita est. Ita civis bene meritus a populo ipso, cuius auctoritatem contra potentiores asseruerat, ingrate desertus, in exilio diem obiit.

45 Per idem fere tempus renovata societas est inter civitates, foedusque denuo ictum. Nec multo post aliud foedus initum est cum Perusinis, et in amicitiam societatemque recepti, mutua sibi auxilia promisere.

46 Versus dehinc ad magnificentiam populus, regionem simul et urbem decorare aggressus, medio ferme spatio inter Arretium ac Florentiam duo condidit oppida, ut forent simul ornamento, simul

bility laid down its arms, and a few of the earlier measures against them were abrogated, thanks more to the authority of the priors than to the consent of the people. So the People then laid down its arms, but they remained armed mentally. Afterwards the People never stopped humbling the nobility, nor did the nobility ever stop trying to recover its lost status. The People were angry with the priors of that time because the latter had favored the nobility. Hence the magistrates were censured when they left office, and the very few concessions they had allowed the nobility were soon revoked and the original Ordinances were restored.[33]

There was, furthermore, pressure from the common people to 44 recall Giano della Bella, as the one citizen who seemed uniquely suited to crush the power of the nobility; they plainly wanted him back because they had seen the recklessness of the nobility and its attempt to abrogate the laws. So when the pressure began to recall him, his adversaries had recourse to Pope Boniface. He instructed the People and the magistrates by letter not to recall from exile either Giano della Bella or his brother Taldo or his nephew Ranieri; not to confer upon them any honor or dignity; and not to let them enter the city. If they did, he would lay heavy penalties upon those responsible and indeed the entire city. The rationale as expressed in the letter was that Giano had been a sower of discord among his fellow-citizens.[34] Giano's return was blocked because of this letter, and thus a citizen who had deserved well of his people and who had safeguarded its authority against the powerful died in exile, deserted by his ungrateful countrymen.

Around the same time the league among the cities was renewed 45 and a new treaty was signed. Soon thereafter another treaty was entered into with the people of Perugia, who became friends and allies, and promised mutual aid.

The People then turned its attention to splendor, and began to 46 embellish the city and the countryside. About halfway between Arezzo and Florence it built two towns, for the sake of adorn-

belli praesidio; et alterum quidem in sinistra Arni ripa situm, cui
nomen dedere a patrono civitatis; alterum trans Arnum a dextra
fluminis parte, quod Francum appellarunt. Intra urbem vero, quoniam aedes quibus tunc priores inhabitabant neque publicae neque
dignae florentino populo videbantur, et formidabatur saepe a prioribus ob potentiam nobilitatis, his de causis aedificium publicum
insigni magnificentia atque fastigio aedificare statuerunt. Locus ad
hoc delectus[66] est eminentissimus cis Arnum, inter Scradii templum ac theatrum vetus. Eius aedificandi causa, privatarum aedium redemptio facta est a dominis locorum, multisque emptioni-
bus, cum solum publicum effecissent, dirutis privatis aedificiis,
palatium fundarunt. Area vero quae circumstat palatium magna ex
parte Ubertorum fuit, quorum iam pridem dirutae aedes, purgatis
tandem ruderibus soloque aequato, aream in usum publicum praebuere. Iacta sunt autem huius palatii fundamenta biennio ante
millesimum trecentesimum annum, turrisque egregia magnitudine
in illo erecta. Nova post haec urbis moenia aedificare adorti (quae
prius designata magis fuerant quam coepta) ab inferiori Arni ripa,
via Pistoriensi, longo et sinuoso ambitu, ad superiorem usque ri-
pam perpetua moenia cum insigni turrium altitudine perduxerunt,
ut non solum muniretur urbs, verum etiam ornaretur. Carcer
quoque per haec ipsa tempora aedificari coeptum[67] est ad portam
gibellinam in solo Ubertorum. Eius ambitus quadrato ferme spatio muris undique cinctus, intusque distinctio facta tricliniorum
diaetarumque. Ad id[68] aedificandum primo statim tempore
quinque millia aeris publici decreta sunt. In his conficiendis biennium fere consumptum.

47   Per idem tempus Bononienses Ferrariensesque, bello iam pridem conflictati, arbitrium pacis concordiaeque in florentinum po-

ment as well as for protection in wartime: one on the left bank of the Arno, named after the patron of the city,[35] and the other across from it on the right side of the Arno, called Castelfranco.[36] Within Florence it was decided to build a public edifice of great height and splendor for the priors, since the buildings they currently inhabited were neither public property nor did they seem worthy of the Florentine People, and the priors were often in a state of fear owing to the power of the nobility. The place chosen for the building was on an elevation on this side of the Arno between the church of San Piero Scheraggio and the old theater. To build it they purchased private dwellings from their owners, and when after many purchases they had created a plot of public land, they tore down the private dwellings and laid the foundations of the palace. The piazza surrounding the palace had mostly belonged to the Uberti, whose dwellings had already been torn down some time before; and when the rubble had been cleared away and the ground made level, the piazza was turned over to public use. The foundations of the palace were laid in 1298, and a tower of extraordinary height was erected on top of it. After this they began to construct the city walls (which earlier had only been laid out, not really begun), bringing them from the lower bank of the Arno, by the Via di Pistoia, in a long and curving arc up to the higher bank of the river, and placing high towers along them at regular intervals, with the aim not only of protecting the city, but also of embellishing it.[37] They also about this time began to build a prison near the Porta Ghibellina on the Uberti land. It occupied an almost square plot of ground surrounded by walls on every side, and its interior was divided up into living and dining quarters. To build it an initial appropriation of five thousand florins was made, and two years were spent finishing it.[38]

Around the same time the peoples of Bologna and Ferrara, who had been fighting a long war, called in the Florentine People to settle their differences and make peace. It was believed that the

1298

47

pulum contulere. Earum civitatum auctoritas quia a romana sede pendere credebatur, visum est non absque pontifice romano quicquam agere, sed eo praesente atque volente. Ita, missi ad pontificem eius rei gratia oratores septem, mixti ex nobilitate plebeque: Rainerius Bondelmontes, Burnetus Burnelletius, Bingerius Tornaquincius, Albicius Corbinellus, Baldus Agulio, Gentilis Altovita, Borgus Rinaldi. Hi, ex auctoritate pontificis, florentini populi nomine, pacem inter populos ex arbitrio pronunciarunt.

48   Sequitur post haec annus christianae salutis trecentesimus supra mille, in quo iubilaeus a Bonifacio pontifice institutus est, cum incredibili concursu fidelium populorum.

49   In eo rursus anno nova turbatio Florentinos pervasit, ac nescio an maxima superiorum omnium, initio huius mali in hunc modum coorto. Genus erat Pistorii per eam tempestatem admodum florens, nec divitiis modo, verum etiam virorum multitudine conspicuum; vulgo Cancellarios nominabant ab auctore eius generis ita vocitato. Huius familiae homines, natis inter se discordiis, in diversum abierant, iamque inimicitiae graves et rixae ad plagas usque et vulnera manus impulerant. Foedati proximorum sanguine atque polluti, per varios favores totam diviserant civitatem; vulgoque, ut fit, nominibus inditis, hi albi, illi nigri appellabantur. Cum ob eas sectas in extremum paene discrimen Pistorium devenisset, suscepta civitatis cura, Florentini, quo id malum aperte iam erumpens, si qua posset ope, comprimeretur, capita factionum amovenda, quoad refrigesceret impetus, factu optimum iudicarunt. Itaque dedita opera ambae partes Florentiam deducuntur. Enim vero ea res non tam Pistorium purgavit, quam Florentiam infecit. Nam simul atque Florentiam pervenerunt homines nobiles, multisque ac magnis affinitatibus in ea subnixi, a propinquis hospitio varie suscepti ac mox favore sublevati, easdem quoque in-

Roman See had authority over these two cities, so it seemed best not to take any action without the participation and approval of the Roman pontiff. Thus seven ambassadors, a mixture of nobles and commoners, were sent to the pope for this purpose: Ranieri Buondelmonte, Brunetto Brunelleschi, Bingieri Tornaquinci, Albizzo Corbinelli, Baldo Aguglione, Gentile Altoviti, and Borgo Rinaldi. Under authority from the pope, these men arbitrated the peace between the two peoples in the name of the Florentine People.[39]

The year following was the thirteen hundredth year of Christian salvation, and Pope Boniface declared a Jubilee, which was attended by incredibly large crowds of the faithful.[40] **48** **1300**

In that year political turbulence once again swept through Florence, possibly the greatest that had yet taken place. The troubles began in the following way. In Pistoia in that period there was a flourishing clan, famous for its numbers as well as its riches. They were called the Cancellieri in the native tongue, after the founder of the clan. Discord had arisen between the members of this family, and they had gone their separate ways; now serious hostilities and brawling had driven them to blows and bloodshed. Having stained and polluted themselves with the blood of their relatives, they had made the whole city divide itself up into factions favoring one side or the other, and (as usually happens) the factions were given demotic names: one was called the Whites, the other the Blacks. When, thanks to these factions, matters had reached a critical state in Pistoia, the Florentines became concerned and set about controlling in any way they could the disease that had now burst into the open. They decided the best thing to do, to cool things off, would be to remove the heads of the factions. So they purposely brought both parties to Florence. The effect of this was less to cure Pistoia than to infect Florence. For the arrival of these noblemen in Florence, where they had numerous powerful blood-relations who gave them succor of various sorts and were soon fa- **49**

cendii faces in proximam civitatem iniecerunt. Ea quidem labes nobilitatem primo irrepsit, alio aliis favente, nec ulla fuit domus paulo insignior quae non bifariam scinderetur. Inde, quoniam huiusmodi controversiae in re publica tractandae saepius erant, in populares quoque, veluti tabes aliqua diffusa, eo validius exarsit quo ampliorem Florentiae quam Pistorii fuerat materiam consecuta. Igitur, divisa civitas, divisae domus,[69] divisae familiae, fratres quoque reperti sunt quorum alius alia sentiret. Ita[70] factio illa quos vocitabant guelfos anceps discinditur, duaeque factiones ex una consurgunt.

50   Erant iam pridem contentiones quaedam inter Circulos et Donatos, ex vicinitate qua se paene intra urbem extraque in praediis contingebant exortae. Ad eas incendendas aptissima fuit discordiarum flamma Pistorio allatarum. Nam ea Pistoriensium pars qui nigri vocabantur, plurimum apud Donatos diversata, immodico familiae eius favore, ut propinqua et hospitio suscepta, iuvabatur. Ea res effecit ut quicumque albis favebant ad Circulos, iam pridem notos Donatorum adversarios, se conferrent. Ita his aut illis omnes cohaeserunt. Et Circulorum quidem familia erat ad pacem aptior: tranquilli homines, maximis praediti divitiis, civili moderatione et innocentia. Donatis autem vetustior nobilitas, mediocris opulentia, belli aptior natura quam pacis artibus.

51   His contentionibus cum tota divisa civitas esset cladesque inde proventura haud dubie timeretur, veriti duces guelfarum partium ne ob hanc divisionem inter suos homines coortam gibellinorum factio in civitate resurgeret, ad Bonifacium pontificem confugerunt; monstratoque periculo, flagitarunt ut huic nascenti malo auctoritate occurreret. Pontifex, intellecta re, Verium Circulum principem eius familiae ad se vocatum multis verbis cohortatus est

voring their causes, meant that they simultaneously spread the same conflagrations to the city next to theirs. The infection first appeared among the nobility, with each one favoring one side or the other, and there was no clan of any distinction whatever that was not split in two. Then, since controversies of this kind very often become matters of public debate, the disease spread also to the popular classes, raging the more violently as it had more fuel to feed on in Florence than in Pistoia. Thus the city was divided, clans were divided, families were divided — there were even brothers who took opposite sides. So the faction that used to be known as the Guelfs was split in two, and two factions arose from one.[41]

There had been for a long time certain quarrels between the 50 Cerchi and the Donati springing from the proximity of their estates in the city and in the countryside, and the flame of discord brought from Pistoia was well adapted to ignite those quarrels. The Pistoian party known as the Blacks had many connections among the Donati, and were entertained like relatives and helped unreservedly thanks to the favor of that family. That was why whoever favored the Whites had recourse to the Cerchi, who had long been known as enemies of the Donati. So everyone attached themselves to one family or the other. The Cerchi were as a family more inclined to peace. They were mild men, immensely wealthy, restrained and blameless in civic affairs. The nobility of the Donati was of more ancient origin. They were only moderately wealthy, and naturally more given to the arts of war than of peace.

When the whole city had been divided by their quarrels, and it 51 was feared that disaster would surely follow, the leaders of the Guelf Party, worried that the Ghibelline faction would rise again in the city because of the divisions that had sprung up between these men, had recourse to Pope Boniface. They pointed out to him the danger and demanded that he use his authority to check the nascent evil. Once he understood the situation, the pontiff summoned Vieri de'Cerchi, the leader of that family, and exhorted

ut, deposita contentione, in gratiam rediret cum Cursio Donato, principe familiae Donatorum; neque enim dubitare se, reconciliata inter eos gratia, ceteros quoque fore secuturos. Ad haec, multa licet pollicitus, flectere hominem nequivit, asserentem se adversus neminem prorsus inimicitias exercere. Ita per Verium stetit, quo minus res interventu pontificis componerentur, quod ad magnum sibi erratum plerique imputarunt. Mentem certe pontificis non mediocriter offendit, praesertim cum adversarius eius Cursius, paulo ante hoc ipsum a pontifice rogatus, se totum in potestate sua respondisset futurum.

52   Simultatibus igitur in dies crescentibus, forte fortuna proximis Kalendis maiis iuvenes utriusque familiae per urbem de more equitabant, comitatum habentes aequalium et amicorum equitum circiter trecentos. Cum in area quae est ad Trinitatis aedem mulierum choream festum diem celebrantium inspecturi utrique constitissent, torve se conspicientes primo, mox, quia mixtis erant equis, alteri alteros urgentes, rixa tandem exoritur et gladiis aperte geritur res; quaedam utrinque inferuntur vulnera; uni etiam Circulorum (Recoverino illi nomen fuit) in ea rixa nasus abscinditur. Fit subito[71] concursus hominum alterutris faventium, non sine tumultu et trepidatione civitatis; aegreque[72] tandem pugna dirimitur. Natis hinc iam[73] gravioribus odiis, armata pars utraque longis agminibus per urbem incedebat, et tota civitas erecta ac solicita gravissimo in metu versabatur.

53   His de causis pontifex non ultra cunctandum ratus, legatum suum Florentiam misit Matthaeum Ostiensem. Is cum urbem intrasset, liberum sibi arbitrium tradi postulavit, quo rem publicam stabilire, simultatesque tollere commodius posset. Circuli et factio eorum per illa tempora multum in re publica praevalebant. Itaque veriti ne voluntas legati ad adversarios inclinaret,[74] operam eius in

him at great length to lay aside his feud and make peace with Corso Donati, the leader of the Donati family. The pope had no doubt (he said) that, once the two of them were reconciled, the rest would follow suit. Despite many promises the pope was unable to persuade Vieri to do this, however; the latter kept claiming that he really had no quarrel with anyone. So, thanks to Vieri, the matter was not settled by papal intervention, and most people set this down against him as a great error. Certainly he gave no little offense to the pope, especially since his adversary Corso, who shortly before had been asked the very same thing by the pontiff, replied that he would do everything in his power.

Thus the feud became worse every day. By chance on the next 52 Calendimaggio[42] some youths of both families were riding as usual through the city, accompanied on horseback by about three hundred friends and companions their age. When both groups stopped in the piazza before the church of San Trínita to watch some women dancing in celebration of the feast, they started glaring at each other; then, as their horses mingled, they started to shove one another; and finally a brawl began. Swords were drawn, and wounds inflicted on both sides. One of the Cerchi, named Recoverino, even had his nose cut off in the clash. Immediately, the men who supported one or the other faction ran up, and the city was wracked with confusion and fear. Finally the fight was with difficulty broken up. Thereafter, still deeper hatreds were born, and both parties marched armed in long processions through the streets.[43]

For these reasons the pope thought he should delay no longer, 53 and sent his legate Matthew of Ostia to Florence.[44] When this man had entered the city, he asked that he be given a free hand so that he could more easily bring order to the commonwealth and stop the feuding. Now the Cerchi and their faction had far greater influence in the commonwealth, and they were afraid that the legate would take the side of their adversaries. Hence they spurned

constituenda re publica aspernati sunt. Itaque, decedens urbe legatus, interdicto illam subiecit.

54   Secutae dehinc graviores contentiones. Nam haud multo post,
cum pars utraque armata funeri mulieris nobilis adesset, e contraria regione se minabundi aspicientes, gladios stringere ac invadere
alterutros voluerunt. Ob eam rem animadversam, trepidatio exorta
est multitudini quae ad funus convenerat, et fuga passim per urbem facta. Ipsi tamen illo in loco non depugnarunt, sed interventu
separati diversis viis domos suas rediere. Circuli ea die concursu
factionis suae adiuti, Donatos invadere statuerunt, et aderant ceterarum familiarum homines, qui nuper una cum illis ad Trinitatis
<aedem>⁷⁵ aut vulnerati fuerant aut graviter offensi. Hi non clam
neque per insidias, sed quasi iustam ad pugnam profecturi, equis
cataphractis insidentes, peditum multitudine circumfusa, Donatorum aedes adierunt. Illi, audita vi quae contra se parabatur, apud
Cursii aedes convenerant et acciverant amicorum manum, fa-
ctoque armatorum globo, venientes adversarios non inviti expectabant, confisi praecipua Cursii virtute, cuius tanta erat constantia et
magnitudo animi ut eo praesente adversariorum conatus omnes facile se arcere posse arbitrarentur. Quod et plane accidit. Nam, ubi
eo pervenerunt adversarii ac magno clamore faces et arma inferre
coeperunt, ruens non minori impetu in eos Cursius, aciem venien-
tium perfregit, multisque vulneribus reiectos terga vertere ad extremum coegit.

55   His ergo et huiusmodi crebro emergentibus civitas tota erecta,
suspicionibus rumoribusque obnoxia erat. Crimina vero et delicta
interdum vindicabat, interdum etiam multitudine delinquentium
subsistebat. Circuli tamen, eaque pars civium qui albi vocabantur,

his offer of help to bring order to the commonwealth. Thus, as the legate left the city, he placed it under interdict.[45]

But still graver quarrels were in store. Shortly afterwards both 54 parties, armed, were attending the funeral of a noblewoman, when, staring threateningly at each other from opposite sides, they became filled with the desire to draw swords and attack each other. When the crowd attending the funeral noticed this, it grew terrified and began to flee through the streets. Yet they did not come to blows in that place, but were separated thanks to mediation; instead, they went back home by their separate ways. The Cerchi that day were reinforced by a gathering of their faction, and decided to attack the Donati. Present also were members of other families who had recently been insulted or wounded at San Trínita, together with the Cerchi. They set out, not in secret or like plotters, but as though marching to a real battle — mailed and on horseback, surrounded by infantry — and closed in on the dwellings of the Donati. The latter could hear the forces being arrayed against them, and, assembling at Corso's house, they summoned bands of their friends. Forming an armed mob, they gladly stood waiting for their oncoming adversaries, trusting Corso's outstanding courage. Such was Corso's constancy and greatness of soul, that they believed they could easily ward off all the assaults of their adversaries, which is exactly what happened. For when their adversaries got there and began to attack with arms and torches and loud shouting, Corso came down upon them with no less force and shattered the line of their advance. In the end, after he had inflicted much bloodshed on them, he forced them to take to their heels.[46]

The whole city was put on edge by mounting incidents of this 55 kind, and was wracked by rumors and suspicion. Sometimes the crimes and misdeeds were punished, sometimes they went unpunished owing to the sheer number of the delinquents. But the Cerchi, and the party known as the Whites, were far more power-

longe plus poterant in re publica: priores quidem et magistratus plurimum ex illorum numero legebantur. Itaque, adversarii graviter id ferentes ac saepius inter se quaesti, demum consultandi gratia in Trinitatis aede convenerunt. Interfuerunt ei consilio quidam e ducibus partium optimarum. Ibi multis dictis agitatisque summa consilii tandem fuit: pontificem adire postulareque uti principem aliquem regii generis Florentiam mittere curaret ad statum civitatis componendum.

56 Id consilium, quia privatim erat habitum de re publica, confestim, ubi rescitum est, diversae factionis homines carpendo atque indignando ad magistratum, quasi conspirationem adversus rem publicam libertatemque populi initam, detulere. Ipsi vero per speciem imminentis periculi ex agro clientelisque armatorum ingentem numerum contraxerunt. Contra vero alia factio et ipsa sese munierat, et collecta armatorum manu, quos e praediis item agroque evocarat, magistratus prioresque adiens minabunda reclamabat. Cum igitur illi quidem conspirationem initam contra rem publicam, hi autem vim et arma publice contra leges sumpta puniendum esse clamitarent, et utraque pars armata magistratibus minaretur, confusio erat et dedecus in re publica, et neque leges neque pudor quicquam valebant.

57 Erat per id tempus in numero priorum Dantes poeta, qui, offensus consilio illo quod de evocando principe aliquo in urbem habuerant, cum id plane ad eversionem libertatis pertinere existimaret, in diversam partem inclinare ferebatur. Quod autem ingenio et eloquentia inter collegas eminebat, voluntatem eius unius nutumque omnes maxime spectabant. Is igitur hanc deformitatem labemque rei publicae abominatus, commotus etiam minis quae contra priores iactabantur, collegis suadet uti animos capessant, populum pro libertate ac tutela rei publicae in arma excitent. Eo

ful in public affairs; most of the priors and magistrates were chosen from their number. Their adversaries were unhappy at this
state of affairs and often complained about it. Finally, they met in
the Church of San Trínita to discuss the situation.[47] Present at the
meeting were certain leaders of the Parte Guelfa. After much discussion and debate, the sense of the meeting was that they should
go to the pope and ask him to have some prince of royal lineage
sent to Florence to bring order to the city.

When it became known that a private meeting had taken place 56
concerning public affairs, the members of the other party angrily
denounced it to the magistrates as a conspiracy against the commonwealth and the liberty of the people. Indeed, the Whites, on
the pretext of imminent peril, assembled a great number of armed
men from the countryside and from among their clients. In response, the Blacks set about defending themselves as well, and
summoning bands of armed men from their own country estates,
they went before the magistrates and the priors with threats and
shouts of protest. With the Whites clamoring for the conspiracy
against the commonwealth to be punished, and the Blacks loudly
demanding punishment for those engaging in illegal armed violence, and both parties, armed to the teeth, uttering threats against
the magistrates, the commonwealth was reduced to an unseemly
state of confusion against which neither laws nor shame could in
the least prevail.

The poet Dante at that time was one of the priors. It is said 57
that he favored the Whites because he was offended by the meeting where the Blacks talked about summoning a prince to the city,
a plan he believed would certainly lead to the destruction of liberty. Because he towered above his colleagues in intelligence and
eloquence, they all showed the greatest respect for his wishes and
direction. He hated the disorder and corruption in the commonwealth and was disturbed, too, by the threats which had been
made against the priors. So he persuaded his colleagues to take

facto, cum principes utriusque factionis ponere arma compulissent, tumultus auctores deiiciendos urbe amovendosque censuerunt, quasi eorum praesentia tranquillitas rei publicae turbaretur. Ergo Cursius Donatus, quem principem consilii fuisse et postea stipatum armatorum caterva per urbem incessisse prioribusque comminatum fuisse constabat, publicatis bonis, in exilium agitur; ceteri vero eius factionis, pecuniis multati, ad tempus relegantur. Fuerunt autem hi Sinibaldus Donatus Cursii frater, Rubeus Tosa, Giachinoctus Pactius, Gerius Spina. Hi omnes equites per eam tempestatem insignes ac suarum familiarum principes, et cum his agnati quidam et proximi singulorum satis magno numero ex ea parte qui nigri dicebantur, in agrum perusinum relegati sunt, et consistere illic[76] iussi donec a populo revocarentur.[77]

58   Ex altera vero factione multati pecuniis et relegati fuerunt Gentiles et Torrigianus Circuli equites et agnati quidam eius familiae, Bascherius Tosa, Baldinaccius Adimar, Naldus Lotti filius Gherardinus, Guido Chavalcantis, Johannes Malespina. Hi Serazanam eodem modo ire iussi, et revocationem populi expectare. Ceterum, haec pars cito revocata est sub praetextu gravioris coeli, ex quibus Guido Chavalcantis morbo confectus interiit, haud multo postea quam reversus est, vir philosophus et inprimis bonarum artium studiis per ea tempora eruditus.

59   Cursius postquam urbe aufugit, nullum intermisit tempus quin ad pontificem se conferret, ut ea quae consultata fuerant sedulo adimpleret. Ubi vero ad pontificem pervenit, instando atque rogando illius mentem incendere non cessabat, et erat facundus vir,

heart and call the People to arms to safeguard the liberty of the commonwealth. Having done this, they compelled the leaders of both factions to lay down their arms, and decreed that the authors of the disturbances should be ejected from the city and sent into exile, as though it was their presence that disturbed the tranquillity of the commonwealth. Thus Corso Donati, who had been the leader of the meeting, who had later paraded around the city with troops of armed men, and who had threatened the priors, was sent into exile and his goods were confiscated. Other members of that faction were fined and temporarily banished. The latter included Corso Donati's brother Sinibaldo, Rosso della Tosa, Giachinotto de'Pazzi and Geri degli Spini. All these men were famous knights of the day and heads of families. With them were banished to Perugian territory a rather large number of so-called Blacks who were blood-relations and connections of the individuals who had been banished. They were told to stay there until such time as they should be recalled by the People.

From the other faction the following men were fined and banished: the knights Gentile and Torrigiani de'Cerchi and certain blood-relations of that family, Baschieri della Tosa, Baldinaccio Adimari, Naldo di Lotto Gherardini, Guido Cavalcanti and Giovanni Malespina. These men were ordered in the same fashion to go to Sarzana and await recall by the People. But this party was quickly recalled on the pretext of an unhealthy climate. Of this group Guido Cavalcanti contracted an illness and died not long after his return. He was a man of philosophical temper and among the most learned men in the liberal arts of his time. 58

After Corso fled the city, he lost no time in resorting to the pope, in order zealously to execute the plan of the earlier meeting. Once he had gained access to the pope, he pressured him and stirred him up with continual requests; he was an eloquent man, with a pleasant and happy face, and very astute when it came to practical affairs. Using his arts he was able to turn the pontiff's 59

laeta atque hilari fronte, et in tractandis agendisque rebus admodum sagax. His artibus tandem effecit ut pontifex ad rem florenti-
nam emendandam mentem animumque converteret. Cum itaque
Siciliam, quae contra romanae sedis voluntatem ab Arragonibus
occupabatur, recipere pontifex statuisset, et in Etruria quoque
multa forent emendanda, Carolum Valosianum regis Francorum
fratrem evocare in Italiam perrexit, multa promittens atque ostentans quo ille venire non cunctaretur. Haec eo anno foris domique
gesta.

60   Proximo dehinc anno Pistorienses, adiuti ab ea parte quae Florentiae praevalebat, nigros expulerunt urbe domosque eorum diruerunt. Auctor novarum rerum Pistoriensibus fuit Andreas Gherardinus eques florentinus, qui Pistorium missus, praeerat civitati.
Is ut erat Florentiae albarum partium, eam quoque Pistorii factionem avide complexus, arma corripere iussit. Mox vocatis adversariis, cum illi metu armorum deterriti non parerent, domos incendit ac subvertit, bona diripuit, hostes iudicavit.

61   Lucae quoque eadem pestis factionum convaluit. Itaque, per
eundem favorem insurgentes albi, ducibus Interminellis, pellere nigros tentaverunt et Obitium quemdam diversae factionis prima-
rium hominem interfecerunt. Sed nigris[78] raptis confestim armis,
non se solum tutati sunt, verum etiam adversarios pepulere. Ita
malum succrescens per singulas civitates spargebatur.

62   Eodem anno circiter Kalendis septembris fulgor quem cometen
dicunt in caelo apparuit. Nec multo post adventus Caroli Valosiani in Italiam secutus est; qui cum ad Bonifacium pontificem
tunc Ananiae residentem magno procerum comitatu venisset, receptus ab eo splendide ac titulis honestatus, magnam spem attule-

mind and spirit to mending the Florentine situation. Since the pope had decided to recapture Sicily, which was being occupied by the Aragonese against the will of the Roman See, and there were also many problems to be solved in Tuscany, he proceeded to summon to Italy Charles of Valois, brother of the king of France, making him many promises and showing him why he should make haste to come. Such were the deeds at home and abroad this year.[48]

The following year the Pistoians, with the help of the party in power in Florence, expelled the Blacks from their city and destroyed their homes. The man who engineered this revolution in Pistoia was Andrea Gherardini, a Florentine knight, who had been sent to Pistoia to take charge of the city.[49] As he was a member of the White faction in Florence, he fervently embraced the same faction in Pistoia, bidding them go to war. Then he challenged their adversaries to a fight, but the latter, being afraid of armed conflict, did not answer his summons. So he burned and destroyed their houses, seized their property and had them declared enemies.[50]

The same plague of factionalism broke out in Lucca, too. Thus under the same auspices the Whites rose up, led by the Interminelli family, and tried to expel the Blacks. They killed a principal member of the other party, a certain Obizzo. But the Blacks immediately seized arms and not only protected themselves, but even expelled their enemies. In this way the growing evil spread through every city.[51]

In the same year around the first of September a shining star, which they call a comet, appeared in the heavens. It was followed soon after by the coming of Charles of Valois to Italy. With a large entourage of barons he went to Pope Boniface, who was then residing in Anagni, and was received splendidly by the pontiff who granted him titles of honor, for Charles had brought with him great hope of brilliant deeds. This prince decided to assemble the

60

1301

61

62

rat rerum praeclare gerendarum. Ad Siciliam igitur invadendam apparatus fieri placuit, quo proximo vere in eam traiiceretur. Interea vero dum hiems obstat, ad pacandam[79] Florentiam[80] a pontifice missus est. Is ergo cum Romam peteret ac inde Florentiam venturus nunciaretur, variae consultationes ab his qui rei publicae gubernacula tenebant habitae sunt; variae insuper curae, ut magis ac magis appropinquabat, susceptae. Erat omnino eius adventus totae factioni eorum qui albi dicebantur molestissimus; nam pulsis adversariis eorum auctoritate res publica nitebatur et nihil innovari conducebat. Sed contra impellebat pontificis simul ac regiae domus auctoritas, quibus obviare ac[81] resistere, praesertim eos qui Guelfos se haberi vellent, inter nefaria putabatur. Et accedebat perhumana Caroli pollicitatio, non nisi commodum et pacem eorum ipsorum hoc adventu suo quaerere affirmantis.

63   Quibus tandem adducti rationibus qui rem publicam tenebant, recipiendum in urbem censuerunt. Ingredienti denique honores magnificos solemnesque impenderunt, magistratibus[82] obviam euntibus et iuventute ludicra equorum hastiliumque exhibente. Ingressus est autem Florentiam die ipso Kalendarum novembrium. Nec multo post concionem petens, astantibus magistratibus et populi multitudine, se pacis causa venisse confirmavit, id quo perficere posset, liberam ad hoc potestatem sibi per populum concedi oportere. Postquam id quoque permissum est, iureiurando edixit se recte pacateque sine cuiusquam iniuria potestatem illam habiturum. Sed illo mox e concione abeunte, publica potestate suscepta, milites eius armati prodierunt, cum in ipso urbis ingressu aliisque superioribus diebus inermes circa se habere consuesset. Ea res, praesertim repentina et insueta, speciem tyranni magis praebuit quam principis.

64   Itaque suspicionibus coortis, itur confestim ad arma. Maxima pars populi ad priorum aedes convenit; obices multis in locis per

equipment to invade Sicily, so as to make a crossing the following spring. But in the meantime, during the intervening winter, the pope sent him to pacify Florence. When he set out for Rome, announcing that he would come next to Florence, various consultations were held by those who controlled the commonwealth, and their concerns multiplied the nearer he came. The whole White party was exceedingly vexed at his coming, since they now controlled the commonwealth, their adversaries having been expelled, and change could not profit them. On the other hand the authority of the pope and the royal house weighed heavily with them, and it was considered wicked to block and resist that authority, especially for persons who wished to be considered Guelfs. Added to this was Charles' very civil promise not to seek by his coming anything other than their own welfare and peace.

At last, the rulers of the commonwealth were persuaded by   63 these considerations and decided to receive him into the city. His entry was attended by solemn and magnificent ceremonies; the magistrates came out to greet him and the youths of the city held a joust. He entered Florence on the first of November. Shortly thereafter he asked for a public assembly, and in the presence of the magistrates and the people he confirmed that he had come for the sake of peace; and in order to achieve it, he said, the People should allow him full powers.[52] After this had been granted, he took an oath that he would exercise that power in a just and peaceful way, without doing harm to anyone. But soon after leaving the assembly and taking up public power, he deployed his troops armed, although it had been his practice during his entry into the city and for several days thereafter to keep them unarmed around his person. This action, especially as it was unexpected and unfamiliar, made him look more like a tyrant than a prince.

The People's suspicions were thus aroused and there was a rush   64 to arms. The largest part of the People converged on the priors' dwelling-place, and barricades were set up in the streets in many

vias opponuntur. Sed apud nobilitatem et plebem magna erat dissensio et mirifica quaedam voluntatum opinionumque confusio, aliis mutationem rei publicae optantibus, aliis formidantibus. His curis anxii, neque ducem neque propositum certum ullum habebant. Cum in hoc tumultu civitas esset, Cursius Donatus cum aliqua manu ad urbem accessit. Ingressus nova moenia, cum veterum murorum portas clausas obseratasque offendisset, circumdata urbe ad faesulanam portulam venit,[83] aedibus suis vicinam. Cum foris[84] perfringeret, amici eius re cognita concurrerunt, portaque intus refracta, gratulabundi susceperunt. Ille, postquam ingressus est, cumulata suorum manu ad priorum aedes profectus (diversae factionis hi erant), confestim publico deturbat, exutosque potestate in privatam redigit[85] formam. Carolus vero, dum haec agerentur, milites suos circa se continuit, neque ob ea quae nunciabantur unquam commotus est, non cum portas effringi, non cum priores pelli,[86] non postea cum totam urbem incendiis rapinisque misceri sentiret. Nam, post priores eiectos, eadem illa manus quae Cursium secuta fuerat, per se iam ipsa suo motu per urbem diffusa, caedes et incendia pluribus locis perpetravit; quae patiendo Carolus, totam rem composuisse creditus est, non sine gravi querela eorum quibus paulo ante pacem quietemque iuraverat. Eadem quoque clades per agrum vagata latius, a nullo genere maleficii temperavit: crematae locupletium hominum villae, homicida pluribus locis facta, rapinis et vulneribus omnia foedata. Post aliquot dies posita sunt arma, et novi priores subinde creati, qui reliquum temporis adimplerent.

places. But there was great dissension among the nobility and the people, and an astonishing welter of views and desires were expressed, with some persons hoping for change in the commonwealth, and others fearing it. The citizens were wracked with anxiety and had neither a leader nor a settled plan. While the city was in this state of uproar, Corso Donati with a band of followers descended on the city. He passed through the new walls, but found the gates of the old ones closed and bolted against him. Circling the city, he came to the Fiesolan Gate near his own houses. As he was smashing his way through it from outside, his friends saw their chance, ran up, broke down the gate from within, and welcomed him with rejoicing. He entered, and, gathering a band of followers, set out for the house of the priors (who were of the opposing faction) and immediately threw them out of the public palazzo, stripped them of power and reduced them to the status of private citizens. While this was going on, Charles kept his soldiers close by him, and remained unmoved by anything that was being told him: that the gates had been broken down, that the priors had been expelled, and, later, that the whole city was embroiled in burnings and plunder. For the same band that followed Corso had now spread by its own impetus throughout the city and was committing acts of arson and murder everywhere. Charles' forebearance in the face of this behavior gave rise to the view that he had devised the whole thing. This was a matter of serious complaint to those whom but a short while before he had sworn to maintain peace and quiet. The same calamity spread widely into the countryside, and evil deeds of every kind were committed without let or hindrance: the villas of wealthy men were burned, numerous murders took place; everything was defiled by looting and bloodshed. After several days they laid down their arms and new priors were then elected who filled out the rest of the term of office.

65   Per hoc idem tempus legatus de quo supra diximus Florentiam
rediit. Eo auctore et adiutore pax facta est inter Circulos et Donatos aliasque familias utriusque factionis. Conanti deinde legato gubernationem rei publicae communem utrique facere, Cursius et hi
qui cum illo sentiebant et ob recentem reditum plus poterant, parere legato in ea renoluerunt. Itaque, uti prius alborum, sic postea
nigrorum facto offensus, urbi interdixit atque abivit. Qua legati as-
peritate etiam prius inter familias composita visa sunt irritari.
Itaque, nec privata quidem pax inter publica duravit odia.

66   Nam haud multo post, Simon adolescens Cursii filius Nicolaum Circulum equitem rus iter facientem secutus, non longe a
porta Casentinati via[87] invasit. Erant utrique comites aliqui, et pugnatum est egregie ab utrisque. Tandem pugnae hic exitus fuit ut
Nicolaus interficeretur; Simon vero ipse, accepto lethali vulnere,
proxima nocte expiraret. Ob haec facta, cum rursus odia gravissima suscitata essent et in peius quotidie laberentur res, stante
adhuc in urbe Carolo, summa tandem[88] calamitas in apertum
prorupit. Quidam enim principes diversae factionis contra statum
rei publicae coniurasse dicebantur, et Petrum quendam Ferantis,
unum ex proceribus Caroli, ad res novandas magnis pollicitationi-
bus pellexisse. Horum sigilla proferebantur; pacta conventa legebantur; rem tamen plerique compositam fictamque putaverunt;
alii invitatos deceptosque a Gallo existimabant fuisse. Ob eam
coniurationem seu fictam seu veram, tres nobilissimi et potentis-
simi cives in periculum vocabantur: Baldinatius Adimar, Naldus
Gherardinus, Bascherius Tosa. Tangebat quoque ea suspicio Ve-

During this period the legate mentioned above returned to 65 Florence. At his initiative and with his support, peace was made between the Cerchi and the Donati and other families of both factions. The legate then tried to set up a power-sharing arrangement between the two factions, but Corso and those who shared his views—and those whose power had increased thanks to his return—refused to obey the legate in this. So the legate took offense at the behavior of the Blacks, just as he had been before at that of the Whites, and left the city, placing it under interdict. The legate's abrasive behavior caused even the wounds that had already been healed between families visibly to reopen, and thus the private peace agreement did not survive the outbreak of public hatreds.

Not much later Simone, the young son of Corso Donati, fol- 66 lowed messer Niccolò Cerchi as the latter was riding out into the country, and attacked him on the road not far from the Casentino Gate. Both men had companions and both sides fought well. In the end, the fight resulted in Niccolò's death, while Simone himself expired the next night of a mortal wound. Thanks to these events the deadliest hatreds were once again revived and the situation grew worse every day, until finally, while Charles was still in the city, the crowning calamity burst out into the open. Certain leaders of the opposing faction were said to be plotting against the stability of the commonwealth, and a certain Pietro Ferrante, one of Charles' barons, had been induced by promises of great reward to start a revolution. His seals were produced and the agreements he had made were read out; and though many believed the plot was concocted and fake, others believed the conspirators had been led on and deceived by the Frenchman. On account of this conspiracy, whether pretended or actual, three of the noblest citizens were put on trial for their lives: Baldinaccio Adimari, Naldo Gherardini and Baschieri della Tosa. Vieri de'Cerchi and other members of his family also came under suspicion. By their advice

rium Circulum ac ceteros eius familiae homines, quorum opera et consilio id factum promissumque fuisse inimici iactabant. Hi omnes ad magistratum vocati, cum adversariorum metu parere non ausi profugissent ex urbe, absentes damnati sunt. Nec posthac modus aliquis fuit in damnandis pellendisque civibus diversae factionis, bonisque eorum vastandis.

67 Per haec ipsa tempora, Dantes poeta in exilium actus est ob eam quam suo prioratu contraxerat invidiam, cuius supra mentionem fecimus. Erat autem per id tempus ad pontificem orator concordiae gratia missus. Sed mox, novis exortis rebus, pulsisque ex urbe civibus eiusdem factionis, cum ipse[89] reus postularetur, absens damnatus est, domusque eius direpta, praedia vastata. Qui albas secuti erant partes, per hunc modum pulsi, exularunt. Carolus, quinque mensibus Florentiae commoratus, tandem abscessit, in Siciliam transiturus.

68 Proxima dehinc aestate Florentini et Lucenses, coniunctis in unum copiis, Pistorium obsederunt, quod nuper, pulsis, ut docuimus, adversariis, albi dumtaxat urbem tenebant, ac eo Lucensium Florentinorumque exules magno se numero contulerant. Dum circa Pistorium essent Florentinorum copiae, manus quaedam exulum superiore Arno bellum tumultuosius commovit, quo non vicina modo, verum etiam remotiora infestabantur loca. Ob eum tumultum duae partes earum copiarum quae Pistorium missae fuerant, confestim in superiorem Arnum traductae, non pepulerunt modo hostem aequis[90] locis, verum etiam castellum quod occupatum fuerat ab exulibus recuperarunt, non sine ingenti detrimento eorum qui se illo incluserant.

69 Inde contra Ubaldinos exercitus ductus, quod hi, receptis exulibus quibusdam, ex castellis bellum haud segniter inferre coepe-

and aid, their enemies charged, the affair had been underwritten and carried out. All these men received summonses to come before the magistrates, but they did not dare obey for fear of their adversaries. So they fled the city and were condemned in absentia. After this there was no restraint whatever when it came to condemning and expelling citizens of the opposing faction and destroying their property.

During this period, the poet Dante was driven into exile owing   67
to the envy he had aroused during his priorate, which we have mentioned above. At the time he was serving as an ambassador, and had been sent to the pope on a peace mission. But after the revolution, when the citizens belonging to his faction had been expelled from the city, he himself was put on trial. He was condemned in absentia, his house was seized, and his estates were looted. In this way the members of the White party were expelled and exiled. Charles, after a sojourn of five months in Florence, finally departed to make the passage to Sicily.[53]

The next summer after that the Florentines and Lucchesi com-   68
bined their forces and laid siege to Pistoia. As we have seen, that   1302
city had recently expelled its adversaries [the Black party], and the White party ruled the city all by themselves, and the exiled Florentine and Lucchese Whites had taken refuge there in great numbers. While the Florentine troops were encamped around Pistoia, a band of exiles was conducting an irregular war in the upper Arno valley, harrassing not only nearby, but even remote places. Thanks to this uproar, two detachments from the troops that had been sent to Pistoia were transferred to the upper Arno, and they not only expelled the enemy from these same places, but also recovered the castle the exiles had occupied, to the extreme prejudice of those within.

Next the army was sent against the Ubaldini, because the latter   69
had harbored certain of the exiles and had begun actively to make war from their castles. In these places, too, the war turned out

rant. His quoque in locis res prospere gesta est, ac fugatis deiectisque hostibus, omnia circum[91] Apenninum loca et mugellanum agrum, qua[92] hostis tenebat, vastaverunt.

70   Inde mox circa Gravem fluvium traductae copiae, Alliarium et Acutum castella (quae et ipsa defecerant) in potestatem redacta everterunt. Copiae victrices, eo anno omnibus ex locis bene ac feliciter gestis rebus, Florentiam rediere.

71   Circa finem huius anni, ob easdem seditiones florentini quidam cives ex praecipuis familiis intra urbem capti, quasi contra rem publicam coniurassent, supplicio afficiuntur. Quo metu et alii complures in suspicionem vocati, sponte sua abierunt absentesque damnati sunt.

72   Cum esset hic status rerum urbanarum ac omnia suspicionibus intra moenia redundarent, exules per eam occasionem, coactis undique suis amicorumque viribus, et a Bononiensibus (quae civitas et ipsa iam hauserat studia factionum) adiuti, magnas copias equitum peditumque confecerunt. Cum his copiis in agrum mugellanum descendentes, regionem occuparunt, sperantes se, alia ex aliis appetendo loca, urbem tandem invitis adversariis intraturos. Et vulgo iactabant eos qui in urbe erant, ob novitates domi exortas, nunquam ausuros obviam exire. Haec seu credulitas seu iactantia multum admodum illis obfuit. Nam, simul atque Florentiam ipsorum adventus nunciatus est, civitas confestim in armis fuit et Lucensium ceterorumque sociorum auxilia evocavit;[93] quae cum propere advenissent, praesidio satis valido ne quis motus suscitaretur domi relicto, reliquas omnes copias ad hostem duxere.

well. The enemy was beaten and put to flight, and all the enemy possessions in the Apennines and in the fields of the Mugello were laid waste.

Soon thereafter the troops were brought down near the river 70 Greve, where they recovered the castles of Aliaro and Montacuto, which had also rebelled, and destroyed them. The victorious troops, having fought well and successfully everywhere that year, returned to Florence.

Around the end of this year, certain Florentine citizens from 71 distinguished families, owing to the same political turmoil, were taken prisoner within the city and put to death as conspirators against the public weal. Many others who had also come under suspicion of the same activity left the city of their own accord and were condemned in absentia.[54]

Such was then the state of the city's affairs. With the whole city 72 awash in suspicion, the exiles seized the opportunity to assemble from every direction their own and their allies' forces. In this they had the help of the Bolognese, as that city, too, had now drunk deeply of the passions of factionalism. So they assembled massive forces of infantry and cavalry. They descended upon the Mugello with these forces and took over the region, hoping, as they attacked one place after another, that they would at last enter the city against the will of their adversaries. They publicly boasted that those inside the city would never dare come out to challenge them because of the domestic uprisings that had taken place. Such remarks, whether uttered from credulity or boastfulness, did them great damage. For, as soon as news of their coming reached Florence, the city immediately took to arms, summoning auxiliaries from Lucca and from the other allies. These forces quickly arrived. A strong garrison was then left in the city to protect it from a coup, while all the remaining troops went out to confront the enemy.

73   Exules per id tempus ad Pollicianum castra habebant, qui adventu Florentinorum Lucensiumque cognito, cum praeter opinio-
nem urbem, in qua metu novarum rerum distineri putabant, reli-
quisse ausos in se valentius ruere viderent, tanta repente in castris
trepidatio est coorta ut magna pars auxiliorum e vestigio dilabere-
tur ac exules ipsi desperatis rebus arriperent fugam, impedimentis
omnibus amissis, nonnulli etiam abiectis armis. In hac fuga quidam exulum capti Florentiam ducuntur. In his fuit Donatus
Alberti filius, vir quondam in re publica magnae auctoritatis, et
Inamis⁹⁴ Ruffolus eius frater, qui primus vexillifer iustitiae fuit, et
alii praecipuarum familiarum, de quibus plerisque civitas supplicium sumpsit.

74   Proximo dehinc anno Florentini et Lucenses, coniunctis inter se
copiis, rursus Pistorium obsederunt. Cum moenia dumtaxat tutaretur hostis nec fortunam proelii tentare vellet, nihil aliud profectum est quam ut agri hostiliter vastarentur.

75   Caritas eo anno ingens annonae fuit, et sustentata multitudo
est importato externoque frumento, curam adhibente civitate, ut e
Sicilia atque Calabria supra viginti septem millia modium⁹⁵ Florentiam adveherentur, pecuniis ad hoc ipsum largiter contributis.

76   Cum et bello et fame civitas premeretur, intestina insuper oritur seditio, haud minor sane pestis quam duo superiora incommoda. Cursius enim Donatus, post reditum in urbem ac pulsos
diversae factionis homines, non satis gratiae sibi existimabat a civibus suae factionis referri; multosque inferiori virtute honoribus ac-
cumulari, se autem praeteriri ac nomen suum velut antiquari, pergraviter ferebat. Hac igitur indignatione permotus, quo res novas

By this time the exiles had encamped near Pulicciano. When   73
they learned that the Florentines and Lucchesi were coming, and
saw that the Florentines, whom they had believed distracted by
fear of a coup, had dared to leave and were now speeding towards
them with a powerful force, great fear suddenly arose in the camp.
A large proportion of the auxiliaries immediately slipped away,
and even the exiles, their affairs in desperate condition, took to
flight, leaving behind all their baggage; some of them even threw
down their arms. In the rout, a number of exiles were captured
and taken to Florence. Among them was Donato Alberti, a man
formerly of great authority in the commowealth, and Nanni
Ruffoli, brother of the first Standard-Bearer of Justice, and other
men from distinguished families. The city exacted reparations
from most of them.

The following year, the Florentines and Lucchesi joined forces   74
and again besieged Pistoia. Since the enemy simply remained safe   1303
behind their walls, unwilling to try the fortunes of battle, the only
outcome of the expedition was that the allies laid waste to enemy
territory.[55]

The same year there was a great famine, and the populace had   75
to be sustained by grain imported from foreign sources. The city
took charge of this, and more than 27,000 pecks were conveyed to
Florence from Sicily and Calabria. Large sums of money were generously contributed for the purpose.

While the city was thus beset by war and famine, internal strife   76
arose as well, a plague hardly less serious than the two former
troubles. After Corso Donati had returned to the city and the
members of the opposing faction had been expelled, he began
to feel that the citizens belonging to his own faction had not
accorded him sufficient influence. He was deeply offended that
many men of lesser virtue were being loaded with honors, while he
himself was being overlooked and his own name had been forgotten. This so angered him that, with a view to starting a revolution,

suscitaret, auctor erat ut pecuniarum publicarum, quas magni quidam in re publica viri non absque infami administratione tractave-
rant, ratio posceretur. Hoc ipsum et diversae factionis homines,
quot aut occulti aut sustentati in urbe remanserant, et alii, quicumque praesentem civitatis statum vel invidia potentiorum vel
iniuria oderant, malevolentia potius quam bono aliquo publico
flagitabant. Itaque nullis opinantibus repente coniunctio facta est
inter eos homines et Cursium Donatum ad rationem deposcen-
dam. Ea postulatio aperte erat contra illos qui per id tempus rem
publicam gubernabant. Et addixerat se postulationi Lottarius
praesul, vir magnae profecto auctoritatis, ceterum non satis sinceri
in rem publicam animi. Postulatio quidem honestam speciem
praetendebat, sed vexatio deiectioque gubernatorum rei publicae et
novarum rerum semina quaerebantur. Ea res intellecta (neque
enim erat obscura) ad resistendum postulationi cives animavit.

77   Contentio tandem ad arma prorupit. Hinc populares eius factionis, quae post adventum Caroli Valosiani rem publicam gubernabant; inde Cursius Donatus alienior factus, cum antea princeps
eius factionis esset: hunc omnes qui praesentem rei publicae statum vel occulte vel palam graviter ferebant, sectabantur. Crebra ab
his proelia intra urbem commissa. Priores enim ac populares eius
factionis arcem tenebant et armatorum multitudine aditus tutabantur. In hos crebri impetus ab adversariis facti sunt, caedesque
et vulnera pluribus locis commissa; confluxerant namque in urbem
rusticorum turbae reorumque et damnatorum ac praeterea latro-
num et sicariorum multitudo ingens; homicidiis rapinisque omnia
foedabantur.

he took the lead in calling for an accounting of public moneys which certain great men in the commonwealth had been administering in a disreputable way. An accounting was also being demanded by members of the opposing faction who had remained in the city through political alliances or by keeping their political sympathies secret, and they were joined by whoever else disliked the current condition of the state either because of injuries done them or because they envied those in power. Both groups were motivated by ill-will rather than by commitment to the public good. Thus, there came about an unexpected alliance between these men and Corso Donati to support the petition for an accounting. The petition was openly directed against the current regime, and was also backed by Bishop Lottieri,[56] a man of great authority, to be sure, but whose motives with respect to the public weal were less than pure. The petition was put forward allegedly in the interests of honest government, but its actual goal was to harrass and bring down the regime and sow the seeds of revolution. This was understood (it was, indeed, obvious), and the citizens roused themselves to resist the petition.

Finally, the quarrel erupted in armed conflict. On one side were the popolani of the faction that had been ruling the commonwealth since the arrival of Charles of Valois; on the other were Corso Donati, the former leader of that faction, now alienated, and his followers, consisting of all the malcontents, secret or avowed. The two groups were constantly getting into fights inside the city. The priors and the popolani held the palace and protected its entrances with a large force of armed men. The enemy frequently attacked these guardmen, and caused murder and bloodshed everywhere. Crowds of criminals and convicts flooded into the city from the countryside as well as an enormous number of thieves and assassins. The whole city was disgraced by murders and looting. 77

78   Multos dies cum ea pestis viguisset, nec modus aut finis ullus
turbationibus cerneretur, et utraque pars obstinate perstaret in armis, tandem unicum per id tempus remedium supervenit, lucensium multitudo civium. Hi vero, utrum suopte ingenio commoti
pro sociorum salute an rogati postulatique advenerint, non satis
exploratum est mihi, verum magno illos numero venisse Florentiam constat, magnasque equitum peditumque copias adduxisse,
ut cuivis parti adhaererent, ad illam haud dubie victoriam inclina-
rent. Intra moenia recepti, partim rogando, partim minitando,
cum proelium diremissent, per praeconem suo nomine edixerunt
uti damnati ac facinorosi urbem purgarent, nemo rapinam, nemo
caedem aliudve maleficium patraret. Inde ad pacandos[96] civium
animos conversi, novos magistratus creari per populum suaserunt
ac rei publicae constituerunt statum. Duodecim priores tunc primum creati sunt, cum antea sex dumtaxat creari mos esset, idque
altero quoque bimestri servatum est. Lucenses compositis Florentiae rebus, bonum ac sociale operati opus, abiere.

79   Per haec ipsa tempora Benedictus pontifex romanus, qui Bonifacio paulo ante defuncto in pontificatu successerat, auditis
Florentinorum discordiis legatum ad pacandam Etruriam Florentiamque delegit, Nicolaum Pratensem, romanae ecclesiae cardinalem, virum sagacem atque industrium. Qui etsi res compositas
a Lucensibus cognovisset, tamen complura superesse ratus et
praesertim reductionem exulum mente cogitans, Florentiam venit tribus fere mensibus postquam Lucenses abierant. Ingressus
urbem, cum arbitrium liberum postulasset, sibi haud difficulter
concessit civitas, sentiens adhuc morbi reliquias nequaquam
contemnendas intra viscera remansisse, quibus medelam cupiebat
afferri.

This plague throve for many days, and no end or moderation of   78
the disturbances was in sight. Both parties obstinately stuck to
their weapons. Finally there appeared on the scene the only remedy possible at that time: a multitude of citizens from Lucca. I
have not been able to find out whether it was their own idea to
come and save their allies, or whether they were asked to. But it is
clear that a great number of them did come to Florence, bringing
with them large forces of infantry and horse, so that whichever
side they took would undoubtedly win. They were taken into the
city, and broke up the fighting with a mixture of pleas and threats.
Then they announced through a herald speaking in their name
that convicts and criminals should leave the city and that no one
should engage in looting, murder, or any other misdeed.[57] Thereupon they set about reconciling the citizens with each other, and,
persuading the people to elect new magistrates, they set in order
the condition of the commonwealth. It was then, for the first time,
that twelve priors were elected — before the custom had been to
elect six only — and this practice was kept in the next bi-monthly
term. The Lucchesi thus settled the affairs of Florence, then left,
having accomplished a good work worthy of an ally.

In this same period Pope Benedict,[58] who succeeded Boniface   79
in the pontificate (the latter had died shortly before) came to hear
of the discords of the Florentines and sent a legate to pacify
Tuscany and Florence, Cardinal Niccolò da Prato, a keen-witted
and industrious man. Although he knew that Florentine affairs
had been set in order by the Lucchesi, he nevertheless believed
that much was left to be done. With the particular intention of restoring the exiles he came to Florence about three months after
the Lucchesi had left. Entering the city, he asked to be granted a
free hand, which the city readily granted him, as it was felt that
not inconsiderable traces of the disease lingered in the city's vital
organs and that these still wanted healing.

80   Legatus igitur, prospecta sagaciter natura civium, cum multifariam civitatem divisam, principem tamen divisionem inter nobilitatem et plebem animadverteret, partes animo complexus est
plebis, sentiens id genus hominum minus pertinax adversus reductionem exulum minusque acre studiis partium reperiri. Confestim igitur huic factioni adhaerens, multa providere ac moliri coepit
quo nobilitatis frangeret animos, plebis vero auctoritatem domina-
tumque assereret; sic enim obnoxiam sibi futuram multitudinem
et nutum eius secuturam arbitratus est. Considerans igitur nobilitatem per se ipsam haud multum posse, nisi clientelis et amicitiis
plebeiorum hominum ad eam[97] concurrere solitorum iuvaretur,
plebeios autem ipsos haud imbecillos fore, si iniuriae singulis illatae ad multos pertinerent, unico utrique rei consilio prospicere
festinavit. Ea de causa sollerti quidem ingenio auctor fuit viginti
societates in urbe creandi, in quas plebem distribuit universam.
Harum societatum trans Arnina tribus continuit quatuor, totidem
Scradiana, reliquae deinceps tribus singulae tres.

81   Ita viginti societates intra urbem factae. Singulis vero societatibus signiferi, singuli praefecti, hisque vexilla sunt tradita variis dis-
tincta insignibus quo quisque sua et internoscere aspiciens et
consequi posset; mandatumque his est ut, quotiens opus foret,
cum vexillis prodirent, et armatam quisque suam adduceret societatem. Designatio autem societatum per vicos parroeciasque est
facta, civesque omnes e plebe descripti, poena gravissima constituta si universi in armis non essent nec vexilla sua, quotiens illa
prodirent, sequerentur. Tempus signifero constitutum fuit mensium sex, et illud additum ne quisquam ex nobilitate in societati-

The legate then made an acute diagnosis of the citizen body, 80
and saw that it suffered from numerous and varied divisions, but
that the principle division was between the nobility and the commons. He took the side of the commons, feeling that men of that
sort would be less bitterly partisan and less obstinate in opposing
the restoration of the exiles. So, attaching himself to this faction
he immediately began to initiate and pass measures to break the
spirit of the nobility and assert the authority and lordship of the
commons, believing that by so doing the multitude would become
indebted to him and would follow his lead. He knew that the nobility could do very little on its own without the help of its clients
and its alliances with those commoners who habitually sought its
aid. The commoners, on the other hand, were by no means weak
in their own right, in cases where injuries to individuals pertained
to the interests of the many. So he hastened to adopt a single plan
addressing the condition of both classes. That was why he inge-
niously promoted the creation of twenty companies in the city into
which the whole commons was distributed. The Oltrarno district
contained four of these companies and the district of San Piero
Scheraggio an equal number, while the rest of the districts contained three apiece.[59]

Thus twenty companies were created within the city. Each had 81
its standard-bearer, each its captain, and each standard was given
its own distinctive device, so that everyone would be able to see
and recognize their own standard and follow it. It was required of
each standard-bearer, whenever need arose, to raise the standard
and lead his company in arms. The companies were designated by
streets and parishes, and all the citizens who were commoners
were enlisted. Heavy penalties were laid down if the whole company failed to muster or follow its standard when it was raised.
The standard-bearer's term of office was fixed at six months, and
it was further stipulated that no member of the nobility should be
enrolled in the companies, nor should any nobleman meddle with

bus censeretur neu se immisceret neve domo abiret, dum vexilla promerentur. Si quis e plebe homo a potentioribus ullo[98] tempore invaderetur, signiferum societatis ex qua is foret auxilium ferre lex iubebat ac vim armis repellere. Si quis e nobilitate plebeium occidisset, ad vindictam proximo agnato societatem assistere; pecunia si opus foret ac propinquus egeret, communi societatis impensa persequendam vindictam statuebat. Si plebeius plebeium invaderet aut occideret, nullae erant partes signiferi neque societatis.

82 Ex quo apparebat et popularium societates esse solum et contra potentiam nobilitatis constitutas solum; ferturque vox illa legati, cum societates creasset, non iam posthac recipiendam fore plebei hominis vocem contra potentiam nobilitatis conquerentis, cum quivis e plebe longe plures habeat iniuriarum vindictaeque consortes quam ulli ex familiis, modo societatum iura institutaque servarent. Eodem fere ordine extra urbem quoque per florentinum agrum vexillationes quaedam sunt institutae, magis ne quisquam ex his locis ad nobilitatem concurreret, quam ut per mutuam sese opem agricolae tutarentur.

83 Roborato plebis statu ac multitudine in suum favorem traducta, legatus iam tempus maturum adesse ratus ea quae cogitaverat adimplendi, reductionem exulum aggreditur. Eius rei causa liberum ab exulibus arbitrium (nam civitas ante concesserat) postulavit. Exulum pluribus locis conventibus actis, summa tamen omnium ad eos qui Arretii erant referebatur; ibi namque Verius Circulus et omnis illa factio ingenti multitudine resederat, ducemque suarum partium sibi constituerat Alexandrum Romenae comitem, consiliariosque et praefectos ex sui corporis civibus. Hi ergo publica deliberatione arbitrium potestatemque rerum suarum permiserunt legato. Fuit in eo consilio Dantes poeta unus e praefectis, et Petrarchae postea incliti poetae futuri pater, qui ambo si-

them or leave his house while the standards were on parade. If any commoner should be attacked at any time by one of the powerful, the law commanded the standard-bearer of his company to succor him and repel force with arms. If any nobleman should kill a commoner, the company was obliged to assist his nearest blood-relative in his vendetta; if the relative needed money to pursue the vendetta he should be supplied from the funds of the company. If a commoner attacked or killed another commoner, neither the standard-bearer nor the company were to take sides.

Hence it was clear that the companies of the popolani were established solely to counter the power of the nobility, and it is reported that, after the companies were created, the legate said he would no longer hear any more complaints of commoners against the power of the nobility, since each commoner had many more allies to avenge his injuries than anyone from the great families — so long as the laws and statutes of the companies were observed. Some companies were also established outside the city in the countryside by a similar ordinance. This was done less for farmers to protect themselves by mutual aid than to prevent anyone in these areas from depending on the nobility for help.[60]

Having strengthened the position of the commons and won the loyalty of the multitude, the legate now considered the time ripe for carrying out his plan to restore the exiles. In aid of this he asked for full powers from the exiles (the city having already conceded such to him). There were conventicles of exiles in many places, but the whole negotiation for all the exiles was turned over to those in Arezzo. For it was there that Vieri de'Cerchi and his whole faction were residing in large numbers, and he had appointed Count Alessandro of Romena the military leader of his faction and citizens of his own band as counselors and captains. After public deliberation the exiles allowed the legate full decision-making powers over their affairs. The poet Dante was present at this meeting as one of the captains, as well as the father of

mili aestu partium eiecti Florentia, Arretii exulabant, ubi et Petrarcha ipse mox natus est.

84   Accepto exulum decreto, legatus syndicis quoque eorum arcessitis propositum intentat; reductionem simul et concordiam enixe aggreditur. Rem per se difficilem longe difficiliorem faciebat, quod ille universam rationem exulum reducendorum ingrediebatur. Hi autem partim erant albi recens pulsi, partim Gibellini, quorum sane durior erat causa; difficultatesque maximae oriebantur vel restituendorum bonorum gratia, vel inimicitiarum privatarum. Quod si albis solum reducendis conatum diligentiamque legatus adhibuisset, haud difficulter ea res videbatur effectum quem optaverat habitura. Sed ille magnitudine animi et favore multitudinis elatus, dum utrumque simul assequi vult, neutrum assecutus est. Adhaeserant tamen familiae quaedam potentiorum legato, postquam propositum eius cognoverunt, ac eius factum vehementer iuvabant. Populares etiam multi pacis avidi eius coepto favebant, quorum ille fiducia nitebatur.

85   Missi ergo ab exulibus syndici, cum Florentiam venissent ac frequentem consultationem apud legatum agerent resque boni profecto exitus spem habere videretur, nova repente turbatio exorta, cuncta prius composita dissipavit. Civibus enim, nihil minus quam tale aliquid suspicantibus, repente nunciatum est maxima exules multitudine, iussu legati, adventare quasi urbem concedentibus repugnantibusve civibus intraturos. Id cum pluribus simul ex locis nunciaretur, trepida civitas arma sumpsit ac magnis in[99] suspicionibus versabatur; legatum vero ut parum sincerum hominem ac ficte compositum formidabat; multi etiam subdolam eius versu-

Petrarch; the son would afterwards become a famous poet. Both of them had become embroiled in the same party struggles and had been banished from Florence. They were then living in exile in Arezzo, where Petrarch was born shortly thereafter.

Having received the decision of the exiles, the legate summoned their representatives as well and presented his plan. He would make an earnest attempt to restore the exiles and simultaneously to reconcile them with the community. He made a difficult proposition much more difficult by advancing a single generic scheme for bringing back the exiles. But these included not only the recently-banished Whites but also the Ghibellines, whose case was really much harder. The greatest difficulties arose either from the requirement to return their property or from private hostilities. If the legate had applied his efforts and diligence to restoring only the Whites, the matter would have turned out as he wished without difficulty. But he was a man of large ideas, carried away by the plaudits of the multitude. Wishing to accomplish two things at once, he accomplished neither. Nevertheless, certain powerful families stuck to the legate after learning of his plan and gave it strong backing. Many popolani, too, eager for peace, favored his undertaking, and he relied on their loyalty. 84

Thus the representatives sent by the exiles, when they had arrived in Florence, held frequent consultations with the legate, and it seemed the business would certainly have a good outcome when a new disturbance arose which shattered all previous arrangements. The citizens, who had absolutely no suspicion that such a thing might happen, were suddenly informed that an enormous body of exiles, on the legate's instructions, was heading for the city as though to enter it, with or without the city's permission. When this was announced simultaneously in a number of places, the frightened city took to arms and was thrown into a state of extreme suspicion. They feared the legate as a man of impure motives and a studied deceiver; many also accused him of treacherous 85

tiam criminabantur. Enim vero legatus se constantissime purgans, neminem a se vocatum fuisse exulum persancte asseverabat; totam rem ab adversariis et malevolis pacisque et quietis publicae hostibus quadam arte compositam querebatur. Atqui constabat litteras legati nomine scriptas exules accepisse, sed an verae vel fictae fuerint litterae, ambigebatur. Nec deerant qui praedicarent a principibus nobilitatis, reditum adversariorum graviter ferentibus, ad pariendas turbas falso litteras fuisse submissas.[100] Nos utrum illorum verum fuerit, in medio relinquimus. Sed qui exulum nomine advenerant, conterriti ea novitate, e vestigio abierunt. Ita negotium pacis interruptum est. Legatus quoque, ut suspicionem minueret, tunc relicta urbe Pratum concessit. Oppidum ingressus, cum eadem postulasset (nam Pratenses quoque iisdem seditionibus agitabantur), nihil ad extremum proficere valuit. Quin etiam dum acrius urgeret, insurgente factione Prato expellitur. Quare Florentiam reversus, expeditionem contra Pratenses indixit. Ad eam rem, cum voluntarios milites rogaret et profiterentur multi, copiaeque iam in urbe crescerent, suspicio iterum coorta est ne sub alio praetextu militem cogere ac res novare aggrederetur. Itaque, adversantibus civibus et arma ponere iubentibus conatus legati in irritum reciderunt.[101] Ea tandem indignatione permotus, Florentiae simul ac Prato interdixit. Ipse irrito labore ad pontificem rediit.

86 Eodem anno pons qui ad Carariam dicitur nimio pondere multitudinis quae ad ludos incubuerat spectandos corruit. Erat vero per id tempus non quemadmodum nunc lapideus est,[102] sed sublicius. Eius ruina multos afflixit.

87 Recessum legati magnae contentiones secutae fuerunt. Pars enim quaedam nobilitatis, stante nuper in urbe legato, sese illi

cunning. The legate for his part insisted on his innocence, swearing by all the saints that he had not summoned a single exile, and protesting that the whole business had been faked by his adversaries and by persons of ill will hostile to peace and public tranquillity. Yet the exiles had clearly received letters written in the legate's name, though whether those letters were real or faked remained in doubt. There were persons who asserted that the letters had been sent under false pretences by leaders of the nobility who were angry at the return of the exiles and wanted to cause political disturbances. For our part we shall leave undecided the issue of where the truth lay. But the representatives of the exiles, terrified by the public reaction, immediately left. Thus the peace negotiations were interrupted. Thereupon the legate, too, in order to relieve suspicion, left the city and withdrew to Prato. On his arrival he found that town being wracked by the same turbulence, and so made similar demands on it, but in the end he accomplished nothing. Indeed, when he became too relentless in his demands, the opposing faction rose up and expelled him from the town. Whereupon he went back to Florence and declared a crusade[61] against the citizens of Prato. He asked for military volunteers for this purpose and many offered their services. But as the legate's military resources in the city grew, suspicion once again arose that under another pretext he was trying to assemble troops for a revolution. The citizens began to oppose him and to demand that he disarm his men, and thus the legate's efforts came to nothing. In the end he angrily placed Florence and Prato simultaneously under interdict and returned to the pope, having labored in vain.[62]

That same year the Ponte alla Carraia collapsed under the 86 weight of a crowd that had gathered there to watch a spectacle. At *1303* that time it was not made of stone, as today, but of wood. Many people were injured in its fall.[63]

The legate's withdrawal was followed by great strife. A certain 87 part of the nobility had allied itself to the legate during his recent

427

coniunxerat ac reductionem exulum intemperanter concupisse visa fuerat. Erat vero fere ex iis familiis quae ad albas partes inclinare putabantur;[103] ea de causa ceterarum familiarum in se contraxerat odia. Ut ergo abiit legatus, reliqua omnis nobilitas in illos surrexit, praeter Cursium Donatum qui, amicis infensus, contra naturam suam quiescebat. Hos popularium quoque duae insignes familiae nigrarum partium assertrices sectabantur, Iunii et Medices. Crescentibus igitur contentionibus, pugna tandem conseritur. Principium vero pugnae ortum est apud Circulorum Garbensium aedes; mox a privatis aedibus in forum delata. Cum ergo novum inter vetusque forum et circa porticum frumentariam pugnaretur, et invicem modo pellerent, modo pellerentur, Nerius quidam Abbas, qui suorum inimicus e tota Abbatum familia in urbe restiterat, et contra Circulos atque alios huius factionis in pugna stabat, contemplatus Boreae vim in adversarios perflantem, "Fax et malleoli afferantur," inquit. "Iam ego hos cum domibus propriis extorres agam." Nec mora delatum ignem in gentilium agnatorumque aedes iniecit, quae non longe a porticu frumentaria sitae fuerunt. Inde, cum eadem face discurrens ad caput veteris fori, Caponsaccorum aedes incendit. Is ignis inter missilia ac tela vires assumens, flatu insuper Boreae adiutus, late pervagatus est; domos et singula carpendo apprehendit. Tabernae venalium rerum magni pretii in his erant locis; eas, cum ignis invaderet, vel incendio cremabantur vel a praedonibus diripiebantur. Urbs eodem tempore ardebat et vicatim oppugnabatur, non secus ac si hostis intrasset. Quo minus homines ferre opem poterant, eo latius vagatus ignis, inter duo fora primum et circa porticum frumentariam omnia consumpsit; inde

stay in the city, and were observed to have had an unhealthy desire for the restoration of the exiles. They were mostly from those families that were thought to favor the White party, and for this reason had brought the hatred of the other families upon themselves. Thus when the legate went away, the rest of the nobility rose against them, with the exception of Corso Donati, who, being now hostile to his former friends, remained, for him, unnaturally quiet. Two distinguished popolani families also followed the champions of the Black party, the Giugni and the Medici. The strife thus grew greater, and battle was finally joined. The battle began near the houses of the Cerchi-Del Garbo, but soon moved from private houses into the marketplace. While the fight was going on between the Old and New Markets around Or San Michele, and the combatants were alternately driving each other out, a certain Neri degli Abati (who as an enemy of his own family had been its only member to remain in the city), stood up while fighting against the Cerchi and other members of that faction and noticed that the north wind[64] was blowing strongly in the direction of his adversaries. "Bring me a torch and some fire-arrows," he said, "now I shall use their own homes to drive them into exile." Immediately fire was brought which he laid against the houses of their kinsmen and blood-relatives which stood not far from Or San Michele. From there he ran with the same torch to the head of the Old Market and set fire to the houses of the Caponsacchi. The fire gathered force amid the spears and darts, and, helped by the north wind, it spread far and wide, attacking homes and private property. There were botteghe full of valuable goods in these places which under the fire's assault were either burned or looted. By this time the city was burning, the fire attacking it street by street like an invading army. The conflagration spread wider and wider as efforts to contain it became less effective, and it consumed everything between the two markets and near Or San Michele. Then, gathering renewed force, it reached

rursus vires assumens, usque ad Arnum pervenit, nec prius finis
cremandi est factus quam supra mille et septingentas aedes uno incendio conflagrarunt. Medicatum fuisse ignem vulgo creditum est.
Nec equidem ab re susceptam credulitatem existimarim, cernens
etiam nunc admirabilem ac prope stupendam illius vim in parietes
etiam ipsos ac lapides, quod reliquiae monstrant, saevientem. Ob
huius incendii damna, pars illa quae Circulis favebat, succubuit,
assumptis Cavalcantum Gherardinorumque et Pulchrorum aedibus, quibus ea factio plurimum nitebatur, et vicinis etiam qui una
sentiebant eversis.

88   Cedentibus igitur victis et civitate ad aliquem modum composita, novum rursus periculum novaque turbatio exoritur. Legato
enim, de quo supra diximus, sinistra admodum ac perversa refe-
rente, cum de suis ipse facinoribus tacens, aliena facinora in crimen vocaret ac pontifici qui illum miserat quasi eius honor spretus
esset ac derisui habitus veluti faces quasdam indignationis admo-
veret, commotus pontifex duodecim potentissimos ea tempestate
cives, principes eius factionis quae tunc urbem tenebat, corripien-
dos statuit. Eos igitur cum ad se citasset, varia consultatio fuit; et
contemnere simul et parere formidabant, quod in altero famae,
in altero status periculum versaretur: famae, si quasi delictorum
conscii non irent; status, si per eorum absentiam motus aliquis in
urbe suscitaretur. Omnibus tandem pensitatis, et ad honestatem
et ad magnanimitatem potius visum est pontificem adire. Quare
profecti omnes, ut vocati erant, viri amplissimi principes civitatis,
Cursius Donatus, Rubeus Tosa, Gerius Spina ac ceteri potentissimarum familiarum supremi, honestum ac decentem comitatum
ducentes, Perusiam, quod tunc ibi[104] pontifex residebat, pervenerunt.

89   Cum pontificem patresque adiissent, ac purgandis diluendisque
criminibus intendunt,[105] Nicolaus pratensis, quem legatum in

the Arno, and before the burning stopped that one fire had destroyed more than 1700 houses. It was commonly held that the
flames had been artificially doctored, and for my part I think the
facts support this belief: one may see still today the remains of its
astonishing violence where it raged even against walls made of
stone. It was owing to the damage caused by the fire that the party
favoring the Cerchi collapsed, as the houses of the Cavalcanti,
Gherardini and Pulci, which had given that faction so much support, as well as the neighborhood that had sympathized with
them, were burned up and destroyed.[65]

So the defeated withdrew and the city returned in some sense   88
to an orderly condition, but soon there arose a new peril and a
new disturbance. To the pope who had sent him the aforemen-   1304
tioned legate gave a perverse and hostile account of what had
happened in Florence, charging other people with crimes while
passing over his own in silence. He got the pope into a rage, representing to him that His Holiness had been dishonored and
mocked, and the angry pontiff decided to rebuke twelve powerful
citizens of the time, the leaders of the faction who controlled the
city. When he had cited them to appear before him, they held a
conference fraught with indecision. They were afraid either to reject the pope's command or to obey it; the former course threatened their reputation, the latter their political position. In the former case, not to go would make them look guilty; in the latter
case, their absence might cause a coup. Finally, having weighed everything, it seemed the more honorable and great-spirited course
to appear before the pope. So they all set out, as they had been
summoned, these eminent men, the leaders of the city — Corso
Donati, Rosso della Tosa, Geri Spini, and other heads of powerful
families, suitably and honorably escorted — and arrived in Perugia,
where the pope was then in residence.

While they were appearing before the pope and the cardinals   89
and attempting to clear their names, Niccolò da Prato, the Tuscan

Etruria fuisse docuimus, inter haec dolum commentus,[106] exulibus clam perscripsit uti repente Florentiam invaderent: nullum quidem tempus rei patrandae aptius fore, cum principes omnes diversae factionis de industria evocati abessent; quibus detractis, ne ausuros quidem esse reliquos cives manum contra attollere, maxima praesertim multitudinis parte (quod pridem experimento viderit) illorum reditum affectante. Hanc exhortationem avide complexi exules, cum alii aliis celeriter significassent, constituta die Florentiam versus undequaque contendere ita improviso atque secreto, ut nil praesentiretur; ita magna multitudine, ut cuncti expavescerent. Fuerunt enim peditum supra novem millia, equites vero ad mille septingentos. Hae copiae maxima ex parte Arretinorum Bononiensiumque fuerunt, quae civitates, iisdem infectae partibus, albis favebant.

90   Cum igitur, vergente iam in occasum sole, non procul ab urbe via Bononiensi primae exulum copiae apparuissent, civitas repente in armis fuit, vigiliaeque ea nocte prope vicatim actae. Addebat terrorem debilitas urbis, quae nondum absolutis novis moenibus, et antiquis propter spem novorum neglectis, non satis valida contra oppugnationem putabatur. Exules prima luce bifariam partitis copiis, ad primum fere lapidem Bononienses in subsidio reliquere. Ipsi vero cum Arretinis ad urbem descendentes, nullo negotio nova transgrediuntur moenia. Inde levia quaedam proelia commissa sunt, in quibus superante multitudine, cum cives dimovissent, ad laevam tenentes iter, non longe a Servorum templo patentiori loco aciem struxerunt. Signo dato, cum ad vetusta moenia discurrissent, contra Viam Gladiariam et portulam, qua via illa

legate, was meanwhile concocting a plot. He wrote secretly to the exiles, urging them to attack Florence immediately. There would be no better time (he said) to commit such an act, since all the leaders of the opposing faction were absent, having been summoned hither by his design; with them out of the way, the rest of the citizens would not even dare raise a hand against the exiles, especially since the majority of the populace (as previous experience had shown) were minded to see them restored. The exiles eagerly embraced this exhortation, and swiftly spread instructions to each other that on the appointed day they would converge on Florence from every direction, so secretly and unexpectedly that Florence would have no warning, and in such large numbers that the whole city would be terrified. They possessed above 7000 foot and about 1700 horse. The majority of the troops came from Arezzo and Bologna, for these cities, which suffered from the same kind of partisanship, favored the Whites.

Thus at sundown one day the advance forces of the exiles appeared on the Via Bolognese not far from the city. The city sprang to arms and established guard-posts in almost every street that night. The weakness of the city added to the terror. The new walls were not yet finished, while the old ones had been neglected in anticipation of the new, so it was thought that the city could not stand up to attack. At dawn the exiles divided their forces in two, leaving behind the Bolognese as reserves near the first milestone. They themselves with the Aretines descended on the city and passed through the new walls without trouble. Then some light skirmishing broke out, in which the populace was bested, and when the citizens had withdrawn, the exiles took the road to the west and set up their line of battle on the more level ground near the church of the Santissima Annunziata. Sounding the trumpet, they charged towards the old walls and made a great attack opposite the Via degli Spadai and the little gate at the end of that street. Its defenders were thrown back and the gate was broken

90

433

claudebatur, maxime impetum fecerunt. Eam cum repulsis defensoribus perfregissent, ingressi antesignani usque ad Martis templum proeliantes pervenerunt, et vexilla quaedam intra portam illata magnum terrorem praebuerunt civibus. Nec ambigitur quin eodem impetu, si secuta fuisset acies, exules illa die victores fuissent. Sed, cunctando extra portam ac exitum pugnae expectando, concurrendi ac se conglobandi civibus facultatem praebuere. Itaque, concursu postea ad eum locum facto, quo hostem intrasse clamabatur, sese cohortantes cives invadentesque extra portam deiecerunt.

91   Sunt qui putent exules non sat unanimis fuisse ad urbem invadendam et albos Gibellinorum vires expavisse. Nam, qua ratione a viris militaribus ac bellorum expertis omissum fuerit vel aciem totam primo impetu irrumpere, vel, cum uno in loco pugnaretur, aliis subinde locis copias[107] admovere? Iam vero Bononiensium copias, quae in urbe conspectae magnum terrorem afferre potuerunt civibus, quo tandem consilio procul ab urbe reliquerunt? Haec et huiusmodi errata suspicionem praebent, quasi mallent quidam exulum urbe non potiri, sed aciem dumtaxat admovere, quo ipsi per pactionem reciperentur. Nam pulsi[108] nuper cives quos vocabant albos non tam voluntas quam necessitas Gibellinis coniunxerat; nec, si facultas esset, passuri sese invicem videbantur. Et relictam de industria procul ab urbe putant Bononiensium[109] aciem, quoniam illa maxime cum Ubaldinis et aliis gibellinae factionis hominibus venisset.

92   Ego vero, quid animi habuerit unusquisque exulum, haud facile existimo quemquam esse dicturum. Verum haec et huiusmodi errata in re militari evenire non alienum puto, ubi non unus dux, sed

down. The advance guard entered and fought its way as far as the Baptistery, terrifying the citizens when it succeeded in carrying its standard inside its doors. And there is no doubt that if the main body of troops had followed them, striking with the same force, the exiles that day would have had the victory. But they delayed outside the gate, awaiting the outcome of the battle, giving the citizens a chance to regroup. Thus, the citizenry came on the run to the place where there were shouts that the enemy had entered, and, urging each other on, they pushed the invaders back outside the gate.

There are those who think that the exiles were not of one mind 91 about invading the city, and that the Whites feared the power of the Ghibellines. For why (they ask) would military men and experienced warriors have failed to use their entire force in the first attack, or, alternatively, why would they not have moved their troops up to attack other places after the battle had been joined in one place? Again, why on earth did they leave the Bolognese forces so far from the city when the mere sight of them near the city would have struck terror into the citizens? These and similar errors raise the suspicion that certain of the exiles preferred not to take control of the city, but merely wanted to bring the army up so that they might themselves negotiate to be taken back. For the citizens who had recently been expelled, the so-called Whites, had joined the Ghibellines less from free will than from necessity, and the two groups would probably not have tolerated each other if they had been able to avoid the association. Some believe the Bolognese army was left so far outside the city by design, because they had close relations with the Ubaldini and other members of the Ghibelline faction.

For my part, I believe it is very hard indeed for anyone to say 92 what any given exile had in mind. But I do know that mistakes of this kind are not uncommon in military affairs where there is no one commander, but only a number of different condottieri, and

multi ductores praesunt, nec miles est qui post signa ingreditur, sed collecticia turba neminis unius imperio consueta. Quae omnia tunc aderant, nam et multi aequales inter se duces erant et manus tumultuaria atque nova. Bononienses simul atque repulsos qui urbem intraverant cognovere, et nunciabant quidam aciem quoque extra portam esse profligatam, confestim signa moventes abiere. Qui vero ante portam in acie stabant, cum a prima luce ad meridiem constitissent, siti atque calore fatigati, labescere iam pridem coeperant. Itaque, postquam abiisse Bononienses audiverunt, quasi deserti a suis, e vestigio secuti sunt tanta trepidatione ut fuga magis quam profectio videretur. Pauci ex civibus post eos egressi, quosdam postremo agmine interfecerunt; reliqui ea ipsa qua venerant via remearunt. Cum superato colle in agrum mugellanum descenderent, obviam illis fuerunt Pistoriensium copiae, quas Tolosanus[110] Ubertus florentinus eques et ipse exul eadem ex causa adducebat. Erant autem equites trecenti, pedites vero circiter octingentos. Ab his Tolosanus[111] cognovit et quid actum esset et quid spei superforet; itaque converso itinere Pistorium reduxit.

93   Per eosdem fere dies quibus haec ab exulibus attentata sunt, Benedictus pontifex romanus vita decessit, magnaeque sunt patrum discordiae in eligendo secutae. Itaque, cives nuper ad pontificem evocati, cognita legati fraude et apud patres conquesti, Florentiam illico redierunt. Versi dehinc ad rem publicam statumque civitatis roborandum, quoniam apparebat magna superesse certamina, societatem renovarunt cum aliis Etruriae populis, qui easdem per id tempus sectabantur partes. Hi fuerunt Lucenses, Volaterrani, Senenses, Pratenses, Geminianenses, Collenses, Ti-

where the soldier does not follow a standard, but there is only a motley mob unused to the command of a single individual. And such was the state of affairs then, for they not only had many commanders serving on an equal basis, but their band of men was also raw and disorderly. As soon as they learned that the men who had entered the city had been repulsed, and received the news that the army outside the gate had also taken to its heels, the Bolognese immediately began to retreat. The men who had been standing in the ranks in front of the gate from dawn to mid-day had suffered much from thirst and the heat, and had long since begun to melt away. And when they heard that the Bolognese had withdrawn, like deserters they immediately began to follow in such a state of fear that it seemed more a rout than a withdrawal. A few citizens who went out of the city after them killed some who were last in the column; the rest of the exile forces returned the way they had come. When they had crossed the ridge and come down into the Mugello they were met by troops from Pistoia which the Florentine knight Tolosano degli Uberti, himself an exile, had led there for the same reason.[66] He had 300 knights and about 800 infantry. When Tolosano learned from the retreating exiles what had happened and how little hope remained, he turned around and went back to Pistoia.[67]

Almost simultaneously with the exiles' attempt on Florence, Pope Benedict departed this life, and great discords followed among the cardinals with respect to his successor.[68] The citizens who had recently been summoned to the pontiff realized that the legate had tricked them; they complained to the cardinals, then left at once for Florence. Upon their return they turned their attention to stabilizing the commonwealth and the condition of the city, and since it seemed to them that great battles remained to be fought, they renewed the league with the peoples of Tuscany who were of their own party at that time. These were the peoples of Lucca, Volterra, Siena, Prato, San Gimignano, Colle Val d'Elsa,

fernates, quos Castellanos vulgo dicunt. Omnes hi simul uno foedere colligati ducem sibi praeficere[112] aliquem maioris auctoritatis statuerunt, cuius auspiciis bellum inferrent.

94   Robertus erat per id tempus filiorum Caroli regis in Italia maximus, insigni iam tunc indole ac magnae spei iuvenis. Hunc deligere ducem placuit. Eius rei gratia missi Neapolim oratores duo: Rainerius Foresii et Borgus Rinaldi. Iverunt et a Lucensibus Senensibusque oratores alii. Qui regem primo, mox iuvenem allocuti, tandem illius adventum in Etruriam impetrarunt huiusmodi condicionibus dictis receptisque: uti Robertus in Etruriam veniret; exercitum Florentinorum sociorumque ductaret; nullam in urbibus oppidisve potestatem haberet; in exercitu vero animadvertendi in eos qui non parerent sibi ius esset; si pecunia damnaret, aerario civitatis oppidive cuius damnatus civis oppidanusve foret, applicaretur; annum integrum in Etruria gerendo bello perstaret, nec inde abiret nisi aut evidens periculum regni paterni aut pontificis iussus moram eius impediret. Contra vero Florentini sociique stipendia equitibus quos adduxisset in menses singulos darent, sibique et familiae diurnam pensionem. Harum pecuniarum maximam omnium partem Florentini ex foedere conferebant, proximam Lucenses, pauciora[113] Senenses, perexiguam deinde Pratenses, Tifernates, Geminianenses et Collenses.

95   His ergo compositis, proximi anni vere primo Robertus in Etruriam venit, ducens equites non amplo quidem numero, sed viros nobiles ad bellum delectos. Civitates, iam consilio habito, Pistorium obsidere constituerant, quod ea urbs per id tempus ab adversariis tenebatur, Florentinisque et Lucensibus bellum assiduum

and Città di Castello. All of these peoples came together in a single federation and decided to appoint a commander-in-chief under whose auspices they would make war.

Robert at that time was the oldest son of King Charles in Italy, 94 and he was already then an outstandingly gifted youth of great promise.[69] It was he whom they decided to choose as their commander. To accomplish this they sent two ambassadors to Naples, Rinieri del Forese and Borgo Rinaldi. Other ambassadores from Lucca and Siena went as well. They spoke first with the king, then with the youth, and finally succeeded in obtaining his coming to Tuscany after agreement had been reached on the following condi- 1304 tions: that Robert should come to Tuscany; that he should command the army of the Florentines and their allies; that he should have no power in any of the cities or towns, but in the army he should have the right to punish those who disobeyed him; if he fined someone, he should apply to the treasury of the city or town of the citizen who had been fined; he should remain in Tuscany to wage war for a full year and not leave unless there was some clear and present danger to his father's kingdom or unless the pope should command him to curtail his sojourn. The Florentines and the allies, on the other hand, were to provide stipends in monthly installments for the knights he brought with him as well as maintenance for himself and his family. According to the treaty the Florentines were to supply the greatest part of the monies, and the Lucchesi the next largest share, followed by the Sienese, with small shares to be paid by the peoples of Prato, Città di Castello, San Gimignano and Colle Val d'Elsa.[70]

The matter being thus settled, in the spring of the following 95 year Robert came to Tuscany at the head of a company of knights. 1305 It was a small company, to be sure, but it consisted of noblemen and elite warriors. The cities now took counsel together and decided to besiege Pistoia, as that city was controlled by their adversaries at that time and had been waging continuous war on Flor-

inferebat. Igitur, postquam Florentiam venit Robertus, coactum paulo post exercitum in Pistorienses duxit. Venerunt alia ex parte Lucenses magna multitudine, ac se Florentinis ceterisque sociis coniunxerunt. Castris non longe positis, cum undique Pistorium cinxissent, expugnare urbem aggrediuntur, sed resistebatur acerrime ab his qui in urbe erant Pistoriensibus. Et aderant florentinorum exulum non contemnenda manus et conducti equites mercede circiter trecentos. Hi cum urbem egregie defenderent, ac ob eam rem longior intercessura videretur mora, Florentini et socii obstinatis animis vallo et fossa urbem circumdarunt, castellisque et turribus opportunis locis munierunt ut nemo ingredi egredive posset. Crebra vero quotidie proelia inter moenia urbis fossasque committebantur.

96 Dum ea geruntur apud Pistorium, Clemens pontifex romanus (is enim Benedicto nuper defuncto in pontificatu successerat) hortatu Nicolai pratensis duos simul legatos in Etruriam misit. Hi, quartum fere mensem postquam obsidio coepta fuerat, cum in castra venissent, Roberto duci exercituique ex auctoritate pontificis edixerunt uti ab armis discederent obsidionemque dissolverent; his nisi parerent, censuras gravissimas protulerunt. Robertus dicto pontificis audiens fuit; id enim ab initio nominatim exceperat. Ceteri quoque populi longiorem militiam veriti, destiterunt. Florentini solum et Lucenses obstinatis animis obsidionem persecuti[114] sunt, conscii non tam ex animo pontificis, quam ex procuratione adversariorum praecepta illa comminationesque prodire, ac paulo ante in principibus experti civibus nihil neque firmi neque sinceri curiam habere. Ea indignatione legatorum praecepta contemnere, nec tantis laboribus coeptam protractamque obsidionem dissolvere statuerunt. Legati, quoniam dicto non parebatur, in Florentino-

ence and Lucca. So shortly after Robert arrived in Florence he assembled an army and led it against Pistoia. A large crowd of Lucchesi came from the opposite direction and linked up with the Florentines and the other allies. They encamped in a tight ring around Pistoia and began to lay siege to the city, but they were bitterly resisted by the Pistoians who held the city. Inside was also a considerable band of Florentine exiles and about three hundred mercenary knights. This force defended the city with distinction, and for this reason it became evident that a longer sojourn was going to be necessary, but the Florentines and their allies obstinately surrounded the city with earthworks and moats, strengthening the fortifications with strongholds and turrets in strategic places so that no one could get in or out. There were pitched battles every day between the city walls and the moat.

While this was happening in Pistoia, Pope Clement[71] (who had recently succeeded to the pontificate after Benedict's death) sent two legates simultaneously to Tuscany at the exhortation of Niccolò da Prato. These legates arrived in the camp nearly four months after the commencement of the siege and commanded Duke Robert and the army, on the authority of the pope, to lay down their arms and dissolve the siege; if they failed to obey, they would incur the gravest ecclesiastical censures.[72] Robert obeyed the pontiff's command, as he had expressly stipulated that he would from the beginning. The rest of the peoples, too, fearing a long campaign, desisted. Only the Florentines and the Lucchesi obstinately continued the siege, knowing full well that these instructions and menaces proceeded not so much from the mind of the pope as from the maneuverings of their adversaries. Shortly before they had learned from the case of their principal citizens that the papal curia's intentions were neither fixed nor sincere. Indignantly they rejected the instructions of the legates and decided not to abandon the siege they had begun and carried on with such effort. The legates, since they were being disobeyed, passed

96

rum Lucensiumque praesides sententiam tulerunt; urbibus autem eorum interdixerunt sacris. Robertus igitur, relicta apud Pistorium maxima parte equitatus quem veniens in Etruriam duxerat, ipse tenui comitatu in Provinciam primo, mox in Galliam transiit, pontifici[115] pro assumptione gratulatum. Florentini vero et Lucenses in obsidione perseverantes, urbem arctius in dies presserunt. Milites, ne longiori afficerentur militia, vicissim mutabantur, ut novi veteribus et integri succederent fessis. Ad undecimum usque mensem protracta obsidio est. Tandem, cum iam necessaria deficerent, qui obsidebantur turbam mulierum et inutilium bello hominum exigere coeperunt. Sed hi cum ad munitiones pervenerant, non minus acerbe a militibus qui stabant pro vallo in urbem reiiciebantur. Ita, longitudine belli domiti Pistorienses, in potestatem venerunt, exulibus qui intus erant incolumibus abire pactis, civibus autem impunitate concessa.

97 Postquam urbe potiti sunt Florentini et Lucenses, moenia undequaque diruerunt, fossas compleverunt, agrum et regionem inter se partiti sunt; urbi vero afflictae ac semirutae communiter imperitarunt. Captum est autem Pistorium V Idus aprilis, anno christianae salutis trecentesimo sexto supra mille, cum superiori Maio obsideri coeptum esset; finemque habuit pistoriense bellum.

98 Haud multo post reductas Pistorio copias, Florentini in agrum mugellanum profecti, Accianicum obsederunt. Id erat castellum Ubaldinae gentis, et situ loci et structura murorum longe munitissimum. Causa obsidendi illa fuit, quod maxima vis exulum eo in castello consederat, a quibus non terrores modo, verum etiam damna finitimis inferebantur. Tribus mensibus omni conatu Flo-

sentence[73] against the military commissioners[74] of the Florentines and Lucchesi and placed their cities under interdict. Robert then left behind at Pistoia the largest part of the cavalry he had brought with him to Tuscany, and with a small escort passed first to Provence, then France, to congratulate the pope on his accession. The Florentines and the Lucchesi persevered in the siege, drawing the noose tighter every day. Their soldiers were relieved by turns to prevent them from becoming worn down by long tours of duty, so that new soldiers relieved the old, and fresh troops replaced exhausted ones. The siege dragged on into its eleventh month. Finally, since their supplies had now run out, the besieged began to expel throngs of women and such men as were useless in battle. But when they reached the siegeworks, sentries standing in front of the moat drove them back to the city with equal harshness. Thus the Pistoians were mastered by the sheer length of the siege and surrendered on condition that the exiles inside were to be allowed to leave unharmed, and that the citizens of Pistoia were not to suffer punishment.

After the Florentines and the Lucchesi had made themselves   97
masters of the city, they threw down the walls on every side, filled up the moat, and divided the countryside and the region up among themselves. But they shared between them the rule of the prostrate and half-ruined city. Pistoia was captured on 9 April 1306, after a siege that had begun the previous May. Thus ended   *1306* the war with Pistoia.[75]

Soon after their troops had returned from Pistoia, the Floren-   98
tines set out for the Mugello to besiege Accianico. This was a castle belonging to the Ubaldini clan, and was extremely well fortified owing to its position and the construction of its walls. The reason for besieging it was that a large band of exiles had taken up residence in that castle who were terrorizing and inflicting damage on their neighbors. For three months the Florentines encamped there, straining every nerve to capture it using catapults and mines. But

rentinus circa illud commoratus, tormentis maxime et cuniculis oppugnationem tentavit. Verum conatus omnes in irritum casuri erant, aspernante munitissimo loco, nisi suspicio inter principes eius familiae coorta certatim compulisset ad deditionem faciendam. Quare, pecunia expromissa, castellum tandem receptum est et ad solum eversum. Incolarum autem pars in subiectam planitiem redacta, et oppidum ibi conditum, quod postea Scarpariam vocitarunt.

99   Eodem anno magistratus noviter creari in urbe coeptus est contra nobilitatem, quem executorem iustitiae dixerunt. In hunc magistratum magna pars eius curae, quae prius ad officium vexilliferi iustitiae pertinebat, translata est. Et quo gratiae metusque abesset suspicio, peregrinum sumere placuit, et quidem extra Etruriam oriundum. Societates etiam populi eodem anno renovatae, una detracta ex tribu Scradiana. Eo factum est, ut pro viginti societatibus decem et novem instituerentur. Ac secuti tunc primum vexilla cives ante diem octavo Kalendas sextiles transmiserunt.

100   Per haec ipsa tempora Nepoleonem Ursinum, romanae ecclesiae cardinalem, Clemens pontifex in Italiam misit ad discordias Etruriae componendas. Huius autem[116] legatio eodem auctore manasse creditur quo superiorum legatorum. Nicolaus enim pratensis nuper his contentionibus imbutus, vel acerrimum patronum[117] apud pontificem agebat pro exulibus reducendis. Gratia vero maxima apud Clementem poterat, quoniam eius pontificis electio ex sinu consiliorum suorum fluxisse credebatur. Nam inclusi nuper apud Perusiam patres, cum magnis inter se discordiis certarent, huius praecipua calliditate in burdegalensem archiepiscopum[118] consenserunt, cui mox Clementi placuit appellari. Ea de causa recenti gratia potens, ubi priores legati re infecta redierunt,

this impregnable place resisted them, and all their efforts would have come to naught, if a climate of distrust had not arisen between the chiefs of the Ubaldini family which forced them into a competition to surrender the castle. Hence money was produced and the castle was at last taken and razed to the ground. A number of the inhabitants were transferred down to a plateau beneath it, and a town was founded there which was afterwards called Scarperia.[76]

In the same year a new magistracy was created in the city, directed against the nobility, which was called the Executor of Justice.[77] A large proportion of the business that formerly belonged to the office of the Standard-Bearer of Justice was transferred to this magistracy. So that there should be no suspicion of fear or favor, it was decided to choose a foreigner; indeed, someone born outside Tuscany altogether. The companies of the People were also revived in that year, and one company was subtracted from the region of San Piero Scheraggio. Thus it came about that there were nineteen companies instead of twenty. It was then, on 25 July, that the citizens first followed the standards in procession.

In this very period Pope Clement sent Cardinal Napoleone degli Orsini to Italy to settle the quarrels of Tuscany. It was believed that this legation could be traced to the same source as the previous one: that is, to Niccolò da Prato, who had recently been meddling in these rivalries and was acting in the pontifical court as an extremely zealous advocate for the restoration of the exiles. He had tremendous influence with Clement, since the latter believed he owed his election as pope to Niccolò's counsels. For, not long since, when the cardinals had been immured in Perugia and had been divided by great rivalries, it was thanks especially to his cunning that their choice had fallen on the archbishop of Bourdeaux, who afterwards took the name of Clement. For this reason Niccolò had recently become powerful and influential, so when the previous legates returned in failure, he persuaded the pope that

Nepoleonem, fiducia quadam generis, in Etruriam persuasit legandum. Ille igitur pontificis iussu Lugdunio movens, cum superatis Alpibus in Italiam pervenisset ac iam Etruriae propinquaret, praemissis Florentiam nunciis adventum suum populo significavit, et sibi parari locum in urbe petiit. Frequenti super ea re consultatione habita, cum varia variis placerent, tandem vicit eorum sententia, qui non recipiendum in urbem censebant, ob superiorum exempla legatorum, a quibus auctae fuerant potius civium discordiae quam aut diminutae aut sublatae.

101   Nepoleo igitur a Florentinis recusatus, Caesenam se contulit. Inde, cum frustra saepius rem tentasset, et principes quosdam civitatis coercere metu censurae niteretur, non parentibus civibus, interdicto urbem subiecit. Sed cum minimum ea quoque re proficeret, quoniam assueta iam pridem civitas longe aspernabatur, vi et armis conandum ratus, parare copias ac bellum inferre constituit. Ea de causa, principio insequentis[119] anni Caesena movens per sarsinatem agrum, superato Apennini iugo, Arretium venit, quod eam urbem ad bellum inferendum parandasque copias aptissimam iudicabat. Receptus ab Arretinis, praeter Florentinorum exules, qui ad eum undique confluxerant, magnum insuper equitum numerum, non ex Etruria modo, verum etiam ex Latio et Sabinia et Umbria contraxit. Cum his copiis ingredi florentinum agrum exulesque vi reducere constituerat. At civitas, cognito legati consilio, copias impigre paravit et socios amicosque rogavit auxilia. Quibus undique affluentibus, cum aliquanto superior copiarum multitudine videretur, minime expectandum putavit quoad legatus fines eius intraret, sed obviam profecta in agrum Arretinum copias misit. Hae per Ambram fluvium euntes, superato ad extremum colle,

Napoleone, whose family name inspired trust, should be sent on legation to Tuscany. Napoleone thus left Lyons at the pope's bidding, crossed the Alps, and entered Italy. He was already nearing Tuscany when he sent messengers ahead to Florence to announce his coming to the people, asking them to prepare a residence for him in the city. Crowded meetings were held on this subject, and various views were expressed, but the view that eventually won out was that he should not be admitted to the city. The proponents of this view held up the example of the previous legates, whose actions had exacerbated rather than diminished or removed the divisions of the citizens.[78]

Having been rejected by the Florentines, Napoleone betook 101 himself to Cesena. There he tried repeatedly but in vain to enter the city and tried to coerce certain leading citizens with fear of excommunication, but the citizens would not obey him and he placed the city under interdict. This, too, was of little profit, as the city had long since grown used to such measures and had contempt for them. So Napoleone, thinking to try violence and arms, decided to raise troops and make war. Thus at the beginning of the following year, he left Cesena and crossed the Apennine passes 1307 in the territory of Sársina, arriving at Arezzo, a city he believed to be well suited as a base for making war and raising troops. The Aretines received him, and, in addition to the Florentine exiles who flocked to him from every direction, he assembled a great number of knights, not only from Tuscany but also from Lazio, Sabina, and Umbria. With these forces he determined to enter Florentine territory and restore the exiles by force. But the City, learning of the legate's plan, vigorously raised troops, calling upon its friends and allies. They poured in from every direction, and, as it appeared that the Florentines enjoyed some numerical superiority, it was thought unlikely that the legate would cross their borders. Instead, they sent their troops out to meet him in Aretine territory. These passed the river Ambra and, climbing to the top

Gargonsam circumsederunt, quod in eo castello paulo ante exules florentini magnos conventus egisse dicebantur, et consilia iniisse in urbem redeundi. Quare honestum magis visum est copias eo ducere quam si contra legatum ipsum, nulla prius lacessiti iniuria, conarentur.

102 Dum circa Gargonsam moratur Florentinorum exercitus et oppugnationi intendit, legatus omnibus copiis Arretio profectus, diversa ab hoste regione, Casentinati via, Florentiam versus ducere contendit. Eius rei tanta repente trepidatio civitatem pervasit ut qui domi remanserant[120] confestim exercitum revocarent; et qui in exercitu erant, audita profectione hostium, sine ullo ordine proriperent se atque abirent. Legatus, cum in media iam esset via, reversionem florentini exercitus cognovit; quare et ipse mutato consilio Arretium copias reduxit. Moratus post haec aliquanto circum[121] ea loca, cum spe vana pacis distineretur, tandem, nulla notabili perfecta re, in Galliam abiit.

103 Civitas gravibus censuris obnoxia remansit, nec absolutionis spes in praesentia suberat nec sane apud cives petendi voluntas. Contumaciter enim maxime per id tempus degebant, experti pontificum voluntates insinceras plane, nec tam pro ratione, quae perpetua est, quam pro eorum qui praesidebant cupiditate mutari. Et accedebat indignatio, quod, cum ipsi fautores romanorum pontificum fuissent, illorum tamen patrocinium ingrate quidem ac perverse pro inimicis stare cernebant. Quamobrem et ipsi quoque dolore conciti, quoniam belli sumptus culpa ecclesiasticorum hominum provenire existimabant, grandia ecclesiasticis religiosisque locis personisque tributa superposuere. Eorum tam acerbe facta per id tempus exactio est ut plus cladis inferret vexatio exactorum quam persolutio ipsa pecuniarum.

of the hill, surrounded Gargonza, since in that castle the Florentine exiles were said to have held large meetings shortly before and to have begun their plan to return to the City. For this reason it seemed more honorable to lead the troops there, rather than make some thrust against the legate himself, who as yet had done them no injury.

While the Florentine army was staying at Gargonza intent on a 102 siege, the legate set out from Arezzo with all his forces, and hastened towards Florence, but through a different region, by the Via Casentina. This caused a sudden shock of apprehension to pass through the citizenry, so that those who had remained behind immediately recalled the army, and those in the army, hearing of the enemy's march, picked themselves up and took off in a disorderly mob. The legate heard of the Florentine army's return when he was halfway there, whereupon he changed his mind and marched his forces back to Arezzo. He stayed for a little while in the area, held there by a vain hope of peace, but finally went away to France without accomplishing anything of note.

The city remained under interdict, nor was there any immedi- 103 ate hope of absolution, nor, frankly, any desire to seek it on the part of the citizens. At this time especially the citizens lived in a state of contumacy, having had direct experience of the impure motives of the popes which fluctuated not so much in accordance with reason (which does not change), but in accordance with the cupidity of those in power. It added to their indignation that, though they themselves were supporters of the Roman pontiffs, they saw their patrons, ungratefully and perversely, treat them like enemies. The pain they felt spurred them on to impose large taxes on ecclesiastical institutions and religious persons, since they felt that the expenses of war had been the fault of ecclesiastics. The taxes were extracted at that time with such rigor that the clergy suffered more from the harassment of the tax collectors than from the payment of monies itself.[79]

104   Proximo dehinc anno quies fuit ab externis bellis; domi autem seditiones insuper coortae graves et a civibus arma sumpta ex huiusmodi causa. Cursium Donatum iam pridem alieno fuisse animo in cives suae factionis diximus. Videtur porro id maxime periculosum in praestantibus viris, quod virtutis meritorumque suorum conscii, arroganter potius requirere honores quam ambitiose petere sustinent.[122] At populorum ea fere natura est ut rogantibus[123] et ambientibus magis concedant. Ea contentio ad arma plerumque et civile bellum prorumpere consuevit, cum et praestantes viri adversus ingratitudinem civium suorum conciti, impetum animi regere nequiverunt, et cives superbiam ac fastidium summorum virorum cavillati, non iam pro civibus, sed pro tyrannis gerere criminantur; quod tunc Florentiae accidit. Neque enim prius cessatum est vel a Cursio indignatione provehi vel a quibusdam civibus illius superbiam inquietudinemque accusari quam ad arma et sanguinem ac civile discidium[124] res prorupit.

105   Coeperat iam pridem[125] Cursius motum omnem rei publicae non cunctanter arripere, ut in postulandis rationibus publicarum pecuniarum supra monstravimus. Eo fiebat ut quicumque magnis in re publica viris infensi resistere vellent, omnes ad ipsum, tamquam ad patronum calamitosorum prohibitoremque iniuriarum concurrerent. Hic vero palam loqui, insectari, protegere, denique lacessere non formidabat. Per has quidem artes nomen eius viri, quod nobilitatis columen esse consueverat, populare iam et plausibile factum erat. Et delectabat plebem excelsa quaedam et invicta[126] magnitudo animi, qua ceteris omnibus illa tempestate praecellere imminereque videbatur. Ipse quoque, hac sublevatus aura, novas res crebro suscitare, tela promere, armatorum catervas domi habere, adversarios deterrere pergebat. His rursus in civitate sic praevalebat ut cunctos et auctoritate et potentia superaret.

The following year there was a respite from foreign wars, but at home grave sedition arose once again, and the citizens took to arms for the following reason. Corso Donati had for a long time, as we have shown, been alienated from the citizens of his own faction. It seems, indeed, that this is a particularly dangerous attitude for great men to adopt: they are conscious of their own virtue and merits and therefore possess the arrogance to demand public honors rather than the political skills to be given them. But it is, generally speaking, the nature of peoples to grant honors by preference to those who seek them in an ingratiating manner. The competition for honors commonly leads to armed struggle and breaks out in civil war, since great men, spurred on by the ingratitude of their own citizens, are unable to regulate their inner drives, and citizens, railing at the pride and arrogance of great men, charge them with acting like tyrants rather than citizens. That is what happened then in Florence. Corso did not stop being overwrought with indignation, and certain citizens did not stop accusing him of restless pride, until the situation erupted into armed struggle, bloodshed, and civic turmoil.

Corso had begun long before to seize eagerly upon every public disturbance, as we showed above when he demanded an accounting of public funds. He did this to the point where anyone who had been offended by one of the great public men and wanted to fight back ran to him as to the patron of the unfortunate and the defender of the injured. Through these arts the man's former reputation as a pillar of the nobility changed, and he became much admired as man of the people. He delighted the commons with his exalted and unconquerable greatness of mind, by which he seemed to excel and overtop all other men of the day. He himself, sustained by popular favor, continued to make trouble, brandish weapons, keep troops of armed men at his house, and face down his adversaries. By these means he grew so strong in the city that he exceeded everyone else in authority and power.

104
1308

105

106   Crescentem in dies virum multaque molientem, adversarii tandem quasi tyrannidis affectatorem criminari coeperunt, occasione freti, quod ille haud multo prius, defuncta uxore, affinitate nova Uguicionem Fagiolanum, hominem potentem domi ac diversarum partium vel praecipuum assertorem sibi socerum adscivisset. Hanc igitur affinitatem, statim ubi de illa auditum est, carpentes adversarii, perinde quasi immineret libertatis periculum, arma propere invaserunt. Ille vim contra se parari sentiens, arma corripuit et vicinas domui suae partes communivit. Sed plebis animos ab eo averterant inimicorum voces, missa profecto auxilia venire a socero asserentes, quibus rem publicam occupaturus esset. Itaque convenit apud eum non multitudo[127] quanta solebat, sed familiarium dumtaxat et amicorum manus; qua etsi exigua fretus, se contra vim populi tutabatur, nec magistratui parebat vocanti, formidans inimicorum calumniam contra se iactatam.

107   Magistratus igitur inimicorum vocibus rumoribusque exagitatus, quoniam ille haudquaquam parebat, armis etiam se tutabatur, quasi reum damnavit, adeo iudiciorum ordine intermisso ut eodem die accusatum, eodem citatum, eodem condemnatum fuisse constet. Ad sententiam mox exequendam ire placuit, ac populi manus ad eam rem ex ordine iustitiae arcessita. Quae postquam apud eum convenit, magistratus a praetorio movens, praeeunte vexillifero iustitiae cum multitudine armatorum et societatibus item sub vexillis sequentibus, populari impetu domos Cursii adierunt. Ille, nihil magis deterritus, omnem vim populi parva ipse manu distinere audebat, et muniverat aditus non armata modo acie, verum etiam impedimentis, quo facilius ruentis in se multitu-

As the man's power increased daily and his plots multiplied, his 106
adversaries finally began to charge him with aspiring to tyranny.
Their charge was given color by the fact that, not long before, after
the death of his wife, he had formed a new marriage alliance by
which Uguccione della Faggiuola, a powerful man in his own lands
and a leading Ghibelline partisan, had become his father-in-law.[80]
As soon as this marriage tie became known, it was seized upon by
his enemies, to the point where they ran to arms as though a crisis
of liberty was at hand. When Corso heard of the preparations to
attack him, he mobilized and fortified the area near his house. But
the words of his enemies had alienated the commons from him.
They claimed that he had assuredly been sent aid by his father-in-
law so that he could take over the commonwealth. Thus the populace did not come to help him in great numbers as before, but he
had only a band of friends and family. Although it was small, it
protected him against the violence of the people, and he did not
obey the summons of the magistrate, fearing that the calumnies of
his enemies would be thrown up against him.

The magistrate therefore was stirred up by the claims and sto- 107
ries of Corso's enemies, and since Corso would not obey him and
was even defending himself with arms, the official condemned him
as a perpetrator, abrogating the normal procedure of the courts to
the extent that he was, evidently, accused, cited, and condemned,
all on the same day. Thereupon the magistrate decided to go and
execute sentence, invoking the Ordinances of Justice to assemble a
band of the People. When they had assembled, the magistrate
went forth from the Palace of the Podestà with the Standard-
Bearer of Justice in the lead, and a crowd of armed men as well as
the companies following their standards; they approached Corso's
dwellings with the vigor characteristic of the People. Corso himself was not in the least intimidated but dared hold at bay the full
force of the People with his tiny guard. He had fortified the entrances not only with armed guards, but also with barricades, so as

dinis impetum arceret. Ad ea loca postquam magistratus pervenit, aliquot horis acriter pugnatum est. Tandem, redundante multitudine populi et cuncta undique complente, effractis proximarum domorum hortorumque parietibus, cum alii aliunde intra munitiones penetrassent, qui contra stabant, omissa defensione aufugerunt. Cursius ipse cum paucis egressus urbe, Casentinati via fugam arripuit. Verum, missa post eum confestim equitum turma, non longe ab urbe fugientem consequitur et proeliando sistere compellit. Ita, circumventus inimicorum multitudine, demum occiditur. Interfecti sunt et alii quidam cum eo, totaque illius factio profligata.

108   Hunc finem habuit Cursius Donatus, vir procul dubio egregius, ceterum inquietior civis quam bonae rei publicae conveniret. Fuisse vero suspicionem vel calumniam potius quod de tyrannide obiiciebatur, vel ex hoc intelligi licet, quod apud collegium partium optimarum nunquam eius nomen ut inimicum vel adversum fuerit annotatum, cum in ceteris huiusmodi damnatis id fieri consuesset, quodque agnati et familia nil diminuta gratia in civitate remanserunt, nec multo post illius necem ulti sunt, tamquam privatam iniuriam publica manu factam.

109   Per idem fere tempus Arretini Tarlatum genus, sic potens opibus ut paene dominaretur, seditione facta, pepulerunt, et guelfarum partium homines, qui iam diu exularant, in urbem revocarunt; quibus rem publicam capessentibus, celeriter pax et societas inita est cum florentino populo, ac superiori contentioni finis impositus.

110   Principio insequentis anni, ortis apud Pratenses seditionibus, altera factio oppido pellitur. Eam rem in tam propinquo loco minime ferendam censuit florentinus populus, sed patrocinio suscepto pulsos restituit. Constabat vero eam turbationem Pistorien-

to ward off more easily the attack of the populace as it came down upon him. There was bitter fighting for several hours after the magistrate arrived, but finally, after successive waves of the people had filled the whole neighborhood, and the walls of nearby houses and gardens had been broken through, when the attackers were penetrating the defenses in all directions, the defenders abandoned the struggle and took to flight. Corso himself escaped the city with a few followers, fleeing up the Via Casentina. But a squadron of knights immediately went in pursuit and caught up with the fleeing man not far from the city, compelling him to stand and fight. Thus, though he had escaped the multitude of his enemies, he was at last killed. Some other men were also killed along with him, and his entire faction was crushed.

Such was the end of Corso Donati, who was doubtless a man 108 of great distinction, but too turbulent to be a citizen in a good republic.[81] His being accused of tyranny was mere suspicion or calumny, as may be inferred especially from the fact that he was never censured by the Parte Guelfa as an enemy or opponent, as was customary in the case of other persons condemned for this crime. Moreover, his family and blood-relatives remained in the city with undiminished status, and shortly thereafter avenged his death as though it were a private injury committed by public force.[82]

Around this same time the Aretines rose up and ejected the 109 Tarlati clan, whose wealth made them almost like lords. Members of the Guelf party who had long been in exile were summoned back to the city. When they had taken control of public affairs, they swiftly made peace with the Florentine People, thus putting an end to the late struggles.[83]

At the beginning of the following year sedition arose within 110 the people of Prato, and another faction was expelled from the 1309 town. The Florentine People could not countenance this happening in a place so near to itself, so it took up their cause and restored the men who had been banished. But the disturbance evi-

ses quoque finitimos commovisse, qui[128] non has modo, sed et quascumque rerum novarum occasiones praecupide arrepturi videbantur, infensi maxime Lucensium dominatu, in quos et vetere odio et recenti dolore incendebantur. Itaque, id veriti Lucenses (eos namque et Florentinos urbem partitos diximus) delendum funditus Pistorium censebant, et Florentinos ad eam rem provocabant. Sed praevaluit mansuetudo apud florentinum populum; misertusque antiquorum sociorum[129] casum, non modo non consensit Lucensium irae, verum etiam Pistoriensibus fecit animos ad se tutandum. Itaque, dempto Florentinorum metu, non viri modo, sed et feminae et pueri et religiosi, omnis denique sexus atque aetatis, die noctuque operi incumbentes, fossas purgare urbis ac diruta nuper moenia festino reficere conatu aggressi sunt; summa denique vigilantia et labore urbem ad aliquem modum communitam a Lucensibus defenderunt. Ita Pistorium in suam rediit potestatem. Nec facile dixerim maiori animo florentinus populus eam urbem ceperit an dimiserit.

III   Eodem anno bellum contra Arretinos renovatum est. Tarlati enim diversae factionis principes, quos superiori anno pulsos Arretio diximus, opera maxime Uguicionis Fagiolani in urbem redierunt, et diversarum partium homines, qui nuper reversi foedus cum florentino populo renovarant, improviso aggressi, post multam caedem eiecerunt. Ea de causa missae confestim equitum peditumque copiae in agrum Arretinum, exulibus coniunctae, magnas regioni intulerunt clades, incendiisque et rapinis cuncta foedarunt. Ita bellum ex integro renascitur.

dently affected their neighbors, the Pistoians, as well. As a people, they seemed eager to seize any and all opportunities for political change, mostly because of their hostility to Lucchese rule; both old hatreds and recent suffering fed the flames of their anger against that people. Fearing revolution, the Lucchesi (who had divided control of the city with the Florentines, as we said) were of the opinion that Pistoia should be entirely destroyed and were challenging the Florentines to do it. But the gentleness of the Florentine People prevailed, and they had mercy on the condition of their former allies. Not only did they not share the ire of the Lucchesi, but they even encouraged the Pistoians to defend themselves. Thus, once their fear of the Florentines was taken away, not only the men of Pistoia, but also the women, children and clergy, of every age and sex, worked night and day trying to clean out the moats and repair rapidly the walls that had recently been torn down. At last, with supreme, unsleeping effort they were able to fortify the city after a fashion and defend it from the Lucchesi. Thus Pistoia became independent once more. For my part, I should not find it easy to say whether the Florentine People behaved more nobly when it took that city or when it allowed it to go free.[84]

In the same year the war against the Aretines began again. The III Tarlati chiefs of the Ghibelline faction (who, as we said, had been expelled the previous year) had returned to the city, thanks largely to the efforts of Uguccione della Faggiuola. The members of the Guelf faction who had recently returned and renewed the alliance with the Florentine People were attacked by surprise and thrown out of the city after much slaughter. For this reason cavalry and infantry detachments were sent immediately into Aretine territory where they joined forces with the exiles and inflicted great damage on the region, pillaging and burning everything. Thus the war started all over again.[85]

112   Per idem tempus, legato romanae sedis contra Venetos bellum gerenti, auxilia equitum Florentini miserunt. Id suo ne ipsi motu an rogatu illius fecerint, quo gratiam reconciliationemque promererent, haud satis compertum habeo. Ceterum is legatus, paulo post Venetis magno fusis proelio, beneficientiae memor, interdictum sustulit et civitati restituit sacra. Hoc tandem modo reconciliata urbs in gratiam rediit.

113   Eodem anno copiae in fines Volaterranorum deductae gravissimas contentiones inter Geminianenses ac Volaterranos pro finibus agrorum coortas, de quibus iam simul digladiabantur, removerunt, ac limites agris ex arbitrio posuerunt, ne amplius de his ambigeretur.

114   Extremo eius anni, equites trecenti ac pedites circiter sexcenti[130] Florentia profecti, per medios Arretinorum fines iter facere perrexerunt, ut Tifernatibus sociis et amicis, qui per id tempus ab Arretinis bello premebantur, opem ferrent. Audax coeptum ac paene temerarium finem habuit prosperum: nam cum, relicto ad laevam Arno, in viam Perusinam descendissent et Cortonam versus iter facerent, Arretini, raptis[131] post eos copiis, quia paucitatem spernebant, nullo neque ordine neque duce, sed sola voluntate, ut quisque celeritatis habuit, delati sunt. Ita, rari et imparati ruentes, aliquot ea die detrimenta susceperunt, et ceciderunt praecipui nominis duo: Vannes Tarlati filius e familia nobili, et Uguicio Gherardinus, exul florentinus. Signa militaria Arretinorum tria victores capta retulerunt.

115   Carolus rex secundus hoc anno decessit. Regnum ad Robertum eius filium pervenit. Proxima dehinc aestate, Florentini et socii, contractis undique copiis, in Arretinos duxere. Cum in agrum

In this same period the Florentines sent mounted auxiliaries to the papal legate who was waging war against the Venetians.[86] I have not been able to ascertain whether they did this at his request or of their own accord, in order to promote reconciliation and gain favor. In any case that legate, after beating the Venetians in a great battle, recognized this generous act, lifted the interdict and restored the sacraments to the city. In this way the city was at last reconciled and returned to favor.

In the same year the Florentines marched their troops to the border of Volterra and put a stop to some serious quarrels that had recently turned to blows. These had arisen between the peoples of San Gimignano and Volterra and concerned the borders of their respective territories. The Florentines arbitrated the border dispute so as to remove any further ambiguities.

At the end of this year, 300 knights and about 600 infantry set out from Florence and marched right through the middle of Aretine territory to help their friends and allies, the people of Città di Castello, who were then being hard pressed in a war with the Aretines. It was an audacious, almost rash, plan, but it had a fortunate ending. For, as the Florentines left behind the Arno to the north and came south along the road to Perugia before marching towards Cortona, the Aretines threw a force together and, heedless of its small size, took off after the Florentines. This force had no leader and no battle order; everyone simply went as fast he could as the spirit moved him. They rushed towards the enemy without preparation and in isolation from each other, and as a result suffered no small losses that day. Two men with great reputations fell: the nobleman Vanni, son of Tarlato, and Uguccione Gherardini, a Florentine exile. The victors brought back three Aretine military standards they had captured.[87]

In this year King Charles II died, and the Kingdom passed to his son Robert. The following summer, the Florentines and their allies gathered their forces and marched to Arezzo.[88] When they

112

113

114

115

1310

Arretinum pervenissent, coniunctis Arretinis exulibus, apud Domum Veterem posuerunt castra. Inde crebris proeliis urbem aggressi, expugnare nitebantur.

116   Dum apud Arretium esset Florentinorum exercitus, oratores Herrici, nuper ad imperium delecti, Florentiam venerunt. Hi cum publicum sibi auditorium postulassent, priores civitatis, vocato amplissimorum civium consilio, dicendi quae afferrent fecerunt potestatem. Oratores, pleraque oratione in laudandis tollendisque virtutibus novi principis absumpta, cum verborum grandiloquentia divino simul humanoque consensu provectum tantae dignitatis ad fastigium demonstrassent, tria subinde proposuerunt: adventum eius in Italiam cum validissimo tremendoque exercitu ex invictissimis illis asperrimisque nationibus, proximo tempore futurum; esse praeterea sui propositi Florentiam adire, pacis constituendaeque urbis causa; itaque, parari sibi receptum iam inde commonuere; insuper molestum esse principi Arretinos bello premi, cum si quid ab illis secus atque[132] deberetur admissum fuisset, ad ipsum potius deferendum iudicem,[133] et sic vindictam exposcere conveniat, quam propria auctoritate ultum ire; quapropter, iubere uti discedant ab armis, Arretinosque ultra prosequi desistant.

117   Responsum est oratoribus datum in hunc maxime modum: laetitiae cunctis esse debere talis principis, qualem ipsi praedicent, assumptionem; quod vero nuncietur eiusdem in Italiam transitus cum ferocissimarum gentium exercitu, id porro vix credibile videri: imperatorem romanum tantam vim barbarorum in Italiam, quasi in hostilem terram, adducere; convenire quidem romano principi Italos contra barbaros, non barbaros contra Italos secum trahere; sperare tamen se qua moderatione, qua iustitia esse dicitur, bene

arrived in Aretine territory, they joined forces with the Aretine exiles and pitched camp at Casa Vecchia. From there they attacked the city in pitched battles, trying to capture it.

While the Florentine army was near Arezzo, ambassadors came 116 to Florence from Henry, who had recently been elected as emperor.[89] They requested a public audience and the priors of the city, summoning a council of the most eminent citizens, gave them leave to speak. The ambassadors devoted most of their speech to praising and extolling the virtues of the new prince, demonstrating in copious language that he had been raised to the greatest heights of honor through a combination of human and divine consent. Afterwards, they set out three propositions: [first,] that he was coming to Italy in the near future with a powerful and awesome army composed of men from those tough and unbeatable nations; [second,] that he purposed, furthermore, to come to Florence to impose peace and order on the city, and so recommended that they begin preparations forthwith to receive him; and [third,] that he was deeply displeased that they were making war on the Aretines, since if the latter had done anything amiss, it should have been submitted to him for judgement; it would have been more fitting to beg vengeance of him rather than seek to avenge themselves on their own authority; wherefore, he ordered them to lay down their arms and desist from further persecution of the Aretines.

More or less the following response was made to the ambassa- 117 dors: that everyone should be happy that a prince such as they had described had come to power; but that the announcement of his passing to Italy with an army of ferocious tribesmen seemed scarcely credible; would a Roman emperor bring so large a force of barbarians to Italy, as though into enemy territory? — was it not more appropriate for a Roman emperor to lead Italians against barbarians, not barbarians against Italians? — yet they hoped he would take good care of everything with the moderation and jus-

cuncta provisurum; quod autem sibi Florentiae parari iubeat, super ea re ita provisurum florentinum populum uti saluti dignitatique suae expedire censebit; exercitum vero Arretium misisse ut Arretinos cives, socios et amicos florentini populi, quos diversa factio immaniter pepulisset, in urbem restituerent; huius tam iusti operis causa neminem sibi succensere posse, praesertim cum ea factio quae urbem teneat, pacem fregerit et ultro intulerit bellum et ad tyrannidem eversionemque eius civitatis manifeste contendat; iustum principem, si eam rem cognoverit, laudaturum esse potius Florentinorum factum quam reprehensurum; sed expectare, quoad illi deferantur querelae, in eo certissimam fore sociorum perniciem, quibus postea, etsi cupiat princeps mederi, non possit.

118 Accepto responso, oratores Arretium profecti, ante quam urbem intrarent, in castra pervenerunt. Ibi quoque ex principis auctoritate cum eadem praecepissent, tantum abfuit ut dicto pareretur, ut etiam in ipsorum oculis solito infestius cuncta hostilia contra urbem intentarent. Et oratores quidem novi principis in hunc modum abiere. Florentini vero aliquandiu circa Arretium commorati, tandem, cum vanum appareret expugnationem tentasse, praesidio apud Turritam, duobus fere passuum millibus ab urbe, opportunissimo loco communito, Arretinisque exulibus in eo relictis ut inde bellum inferrent, ipsi vastato circa urbem agro omnibusque vicis exustis Florentiam copias reduxere.

119 Herrici fama per id tempus in dies magis crescebat, variique rumores afferebantur. Etiam ex Germania in Galliam transiisse asseverabant, circaque Rhodanum Lemanumque lacum, audiendis civitatum legationibus comparandisque copiis quas traduceret, immorari. Legati vero frequentes ab Italia ad illum currebant; exules

tice that had been attributed to him. They responded, further-more, that with respect to the command to prepare for his coming, the Florentine People would take such steps as it believed comported with his welfare and dignity; but that they had sent their army to Arezzo to restore Aretine citizens, allies and friends of the Florentine People, to their city after those Aretines had been cruelly expelled by the opposing faction; that no one could take offense at so just a cause, especially as the faction which controlled the city had broken the peace and made war into the bargain, and was manifestly pressing for tyranny and the destruction of that city; that a just prince, if he understood the situation, would rather praise than condemn the act of the Florentines; but that to wait until complaints could be laid before him would most certainly lead to disaster for their allies, after which matters could not be healed, however much the emperor might wish to do so.

Having received this response, the ambassadors set out for Arezzo. Before entering the city, they came to the Florentine camp, and there, too, gave out orders on the authority of the emperor. But the Florentines were so far from obeying his commands that, before the very eyes of the ambassadors, they even threatened hostile action against Arezzo more ferociously than usual. So the ambassadors of the new emperor took their leave. The Florentines spent a little more time near Arezzo, but finally, when it was clear that the siege had been mounted in vain, they established a garrison in a fort near Torrita, about two miles from Arezzo, and left the Aretine exiles there to carry on the war. They themselves laid waste to the land around the city and burned all the villages, then marched back to Florence.[90]

At this time Henry's fame was growing every day, and various rumors were reported. It was even asserted that he had gone from Germany to France, and was staying near the Rhone and Lake Leman, to receive legations from the cities and to raise the troops he would lead across the Alps. Numerous ambassadors

florentini, quoscumque non impediebat egestas, ad eum confluere
dicebantur.

120   In hac suspicione civitas quid agendum foret consultabat. Erant
quibus optimum videretur legationem mittere, ne principis maiorem in modum alienaretur animus; inclinare quidem illius mentem
haud difficile fore, praesertim pecuniarum indigentem, quas ab
exulibus sperare nequaquam possit; barbarorum animos cupiditate
et auro singula metiri. Aliis periculosum id consilium videbatur,
quoniam nomen ipsum imperii alienum inimicumque suis rationibus esset, neque conduceret pacis reconciliationisque auctorem illum assumere, missioque ipsa legatorum hanc praebere ansam videretur. Praeterea, si receptum in urbem petat, quod ante oratores
sui denunciarunt, negaturi ne sint legati an concessuri? Atqui si
negaturi sint, ad manifestam indignationem; si concessuri, ad manifestam perniciem mittere. Nam, si urbem introeat, quis tempe-
raturum confidat?

121   Huius deliberationis cum utraque pars rationem haberet probabilem, utraque suo tempore pervicit. Nam ab initio praevaluit eorum sententia qui mittendam legationem censebant; itaque, non
delecti modo oratores, verum etiam apparatus omnes facti. Ad extremum mutata sententia et non mittere decretum. Inclinavit autem maxime ad id consilium Roberti Siciliae regis cognita voluntas, qui inimico esse animo in Herricum ferebatur. Itaque, perinde
quasi ageretur de partium studiis, huic inhaerendum, illi repu-
gnandum esse statuerunt. Robertus autem ipse haud multo post
Florentiam venit. Redibat autem a pontifice tunc in Gallia com-
morante, a quo, nuperrime defuncto patre Carolo, concessionem
regni coronamque susceperat. Is igitur et sua gratia, quod antea
pistoriensi bello propensissima cognitus fuerat benevolentia in

were streaming to him from all over Italy, and those Florentine exiles not constrained by poverty were said to be flocking to him.

In this state of uncertainty the city took stock of what it should 120
be doing. There were those who thought it would be best to send
a legation of its own so as not to alienate still more the emperor's
attitude; it would not be difficult to influence him (they said), especially as he needed money, which he could have no hope of getting from the exiles; the barbarian mind measured everything by
greed and gold. Others thought this counsel dangerous, since the
very name of empire was alien and inimical to their own system,
and it would be useless for him to take charge of peace and reconciliation; the very act of sending ambassadors would let him get
his foot in the door. Moreover, if he sought to be received into the
city, as his ambassadors had earlier announced, should the ambassadors agree to this or refuse it? If they refused it, it would lead to
manifest anger on his part; if they agreed to it, it would lead to
manifest destruction on theirs. If he should enter the city, who
would trust him to act with moderation?

Since both sides of this debate had some degree of reason, both 121
sides stood in the ascendent for a time. In the beginning those
who favored sending ambassadors prevailed, and the ambassadors
were not only chosen, but all their gear was made ready. In the
end, however, opinion changed, and it was decided not to send
ambassadors. What was most influential in changing their minds
was learning the wishes of King Robert of Sicily, whose attitude to
Henry was reported to be hostile. Thus, once it became a partisan
issue, it was decided to stick with Robert and reject Henry. Robert
himself, in fact, came to Florence soon after. He was returning
from the papal court, at that time based in France, where he had
very recently been granted the crown and investiture of the Kingdom after the death of his father Charles. He was received by the
city with the greatest honor, both thanks to his own popularity,
because he was known to have shown great goodwill towards the

Florentinos, et paterno simul avitoque favore summis honoribus a civitate recipitur. Confirmandis civium animis contra novi principis terrorem simultatibusque tollendis mense fere integro Florentiae commoratus, societatem foedusque renovandi auctor fuit civitatibus adversus Herrici potentiam, et se missurum auxilia, cum tempus expeteret, pollicitus est.

122 Dum haec Florentiae geruntur, Arretini exules, qui in praesidio contra urbem munito relicti erant, quotidianis prope incursibus usque ad Arretii moenia infestabant. Horum[134] assiduam vexationem non ultra ferendam hostes rati, praesidium expugnare adoriuntur. Cum fortiter ab exulibus resisteretur, neque capi praesidium posset, fame et obsidione pervincere constituerunt, putantes (id quod erat) non multum commeatus intra munitiones teneri, sed dietim fere ex proximis castellis, quae ad exules defecerant, importari. Hac igitur fiducia circumsistentes praesidium obsidebant, telisque et machinis oppugnabant.[135] Ob id periculum sociorum, missa rursus a Florentinis auxilia equitum, cum ex amicis oppidis peditem coegissent, liberare obsessos pergunt. Cum iam appropinquarent praesidio, et hi qui obsidebant sese unum in locum conglobassent, exules desertis munitionibus incolumes ad florentinum equitatum evaserunt. Ita, liberati periculo in proxima castella deducuntur. Hostes quoque, incenso ac diruto praesidio, redierunt in urbem. Et bellum quidem ab Arretinis exulibus acriter inferebatur; Florentini vero auxilia submittebant; interdum quoque maioribus copiis profecti, usque ad Arretii moenia infesto agmine populabantur.

123 Ceterum, ab[136] hoc Arretino bello maior insuper cura mentes hominum avocabat. Herricus quidem superatis Alpibus in citeriorem Galliam descendisse nunciabatur, et quidquid ubique fuerat exulum florentinorum ad illum concurrisse, adeo spe firma victoriae ut iam inde bona inimicorum inter se partirentur. Extat

Florentines before the war with Pistoia, and because of the esteem for his father and grandfather. He spent nearly a full month in Florence, settling feuds and strengthening the citizens' resolve against the threat of the new emperor. He took the lead in renewing the alliance and federation among the cities against Henry's power, and promised to send help, if the occasion should demand it.[91]

While this was going on in Florence, the Aretine exiles, who   122 had been left to garrison the fort[92] facing Arezzo, were making raids nearly every day, right up to the walls of the city. The enemy decided it could no longer endure their continual harassment and rose up to attack the fort. The exiles put up brave resistance and the fort could not be captured by force, so they decided to starve them out with a siege, thinking (quite rightly) that they had few provisions inside the fortifications, but brought them in almost on a daily basis from nearby castles which had defected to the exiles. In this belief they surrounded the fort and laid siege to it, attacking it with missiles and siege-engines. The danger to their allies made the Florentines once again send out some mounted auxiliaries, which, when they had rounded up some infantry from friendly towns, went on to free the besieged exiles. As they neared the fort, the besiegers clustered in one place to resist them, whereupon the exiles abandoned the fort and escaped unharmed to the Florentine cavalry. Being thus freed from peril, they were brought to a nearby castle. The enemy, too, having burned and destroyed the fort, returned to Arezzo. Still, the Aretine exiles continued bitterly to make war. The Florentines supplied them with auxiliaries, and would sometimes send larger forces in a marauding column to devastate the land right up to the walls of Arezzo.

But greater concerns were drawing the attention of men away   123 from this Aretine war. The news came that Henry had crossed the Alps and had come down into Lombardy. Florentine exiles were flocking to him from every direction, with such confidence in victory that they were already dividing up among themselves the pos-

Dantis poetae epistola amarissimis referta contumeliis, quam hac inani fiducia exultans, contra Florentinos, ut ipse vocat, intrinsecos scripsit, et quos ante id tempus honorificentissimis compellare solebat verbis, tunc huius spe supra modum elatus, acerbissime insectari non dubitat. Quod equidem nec levitati nec malignitati praestantis ingenio et doctrina viri tribuendum puto, sed tempori: est enim naturae proximum ut victores cum aliqua increpatione verborum ulciscantur. Ille vero in hoc deceptus, quod se iam inde putabat victorem. Exules ergo florentini certa spe tenebantur; civitas autem suspensa metu, comparandis societatibus delectisque habendis oppidisque firmandis, magno opere intendebat. Harum vero conficiendarum rerum facultatem maximam praebuit implicatio hostis, annum fere totum circa Mediolanum et Cremonam et Brixiam commorantis.

124   Principio insequentis anni salutaris provisio facta est a civitate circa exules reducendos. Cum enim magna civium multitudo exularet ac diversa multorum condicio esset, cuncti tamen ad Herricum desiderio reditus cohaesuri viderentur, ad minuendam eam manum, placuit decreto publico revocare eos, quorum nec insigne odium in praesentem rei publicae statum nec periculosa reductio foret. Prioribus igitur potestas a populo tradita uti una cum duodecim viris a se delectis nominationes facerent eorum qui reducendi ab exilio viderentur pacique et concordiae civium providerent.

125   Fuit tunc in numero priorum Baldus Agulio iurisperitus. Is privatim odio in quosdam accensus, ut est id genus hominum subtile ac maleficum, deprehendit posse etiam in beneficio populi locum esse nocendi, si non ii nominarentur quibus dabatur beneficium, sed ii et ipsorum genera quibus adimebatur ut sic perpetua illis nota inureretur. Hac itaque mente formulam provisionis sic insti-

sessions of their enemies. A letter of the poet Dante is extant, filled with the bitterest insults, which he wrote against what he calls 'intrinsic Florentines'[93] while exulting in this hope. Elated beyond measure by his expectation of success, he does not hesitate to attack in the most violent language the men whom previously he used to address in the most honorable terms. I think this should not be set down to frivolity or malignity, since we are dealing with a man of exceptional intellect and learning, but rather to the times. It is not unnatural for victors to take their revenge with a certain amount of scornful talk. Indeed, he was deceived in thinking himself already a victor. The Florentine exiles were borne up in confident hope, while the City hung on a thread of fear, making great efforts to muster its alliances, levy troops, and strengthen its towns. The entanglements of the enemy, who spent nearly a year around Milan, Cremona and Brescia, gave them a great opportunity to make preparations of this kind.[94]

At the beginning of the following year, the city made a salutary provision concerning the restoration of exiles. A great number of citizens had been exiled for many different reasons, yet it seemed that all of them were siding with Henry out of hope of restoration. To reduce this number, it was decided to recall by public decree those who had no great quarrel with the present regime and whose return presented no threat. The People therefore gave the priors, and a board of twelve men selected by them, the power to nominate persons who might be brought back from exile, and to provide for the peace and harmony of the citizens. 124
1311

One of the priors at that time was the jurist Baldo D'Aguglione.[95] He nursed private grudges against certain persons, and, as is the way with this subtle and malicious sort of person, he discovered an opportunity to cause harm even in a popular act of amnesty. He realized that if they named, not those who were being given the amnesty, but those to whom it was being denied, that the latter would be branded with perpetual infamy. He designed 125

tuit ut et reditum ab exilio et cetera pacis concordiaeque beneficia omnibus tribueret, praeter eos qui exciperentur. Ita in prima legis parte qua beneficium datur, neminem expressit; in secunda vero qua adimitur, nomina singulorum et familias longo et sinuoso ordine per tribus annotavit. Ea res posteris temporibus multis nocumento fuit.

126   Exulum igitur pars beneficio populi revocata in urbem rediit; alia pars reiecta in exilio remansit. In ea fuerunt omnes iam inde post primi adventum Caroli ex prioribus illis seditionibus exules, quorum nemini penitus lex prospexit, et praeterea recens pulsi, quos vocitarunt albos; horum longe mitior erat causa. Denique, non studio partium contra istos, sed privatis fere simultatibus certabatur. Itaque, horum pars tunc restituta in urbem rediit; pars vero omnino reiecta, in qua Circulorum, Adimariorum et Tosingorum, vel guelfissimarum quondam gentium, aliqui remanserunt; filii praeterea Baldi Ruffoli, quem primum vexilliferum iustitiae fuisse ostendimus, fratres insuper et nepotes Iani Labella, Dantes Alagherii, Palmerius Altovita et alii permulti ex nobilitate et plebe, quos nominare longum esset.[137]

127   Post haec renovata societas est inter civitates. Fuerunt autem hae: Florentini, Lucenses, Senenses, Pistorienses, Volaterrani et ceteri qui in superiore societate nominantur. Accesserunt Tifernates et Bononienses et horum omnium[138] princeps, Robertus Siciliae rex. Hi omnes unanimiter foederati bellum contra novum principem aperte[139] susceperunt.

the form of the provision with this in mind, so that return from exile and other benefits of peace and harmony would be granted to everyone, except those who were being excluded. Thus in the first part of the law where the amnesty is given, no one is named, but in the second part where it is being taken away, he gave a long and tortuous list of the names, by parish, of each individual and their family. This act was a great source of harm to many people in later times.[96]

Thus a part of the exiles returned to the city after being recalled 126 by the amnesty of the People; another part that had been rejected remained in exile. In the latter group were all those who long ago, after the coming of Charles I, had become exiles as a result of those earlier revolts; not a single one of these were taken into consideration by the law. There were in addition those men known as the Whites, who had been more recently banished; their case was much milder. Opposition to them came not from partisanship but from private feuds. Thus, part of this group were restored and returned to the city, but part was completely rejected, including some of the Cerchi, Adimari and Tosinghi[97] — who at one time were considered the most Guelf of all clans — as well as the sons of Baldo Ruffolo (who as we have shown was the first Standard-Bearer of Justice), the brothers and nephews of Giano della Bella, and Dante Alighieri, Palmieri Altoviti, and many other commoners and noblemen too numerous to name.[98]

After this the alliance among the cities was renewed. This in- 127 cluded the peoples of Florence, Lucca, Siena, Pistoia, Volterra, and the others named in the earlier alliance.[99] In addition there were the peoples of Città di Castello and Bologna. King Robert of Sicily was their leader. All these peoples, united in purpose, joined together to embark upon open war with the new emperor.

Note on the Text and Translation

᛭᛬᛭

The Latin text of Bruni's *History of the Florentine People* survives in about sixty manuscripts and has been printed three times, in editions by Sixtus Bruno (1610), by a commission of the Accademia di Scienze, Lettere ed Arti of Arezzo (1855–60), and by Emilio Santini for the series *Rerum Italicarum Scriptores* (1914–26).[1] None of these editions can be considered a proper critical edition and none of the three includes a critical apparatus. Sixtus Bruno used two manuscripts, one of which was certainly Pal. lat. 941 (*P*); the other has not been identified. The Aretine Commission, despite claims to the contrary, simply reproduced the 1610 edition. Santini's edition represented an improvement in most respects on the two previous texts. He located twenty-five codices of the *History* and was able to identify two of them (*B* and *L*) as codices that had once belonged to the Florentine Signoria. His edition of Books I–VI is in principle based on Bologna Univ. 353 (*B*), while Books VII–XII follow *L*, Laur. 65, 4 (the second half of a codex whose first half is Laur. 65, 3). One must say 'in principle', because in fact Santini sometimes gives the reading of the Aretine Commission text instead of *B*, probably through inadvertence.[2] Santini's text, moreover, is marred by numerous typographical errors as well as by silent conjectural emendations, most of which are superfluous.

The text presented in this volume cannot claim to be a critical edition as there has been no attempt to survey the manuscript tradition as a whole nor to construct a full recension of the witnesses. My aim has been simply to provide a reliable working edition to serve as a basis for the translation. The text of Santini has been corrected against the selection of authoritative manuscripts listed below; these, owing to the circumstances of their transmission, are

highly likely to be close to the author's archetype if not direct copies of it.

Collation of these witnesses[3] has disclosed that Santini's working assumption in preparing his edition was flawed. Santini assumed that, given its provenance, B could serve as a *codex optimus* because it was almost certainly a direct copy of the author's archetype. Although there is reason to believe Santini was correct in his assessment of the importance of B (and his case is made even stronger by the presence of occasional corrections in Bruni's own hand, which Santini did not recognize as such), it does not follow that B represents the final state of Bruni's text. In fact, as in the case of Bruni's other works, the textual tradition reveals a long process of correction and redaction.[4] It is moreover likely that, in accordance with Renaissance practice, not all of Bruni's own authorial interventions subsequent to the circulation of the earliest version of his text were entered in his own archetype; some of them may only be preserved in the form of authorial *correctio* in presentation copies.

The assumption of the present working edition, based partly on paleographical and partly on internal textual grounds, is that B represents the earliest version of the text, possibly a redaction to be associated with the numerous six-volume copies of the text. P, on the other hand, seems in numerous places to represent a more polished version of the text. CM agree more frequently with P than with B, while F is closer to B. A complication is added by the evident fact that P was copied from an uncorrected or partly corrected intermediary of B. I have nevertheless treated all five witnesses as independent copies of the archetype, which seems to be the only prudent course until a full recension of witnesses has been constructed. Where BF and CMP disagree, I have generally followed the readings of what I take to be the later stage of the tradition.

The more obvious errors in Santini's edition have been corrected silently, though I have occasionally given his readings or conjectures where they might conceivably be of use to reader. Capitalization and punctuation have been modernized, as has been Bruni's orthography, with the exception of proper names. In the case of the latter I give Bruni's spelling in the Latin text but the modern English or Italian form of the name in the translation.

The translation of Donato Acciaiuoli (1473), though quite free, is of course not irrelevant to establishing the text.[5] This volgare version survives in nineteen manuscripts and five printed editions. I have consulted Acciaiuoli's version in preparing my own English version, and occasionally noted instances where Acciaiuoli's text corroborates a reading of the Latin witnesses. I have also made use of Renée Neu Watkin's translation of the Preface, Book I, and Giano della Bella's speech from Book IV,[6] often following her rendering word-for-word where it seemed to me felicitous. The source notes are heavily indebted to those in Santini's edition as well as to the works of Robert Davidsohn and Anna Maria Cabrini cited in the Bibliography.

ABBREVIATIONS

B   Bologna, Biblioteca Universitaria MS 358, written by the Florentine scribe Antonio di Mario in 1429, probably for the Florentine Signoria, with marginal corrections in Bruni's hand. It is the oldest dated manuscript. Possibly one of the two manuscripts of the six-book version owned by the Signoria and identified as in the possession of Pope Eugene IV in an inventory notice of 1444 (Florence, Archivio di Stato, Carte di Corredo, vol. 65, f. 34v). See also A. C. de la Mare, "New Research on Humanistic Scribes in Florence," in Annarosa Garzelli, ed., *Miniatura Fiorentina del Rinascimento, 1440–1525: Un*

primo censimento (Florence, 1985), p. 482; *Repertorium Brunianum*, no. 164.

C   Florence, Biblioteca Mediceo-Laurenziana Plut. 65, 5, copied *ex originali* by Antonio di Mario in 1444, probably for Cosimo de'Medici; it carries the ex-libris of Piero de'Medici, who had acquired it at the latest by 1456. See F. Ames-Lewis, *The Library and Manuscripts of Piero di Cosimo de'Medici* (New York: Garland, 1984), pp. 289–90; de la Mare, "New Research," p. 482; *Repertorium Brunianum*, no. 518.

F   Florence, Biblioteca Mediceo-Laurenziana Plut. 65, 3, containing books I-VI only, copied by Giovanni da Stia and Antonio di Mario (both copyists who worked closely with Bruni) probably for the Florentine Signoria. Only the second half of this copy (Plut. 65, 4 = Santini's L), containing books VII-XII, was collated by Santini for his edition. See de la Mare, "New Research", pp. 483–84, 499; *Repertorium Brunianum*, no. 516.

M   Florence, Biblioteca Mediceo-Laurenziana, Ashburnham 869. Florence, 1430s. See *Repertorium Brunianum*, no. 650.

P   Vatican City, Biblioteca Apostolica Vaticana MS Pal. Lat. 941, owned by Bruni's student Giannozzo Manetti. See *Repertorium Brunianum*, no. 2626.

Acc   The Italian translation of 1473 by Donato Acciaiuoli

Sant   The text of Emilio Santini

NOTES

1. For fuller bibliographical information on the manuscripts, see my *Repertorium Brunianum: A Critical Guide to the Writings of Leonardo Bruni*, Istituto Storico Italiano per il Medio Evo, Fonti per la Storia dell'Italia Medievale, Subsidia 5 (Rome, 1997).

2. Hence the occasional correspondences of *Sant* with *P*.

3. As indicated in the Introduction, the collations were done by my assistant, Paola Tartakoff. I have, however, verified against microfilm copies of the witnesses all the variants she has identified.

4. See my study "Remarks on the Textual Tradition of Leonardo Bruni's *Epistulae familiares*," *Filologia umanistica per Gianvito Resta*, ed. V. Fera and G. Ferraú, 3 vols. (Messina, 1997), vol. II, pp. 1023–62.

5. On Acciaiuoli's sources for this text, see Rosella Bessi, "Un traduttore al lavoro: Donato Acciaiuoli e l'elaborazione del volgarizzamento delle *Historiae*," in *Leonardo Bruni Cancelliere della Repubblica di Firenze*, ed. P. Viti (Florence, 1990), pp. 321–338.

6. Published in *Humanism and Liberty: Writings on Freedom from Fifteenth-century Florence*, tr. Renée Neu Watkins (Columbia, South Carolina, 1978).

Notes to the Text

❧❧❧

1. convenirent C
2. multo *Sant*
3. nominumque *Sant*
4. quaque *M, Sant*
5. eius *CM*

BOOK I

1. honoresque et *P*
2. proxima *P*
3. admixto *C*: admisso *before correction in P*
4. quietos *P, Sant*
5. instituere *CMP*
6. in dies *omitted in BF*
7. ostiis *M*: hostiis *BCFP*: ostis *Sant*
8. Roma *sic P: before correction in B, as it would appear*
9. vero *added superscript by another hand in P*
10. consiliumque *P*
11. et *Sant*
12. ego tibi *BCFMP*: tibi ego *Sant, Virgil*
13. incolit *Virgil*
14. insedit *Virgil*
15. superbo *Virgil*
16. huius *BF*
17. *omitted in C*
18. Romanae *P*
19. ferme *P*
20. ipsis *P*
21. discursiones *C*
22. actum *P*
23. ferunt *in P, after correction:* sunt *BCFM*
24. *cancelled by another hand in P, as it would seem*
25. in proelio *BF*
26. Manilium *MSS*: Mamilius Octavius Tusculus *Livy*
27. Manlius *Sant, Livy*
28. dixit *BF*
29. reliquis *CM*
30. tum *BF*
31. conferto *Sant*
32. tamen *C*
33. tum *F*
34. hostium *P, Sant*
35. lenta *CM*
36. opes Etruscorum *BF, Sant*
37. -rato *MSS*
38. et quos odissent *added in the margin of B, omitted by P*

39. tandem *P, and B before correction, as it would appear*

40. est *omitted in CP, Sant: added in the margin of B*

41. -erant *BF*

42. *omitted in P, added in the margin of B*

43. *omitted in BCF*

44. temporibus *P, Sant*

45. implent *F*

46. animis *P, Sant:* armis *BCFM*

47. quidem *C*

48. -erat *BCP*

49. incoluerunt *after correction in C*

50. Meot(h)idam *MP*

51. *I should prefer* Illyricoque

52. missi *P*

53. Romanorum *CFM, omitted by P, added in the margin of B in Bruni's hand, as it appears*

54. ac ut – obtinuit *omitted in BC*

55. *i.e.* Amalasuntha

56. saevitate *P*

57. Urbes multas – delevit *omitted in BC, Sant, added in the margin of F*

58. fere *M*

59. *i.e.* Clephonem

60. atque *BFM*

61. sibi *M, Sant, omitted in BCFP*

62. populus ro. *P, B before correction*

63. meruit *F*

64. eo *P*

65. in tempore *P, B before correction*

66. superfuerunt *P, B before correction*

67. in dies *omitted in BCF*

68. *i.e.* Tarquinii

69. *i.e.* Capena

70. *i.e.* Falerii

71. -que *omitted in F: added in the margins of BCM*

72. splendore *P, B before correction*

73. et olim *M*

74. autem *P*

75. autem *P*

76. fontem *F*

77. omnibus *F*

78. huius *P*

79. sibi *after* quod *in P, erased in B, as it would seem*

80. favebant *P, before correction in B, as it would seem*

81. ipsa *P:* ipse *BCFM*

82. modo *MSS:* motu *Sant*

BOOK II

1. ad honoris antecellentiam *P*

2. ingred- *P*

3. igitur *C*

4. subitanea *after* expeditio *M*

5. habitandum *P*

6. hostes *FP*] hostem *BC*

7. florentini populi]
Florentinorum *P*

8. gubernabant *P*

9. cura *F*

10. Aldobrandini *P*

11. Florentini *Sant*

12. Senenses *Sant*

13. legitimus *B*

14. creditur extinctus *transposed
in B*

15. sese *M*

16. animi *Sant*

17. commoverunt *P*

18. providentur *BM, after
correction in F*: providerentur *P*

19. angerent *BF*

20. totam *Sant*

21. aperte *P*

22. Farinata *P*

23. filio *F*

24. nostra *P*

25. referatur *C*

26. iam *before* inde *P*

27. ampla spe rem] amplam
spem *F*

28. *corrected from* propriorem *in
CFP*

29. -que] quoque *F*

30. decurritur *Sant*

31. quot *BFMP*: quod *Sant*

32. celerissima *MSS*

33. tandem *P*

34. opem *P*

35. complures *Sant*

36. Silvani *P*

37. partium *P*

38. de consilii temeritate *omitted
in BF, Sant*

39. exprimere *Sant*

40. nobis *P*

41. de me *added in the margin of
B, omitted by P*

42. temporis *F*

43. hostes *Sant*

44. ego igitur *transposed by Sant*

45. hostes *Sant*

46. dum si *BC, Sant*

47. magis *omitted in P, added in
the margin of B (perhaps in
Bruni's hand)*

48. esse *P*

49. experiundum *BP*

50. et *BCF*

51. Quid *Sant*

52. procedat *Sant*

53. hominum *omitted in BCF*

54. diffisae *BF*

55. *thus MSS: one should perhaps
read* quidam

56. nec *Sant*

57. vero *C*

58. sint *P, Sant*

59. ipsos *omitted in P, Sant*

60. haec *M*

61. -quimur *C*

62. inquis *Sant*

63. eos *omitted by Sant*

64. petiamur *Sant*

65. nunc *P*
66. tamen *Sant*
67. mercede *omitted in BCF, Sant*
68. viderentur *BCF*
69. vix *BM, Sant*] vis *FP*
70. illis *CF*
71. nunc *F*
72. tradant *BCFM*
73. pontifex *after* quartus *B*
74. Gallus *Sant*
75. sunt *after* agitataque *C*
76. novatus *P*
77. ipsiusque *M*
78. vix tum *Sant*
79. *omitted in BCF*
80. -que *omitted in P*
81. erat *Sant*
82. nostris *F*
83. omnis *BPM*] eius *F*: hominis *Sant*
84. hostium *F*
85. subierunt *added in the margin by another hand in M*
86. degentes *C*
87. iam inde] commode *P*
88. appareret aequitas *transposed in B*
89. factum *Sant*
90. cum *post* postridie *Sant*
91. divisa *BFM*] diversa *P, Sant*
92. armaque *BFM*] et arma *P, Sant*
93. nobilem *P*
94. praeferenda *after correction in M*: anteferre *BCFP*
95. manus *Sant*
96. modo *omitted in BCF*
97. inficiam ego *Sant*
98. pervenire *BCF*
99. exulibus *omitted in BCFP, Sant*
100. indictum *Sant, before correction in F*
101. circum *after correction in M*: circa *BCFP, Sant*; cuncta *omitted in C*
102. ut *P*
103. castra *P*
104. *corrected from* Mutronem *in B*

BOOK III

1. hos et *transposed in MP*
2. pacataque *F*
3. favere *Sant*
4. exemplo *P, Sant*
5. exteram *F (after correction)*
6. circum *BFM*] citra *P*: circa *Sant*
7. totus *Sant*
8. eventis *Sant*
9. miserat *P, Sant*
10. Magna *P*
11. *omitted in BF, Sant*
12. radicibus *Sant*
13. favore *P*

14. intenderant *B*
15. ipsum *omitted in MP*
16. propius *M, after correction in P*: proprius *BF, Sant*: più dapresso *Acc*
17. quo *BF*
18. inulto *Sant*
19. maximo *Sant*
20. quorum *BF*
21. commonent *BCF*
22. nobis illorum *transposed in Sant*
23. ergo *MP*
24. *omitted in Sant*
25. tua benignità *Acc*
26. in se *Sant*
27. contemni a se dictas *BF*
28. bonaque quae *Sant*
29. integre *P*
30. fere *omitted in BF*
31. qui *Sant*
32. Ut quoque *Sant*
33. Latinus *after* viam *MP*
34. exinde *M*
35. viros *P*: virorum *Sant*
36. praeessent *Sant*
37. dubitabatur *Sant*
38. fuerunt *MP*
39. iudicare *F*
40. ob *Sant*
41. complures *P, Sant*
42. queant *BF*
43. pupillasque *BFM*

44. -ve *Sant*
45. habeatur *Sant*
46. in Italiam *omitted in BF*
47. -ret *Sant*
48. amicorum *omitted in BF*
49. cum *BF*
50. ictum est foedus *BF*
51. autem *BF*
52. Lucanos *BF*
53. habuissent *P*
54. certissime *M*
55. imminentis *F*
56. ipse *omitted in BF*
57. oppugnati *P*
58. ac *MSS*: a *Sant*
59. hostem *Sant*
60. intrarunt *BFM*
61. et *BF*
62. -sent *BFM*
63. dimisere *BFM*
64. dominantes *Sant*
65. fuit *added by Sant*
66. incendio ... coorto *P*
67. quod *Sant*
68. -erunt *P*
69. fieri *omitted in BF*
70. praesertim *omitted in P, Sant*
71. citissime *Sant*
72. a victoribus *omitted in P*
73. belli *P*
74. se ne *Sant*
75. cum praesertim *Sant*
76. inter *P*

BOOK IV

1. circa *Sant*
2. propterea *F*
3. expertem *Sant*
4. sunt *P, Sant: C before correction*
5. autem *F*
6. cedentem *M*
7. hostes *Sant*
8. primo impetu *P, BC before correction*
9. cedentes *Sant*
10. Sin autem *F*
11. -erunt *CF, B before correction.*
12. Florentiam *P*
13. fuisse *C*
14. paene *C*
15. necaretur *P*
16. -erant *MP*
17. illi quandoque] aliquando *P*
18. creari *P*
19. vocantur *P*
20. videbantur *CP*
21. *omitted by Sant*
22. recusarent] noluissent *added in the margin by another hand in F*
23. -retur *P, Sant*
24. *Sant corrects to* ab
25. octavum *P:* octavo *BCFM, Sant*
26. iuniarum *P*
27. graviter *P*
28. Pisas *P*
29. prudentissimus *F*
30. veluti honesta *P*
31. paraturos *F*
32. ut *P: B before correction*
33. ac *BCF*
34. tuas *Sant*
35. nostra *P*
36. -iores *Sant*
37. -iores *P, Sant*
38. restituendae *P*
39. om. *CF: added in the margin of B*
40. -iores *P, Sant*
41. -iores *Sant*
42. et *Sant*
43. alacres *Sant*
44. nobis *P, Sant*
45. prima illa *FMP:* illa prima *B:* prima *omitted in C*
46. -erunt *P, B before correction, Sant*
47. quoque *after* ipsi *P*
48. Guadagnius *M:* Guadagnus *BCF:* Guadignius *P*
49. proprias vires *BCF, Sant*
50. quam *P:* quem *BCFM:* quae *Sant (perhaps correctly)*
51. nunc *P*
52. licet *P*
53. -bantur *Sant*
54. -erant *F, Sant:* -erat *BCMP*
55. -erant *F, Sant:* -erat *BMCF*
56. tunc bello pisano *BCF, Sant*
57. castris *P, B before correction (as it would appear)*
58. captisque *P*

59. adversum *P*

60. -erat *MP*

61. redigerant *P*

62. *omitted by Sant*

63. moveret] movere posset *C*

64. saxis – communiverat *omitted by BCF, Sant*

65. *omitted by MP*

66. electus *P*

67. *corrected to* coeptus *by Sant*

68. *corrected to* eum *by Sant*

69. divisae domus *omitted by Sant*

70. Itaque *F*

71. subitus *F*

72. -que *omitted in P*

73. tandem *BCF*

74. reclinaret *P*

75. *added by Sant*

76. illis *Sant*

77. vocarentur *P, BM before correction*

78. *corrected to* nigri *by Sant*

79. placandam *Sant*

80. Etruriam *M*

81. ei *Sant*

82. magistratus *Sant*

83. devenit *Sant*

84. fores *Sant*

85. rediit *P*

86. expelli *P*

87. vi *Sant*

88. tamen *C*

89. ipse] et ipse *P*

90. aequis *MSS*] ab eis *Sant*

91. circa *BCM*

92. quae *Sant*

93. evocarunt *P, B before correction, Sant*

94. Inarmis *CF:* Inarcus *P:* Nanni *Acc*

95. modiorum *P, Sant*

96. pacandum *BCF, Sant*

97. eos *MP*

98. illo *Sant*

99. in *omitted in P*

100. transmissas *BCF, Sant*

101. redierunt *P, Sant*

102. est *omitted in P:* est lapideus *C*

103. videbantur *BCF*

104. tunc ibi *BF:* ibi tum *M:* ibi tunc *P:* ibi *omitted in C*

105. intendunt *MSS: corrected to* intenderent *by Sant*

106. committens *Sant*

107. copias *after* locis *M: omitted by BCFP, Sant*

108. *corrected to* pulsos *by Sant, perhaps correctly*

109. putant Bononiensium *BF* (Bonon. *added in the margin of* B): putabant Bonon. *C:* Bonon. putant *MP, Sant*

110. Tosolanus *BCFM:* Tolosanus *P, Sant:* Tolosano *Acc*

111. Tosolanus *BCFM:* Tolosanus *P, Sant:* Tolosano *Acc*

112. proficere *BF, C before correction*

113. pauciorem *Sant, perhaps correctly*
114. prosecuti *Sant*
115. pontificem *P*
116. enim *P*
117. patrocinium *P*
118. episcopum *F*
119. sequentis *P, Sant*
120. permanserat *P*
121. aliquantum circa *P, Sant*
122. substinerent *P, Sant*
123. regnantibus *P*
124. bellum *P*
125. enim iam pridem *P*
126. iniuncta *BCF*

127. *BCF transposes* multitudo *after* convenit
128. qui] qui et *P*
129. sociorum antiquorum *BCF*
130. *corrected to* sexcenti *by Sant:* sexcentos *MSS*
131. captis *C, Sant*
132. quam *P, Sant*
133. iudicium *Sant*
134. Hanc *Sant*
135. impugnabant *P, Sant*
136. ob *C*
137. est *Sant*
138. omnia *Sant*
139. unanimiter *C*

Notes to the Translation

❦❧❦

1. The town known in modern times as Fiesole, situated on a mountain overlooking Florence in the Arno valley below.

2. Cicero, *Catilinarian Orations* II, 9, 20; III, 6, 14; *Pro Murena* 24, 40.

3. The Latin word for allies is *socii*, hence 'Social War'.

4. A province known today as the Marche.

5. Florus, *Epitome* II, 6.

6. Pliny the Elder, *Natural History* III, 5.

7. Cicero, *Catilinarian Orations* II, 9, 20.

8. Sallust, *The Catilinarian Conspiracy* 24, 2; 27, l; 30, 1.

9. Cicero, *Catilinarian Orations* II, 9, 20.

10. Sallust, *The Catilinarian Conspiracy* 24, 2; 27, l; 30, 1. Pistorium is the modern city of Pistoia.

11. In his *Epistula* X, 5 (ed. Mehus), Bruni identifies the sources from which he has reconstructed Etruscan history: chiefly Livy, but also Plutarch, Virgil, Servius, Horace, Pliny, and Dionysius of Halicarnassus.

12. I.e. their art of divining the future from the flight of birds.

13. Livy V, 33.

14. *Aeneid* VIII, 475–482.

15. Compare Cicero, *De legibus* I, 1, 4–5.

16. Livy I, 2.

17. Livy V, 34.

18. Livy I, 8.

19. Livy IX, 36.

20. Livy, I, 14.

21. Ibid.

22. Livy I, 23, 24, 26.

23. Livy I, 42.

24. Livy I, 55, 60; II, 6, 7, 9.

25. Livy, II, 10, 11. Bruni gives a deflationary version of a famous story from Livy, which describes how Horatius Cocles sacrificed himself in a single-handed defense of the Pons Sublicius, thus giving his countrymen the chance to destroy it behind him and save themselves from the Etruscan attack.

26. Livy, II, 12, 13. Bruni alludes again to a famous story: the Roman youth Mucius Scaevola was said to have stolen into the Etruscan camp with the aim of assassinating Lars Porsenna, but killed the king's secretary instead by mistake. Captured, he showed his indifference to torture by thrusting his right hand into a fire (hence his name 'Scaevola', 'left-handed').

27. Traditionally the northern side of the Tiber between Trastevere and the Borgo.

28. Livy II, 14, 15.

29. Livy II, 42–43, 45, 47, 49–52.

30. Livy IV, 58.

31. Livy, V, 1, 19, 20, 24.

32. The Lacus Vadimonis, now drained, stood between Orte and Bomarzo; Sutri was a small Etruscan town 45 kilometers northwest of Rome.

33. Livy V, 27, 31, 34.

34. Livy VI, 4; IX, 37.

35. The following passage may be compared to a similar passage in Bruni's earlier (1403/4) *Laudatio Florentinae urbis*, ed. S. U. Baldassarri (Florence, 2000), pp. 16–19.

36. Seneca, *On Clemency* I, 11, 2.

37. Orosius, *Against the Pagans* I, 16; VI, 2, 16; VII, 23, 4.

38. Ibid. VII, 28.

39. The battle of Hadrianople, 9 August 378 A.D.

40. Ibid. VII, 34–36

41. Such was the date traditional in Florence, about which Bruni expresses doubt immediately below. The correct date, 23 August 406, is noted by Davidsohn, *Storia*, I, 61.

42. A footrace was held on the feast of St Reparata in Florence on October 8 in honor of Stilico's victory over Radagaisus; see Giovanni Villani, *Cronica* III, 85, and Davidsohn, *Storia*, VII, 569.

43. Orosius, *Against the Pagans* VII, 37.

44. Ibid. VII, 37.

45. Ibid. VII, 40; compare Virgil, *Aeneid* VIII, 334, "Fortuna omnipotens et ineluctabile fatum," a line much brooded over by Petrarch.

46. Orosius, *Against the Pagans* VII, 38–43; Petrus Diaconus, *Roman History* XII, 14; XIV, 2, 8.

47. Ibid. XIV, 2.

48. St Leo I, called 'the Great', reigned A.D. 440–461.

49. Ibid. XIV, 5–12.

50. Ibid. XIV, 16–19.

51. Ibid. XV, 8.

52. I.e., the Ostrogoths

53. Near modern Trieste.

54. Petrus Diaconus, *Roman History* XVI, 12; Procopius, *Gothic War* I, 4. For questions regarding Bruni's use of Procopius, see Cabrini, "Le *Historiae* del Bruni," pp. 262–63. Cabrini instead identifies the source of the passage regarding Totila immediately following as the continuator of Marcellinus Comes, in Marcellinus Comes, *Chronicon . . . cum additamento ad annum DXLVIII*, in *Chronica minora*, Monumenta Germaniae Historica, Auctores antiquissimi XI.2 (Berlin, 1894), p. 108.

55. Petrus Diaconus, *Roman History* XVI, 14.

56. Ibid. XVI, 22; Procopius, *Gothic War* III, 20, 22; Giovanni Villani, *Nuova Cronica*, ed. G. Porta (Parma, 1990), III, 3.

57. Petrus Diaconus, *History of the Lombards* II, 5.

58. Ibid. II, 4, 25

59. Ibid. II, 28.

60. Hadrian I, reigned 772–795 A.D. Charles the Great is better known as Charlemagne.

61. Leo III, reigned A.D. 795–816, who transferred the Roman Empire to the Franks.

62. Ibid II, 28 and Giovanni Villani, *Cronica*, III, 13, 15.

63. Einhard, *Life of Charlemagne*, 5–7, 10, 13, 25, 28.

64. Giovanni Villani, *Cronica*, III, 15.

65. Giovanni Villani, *Cronica* IV, 1–4; Procopius, *Gothic War* III, 20, 22.

66. One of the defining marks of a city-state (*civitas*) according to Roman law is the possession of a territory (*ager*).

67. Giovanni Villani, *Cronica* II, 9–19.

68. Ibid. VI, 38, 39.

69. Frederick II (1194–1250), of the House of Hohenstaufen, king of Germany and Holy Roman Emperor. He was the grandson of Frederick I Barbarossa and the son of Henry VI.

70. Honorius III (reigned 1216–27); Gregory IX (reigned 1227–41); and Innocent IV (reigned 1243–54).

71. Ibid. VII, 14, 15–25, 33–34.

BOOK II

1. I.e., men belonging to the Ghibelline party. Bruni usually, but not always, denotes the Ghibellines with the phrase 'the opposite faction', probably out of a fastidious desire to avoid the barbarous word 'Ghibelline'; this is an example of 'the harsh-sounding names that . . . hardly allow of elegant treatment', mentioned in Pr. 2.

2. Giovanni Villani, *Cronica*, VII, 39, 42.

3. Ibid. VII, 43.

4. Ibid. VII, 47, 48.

5. Ibid. VII, 49.

6. Ibid. VII, 51, 52.

7. Ibid. VII, 55. See Florence, Archivio di Stato (hereafter ASF), Archivio della Repubblica, Capitoli XXIX, ff. 348–353 (cited by Santini) which is the probable source for Bruni's precise knowledge of the terms.

8. Giovanni Villani, *Cronica* VII, 56, 57. Compare Bruni, *Laudatio*, p. 26.

9. Ibid. VII, 58.

10. The building is now known as the Bargello, and contains the National Museum of Sculpture. Villani gives the date of its construction as 1250 (VII, 39).

11. Compare Marchionne di Coppo Stefani, *Cronaca fiorentina*, ed. N. Rodolico (Città di Castello, 1903), rbr. 110.

12. I.e., for their podestà, the chief legal officer of the town.

13. ASF, Archivio della Repubblica, Capitoli XXIX, f. 189 (cited by Santini).

14. Ibid.

15. The Holy Roman Emperor Frederick II.

16. Innocent IV (reigned 1243–1254), born Sinibaldo Fieschi of Genoa.

17. I.e., the Kingdom of Naples in southern Italy and Sicily, usually referred to in early Italian sources simply as the *Regno* or "the Kingdom."

18. Giovanni Villani, *Cronica* VII, 41, 44, 45.

19. A region of southern Italy north of Taranto, roughly identical with the modern province of Basilicata.

20. Alexander IV (reigned 1254–1261), born Rinaldo, count of Segni, a nephew of Gregory IX.

21. Giovanni Villani, *Cronica* VII, 46.

22. Ibid. VII, 62, 63.

23. Ibid. VII, 66.

24. I.e., persons belong to the social class referred to as the *popolo*. See Introduction, p. xiv.

25. Giovanni Villani, *Cronica* VII, 65.

26. ASF, Archivio della Repubblica, Capitoli XXIX, f. 318 (cited by Santini).

27. Giovanni Villani, *Cronica* VII, 74.

28. Stefani, *Cronica*, rbr. 130.

29. Giovanni Villani, *Cronica* VII, 74.

30. Ibid. VII, 75.

31. I.e., the campaigning season, which lasted generally from May till November.

32. Ibid. VII, 76.

33. Ibid. VII, 77.

34. Cicero, *Familiar Letters* 6.4.1; Livy 10.28.

35. Spedito, a populano who was serving as one of the Anziani; see Davidsohn, *Storia*, II, 690–91.

36. The Abati family were prominent Florentine Ghibellines of the magnate class. Bocca was the son of Ranieri Rustici; on him see Davidsohn, *Storia*, II, 693.

37. Giovanni Villani identifies him as Jacopo del Nacca de' Pazzi.

38. This was the Florentine *carroccio*, a great wooden cart used to carry the city's battle standard and guarded by a special body of picked troops. It was the republican equivalent of a king's personal horse-guards; similar carts were widely used as civic symbols by citizen armies in central and northern Italy from the eleventh century to the fourteenth century.

39. Giovanni Villani, *Cronica* VII, 78, 79.

40. Lit. 'their household gods', a classical touch.

41. Usually known as the battle of Montaperti, though referred to by Bruni as 'the battle of the Arbia'. Dante mentions it in *Inferno* X, 85–86, as 'lo strazio e il grande scempio che fece l'Arbia colorato in rosso.'

42. Ibid. VII, 79.

43. Ibid. VII, 81.

44. Ibid. VII, 82–83.

45. Ibid. VII, 85.

46. Stefani, *Cronica*, rbr. 132.

47. I.e., by the Modenese Guelfs.

48. Giovanni Villani, *Cronica* VII, 86.

49. I.e. Cisalpine Gaul, which in Roman geographical parlance refers to Italy north of the Apennines.

50. Urban IV (1261–64), born Jacques Pantaléon, son of shoemaker of Troyes, later patriarch of Jerusalem. He is most famous as the pope who made the fateful decision to transfer the crown of Sicily from the Hohenstaufen to the Angevins.

51. Charles, count of Anjou (1226–85), brother of St. Louis IX, King of France. In addition to expelling the Hohenstaufen from southern Italy, Charles sought to re-establish the Latin Empire in Constantinople, but was prevented from doing so when Peter III of Aragon seized Sicily after the Sicilian Vespers (see below, III.65 ff.).

52. Giovanni. Villani, *Cronica* VII, 87, 88.

53. See Pliny, *Natural History* II, 89–94.

54. Clement IV (reigned 1265–1268). After his wife's death he became bishop of Le Puy in 1257, archbishop of Narbonne in 1259, and cardinal bishop of Sabina in 1261. He continued Urban IV's policy of using the House of Anjou against the Hohenstaufen in Italy.

55. Giovanni Villani, *Cronica* VII, 91; VIII, 2, 3.

56. See below, II.117, for the founding of the Guelf party, a patriotic institution controlled by the Florentine oligarchy and used to restrain its political adversaries. Bruni's classicizing term for the Parte Guelfa, *optimae partes*, is reminiscent of the Ciceronian term *optimates*, denoting the aristocratic element in a state.

57. Giovanni Villani, *Cronica* VIII, 3, 2, 4.

58. That is, after his anticipated victory.

59. Ibid. VIII, 5.

60. I.e., *princeps*, one of the imperial titles assumed by the Emperor Augustus and his successors.

61. See above, I.82.

62. A town built on the lower slopes of Mount Cairo below the monastery of Monte Cassino. Destroyed in the Second World War, its ruins lie partly beneath the modern town of Cassino.

63. Villani, *Cronica* VIII, 6.

64. A region in the north of Campania, adjacent to Lazio, south of Montecassino.

65. Ibid. VIII, 7, 8.

66. The battle is commonly known as the Battle of Benevento.

67. Ibid. VIII, 9.

68. Ibid. VIII, 13.

69. Stefani, *Cronica*, rbr. 134.

70. Bruni's Latin here refers to the Baptistery 'the temple of Mars', a classicizing touch based on the old legend that the Baptistery was built on the site of a temple of Mars; see I.4, above.

71. Giovanni Villani, *Cronica* VIII, 14, 15.

72. Bruni is referring to the college of the Twelve Good Men (Dodici Buonuomini), later one of the advisory colleges of the Town Council (Signoria).

73. Bruni's language implies that the law was passed at a *parlamento* or public assembly of the entire citizen body.

74. Giovanni Villani, *Cronica* VIII, 15, 16.

75. The source of the following account is identified by Cabrini ("Le Historiae," p. 285) as pseudo-Brunetto Latini, *Cronica fiorentina*, in *Testi fiorentini del Dugento e dei primi del Trecento*, ed. A. Schiaffini (Florence, 1954), 117–19.

76. The penalty established for breaking the marriage contract (see below).

77. Acciaiuoli's translation of Bruni's Latin. The meaning is roughly: 'A *fait accompli* has a mind of its own'; or 'what's done is done'.

78. Giovanni Villani, *Cronica* VI, 38, 39.

79. Ibid. VIII, 19.

80. Ibid. VIII, 19.

81. The comparison implied by the classicizing language is to the ancient Roman censorship, a magistracy generally held by respected senior statesmen who exercized oversight of the morals and conduct of Romans of high rank.

82. Ibid. VIII, 17.

83. Ibid. VIII, 21.

84. Ibid. VIII, 22.

BOOK III

1. Charles of Anjou, who had claimed the title King of Sicily.

2. I.e., he was made chief judicial and police magistrate. In Rome, the official known elsewhere in Italy as the *podestà* or governor was called the 'Senator'.

3. Giovanni Villani, *Cronica* VIII, 10, 11

4. Ibid. VIII, 23.

5. Ibid. VIII, 24.

6. I.e., threats of excommunication.

7. Ibid. VIII, 25. The battle described below occurrred at Tagliacozzo, in the province of Aquila, on 23 August 1268.

8. Ibid. VIII, 26, 27, 29, 30.

9. Ibid. VIII, 31.

10. Ibid. VIII, 32, 33, 35.

11. The Ponte alla Carraia.

12. Ibid. VIII, 34.

13. In fact the cardinals remained in conclave for nearly three years; they were shut up in the papal palace and threatened with starvation by the civil authorities, who were incensed by the prelates' failure to choose a successor. By a later decree, *Ubi periculum* (1274), the cardinals when electing a pope are confined without contact with the outside world until they have chosen one.

14. I.e., the Crusades. King Louis IX of France (1214–70) launched the Crusade of Tunis in 1270. He was canonized by Pope Boniface VIII in 1297.

15. See II.88, above.

16. Giovanni Villani, *Cronica* VIII, 36; compare Stefani, *Cronica*, rbr. 142.

17. I.e., on the plain beneath the hilltop site of the original town.

18. Stefani, *Cronica*, rbr. 150

19. Philip III "the Bold" (1245–85).

20. Tedaldo Visconti of Piacenza (c.1210–76), elected to the papacy on 1 September 1271. He learned of his election in Acre while on crusade with the future Edward I of England and was consecrated as pope in Rome (not Viterbo) on 27 March 1272.

21. Giovanni Villani, *Cronica* VIII, 38, 39, 42.

22. Bruni's Latin in the following speech imitates the archaizing, Biblical style of papal discourse, a style he had learned to write as papal secretary from 1405 to 1414.

23. Luke 10:5.

24. Luke 11:17.

25. Luke 6:29; Matt. 5:39.

26. Giovanni Villani, *Cronica* VIII, 42; Stefani, *Cronica*, rbr. 5. The church of San Gregorio de'Mozzi stood near the the palazzo de'Mozzi (the site of the present Museo Bardini) where Gregory X and later Cardinal Latino (see below, III.52–54) were guests while in Florence. The cornerstone of the tiny church was laid by Gregory X and it was consecrated by Cardinal Latino in 1279 as a monument to the peace between Guelfs and Ghibellines.

27. Giovanni Visconti of the Pisan Visconti, who held the Judgeship of Gallura in the island of Sardinia, at that time a Pisan possession.

28. See above, III.24.

29. Giovanni Villani, *Cronica*, VIII, 44, 45, 47, 49, 43. At the Council of Lyons (1274) the Greek party under Emperor Michael VIII Palaeologus accepted papal primacy, assented to the Roman creed, and agreed to support the planned Crusade in return for protection against King Charles and his ally Baldwin II, the exiled Latin emperor of Constantinople. In defiance of the French party in the curia, Gregory also tried to build up Rudolf I of Hapsburg (1218–91; reigned as King of Germany, 1273–91) as a counterbalance to King Charles, a policy reversed under Gregory's successor, Innocent V.

30. Gregory X was buried in the Duomo in Arezzo where a cult sprang up to preserve his memory. He was placed in the Roman martyrology by Benedict XIV.

31. Giovanni Villani, *Cronica* VIII, 50. Innocent V (21 January–22 June 1276), the Dominican theologian Pierre of Tarentaise, was born in Savoy *c.* 1224.

32. Ibid. VIII, 51.

33. Nicholas III (reigned 1277–1280) was born in Rome *c.* 1210 as Giovanni Gaetano of the house of Orsini. The major theme of his pontificate was to establish the independence of the papacy vis à vis the House of Anjou. Dante placed him in Hell (*Inferno* XIX, 61ff.) as an example of clerical avarice and nepotism.

34. Giovanni Villani, *Cronica* VIII, 51, 54.

35. Latino di Angelo Malabranca, cardinal-bishop of Ostia (d. 1294).

36. Ibid. VIII, 56.

37. Stefani, *Cronica*, rbr. 154; ASF, Archivio della Repubblica, Capitoli, XXIX, f. 325 (cited by Santini).

38. Giovanni Villani, *Cronica* VIII, 56, 58.

39. Martin IV (reigned 1281–85), born Simon de Brie, former chancellor to King Louis IX of France.

40. I.e., Pope Nicholas III.

41. Ibid. VIII, 77, 78.

42. Ibid. VIII, 88.

43. Ibid. VIII, 85.

44. Afterwards known as the "Sicilian Vespers".

45. Ibid. VIII, 57, 61

46. King Peter III of Aragon, who succeeded his father James in 1276. In 1262 he married Constance of Hohenstaufen, and through her claimed the throne of Sicily. He was made King of Sicily by acclamation at Palermo on 7 September 1282.

47. Ibid. VIII, 64, 65, 69, 75.

48. Ibid. VIII, 89. *Compitalia* (here translated 'street-festivals') were Roman festivals held at cross-road shrines in late November or early December to celebrate the end of the agricultural year. See *Der Neue Pauly: Enzyklopädie der Antike*, vol. 3 (Stuttgart—Weimar, 1997), pp. 110–112. Given the date, Bruni may be referring to Advent festivals.

49. Giovanni Villani, *Cronica* VIII, 98.

50. Ibid. VIII, 99.

51. Ibid. VIII, 95.

52. Ibid. VIII, 110, 112, 113.

53. Called Guelfo di Luca in Anon., *Annales Arretinorum maiores et minores*, ed. A. Bini and G. Grazzini, in Rerum italicarum scriptores, vol. XXIV (Città di Castello, 1909), p. 861.

54. *Tyrannis*: Acciaiuoli translates: 'signore della città'.

55. Giovanni Villani, *Cronica* VIII, 115.

56. Dino Compagni, *Cronica*, ed. I. Del Lungo (Florence, 1889), I, 6.

57. Giovanni Villani, *Cronica* VIII, 116, 118.

58. Ibid. VIII, 120, 124.

59. Ugolino Visconti, known as Nino, who held the Judgeship of Gallura after 1276. See Davidsohn, *Storia*, II, p. 432.

60. Giovanni Villani, *Cronica* VIII, 121.

61. ASF, Archivio della Repubblica, Signori, Provvisioni I, f. 109 (cited by Santini).

62. A. Gherardi, *Le consulte della repubblica fiorentina*, 2 vols., Florence 1896–98), I, 381–383.

63. Giovanni Villani, *Cronica* VIII, 127.

64. Ibid. VIII, 126.

65. Ibid. VIII, 127, 128.

BOOK IV

1. I.e., the son of King Charles of Anjou.

2. Giovanni Villani, *Cronica* VIII, 130.

3. The letter of Dante referred to by Bruni does not survive.

4. Suetonius, *Life of Domitian* VI, 2.

5. Giovanni Villani, *Cronica* VIII 131.

6. See above, IV.1

7. I.e., the Baptistery; see the note 70 to II.101, above.

8. Giovanni Villani, *Cronica* VIII, 132.

9. Ibid., VIII, 137.

10. Ibid., VIII, 138.

11. Acciaiuoli translates 'inertes' (without a trade) here as 'gli scioperatori,' a term freighted with negative overtones, indicating persons who chose not to work for a living, *rentiers*. Florentine communal law prohibited rich men who did not exercise a trade and did not belong to one of the craft guilds from holding public office. 'Iners' etymologically means 'lacking art'; *arte* is the Italian word for 'guild.' *Ars* is here translated as 'trade,' but it should be kept in mind that for medieval Italians, the *artes* could include métiers such as banking, international trade, manufacturing, medicine and law.

12. The podestà.

13. The Captain of the People.

14. The city at that time was divided into *sestieri* or sixths, of which the old city center near San Piero Scheraggio and the Oltrarno district were the most populous.

15. The Standard-Bearer in later times became the ceremonial head of state in Florence with certain executive powers and lived in the Palazzo Vecchio with the Priors.

16. I.e., the *divieto*, from *divietare*, to forbid.

17. Ibid., VIII, 140.

18. Ibid., VIII, 141.

19. Ibid., VIII, 148.

20. Ibid., VIII, 154.

21. Bruni seems to indicate an outdoor *parlamento* of the entire people rather than a restricted political meeting inside the public palace.

22. Ibid., IX, 1.

23. I.e., their podestà, the chief judicial and police magistrate, an official who was normally a foreigner, not a native citizen of the town or city where he served.

24. Acciaiuoli translates: 'I Fiorentini fossero esenti dalle gabelle per le robe che conducessero o traessero per la via di mare."

25. ASF Capitoli XLI, f. 35, ed. Dal Borgo, *Diplomi*, p. 279; see Davidsohn, *Storia* III, p. 688.

26. Bruni is presumably summarizing here the tenor of an ambassadorial report contained in the archives of the Signoria. The last phrases seem to indicate that the ambassadors had not yet worked out an understanding about the release of the hostages: they might be released at Pontedera, and Pecciole would then be handed over eight days later, or the hostages might be exchanged at the more distant Pecciole when the Florentines turned over that castle to the Pisans.

27. Villani, *Cronica* IX, 2; ASF, Archivio della Repubblica, Capitoli XL, ff. 35–36 and Provvisioni III, f. 142 (cited by Santini).

28. The documents used by Bruni are published in Gherardi, *Le consulte* I, pp. 372–74.

29. Pope Celestine V (reigned 5 July–13 December 1294) was an eighty-five-year-old ascetic, miraculous healer and monastic reformer named Pietro del Morrone. He was elected after Cardinal Latino Malabranca revealed a prophecy of divine retribution against the church should the cardinals leave Perugia without a pope.

30. Boniface VIII (reigned 1294–1303) born around 1235 at Anagni as Benedetto Caetani. He studied law at Bologna, became a papal notary, then was created cardinal deacon in 1281 by Martin IV. Though intellectually gifted he was also arrogant and cruel, taking the most extreme positions possible on the supremacy of the Church; Dante represents him in Hell in *Inferno* XIX, 53.

31. Giovanni Villani, *Cronica* IX, 5–7.

32. The Ponte Rubaconte.

33. Ibid., IX, 8, 12.

34. ASF, Capitoli XLI, f. 77; see Davidsohn, *Storia* III, 733–34.

35. San Giovanni Valdarno, about 8 kilometers southeast of Figline Valdarno, on the south bank of the Arno. It was begun in 1296 following (according to tradition) a project of Arnolfo di Cambio, the architect of the Florentine Duomo. The patron saint of Florence is St John the Baptist.

36. Castelfranco di Sopra, about 8 kilometers due north of S. Giovanni Valdarno in the Pratomagno, on the northern side of the Arno. It was begun in 1296, following designs of Arnolfo di Cambio, according to tradition. Bruni's terminology of 'left' and 'right' banks seems to disclose an Aretine view of the Arno valley.

37. Giovanni Villani, *Cronica* IX, 17, 27, 31.

38. ASF, Archivio della Repubblica, Provvisioni X (1299), f. 165 (cited by Santini).

39. ASF, Archivio della Repubblica, Provvisioni IX, f. 154 (cited by Santini).

40. Giovanni Villani, *Cronica* IX, 36.

41. Ibid., IX, 38.

42. A spring holiday held on the first of May.

43. Ibid., IX, 39.

44. The legate was in fact Matthew of Acquasparta, cardinal-bishop of Porto, a distinguished theologian and General of the Franciscan Order. Dante criticized him in the *Paradiso* (XII, 124) for having abandoned the Franciscan Rule through an excessive attachment to money.

45. Ibid., IX, 40.

46. Ibid., IX, 41.

47. Ibid., IX, 42.

48. Ibid., IX, 42–43.

49. Presumably as their podestà, an official who was appointed by the Florentines in that period.

50. Ibid., IX, 45.

51. Ibid., IX, 46.

52. Ibid., IX, 49; Compagni, *Cronica* II, 13; Stefani, *Cronica*, rbr. 225.

53. Giovanni Villani, *Cronica* IX, 49–50.

54. Ibid., IX, 52–53, 59.

55. Ibid., IX, 60, 65.

56. Lottieri della Tosa, who became bishop of Florence in February, 1302.

57. Ibid., IX, 68.

58. Benedict XI (reigned 22 October 1303–7 July 1304), born Niccolò Boccasino in 1240, a Dominican theologian, later cardinal-bishop of Ostia.

59. See note 14, above.

60. Ibid., IX, 69.

61. The word *expeditio* used by Bruni here is a common humanist equivalent of *passagium*, the barbaric medieval word for crusade.

62. Ibid., IX, 69.

63. Ibid., IX, 70.

64. Acciaiuoli translates 'il vento dalla tramontana.'

65. Ibid., IX, 71.

66. I.e., to attack Florence.

67. Ibid., IX, 72, 82.

68. Ibid., IX, 80.

69. Robert of Anjou (1278–1343), son of Charles II of Anjou, Duke of Calabria, later King of Naples (1309–1343), patron of Giotto, Simone Martini, Petrarch and Boccaccio.

70. Ibid., IX, 82, and ASF, Archivio della Repubblica, Capitoli XLI, f. 85, cited by Santini and Davidsohn, *Storia*, IV, 405.

71. Clement V (reigned 1305–1314), born Bertrand de Got *c.* 1260 in Gascony, since 1299 archbishop of Bourdeaux; as pope, he was largely a puppet of the French crown.

72. I.e., they would be excommunicated.

73. I.e., excommunicated.

74. Acciaiuoli translated *praesides* here as 'commissari'; in Bruni's time these were civilian officials appointed by the Signoria or by *balìe* (emergency war governments) to oversee military affairs and provide liaison with the city's condottieri.

75. Giovanni Villani, *Cronica* IX, 82.

76. Ibid., IX, 82, 86.

77. I.e., the Executor of the Ordinances of Justice, a foreign official, who like the podestà exercised judicial and police functions.

78. Ibid., IX, 85–88.

79. Ibid., IX, 89.

80. Uguccione della Fagiuola was a powerful Ghibelline warlord with estates bordering on Umbria, the Romagna, and Tuscany. He had been the Ghibelline podestà of Arezzo at the time of Campaldino and later became lord of Pisa, dying in 1319.

81. Ibid., IX, 96.

82. I.e., they were permitted to carry out a legal vendetta, which would not have been the case had Corso's death been considered a legally executed sentence for tyranny.

83. Ibid., IX, 99.

84. Ibid., IX, 106, 110–11.

85. Ibid., IX, 107.

86. I.e, Niccolò da Prato

87. Ibid., IX, 110, 115–116, 118.

88. Ibid., IX, 108, 112.

89. Henry VII (1274–1313), formerly Count of Luxembourg, elected Holy Roman Emperor in 1308 as an alternative candidate to Charles of Valois.

90. Ibid., IX, 101, 119–120.

91. Ibid., X, 7–8.

92. I.e., the castle of Torrita; see IV.118, above.

93. I.e., Florentines inside the walls of Florence. Bruni is citing the rubric of *Epistula* VI, dated 31 March 1311, in *Le lettere di Dante*, ed. A. Monti (Milan, 1920), p. 132.

94. Giovanni Villani, *Cronica* X, 9, 14–15.

95. The best-known Florentine legal mind of the period. Baldo originally collaborated with Giano della Bella on the Ordinances of Justice, but later betrayed him.

96. The amnesty of 2 September 1311, the so-called Reform of Baldo d'Aguglione, is preserved in ASF, Libro del Chiodo, ff. 137–149; see Davidsohn, *Storia*, IV, 619–21.

97. The Tosinghi were also known as the Della Tosa

98. Giovanni Villani, *Cronica* X, 16.

99. See IV.93.

Bibliography

❧❦❧

EDITIONS OF THE LATIN TEXT

Historiarum Florentinarum libri XII, quibus accesserunt Quorundam suo tempore in Italia gestorum et De rebus graecis commentarii, ab interitu vindicati, nec non a mendis repurgati et ex manuscriptis in lucem editi, ed. Sixtus Bruno. Strasbourg: Lazarus Zetznerus, 1610. Pp. 1–248 contain the *History,* without Bruni's preface.

[Arezzo, Accademia di Scienze, Lettere ed Arti.] *Leonardi Arretini Historiarum florentini populi libri XII. Istoria fiorentina di Leonardo Aretino, tradotta in volgare da Donato Acciaiuoli, col testo a fronte.* 3 vols. Florence, 1855–60. With "Aggiunte e correzioni alla vita di Leonardo Bruni," signed by G. Mancini.

Leonardo Bruni Aretino. *Historiarum florentini populi libri XII e Rerum suo tempore gestarum commentarius.* Ed. Emilio Santini and Carmine Di Pierro. Rerum Italicarum Scriptores, vol. XIX, part III. Città di Castello, 1914–26.

ITALIAN TRANSLATION BY DONATO ACCIAIUOLI

Historia universale di Messer Lionardo Aretino. Venice, 1476. Photo-reprint, Arezzo, 1984.

Le Historie Fiorentine. Florence 1492.

Historia universale di Messer Lionardo Aretino. Venice, 1560.

La historia universale de suoi tempi di Messer Lionardo Aretino. Venice, 1561. Despite the title, this imprint contains only the *History of the Florentine People* in Acciaiuoli's translation, not the *Rerum suo tempore gestarum commentarius.*

The edition of the Accademia di Scienze, Lettere ed Arti of Arezzo, as in previous section.

Istoria Fiorentina di Leonardo Bruni, tradotta in volgare da Donato Acciaiuoli. Florence, 1861. A reprint of the previous edition, without the Latin text.

SELECTED MODERN STUDIES

Baron, Hans. *The Crisis of the Early Italian Renaissance: Civic Humanism and Republican Liberty in an Age of Classicism and Tyranny.* 2 vols. Princeton, 1955; revised edition in one volume, Princeton, 1966.

———. *In Search of Florentine Civic Humanism: Essays on the Transition from Medieval to Modern Thought.* 2 vols. Princeton, 1988.

Cabrini, Anna Maria. "Le *Historiae* del Bruni: risultati e ipotesi di una ricerca sulle fonti." In *Leonardo Bruni cancelliere della Repubblica di Firenze,* ed. Paolo Viti, pp. 247–319. Florence, 1990.

Cipriani, Giovanni. *Il mito etrusco nel Rinascimento.* Florence, 1980.

Cochrane, Eric. *Historians and Historiography in the Italian Renaissance.* Chicago, 1981.

Davidsohn, Robert. *Storia di Firenze,* 8 vols. Florence, 1977.

Fubini, Riccardo. "Osservazioni sugli *Historiarum Florentini populi libri XII* di Leonardo Bruni." In *Studi di storia medievale e moderna per Ernesto Sestan,* pp. 403–48. Florence, 1978.

Green, Louis. *Chronicle into History: An Essay on the Interpretation of History in Florentine Fourteenth-century Chronicles.* Cambridge, 1972.

La Penna, Antonio. "Il significato di Sallustio nella storiografia e nel pensiero politico di Leonardo Bruni." In his *Sallustio e la 'rivoluzione romana,'* 3rd ed., pp. 409–31. Milan, 1968.

Rubinstein, Nicolai. *Studies in Italian History in the Middle Ages and the Renaissance.* 3 vols. Rome, 2001.

Santini, Emilio. *Leonardo Bruni Aretino e i suoi "Historiarum Florentini populi libri XII".* Pisa, 1910.

———. "La fortuna delle *Storie fiorentine* di Leonardo Bruni nel Rinascimento." *Studi storici* 20 (1911–12): 177–95.

Ullman, Berthold Louis. "Leonardo Bruni and Humanist Historiography." *Medievalia et Humanistica* 4 (1946): 45–61. Reprinted in Ullman's *Studies in the Italian Renaissance.* Rome, 1955.

Wilcox, Donald. *The Development of Florentine Humanist Historiography.* Cambridge, Mass., 1969.

Index

❧❧❧

References are by book and paragraph number. Pr = Preface.